The University of Michigan
Center for Chinese Studies

Michigan Monographs
in Chinese Studies

Volume 61

Taoist Meditation and Longevity Techniques

edited by
Livia Kohn
in cooperation with
Yoshinobu Sakade

Ann Arbor

Center For Chinese Studies
The University of Michigan

1989

Library of Congress Cataloging-in-Publication Data:

Taoist meditation and longevity techniques / edited by Livia Kohn in
  cooperation with Yoshinobu Sakade.
    p. cm. - (Michigan monographs in Chinese studies ; v. 61)
    Bibliography: p.
    Includes index.
    ISBN 0-89264-084-7. - ISBN 0-89264-085-5 (pbk.)
  1. Longevity. 2. Meditation-Taoism. 3. Medicine, Chinese.
  I. Kohn, Livia, 1956– . II. Sakade, Yoshinobu. III. Series:
  Michigan monographs in Chinese studies ; no. 61.
  RA776.75.T36 1989
  613--dc19   89-806
                                                                        CIP

Cover design by John Klausmeyer
Manufactured in the United States of America

10   9   8   7

Contents

Editor's Preface

The study of ancient Chinese religious and health practices was first brought to scholarly attention by the work of Henri Maspero, more specifically by his article "Methods of 'Nourishing the Vital Principle' in the Ancient Taoist Religion," which was first published in 1937 (Maspero 1981: 443–554). But it took some twenty odd years and a new enthusiasm for the study of Taoism in general before serious inquiry into this important area of ancient Chinese culture began its present boom. In the 1960s, numerous scholars in both France and Japan turned their attention to the field. They were greatly helped by the better knowledge of Chinese religious history in general and Taoism in particular but were also stimulated by a deep concern for a more concrete and practical understanding of the behavior of the ancients.

The 1970s and 1980s duly saw the publication of several highly qualified studies on the subject, all of which are cited again and again in the contributions to this volume. There was Nathan Sivin's work on the alchemy of Sun Simiao (1968), Catherine Despeux's study of Taiji quan (1976), then Isabelle Robinet's work on Taoist meditation (1979), Michel Strickmann's analysis of the alchemy of Tao Hongjing (1979), and Farzeen Baldrian-Hussein's volume on inner alchemy (1984). My own study of mystical states in Tang Taoism and Ute Engelhardt's book on the physical practices of the same period were only published in 1987.

All these studies have in common that they clarify sections of the religious history of China without confining themselves to textual studies and general political occurrences. They try to gain an impression of what the concrete, everyday practices and mental perspective of the individual practitioners were like—to look into their heads and hearts and make them come to life as people rather than mere conduits for texts or ideas. It goes without saying that such a line of inquiry is only possible against the background of textual and historical studies, and we certainly would know a great deal less about ancient practices if scholars hadn't spent so much time and effort elucidating the origin and structure of the materials and the historical and social circumstances of the times.

Taoist studies have for a long time been centered in France, especially in Paris, and Japan, both in Tokyo and Kyoto. As a result, most of the works cited above as well as the impressive Japanese contributions to the field of traditional Chinese practices, which Yoshinobu Sakade outlines in great detail below, have remained largely inaccessible to a wider English reading audience. In this country, with the exception of the work of Michel Strickmann of the University of California at Berkeley and Nathan Sivin of the University of Pennsylvania, ancient Chinese religious and health practices are hardly touched upon at all. The Europeans and Japanese have traditionally been in close contact with each other. In fact, it was the translation of Maspero's volume in 1966 that sparked off a heightened interest in the study of longevity and other Taoist techniques in Japan; conversely, the recent work on Han dynasty medical manuscripts done in Japan (Yamada 1985) is having an increasing impact on our view of early religious practices.

A few years ago, the Japanese Ministry of Education sponsored a series of conferences on the subject of ancient Chinese longevity techniques. A group of about twenty Sinologists from all over Japan formed the organizational committee, and for three years about four meetings were held annually. At each meeting one specific aspect of the study of longevity techniques was discussed, with much general emphasis placed on medical and scientific subjects. Specialists from many different fields were invited, so that the range of discussion, though always centered on ancient Chinese ideas and practices of long life, would include textual studies, historical analyses, natural sciences, and comparative approaches. Interested foreigners residing in Japan were cordially invited to join, and so it happened that the idea for this volume was born. In many ways it is the (smaller) sister of the monumental *Nourishing Vitality in Ancient China: Comprehensive Studies on Theory and Practice*, which was edited by Yoshinobu Sakade and appeared in 1988 (for details see chapter 1).

Why not, we thought, present a comprehensive volume of a variety of papers dealing with different aspects of Taoist meditation and Chinese traditional longevity techniques to a wider, English-reading audience? We hoped, of course, to spread our enthusiasm for this field and perhaps encourage more people to specialize in the area, but most of all we wished to acquaint a larger audience with its situation and problems. Thus the book is not primarily directed at the specialist in Taoist studies or ancient Chinese medicine who is familiar with European and Japanese scholarship anyway and whom we have nothing new to tell. Rather, it addresses itself to the China area specialist or the scholar of religion and the history of science who wishes to know more about (and perhaps even must teach) aspects of Chinese culture that involve Taoism and traditional medicine.

All the chapters have therefore been structured as clearly and straightforwardly as possible. They were all written by specialists in the field on the basis of their own ongoing research.[1] They always include summaries of basic information and keep complicated textual analysis to a minimum (a minimum that may still be much too much for the uninitiated). In all cases ample bibliography has been provided so that interested readers can easily go on to related publications in English or the more specialized literature in French, German, Japanese, or Chinese.

The volume covers the major areas of Taoist meditation and longevity techniques in roughly chronological order. It could be, although for reasons that are explained below it is not, formally divided into four sections.

First, general introductory outlines. This includes Yoshinobu Sakade's description of the history of Chinese physical practices in Japan and the development and present situation of modern studies as well as Hidemi Ishida's study of the body and mind in pre-Han and Han philosophers and medical texts (materials dating from the fourth century B.C. to the second century A.D.). Both set the stage, so to speak, for what comes, and both are marginal and yet fundamental in that they show the framework in which traditional techniques are discussed nowadays.

Second, early development and interaction of Taoism and longevity practices. Here we have Akira Akahori's contribution on drug taking and immortality and Toshiaki Yamada's study of dietetics in one of the earliest Taoist scriptures, the *Lingbao wufuxu*. Both these articles deal primarily with the Han and post-Han periods (roughly second century B.C. to fifth century A.D.), and they both concentrate on the practices undertaken by ancient Chinese ascetics (*fangshi*) and the impact these had on religious Taoism after it had first formed in the second century. The importance of careful textual analysis and dating of the materials is made especially clear in Yamada's work.

Third, Taoist meditation. Divided typologically according to concentrative, ecstatic or shamanistic, and insight meditations, this includes my papers on "guarding the One" and on *neiguan* as well as Isabelle Robinet's work on Shangqing ecstatic excursions. The period covered here is mainly Six Dynasties to Tang, that is, third to ninth centuries. The variety of Taoist mental practices is shown, along with the changes they underwent through the ages. In all cases, the meditation practice is aimed at establishing a

---

1. The contributions by Sakade, Ishida, and Miura are revisions of works that have also appeared in Japanese. Sakade's introduction combines parts of his works listed under the dates 1986, 1986a, and 1988 below. Ishida's work has appeared as the second section of his recent book (1987), and Miura's article was published in 1986.

new world for the practitioner: from a limited individual he or she develops to be at one with the cosmos at large. A universal higher personality is attained.

Fourth, physical practices. Four papers are included in this section, covering the full range of history from before the Han to contemporary China. Catherine Despeux outlines the sources and history of gymnastics (*daoyin*) from the Han to the Tang, Ute Engelhardt shows how the whole variety of longevity techniques is organized and practiced in the Tang, Isabelle Robinet discusses the concepts of inner alchemy, which inherit a great deal from all earlier practices, not just the physical ones,[2] and Kunio Miura finally gives a survey of exercises involving *qi* (Qigong) as understood by the Chinese nowadays. The amazing continuity of the same practices is demonstrated in these contributions: the exercises found in the *Gymnastics Chart* at Mawangdui and dating from the second century B.C. are astonishingly similar to those the Qigong practitioner undertakes today. Different systems and combinations have been employed throughout the ages, but the tradition of physical exercises as a whole is vigorous and very much alive indeed.

This arrangement, though far from giving a complete survey of all there is in Chinese religious and health practices (the biggest gap probably being Ming and Qing systems), should enable readers to use the book as a basic textbook, going systematically from one chapter to the other without breaking the continuity too much at any given point. In every case it will be quite clear and has been emphasized by all the authors that the techniques are hard to separate either chronologically or phenomenologically. They are all to be practiced in conjunction with one another, and the dimensions frequently merge. An example is the practice of "ingesting the five sprouts," which is done by visualizing the different-colored energies of the five directions and guiding them by way of one's mouth to the corresponding inner organ where they belong. According to our categories this is a meditation technique; according to the Chinese it is used to nourish one's body and should therefore be considered one of the physical practices. This is why a basic understanding of the Chinese perspective on body and mind is so essential. It is also why it is quite impossible to classify any of the practices formally as meditative or physical and why we have not done so here.

---

2. The contribution on inner alchemy has been included in this section and not under Taoist meditation (where, strictly speaking, it belongs) for two reasons. First, it is in many ways the link between Tang practice and contemporary exercises and belongs here chronologically. Second, it cannot be properly understood without a background in physical exercises, since it draws at least as much on Tang Qigong as it continues *neiguan* to be placed directly after only one of them.

Some remarks on the forms used here are in order. Chinese and Japanese names have been given in their original order—that is, surname first. Chinese characters for titles of texts and names of people have always been added to the first mention of a title or name in every chapter. Technical terms have been translated and characters added, sometimes with and sometimes without transliteration, depending on the author. Citation of the Taoist Canon has been clearly defined in every given instance.

With the exception of my chapters and those by Akira Akahori and Ute Engelhardt, all the contributions have been translated from either Japanese or French, and inconsistencies or problems may therefore be due to me rather than to the author. All the authors have been extremely kind in their reworking of my translations and extraordinarily cooperative and prompt in submitting and later sending back manuscripts. If, as Sakade points out in his introduction below, more cooperation among specialists of different areas and countries is needed in this field, it should definitely be cooperation of the kind I had the good fortune to experience here. A great wave of mutual learning and unfailing support carried the editing speedily and cheerfully along. I wish, at this point, to thank the contributors with all my heart.

Also, I wish to express my deep gratitude to the Center for Chinese Studies at the University of Michigan and there especially to Professor Kenneth J. DeWoskin, whose support has given me the opportunity to proceed so unhindered in my work. Moreover, I wish to thank especially and personally all the many friends and colleagues who have helped this volume on its way: Ruth Ann Brevitz, Terre Fisher, Griffith Foulk, Maxime Kaltenmark, JoAnne Lehman, Donald Munro, Willard Oxtoby, and, most of all, my husband, Detlef Kohn.

References

Baldrian-Hussein, Farzeen. 1984. *Procédés secrets du joyau magique*. Paris: Les Deux Océans, 1984.

Despeux, Catherine. 1976. *Taiki k'iuan: technique de combat, technique de longue vie*. Paris: Institute des Hautes Etudes Chinoises, 1976.

Engelhardt, Ute. 1987. *Die klassische Tradition der Qi-Übungen: Eine Darstellung anhand des Tang-zeitlichen Textes Fuqi jingyi lun von Sima Chengzhen*. Wiesbaden: Franz Steiner, 1987.

Kohn, Livia. 1987. *Seven Steps to the Tao: Sima Chengzhen's Zuowanglun*. St. Augustin: Monumenta Serica Monographs 20, 1987.

Maspero, Henri. 1981. "Methods of 'Nourishing the Vital Principle' in the Ancient Taoist Religion." in *Taoism and Chinese Religion*. Amherst: University of Massachusetts Press, 1981, 431–554.

Robinet, Isabelle. 1979. *Méditation taoiste*. Paris: Dervy Livres, 1979.

Sakade, Yoshinobu. 1986. "The Taoist Character of the 'Chapter on Nourishing Life' of the *Ishinpō*." *Kansai daigaku bunka ronshū*, 1986, 775–798.

Sivin, Nathan. 1968. *Chinese Alchemy: Preliminary Studies*. Cambridge, Massachusetts: Harvard University Press, 1968.

Strickmann, Michel. 1979. "On the Alchemy of T'ao Hung-ching." In *Facets of Taoism*, pp. 123-192. Edited by H. Welch and A. Seidel. New Haven & London: Yale University Press, 1979.

in Japanese

Ito Festschrift
Itō Sōheikyōjū taikan kinen Chūgokugaku rombunshū
伊藤瀬平教授退官記念中國學論文集
Tokyo, 1986.

Miura Kunio 三浦國雄 1986
"Ki no fukken: Kikō to dōkyō" 氣の復權：氣功と道敎
Itō Festschrift, 203–233.

Sakade Yoshinobu 坂出祥伸 1986a
Introduction, *Dōin taiyō* 導引體要
Tokyo: Taniguchi, 1986.

Sakade Yoshinobu 坂出祥伸 1988
Chūgoku kodai yōsei shisō no sōgōteki kenkyū
中國古代養生思想の總合的研究
Tokyo: Hirakawa, 1988.

Yamada Keiji 山田慶兒 1985
Chūgoku shinhakken kagakushi shiryō no kenkyū
中國新發現科學史資料の研究
2 vols. Kyoto: Jimbun Kagaku Kenkyūjo, 1985.

Chapter One

Longevity Techniques in Japan:

Ancient Sources and Contemporary Studies

Yoshinobu Sakade

The Transmission of Chinese Longevity Techniques to Japan

Japan began to receive a strong influence of Korean medicine in about the fifth century, but Chinese medicine was transmitted directly from China to Japan only from the seventh century onward. In the Nara period, numerous Japanese monks went to China in order to study Buddhism as well as traditional Chinese methods of healing. More than that, Chinese monks also came to Japan to spread the dharma; among them was the famous Jianzhen 鑑真 (689–763), after whom the Kobe–Shanghai ferry is still named today. *Nolens volens*, these monks also brought with them a rich knowledge of traditional Chinese pharmacology, medical practices, and longevity techniques. Throughout the Nara and the first half of the Heian periods—that is, well into the tenth century—Chinese medicine of the Sui and Tang thus occupied the position of official court medicine in Japan.

The first Japanese work on medicine was compiled around this time: the *Daidō Ruijuhō* 大同類聚方 (Classified Collected Prescriptions of Great Unity), by Izumo no Hirosada 出雲廣貞 and Abe no Manao 阿部真直. The book was a lengthy collection of 160 scrolls and was first completed in 808. With it, the native Japanese tradition of oriental medicine and longevity techniques was first established.

Later there appeared the *Kinranhō* 金蘭方 (Golden Orchid Prescriptions), in fifty scrolls, compiled under imperial auspices by Sugawara no Minetsugu 菅原岑嗣 and others. Ordered by Emperor Seiwa around the year 860, the book was first completed in 868. It was largely an imitation of its Chinese counterpart, the *Qianjin fang* 千金方 (Prescriptions Worth a Thousand Ounces of Gold), by the physician-alchemist Sun Simiao 孫思邈 of the seventh century.

Both, the *Daidō Ruijuhō* and the *Kinranhō* are lost to us today.

Gradually, in the wake of these works, more books on medicine, pharmacology, and longevity techniques began to appear in Heian Japan. Among these, the first book that dealt primarily with longevity techniques was the *Setsuyō yōketsu* 攝養要訣 (Essential Formulas of Nourishing Life), by Mononobe no Kōsen 物部廣泉 , in twenty scrolls. It came out under Emperor Junna, who reigned between 823 and 833. Next, there was Fukane no Sukehito's 深根輔仁 *Yōjōshō* 養生抄 (On Nourishing Life), in seven scrolls. It was presented in 890 under Emperor Uda. Neither of these two important early works is extant today.

One year later, in 891, the oldest Japanese bibliography of Chinese works was completed. Entitled *Nipponkoku genzaisho mokuroku* 日本國見在書目錄 (Bibliography of Works Extant in Japan), it consists of one scroll and was compiled by Fujiwara no Sukeyo 藤原佐世. In section 37 of this bibliography, medical works are treated. Altogether it lists 170 different works in 130 scrolls, the great majority of which had been imported from China. They were kept in the Imperial Palace, and their numbers continued to increase.

A great many medical works are listed in this bibliography, which makes the absence of Taoist works astounding. Yet in the medical textbooks themselves a number of Taoist practices and important notions of the Taoist world view were transmitted to Japan. A good example of the role of Taoist-influenced materials in Heian Japan is the fact that in the Imperial Office of Medicine where all officials who had dealings with medicine and drugs were educated, the *Huangdi neijing taisu* 黄帝内經太素 (Inner Classic of the Yellow Emperor: Great Simplicity) was used as a textbook. The commentary to this book by Yang Shangshan 楊上善 of the Sui emphasizes visualizations and meditations on the divinities residing in the human body as an important way to wellness. Another textbook of the Imperial Office of Medicine was the *Xinxiu bencao* 新修本草 (Newly Revised Materia Medica), which explains in great detail the various vegetable and mineral drugs used for prolonging life as well as methods for ingesting and applying them.

All in all, Japanese medicine in the Heian period was an imitation of Chinese medicine of the Sui and Tang. It was mainly practiced among the aristocracy and at the imperial court. In those days, the specially trained court physicians employed by the Imperial Office of Medicine possessed tremendous power. They tended to be largely recruited from two powerful clans, the Wake and the Tamba. A member of the latter family was the author of one of the most important documents on traditional Chinese medicine, of the *Ishinpō*.

Tamba no Yasuyori's *Ishinpō*

The *Ishinpō* 醫心方 (Essential Medical Methods) is the oldest extant work on Japanese traditional medicine. Compiled by the official acupuncturist at the imperial court, Tamba no Yasuyori 丹波康輔 (912–995), it was presented to Emperor Enyu on the twenty-eighth day of the eleventh month in 984.

Looking at the *Ishinpō* from the viewpoint of Sui and Tang influence on Japanese medicine, one finds that it functions like a distant mirror. It quotes passages from 204 different ancient sources, some of which are Japanese or Korean but the majority of which are Chinese, imported from the Sui and Tang court. In many respects, one may say, the *Ishinpō* continues the lineage of traditional Chinese medicine.

In content it closely follows the classification of diseases found in the *Zhubing yuanhou lun* 諸病源候論 (On the Origins and Symptoms of All Diseases). This medical work was presented to Emperor Yang of the Sui dynasty in 610 A.D. It supposedly was compiled on imperial decree by a special editorial committee consisting of physicians and literati. The *Ishinpō* generally proceeds by first listing the causes and symptoms of diseases, and then discussing various healing methods. Here it relies strongly on Sun Simiao's *Qianjin fang* and Chen Yanzhi's 陳延之 *Xiaopin fang* 小品方 (Prescriptions for Small Items). The latter is dated to the fifth century.[1] In addition, the *Ishinpō* quotes a large number of Tang prescription manuals that were developed by Chinese physicians in a certain atmosphere of secrecy. Since the book is based so extensively on earlier sources, the personal preferences of the author and standard viewpoint of Heian medicine hardly show through at all.

---

1. A Kamakura copy of the introduction and first chapter of this text, entitled *Jingfang xiaopin*, was discovered recently in the Sonkeikaku Library in Tokyo. Judging from the reference titles quoted in the introduction, its original date of compilation can now be determined more precisely. It stems from the latter half of the fifth century. For more details see Kosodo 1985.

In the *Ishinpō* medical methods influenced by Indian and Central Asian practices can also be detected. It uses Buddhist concepts, speaks of magical prohibitions and quotes from Taoist alchemical practices. In this respect it is a text of special interest. However, its highest value lies in the fact that it quotes from 204 different sources, among which are found numerous Chinese medical works that were lost early in China proper. These works can be reconstructed with the help of the *Ishinpō*. In addition, even many of the medical works that survive today were revised and supplemented in the Tang or Song dynasties, and it is only through the *Ishinpō* that we know the shape they were in before revision. This point must be especially noted: the *Ishinpō* is a valuable treasury of old Chinese medical materials.

Overall Contents of the Text

The thirty chapters of the *Ishinpō* cover a broad range of subjects. The first chapter is a general overview. It emphasizes principles of healing and fundamental rules to follow when dealing with drugs. It also provides a table of corresponding Chinese and Japanese names of drugs.

The second chapter deals with acupuncture and moxibustion. Taking the *Huangdi neijing mingtang*   黃帝內經明堂   (Inner Classic of the Yellow Emperor: Hall of Light) as its basis,[2] it reports on the circuits and their main pressure points and gives instructions on how to find them. More than that, it describes the different levels of stimulation of pressure points as well as the effect such stimulation has on a variety of diseases.

Chapters 3 through 14 contain lists of internal diseases and complaints, as follows:

> 1. diseases caused by wind and their asymptoms (chap. 3)
> 2. diseases of the hair, head, and face (chap. 4)
> 3. diseases of ears, eyes, mouth, teeth, and the throat (chap. 5)
> 4. diseases of the breast, the abdomen, and the organs (chap. 6)
> 5. diseases of the private parts and tapeworms (chap. 7)
> 6. diseases of the four limbs (chap. 8)
> 7. diseases of the respiratory organs and the stomach (chap. 9)
> 8. liver diseases liver and tumors (chap. 10) diarrhea (chap. 11)
> 9. excrements (chap. 12)
> 10. tuberculosis (chap. 13)
> 11. nervousness and fever (chap. 14)

---

2. This text was allegedly edited by Yang Shangshan of the Sui. It was lost in China at an early date, but we know that it served as an official textbook in Japan in 701, when the Fundamental Law of Japan was established.

Chapters 15 to 18 concentrate on the various healing methods for external diseases and complaints. Chapters 19 and 20 deal with the ingestion and application of mineral drugs. Chapter 21 concentrates on gynecology, chapters 22 through 24 deal with obstetrics, and chapter 25 is concerned with pediatrics.

In chapter 26, we find various odd methods of nourishing life, such as facial treatments, magical methods for being in love, and abstention from cereals. Chapter 27 concentrates on the arts of extending one's life span and perfecting one's health, it is here that longevity techniques in the more narrow sense are found. Chapter 28 deals mainly with the sexual techniques of immortality, and the two last chapters, 29 and 30, mainly emphasize ways of nourishing life by means of dietetics.

Editorial History

After the *Ishinpō* was presented to Emperor Enyu by Tamba no Yasuyori in the year 984, it was kept as it was—in its handwritten form—in the palace for a very long period. In the following centuries it was frequently saved from fires during military raids. Only in the sixteenth century was the book removed from the palace grounds. Nakarai Mitsushige 半井光成 , head of the Imperial Office of Medicine under Emperor Ogimachi (1558–1586), received it from the emperor by imperial decree. Then, for many generations the text was then transmitted within the Nakarai family. Toward the end of the Edo period, the Tokugawa Shōgun borrowed the handwritten manuscript from the Nakarai family and had it copied and officially printed and published. It appeared in 1860 as a monumental work in thirty volumes and 2,784 pages.

During the Meiji period, the Bun'enkaku Asakuraya 文淵閣淺倉屋 , an antique book shop in Tokyo's Asakusa district, acquired a copy of the Ansei edition of the *Ishinpō* and in 1909, it published a second edition, which became known as the *Asakuraya ban Ishinpō*. The edition that is most easily accessible today is a revision of this 1909 version, published in 1955 by the Renmin Weisheng Publishing Company of Beijing in two paperback volumes.

Longevity Techniques in the *Ishinpō*

Longevity techniques are mentioned in different places throughout the *Ishinpō*. For example, in chapters 19, 20, 26, 28, 29, and 30 we find citations relating to the arts of nourishing life. Especially in chapters 19 and 20, there are references to ingesting and applying mineral drugs—the longevity technique most strongly favored in Ge Hong's 葛洪 *Baopuzi* 抱朴子 (Book of the Master Who Embraces Simplicity). However, unlike the more religiously oriented texts, the *Ishinpō* also emphasized the poisonous nature of prescriptions based on mineral drugs and strictly prohibits their ingestion. So it is perfectly reasonable that Tamba no Yasuyori should exclude all ingestion and application of mineral drugs from his specific treatment of longevity techniques in chapter 27. Books dealing with longevity practices that were written in the wake of the *Ishinpō* similarly exclude the discussion of mineral drugs. This point is of great interest and requires further study. Let us now look at the contents of chapter 27, the "Chapter on Nourishing Life." It is divided into eleven sections:

1. "General Overview"
2. "Cultivating the Spirit"
3. "Nourishing the Body"
4. "Applying the Breath"
5. "Gymnastics"
6. "Daily Regimen"
7. "Sleep"
8. "Proper Language"
9. "Clothing"
10. "Dwellings"
11. "Various Prohibitions"

The "General Overview" deals with the fundamental principles of nourishing life. Citing the *Qianjin fang*, it explains that the attainment of longevity first of all means the healing of latent diseases, in other words, that its practice serves mainly preventive purposes. Moreover, perfecting the good qualities of one's character is claimed to be effective for the prevention of calamities. The fact that the theory of nourishing life proposed by Sun Simiao is placed in the first section of the chapter indicates that Tamba no Yasuyori's personal viewpoint is identical with his. Tamba does not explain his personal ideas in his own words, relying entirely on quotations from other sources throughout the whole chapter. Even so, it is possible to glean his position.

From the *Wenzi* 文子, a Han dynasty Taoist work, he quotes the following:

> It is most important to nourish the spirit, it is of secondary importance to nourish the body. The spirit should be pure and tranquil, the bones should be stable. This is the foundation of long life.

From this quotation it seems evident that he understood longevity techniques to consist of two separate sets of practices: nourishing the spirit and nourishing the body. He also clearly considered the former to be more valuable.

He also cites the *Yangsheng yaoji* 養生要集 (Compendium of Essentials on Nourishing Life):[3]

> The *Shenxian tu* [Immortal's Chart] says: "In order to cultivate the arts of nourishing life one must first of all practice meditation. During all everyday activities such as walking, standing, eating, drinking, sleeping, and resting, one must continuously meditate. It makes no difference whether it is night or day. One always preserves one's essence and breath in their entirety, thus one always prevents the divinities of the body from leaving. Thereby long life is attained."

Meditation refers to the practice of concentrating one's mind and spirit on the divinities who reside in one's body. By and by one becomes fully one with them. Tamba no Yasuyori here not only shows a high opinion of the practice of meditation, but also emphasizes that the concentrated mind should be maintained constantly throughout one's everyday activities. In his prohibition of drugs as well as in his preference for meditation, Tamba places the *Ishinpō* squarely in the tradition of the *Yangsheng yaoji*.

"Cultivating the Spirit" is an expression originally taken from chapter 6 of the *Daode jing*: "The spirit of the valley does not die." Following the interpretation of Heshang gong 河上公 , the *Ishinpō* reads: "If one nourishes the spirit, one will not die." This spirit is not merely the spirit of human beings. The term also refers to the divinities of the five inner organs and of the cinnabar fields. This means that Tamba no Yasuyori maintained the notion that one could preserve one's spirit by nourishing and preserving the divinities within the body.

"Nourishing the Body" refers to various ways of preserving one's physical body in strict accordance with the four seasons and the alternations of heat and cold. In particular, careful attention should be paid to the five senses. At regular intervals, baths should be taken, so that the health of the physical body can be promoted.

"Applying the Breath" deals with breath as the basic human life force just as water is the element of fishes. Human beings must take great care tp be aware whether the air around them is dirty or not, whether it is thin or not. They must always apply the breath of life and see that they avoid the breath of

---

3. This text was completely lost in China after the rebellion of An Lushan. As the title Compendium suggests, it originally consisted of quotations and summaries of ancient sources, materials dating from the Han to the Jin, from the second century B.C. to the fourth century A.D. It is ascribed to Zhang Zhan of the Eastern Jin (Sakade 1986a).

death. Thereby they will not be attacked by untimely death, evil winds, fierce cold, or intense heat. One practices application of breath by lying down flat on one's back, closing the eyes, and forming fists with the hands just as a baby does in the womb. With the mouth firmly closed, one breathes entirely through the nose.

"Gymnastics" means physical exercises for the purpose of expelling all evil breath from the limbs, the joints, and the bones of the body. In its stead, healthy, good energy or breath is to be preserved. The practice should be undertaken three times a day, but only on days when the energy of heaven is harmonious and warm, when the sun and the moon are clear. In addition, the time must be particularly quiet. Grinding the teeth and massaging oneself are also part of the practice of gymnastics.

"Daily Regimen" describes the proper deportment and activities of daily life.

"Sleep" concentrates on the correct way of sleeping. For example, in spring and summer one should sleep with one's head to the East, during winter and fall, with the head to the West.

"Proper Language" deals with the instances when one must speak. One should then speak only little and never in a loud voice. Similarly, one should not use vulgar language or utter curses. If one uses improper language, the lungs and the kidneys will be weakened and the deities residing in them will be placed in a state of unrest.

"Clothing" describes the proper thickness of clothes for various occasions.

"Dwellings" admonishes the practitioner to keep his dwellings pure and simple and not to adorn or embellish them. They should suffice to protect him from wind, rain, heat, and humidity. Especially in the southern regions, where high humidity prevails, the bed should be built high and wide so that the energy of the earth won't reach it and the bad, pathogenic energies cannot enter. This latter piece of information is cited from the *Yanshou chishu* 延壽 赤書 (Auspicious Scripture on Extending Life) by Pei Yu 裴煜 , a work probably dating from the Tang dynasty. Interestingly enough, the exact length of the bed is given as three feet six inches.

"Various Prohibitions," the last section, describes the regulations for the minor details of everyday activity. For instance—quoting the *Yangsheng yaoji*—one should never exhaust one's essence and energy, one should not overeat, nor should one take too deep breaths. All such actions are injurious to one's life and health.

The various longevity techniques described in the *Ishinpō* cover the range of traditional Chinese ways of prolonging life and approaching immortality, with the one exception of mineral drugs. Alchemy and related practices seem not to have been particularly popular among the medical giants of ancient Japan. This certainly has to do with the fact that their primary concern was the nourishing of this life and not the more or less immediate transportation into another. The religious zeal associated with certain traditions of longevity in China is replaced here by a concern for the welfare of the patient, but, as noted above, not to the entire exclusion of all Taoist thought and practices.

Japanese Sources from the Eleventh to the Nineteenth Century

The *Ishinpō* exerted a tremendous influence on later Japanese medicine. Its impact was so strong, in fact, that throughout the Kamakura and Muromachi periods (that is, from the twelfth to the sixteenth century) virtually no new works on longevity techniques were written. Outside of the Tamba family, who continued to be among the top physicians in the country, there was an innovation in the field by the monk Yūsai 榮西 (1141–1215). He wrote a book entitled *Kissa yōjōki* 喫茶養生記 (Drinking Tea and Nourishing Life), in which he described methods of drinking tea in relation to prolonging life. Another work of the same period is Kajihara Shōzen's 梶原性全 *Ton'ishō* 頓醫抄 (On Immediate Relief), in fifty scrolls, of the year 1303. It discusses various means of nourishing life especially in everyday activities such as rising, resting, eating, drinking, and sex. In terms of medical therapy Kajihara favors acupuncture and moxibustion, but as far as gymnastics and breathing exercises are concerned he did not go beyond the limits of the *Ishinpō*.

During the reign of Emperor Gomurakami (1339–1368), the monk Yūrin 有鄰 of the Nanzenji Temple in Kyoto wrote the *Fukudenhō* 福田方 (Prescriptions of the Fields of Blessedness) sometime between 1362 and 1367. This is the first book that does not follow the pattern set in the *Ishinpō*. In other words it does not strictly imitate mainland Chinese or Korean works and methods. Yūrin claimed that all medical therapy should bear an immediate relation to one's personal experience. Following this proposition, he came up with some rather original statements. His essay, though, is limited to the more medical aspects of longevity techniques; he does not touch on gymnastics, breathing, or meditation. It appears that at that time the distinction between longevity techniques and medicine made by mainland physicians of the Jin and Yuan was already exerting a certain influence on their Japanese counterparts.

Under the Ming, in the late fourteenth century, a Japanese physician traveled to China. Takeda Shōkei 武田昌慶 , successful physician of Emperor

Gokomatsu (1392–1412), was awarded several high official ranks due to his successful curing of the Shōgun. In 1456 he published a volume entitled *Enju ruiyō* 延壽類要 (Classified Methods of Prolonging Life), of which a Muromachi original still survives in the Palace Library in Tokyo. He classifies longevity techniques according to "Nourishing One's Nature," "Active Cultivation," "Prohibited Actions," "Clothing and Food," "Sexual Behavior," and so on. Physical exercises and breathing techniques are discussed under "Active Cultivation," but he limits his account to a quotation from the *Yangsheng yaoji.* Again, the scope of the *Ishinpō* is not widened or developed.

Physical Exercises in the Momoyama Era

In the sixteenth century, a new trend in Chinese medicine following the tradition of Li Dongyuan 李東垣 and Zhu Danqi 朱丹溪 of the Yuan dynasty was introduced to Japan. There its major exponent was Manase Dōsan 曲直瀬道三 (1507–1595), whose teachings spread to a large number of people and became the dominant medical tradition of the time. His major work was a book entitled *Keiteki shū* 啟迪集 (Collection of Medical Treatments for Diseases), in eight scrolls, in which he listed a considerable variety of diseases and discussed their symptoms and therapy. On the subject of longevity techniques he published the *Yōjō hishi* 養生秘旨 (Esoteric Instructions on How to Nourish Life) and the *Jufuku shichichin* 壽福七珍 (Seven Marvels of Longevity and Happiness). Dōsan's adopted son and heir Manase Gensaku 玄朔 (1598–1631) not only continued the tradition established by his father, but brought it to new heights of excellence and fame. He wrote the *Yōjō monogatari* 養生物語 (The Tale of Longevity; one volume). Describing the essentials of nourishing life in dialogue form, it is a very straightforward and delightful account of longevity ideas and practices. For example, it says:

> When you get up in the morning, first sit on your bedding and meditate quietly for a little while. Then loosen your belt and rub your body from head to feet and stretch and bend your legs a couple of times. Only thereafter should you get dressed and belted and begin the routine of the day.
>
> After the meal, massage your waist and stomach area with both hands. The two thumbs should be pointed outward, the four other fingers should face in towards the abdomen. With the hands in this position, massage the belly about 20 or 30 times. This done, get up and go for a walk of about 200 to 300 paces. Should it be impossible for you to go out, then take the broom and sweep the floor. Thereafter you may rinse your mouth, wash your hands and go back to your occupation.

These instructions are clearly taken from Chinese physical exercises. They represent a Japanese adaptation of Taoist gymnastics.

In another work, the *Enju satsuyō* 延壽攝要 (Assembled Essentials of Extending Life), of the year 1599, Gensaku explained more meditative practices. One should nourish one's spirit and energy, curb passions and desires, and gain control over the senses. The organization of his work is similar to Takeda's *Enju ruiyō* mentioned above. First a general survey is given, followed by "Cultivation of Speech and Action," "Eating and Drinking," and "Sexual Techniques." Physical exercises are discussed under "Cultivation of Speech and Action," which includes the following:

> Some time after midnight, if possible around the fifth watch but also at any other convenient time of quiet and leisure, take off your belt and loosen your garments. Then carefully begin to exhale the turbid energy from your stomach. Repeat the exercise nine times if possible, but at least five or six times. Then concentrate your mind, close your eyes, and grind your teeth together thirty-six times. Thereby your eyes will be bright and all cold within the body will be expelled.
>
> The next exercise begins by pressing the outside of the right and left nostril about seven times. Then you should rub your two hands together until they are well warmed, if not actually hot. Hold your breath by closing nose and mouth and massage your face with your hot hands. This will take care of any hearing problems you might have.
>
> After having completed this, curl up your tongue so that it touches the gums behind your upper front teeth. Let the saliva accumulate in the mouth and then swallow it in three gulps. Repeat the exercise three times, so that you perform nine swallowings altogether. This exercise serves to kill the germs in the body and to replenish energy deficiencies.
>
> In your ordinary life avoid spitting out saliva. Saliva is an important body fluid which, when treated correctly, will return to its inner origin, the kidneys. As such it has to be treated with special care. Also, other useful exercises are to beat the hips with both hands or to massage the pressure point called "Gushing Spring" in the center of the soles of the feet. These practices will help the blood and energy circulation, cold and heat will be driven out from the body, and all complaints of the hips and the legs will be cured.

Again, these gymnastic instructions describe fairly standard, traditional Chinese practices, they do not go significantly beyond the account found in the *Ishinpō*. The one major difference is the emphasis placed on the pressure points used in acupuncture and moxibustion, but this is probably due to

Jin/Yuan dynasty influence. Gensaku, like many of his noble predecessors, was not an original gymnast.

Gensaku's type of medicine has recently been criticized as being a mere replica of modern Confucian-oriented medicine, whose primary emphasis is on the control and reduction of desire. However, his claim that one should lessen one's desires and calm one's mind is not in fact influenced by Confucian thought. The same claim has been made in traditional Chinese medical and Taoist sources since ancient times. There is a fundamental difference between the more Confucian and the more religious, perfection-oriented view. The warning against too many desires in Taoist philosophy and religion is made with the aim of perfecting body and mind, with individual yet cosmic salvation in view. In Confucianism, on the other hand, one nourishes life not for one's own good but as an effort toward a higher public spirit, as a service to a better integrated and more harmonious society. Longevity techniques in the medical and Taoist traditions aim at perfecting health and transcending the human state, which is ultimately a tendency away from society and this world. Taoists were for this very reason severely criticized by their Confucian contemporaries. Lu Jia 陸賈 of the Han dynasty, for example, said:

> Laboring oneself and tiring the body by entering into the depth of the mountains in search of immortality means the rejection of one's kin, the negation of physical necessities, the abstention from cereals, the abandonment of poetry and history. People who do this turn their backs on the treasures of heaven and earth. They search for no-death, but this in truth cannot be had without facing the wrongs of this world. (*Shishuo xinyu*)

Longevity Techniques under the Edo Shogunate

In the last few centuries of Japanese history, several new books on physical exercises and longevity techniques have appeared, but they have rather strictly separated medicine and therapeutic, life-enhancing practices. Nevertheless, there were numerous physicians who held gymnastics, breathing exercises, and massages in high esteem and used them in curing their patients. At the same time quite a number of gymnastic and massage specialists without any specific medical training were practicing in the cities and earning their livelihood by their craft alone. Representatives of this group were Onitsura 鬼 貫 and Old Woman Tessai 鐵齋老婆 .

In 1648, the official acupuncturist Yamawaki Dōsaku   山脇道作 compiled a work on longevity techniques under orders from Emperor Gomizuo. This work, the *Juyōroku* 壽養錄 (On Nourishing Longevity), in four scrolls, was a comprehensive collection which in its organization closely followed the section on longevity techniques in Zhang Jiebin's 張介賓 *Leijing* 類經 (Encyclopedia) of the Ming.

Hayashi Masakatsu's 林正旦 *Dōin taiyō* 導引體要 (Essential Formulas of Gymnastics) was published in March of the same year. A specialized work on physical exercises, this book yet omits much traditional information that should have been available at the time. It does cite relevant passages from the *Huangdi neijing suwen* 黃帝内經素問 (The Inner Classic of the Yellow Emperor: Fundamental Questions) and commentaries found in the *Leijing*, but in general it limits itself to the statement that physical exercises played an important role in traditional medicine, without ever indicating which practices these exercises involved.

In 1692, Takeda Tsūan 竹田通庵 published his *Kokon yōjōroku* 古今養生録 (Ancient and Modern Ways of Nourishing Life), in fifteen scrolls. His biography is only known in its bare outline. He came from a place in modern Gifu Prefecture near Nagoya and studied medicine under Nakarai Zuiken 半井瑞堅 . Among his other works are the *Naikyō yōgo shūchū* 内經要語集註 (Collected Commentaries to Essential Sayings of the Inner Classic) and the *Naikyō yōgo iyoku* 意翼 (Interpretation of the Meaning of Essential Sayings of the Inner Classic).

The *Kokon yōjōroku* in particular is one of the most complete works on longevity techniques that has ever appeared in Japan. It covers all the related areas and describes the practices lucidly and with much practical detail. The fifteen scrolls are divided into eighteen sections: "General Overview," "Nourishing Life in Accordance with the Seasons," "Morning and Evening Practice," "Dwellings," "Clothes," "Food Storage," "Drinking Wine," "Drinking Tea," "Prohibitions Regarding Food and Drink," "Emotions and Intentionality," "Gymnastic Exercises," "Various Longevity Techniques," "On Women," "On Children," "Various Diseases," "Spells and Incantations," "Acupuncture and Moxibustion." In the course of his discussion he cites fifty-five different books. The completeness and thoroughness of the work show Takeda's deep concern with longevity techniques as well as his qualities as a compiler.

Another important source for longevity techniques contained in this book is a set of twenty-four pictures that was first appended to the *Huangdi neijing suwen* and later included in the *Qianjin fang* and the Taoist encyclopedia *Yunji qiqian* 雲笈七籤 (Seven Slips from a Cloudy Satchel). In the Qing, the twenty-four pictures were reedited by Cao Ruoshui 曹若水 in his *Wanshouxian shu* 萬壽仙書 (Immortality of Ten Thousand Years). The same collection also contains a set of fifteen pictures of the Five Animals Pattern of the Han dynasty physician Hua Tuo. Takeda included these in his work as well.

The various longevity encyclopedias of the Edo period all closely follow the tradition of Japanese medicine that was established in the Heian era. Unlike Chinese works after the Tang, Japanese books do not assign dietetic techniques an important role. This lack of emphasis on diet, drugs, and alchemy is the major distinguishing mark of Japanese medicine and longevity techniques.

Almost simultaneously with the publication of Takeda's encyclopedic collections, Taniguchi Ichi'un 谷口一雲 educated himself in Taoist practices and began to teach alchemical techniques and the arts of spells and talismans to an assembly of disciples. He died in 1720 at the age of fifty-nine. Although the practices he taught were traditionally considered a part of the longevity methods in the Chinese tradition, in Japan they were quite independent and definitely a more strictly religiously oriented enterprise. Nor were they widely popular. One finds the active practice of such Taoist methods among isolated individuals rather than organized groups, religious or professional.

Another important work of approximately the same period is the *Tsūsen enju shimpō* 通仙延壽心注 (Essential Methods for Attaining Immortality and Prolonging Life), of unknown authorship, which appeared in 1695. Its second scroll includes two sections on longevity techniques, where instructions in a variety of gymnastic exercises, breathing techniques, and massages can be found.

A few other books should also be mentioned here. There is first of all the *Kokon dōin shū* 古今導引集 (Collection of Ancient and Modern Gymnastics), in two scrolls, written by Okubo Dōko 大久保踏古 and published in 1707. It contains a comprehensive description of the various practices, including also the refinement of one's essence and energy and the healing of diseases by means of exercises. Then there is the *Zōfu idō jitsuyō kōmoku* 増補醫道日用綱目 (Revised List of Everyday Medical Treatments), published in 1707, with a preface by Hongō Masatoyo 本郷正豐 . This book, which only survives in its Chinese translation, describes the personal efforts of its original author in healing himself. He wrote in order to spread the benefits he received from various gymnastic exercises directed at increasing and balancing the energies of the various inner organs. His techniques include gymnastics and massages, and they are solidly rooted in the ancient Chinese and Japanese tradition.

We also have Miyawaki Chūsoku's 宮脅仲策 *Dōin kōketsu jo* 導引口訣序 (Oral Formulas Regarding Gymnastics), in two scrolls, which was published in 1713. Depsite its title, this is in fact a popular and rather simplified exposition of easily practicable massages.

The same year, 1713, also saw the publication of Kaibara Ekken's 貝原 益軒 *Yōjōkun* 養生訓 (On Nourishing Life), in eight scrolls. This is still used today as a major textbook and is indeed one of the most famous volumes on the subject. It classifies longevity techniques according to "General Survey," "Food and Drink" (including smoking and excitements), "The Five Senses" (including basic hygiene), "Ailments Due to Excitement," "Treatments," "Prescriptions," and "Geriatrics." The primary practice in this collection is the nourishing of the "energy of the mind," which is done first of all by controlling and curbing desires and emotions. Among the more physical techniques we find massages, breathing exercises, gymnastics, grinding of the teeth, and others.

Kitamura Toshikatsu 喜多村利且 , also in 1713, published a new edition of Hayashi Masakatsu's *Dōin taiyō*. He added his father's, Gengensai's, supplement to it, a text entitled *Dōin taiyō furoku* 導引體要補錄 (Supplemented Essential Formulas of Gymnastics), which contains numerous illustrations of gymnastics with detailed explanations. Eight major series of exercises are described: the Elegant Exercise in Eight Sections, the Five Animals Pattern, Chen Xiyi's 陳希夷 twenty-four sitting exercises, Chen Xiyi's sleep practices, Indian massages, Brahmanic gymnastics, the Eighteen Arhats' exercises, and Bodhidharma's techniques for health.[4] The year 1713 is thus an important date in the history of longevity techniques in Japan.

In 1758, the Zen master Hakuin 白隱 published his *Yasen kanna* 夜船 閒話 (Leisurely Conversations During a Nightly Boating), where he describes certain sitting-style gymnastics and massages to be practiced in conjunction with meditations of the inner vision type. What is truly amazing about this work is that to this day Japanese practitioners of traditional Chinese medicine use the meditations described by Hakuin as therapy.

Among the gymnastics that are still practiced in Japan today the styles of Onitsura and Old Woman Tessai are the most popular. Onitsura lived in the late seventeenth century and propagated a simplified routine of exercises that could be performed even by children. His style is still well known in the Osaka area as the Onitsura Gymnastics. Old Woman Tessai was originally from Nagasaki, where she died in 1794. Her major disciple, who greatly propagated her work, was Utsumi Tatsunoshin 内海辰之進 . Her techniques came to be generally known as Tessai School Gymnastics and they are described in detail in the *Anfuku den* 按腹傳 (On Stomach Massage) of the year 1800.

---

4. The volume was recently reprinted with an introduction, from which this survey of Japanese sources was originally taken (Kitamura 1986).

After the Meiji Restoration in 1868, with the introduction and spread of Western medical ideas and practices in Japan, especially through the formal schooling system, traditional gymnastics, acupuncture, and pharmacology were relegated to a secondary position and lost quite a bit of their influence. Nevertheless, a certain number of popular practices continued to be developed and applied. There were especially Okada Takehiko's 岡田武彦 method of quiet sitting, Muraki Hiromasa's 村沐弘昌 cinnabar field respiration, Ishihara Yasuhide's 石原保秀 healing through dry bathing (self massages), and Morita Seima's 森田正馬 inner observation method. All of these were based on the ancient tradition and were undertaken in conjunction with acupuncture and moxibustion.

In recent years a new wave of Chinese imports has hit the Japanese health scene. Qigong and Taiji quan, propagated and widely publicized especially by people like Hoshino Minoru 星野稔 , are becoming increasingly popular. Famous Chinese masters frequently come to lecture and give demonstrations, among them such celebrities as Jiao Guorui and Zhou Nianfeng.[5] The populace is thus increasingly confronted with a revival of the ancient Chinese tradition at home and abroad. Since these various *qi*-techniques, with their combined application of gymnastics, breathing, and meditation, most certainly have a beneficial effect on health be it by curing diseases or by generally improving one's wellness, a further widening of their popularity and influence can be expected.

Modern Studies: General Considerations

The scholarly study of longevity techniques, another way in which the ancient tradition is continued nowadays, is mostly historically oriented. The first important contributions to this field were made as early as the 1930s when works like Ishihara Yasuhide's *Historical Studies of Chinese Medicine and Gymnastics*[6] (1933) were published. Although still limited in scope and intensity, those books were important milestones on the road to present scholarship. Over the past sixty years the discipline has continuously progressed and prospered, leading this year to the publication of two comprehensive volumes in different parts of the world—this volume and my own *Nourishing Vitality in Ancient China: Comprehensive Studies on Theory*

---

5. For details on the Qigong boom see the last chapter in this volume, "The Revival of *Qi*: Qigong in Contemporary China."

6. For full quotations in Japanese see the references below.

and Practice (1988). To explain the position of these two volumes in the overall situation of Chinese longevity studies, let me begin by outlining some of the basic conceptions and problems involved in longevity theory.

The basic idea of traditional Chinese medicine is expressed in sentences like "A good physician cures diseases which are not really diseases" (*Huainanzi*) and "The sage does not cure diseases after they develop, but well before they have manifested as diseases" (*Huangdi neijing suwen*). In the Chinese context disease is understood as any trace of disharmony within the body that occurs a long time before any outward symptoms become visible. For this reason, Chinese traditional medicine is fundamentally preventive, more concerned with "nourishing life" than with reestablishing physical health that is already broken down. Thus, in the very first chapter of the *Huangdi neijing suwen*, the Yellow Emperor is described as saying:

> As I have heard the true men of old followed the transforma-
> tions of heaven and earth, held on to the rhythm of Yin and
> Yang; their respiration was of essence and energy, they kept
> the spirit in the body without relying on outward means, thus
> they were able to keep their bodies from decay. For this reason
> the true men of old emulated heaven and earth in their
> longevity and they never perished. They had what is meant by
> the perfectly realized body.

Even in the ancient texts, the fundamental theme of traditional Chinese medicine is the pursuit of longevity, of the perfection of the body.

On the other hand, medicine and longevity or immortality techniques cannot be classified as exactly the same. They are two entirely different sides of the same coin—that is to say, they are today as they have been for thousands of years of Chinese history. Medicine is first of all the art of alleviating and healing the physical and psychological sufferings of humankind, while longevity techniques serve to maintain and perfect a state of health and harmony that has already been attained. Passages like the one quoted above from the *Suwen* are best understood as the principles and guidelines medicine ought to have once it has gone beyond curing the shortcomings of human health. The section on "magical techniques" in the bibliography of the *Hanshu* 漢書 (History of the Han Dynasty) lists medical treatises dealing with physiology and acupuncture side by side with books on sexual longevity techniques, measures for immortality, and the like. Close as this makes medicine and longevity seem, they are still described differently and represent two fundamentally distinct ways of dealing with the purpose and ideal of human life.

They both share a basic conception of what it means to be fully human—they have in common their fundamental understanding of the structure and makeup of the human body. Life is constituted by *qi* (breath or energy), a force that manifests in respiration and that can be felt circulating around the body. The circulation routes of the *qi*, the conduits (or *meridians* as they are traditionally called in translations) are well defined and put to use by both physicians and aspiring immortals. Their beliefs about the relationship of body and mind are basically the same.

These beliefs have been particularly studied by Ishida Hidemi, "The Expanding Spirit: Questions Regarding Body and Mind in Ancient China" (1982) as well as in his *Qi: The Flowing Body* (1987),[7] by Harada Jirō, "Expressions of the Body among Chinese Longevity Seekers" (1987), by Miura Kunio in his "The Revival of Qi: Qigong and Taoism" (1986)[8] by Maruyama Toshiaki in *Qi: From the Analects to the New Science* (1986), especially part 3, "The Life Science of *Qi*," and also by Kanō Yoshimitsu in *The Birth of Chinese Medicine* (1987).

It is quite impossible to gain a proper understanding of Chinese medicine without taking into account the ideas and practices of longevity techniques. After all, both adhere to a fundamental belief in the basic energy, *qi*, which makes up the human body and allows human beings to gain and retain life. Not only physical exercises and meditations deal with the *qi*, but drugs and concoctions also are aimed specifically at nourishing it and enhancing its functioning. The *Shennong bencao jing*　　神農本草經 (Shennong's Materia Medica) lists numerous plants and minerals that are particularly effective in strengthening the healthy *qi* and expelling its pathogenic counterpart. A most instructive example is found in its description of cinnabar, a mineral drug thought most powerful in the nourishing of life.

> Cinnabar. Sweet taste, slightly cool. Cures all diseases of the five inner organs of the body, nourishes the spirit, calms the souls, strengthens the *qi*, and brightens the eye. All evil influences and demons will be exterminated by its use, the light of the spirit will become all-pervading, old age will be avoided completely. If mutated, it turns into mercury. Found especially in deep ravines in the mountains.

Helpful as a drug to heal and strengthen, cinnabar later became the central means for attaining longevity and immortality. As such it was especially praised in Ge Hong's *Baopuzi*.

---

7. The second section of his new book appears as chapter 2 below, "Body and Mind: The Chinese Perspective."

8. A revised version of the latter article appears below as chapter 11, "The Revival of *Qi*: Qigong in Contemporary China."

The ultimate aim of traditional longevity ideas lies in the free manipulation of the *qi* of the individual. Although the basic notions relating to this have been studied and well-known for quite some time, it is necessary to gain a more practical access to them. The concrete methods by which longevity was thought possible can be understood only on the basis of a thorough knowledge of medicine and pharmacology. Both these fields have much in common with the ideas and practices of longevity and immortality in China.

Any fruitful discussion of Chinese longevity ideas must take a variety of notions and practices into account. There is first of all the concept of the body as a microcosm, as an immediate replica of the larger cosmos of the universe, and the notion that the two cosmos can and should be harmonized if not ultimately united. Then there is the specific way of guiding the *qi* around the body, of strengthening its spiritual relations with the help of meditation techniques such as "inner observation." The *qi* is made to pervade the entire body along its specific channels or conduits, and it is also gathered and accumulated in certain places. The power to manipulate the cosmic and personal *qi* at will is the primary aim of immortality concepts and practices. Given all this, it is imperative to study any concept or practice that bears even a distant relationship to longevity from both theoretical and practical perspectives.

Longevity Studies and Related Fields

Of course, it is not the case that Chinese longevity concepts and practices have never been seriously studied before. The philosophy of the Lao-Zhuang tradition, the concepts found in the various texts that followed and were based in one way or another on the ancient Taoist philosophers Laozi and Zhuangzi and the worldview of the Han, as well as immortality ideas and techniques in the more limited sense, have gradually come to be better understood over the years. However, most studies of these subjects have been rather specialized and have tended to single out one or the other aspect of the wider area of ancient Chinese thought that interests us here. There has as yet been no single attempt to collect all the evidence and analyze the overall position of longevity ideas and practices in ancient Chinese thought. This is true not only in Japan, but also in China and in Europe and America. The fundamental obstacle to such a comprehensive analysis is the complexity of the problem and especially the close interrelation of longevity and a great many areas of Chinese culture that belong to different fields of study. We may use the general expression longevity ideas and practices to refer to the phenomenon, but this includes such widely diverse areas as philosophy, religion, calisthenics, alchemy, medicine, and pharmacology.

Medicine

Especially where problems related to Chinese traditional medicine are concerned, a thorough knowledge of the medical classics of the Yellow Emperor, the *Suwen* and the *Lingshu* 靈樞 (Numinous Pivot), is absolutely indispensable. One must furthermore be intimately familiar with traditional pharmacology as it is expressed in the *Shennong bencao jing* and related materials—and that, in turn, is quite impossible without some background in modern pharmacology, botany, biology, and even chemistry. Then, in order to understand texts like Ge Hong's *Baopuzi* that praise the ingestion of an alchemical elixir as the most direct way to immortality, the scholar requires a working knowledge of alchemy. That includes mineralogy and chemistry, the exact ways in which basic chemical substances react with one another and how they can and should be treated. Once a complex text such as the *Zhouyi cantongqi* 周易參同契 (Tally to the Book of Changes) is focused on, additional knowledge of Han dynasty divinatory speculation on the basis of images and lines of the hexagrams in the *Book of Changes* as well as a thorough familiarity with basic alchemical terminology is necessary. The scholar has to decide, for example, whether the text deals primarily with operative alchemy or with inner alchemy and on which level at each given point in the text certain symbolic expressions are being used.

Here is the crux of the problem. The need to have recourse to such widely different fields of study is what has stood in the way of a more comprehensive and encompassing appreciation of Chinese traditional longevity ideas and practices.

Taoism

Longevity techniques also played an important role in the various schools of religious Taoism that developed in the Later Han and succeeding dynasties. Consequently, a student of Chinese longevity should have a basic knowledge of Taoist texts and the history of Taoism in order to be able to shed light on the religious aspect of the subject. Especially since Kawakatsu Yoshio's 川勝 義雄 translation of Henri Maspero's classic *Le Taoisme et les religions chinoises* into Japanese in 1966. Taoist scholars, who were and in large part still are preoccupied with the formal textual history and philological study of the scriptures, have been placing a greater emphasis on the longevity ideas and practices referred to in the texts.

In the Six Dynasties, Sui, and Tang periods, the number of outstanding physicians and pharmacologists who were also fervent believers in Taoism increased dramatically. One should especially mention Tao Hongjing 陶弘景 (456–536), who wrote a commentary to the *Shennong bencao jing*, in seven scrolls; Sun Simiao, recluse on Mount Taibai, with his *Qianjin fang*; and Yang Shangshan of the Sui and early Tang dynasty, distinguished commentator of the *Huangdi neijing taisu*, who may or may not have been a Taoist practitioner but whose writings certainly bear a strong imprint of Lao-Zhuang and Taoist thought.

The Sui and Tang dynasties were the heyday of alchemy. As an area of inquiry alchemy is especially obscure, because the texts are replete with esoteric vocabulary, usually do not include any author's name, and can hardly be dated at all. Worse, even when there are an author's name and a date, the text may very well be a later forgery. In recent years some materials have been properly placed thanks to the outstanding work of Chen Guofu (1983), who analyzed the rhyme structure of alchemical poems. So scholars of longevity ideas and practices must know traditional Chinese phonology as well as botany, mineralogy, and chemistry.

Around the same period, the techniques of inner alchemy were developed. In inner alchemy one uses the same ingredients as in operative or outer alchemy but identifies them with certain energies within the body, such as essence, breath or energy, and spirit. It is from these inner substances that the cinnabar elixir of immortality is produced. Ever since the *Huangdi neijing suwen*, the focus of Chinese notions of the body have been on the five inner organs or orbs. These five were now integrated into a system of circulating the energy and visualizing one's inner makeup. The texts of inner alchemy are largely composed in an esoteric language, and the teachings were traditionally handed down from master to disciple orally which indicates that inner alchemical practice was probably accessible only to a few carefully prepared initiates.

Buddhism

Certain Buddhist concepts were integrated into inner alchemical theory, especially the ideas and practices of meditation of the Tiantai and Chan schools, so, in order to thoroughly understand the later developments of Chinese longevity techniques a basic knowledge of the history, concepts, and practices of Chan Buddhism is necessary. Fukui (1987) has shown the Buddhist influence convincingly in the case of Zhang Boduan's 張伯端

Wuzhen pian 悟真篇 (Awakening to Truth) of the Song dynasty. I myself have described the impact of Chinese Chan Buddhism on inner alchemical practices of the Complete Perfection movement of the Southern Song as well as on Taoists of later periods like Wu Shouyang 伍守陽 and Liu Huayang 柳華陽 (Sakade 1987).

Looking at the interaction of Buddhism and Taoism from the perspective of longevity techniques leads to ancient Indian medicine and its impact on religious thought and practice as well as to typically Indian practices such as Yoga and Tantric forms of meditation. In recent years, Yogic and Tantric practices—physical exercises as well as visualizations and mandala meditations—have come under closer scholarly scrutiny. Indian or more specific Buddhist medicine, on the other hand, is not very well known. Since Buddhist scholars tend to be involved with one or the other school in particular and, in the case of Japanese scholars, often are already born and raised in a given community, their concerns are limited to those specific doctrines and rituals. A broader perspective on Buddho-Taoist and Hindu-Buddhist interactions could benefit scholars in a whole variety of disciplines.

A Comprehensive Approach

So far we have enumerated quite a number of fields related to the study of Chinese longevity techniques. It goes without saying that a thorough familiarity with the traditional Chinese worldview is also a must. Subjects like astrology, magic, geomancy, cookery, and physical education (gymnastics, mountain climbing), are in the broadest sense related to longevity techniques, and to undertake a truly comprehensive study of the latter one has to take all these former into consideration—an undertaking quite obviously too grand for any one single scholar. A concerted effort of similarly interested and enthusiastic students of Chinese worldview and practices is needed. The more scholars of different fields and countries cooperate, the more overall insights and far-reaching results of the inquiry there will be. The two-year series of conferences of our Study Group on Traditional Chinese Longevity Techniques, sponsored by the Japanese Ministry of Education, was only a drop in the ocean, but it has produced some exciting results and has certainly stimulated ongoing and newly developing research. A volume summarizing our results, *Nourishing Vitality in Ancient China: Comprehensive Studies on Theory and Practice*, has recently been published in Japan (Sakade 1988).[9]

---

9. The book divides into five parts, dealing with the relationship of the concepts and practices of nourishing vitality in traditional China to medicine, philosophy, Taoism, Buddhism, and medical traditions other than Chinese.

Lao-Zhuang Thought and Longevity Ideas

The field that is usually considered relevant for the study of Lao-Zhuang thought is philosophy rather than religion. A good example of this outlook is Fukunaga Mitsuji's *Zhuangzi: Ancient Chinese Existentialism* (1964). As the subtitle suggests, the ancient texts here are interpreted as dealing with "a fundamental realization of the true existence of the actual world." It is a philosophy that purports to describe the perfect human being's, the true man's, way of looking at the world, a realm of pure existence.

I remember very clearly how, about twelve years ago, at the twenty-seventh meeting of the Japanese Society for the Study of Taoism (Nippon dōkyō gakkai 日本道教學會), Mori Mikisaburō 森三樹三郎 was severely criticized by the late Kimata Norio 木全德雄 for a presentation entitled "The Relation Between Taoism and Lao-Zhuang Thought."[10] The controversial idea was this one:

> The intimate merging of Taoism and Lao-Zhuang thought was not found in the context of Chinese culture outside the circle of Taoist believers. The relation between the two was consequently studied especially by scholars interested in understanding the Taoist tradition, and in particular by Henri Maspero and the French Sinologists who followed him as well as a few members of the Japanese scholarly community. At this point, and in the wake of Maspero's work, I would like to again raise the issue of the relation between the two traditions of ancient China. (*Tōhō shūkyō* 49 (1977): 77)

Maspero's epoch-making *Taoism and Chinese Religion* (French 1950 and 1971, English 1981) was translated by Kawakatsu Yoshio and published by Tōkai University in 1966. I don't recall all the details of the ensuing discussion at the conference, but I know that Kimata pleaded with Mori, saying: "According to the *Zhuangzi*, the true man can enter fire and not be burned, can enter water and not be drowned—if that isn't Taoism, what is it?"[11]

---

10. An abstract of the presentation can be found in volume 49 (1977) of the *Tōhō shūkyō*, the publication of the Dōkyō gakkai that has appeared twice a year since 1951.

11. The paper was, naturally, not published at the time, but was later considered in "Lao-Zhuang Thought and the Two Religions Buddhism and Taoism" and "The Origin and Development of Taoism," contained in Mori 1986. The gist of the theory proposed here is that Taoism developed from the belief in immortality centering itself on longevity techniques. In the early Taoist movements of the second century, this was then integrated with so-called philosophical Taoism—that is, with the ideas of the *Daode jing* and the

The position that there is a strong fundamental difference Between Lao-Zhuang thought and the Taoist religion, represented especially by Fukunaga and Mori, became more and more tenuous as Taoist scholarship developed. This process was greatly stimulated by the translation of Maspero's *Taoism*, but it was also furthered by the more intensive study of Lao-Zhuang thought itself, which, especially in recent years, has increasingly focused on the more religious and practical aspects of this tradition. The work of Akazuka Kiyoshi is especially noteworthy. In two chapters of a recent book (1987), "The Origins and Structure of Philosophical Taoism" and "Ancient Religious Experience and Forms of Taoist Argumentation," he shows the degree to which the argumentation of the texts of philosophical Taoism is influenced by religious experience. Whether or not his discussion is influenced by Maspero, it certainly shows how irrevocable the spell that insisted on Lao-Zhuang thought as a form of metaphysical philosophy has been broken. Another author who interprets Lao-Zhuang thought as basically religious is Kaga Eiji. He says:

> Nowadays it is generally accepted that the philosophy of both Laozi and Zhuangzi places a strong emphasis on longevity. How should this fact be interpreted? It should by now be obvious to everyone concerned that there is nothing much left of Lao-Zhuang thought when one takes out the longevity aspect. I personally tend toward the conviction that the concern with longevity and immortality is at the root of Lao-Zhuang thought and not vice versa. (Kaga 1982/83)

In his work, Kaga reinterprets a large number of scholarly theories regarding longevity ideas in ancient China in light of this view. For instance, he states:

> Longevity in the *Zhuangzi* does not only refer to longevity in the concrete sense, i.e., to the preservation and perfection of the physical body. It also includes a certain persuasion about the way human beings should live in the world, the process by which an individual, beginning with the realization that life and death are one, arrives at the absolute, the original state and thereby becomes a perfect, a spirit man. (Kaga 1982/83)

To me this perspective makes much more sense than Mori's conviction that

> Zhuangzi's original position is found in the ultimate equalizing of life and death, in the complete transcendence of all opposites, of all choice. It is without doubt in this devotion to

---

Zhuangzi. In later Taoism, Buddhism merged with this already complex structure to form the fully developed religion of the Shangqing, Lingbao, and other schools.

the original ideas of Zhuangzi that longevity ideas and practices found their beginning. (Mori 1959: 7)

Not much has been said in recent publications about the relation of political order and longevity techniques—of the individual's preservation of his or her own body versus the communal salvation of humankind through the establishment of a perfect society. Nevertheless, in numerous traditional longevity theories a direct relation, if not actually structural equality, is seen between the body of the individual and the entirety of the human community. This may be a reflection, at the level of longevity ideas, of the unification of China into one great empire. Certainly the concept needs much further study.

Among recent studies that emphasize the direct relationship of Lao-Zhuang thought and ancient longevity practices there are Sawada Takio's "An Examination of Longevity Ideas Before the Qin" (1965), his *Zhuangzi's Longevity Ideas* (1983), and Shibata Kiyotsugu's "Longevity and Political Theories in the *Lüshi chunqiu*" (1982). Views presented in these publications range between Kaga's and Mori's: some advocate a more philosophical and others a more religious standpoint. What all of them have in common, however, is that they increase our knowledge of the origins and conceptualizations of longevity ideas.

Incidentally, Kaga's argument that longevity techniques are at the root of Lao-Zhuang thought was already formulated by Tsuda Sōkichi in his "Studies on Immortality Thought," originally of 1934. He says:

> The central point of the *Zhuangzi* is the pursuit of longevity, the nourishing of life. One may say that this is the theme that pervades the entire volume. More than that, even the *Daode jing* contains passages that deal with longevity and the perfection of life. (Tsuda 1964: vol. 13:191)

The same viewpoint is also expressed and detailed in other writings by the same author, notably in the chapters dealing with "Hedonism and Longevity Ideas" and "Longevity Ideas and the Concepts of Life and Death" in his book *Philosophical Taoism and Its Development* (1964: vol. 13), which was originally published in 1926.

To summarize, the understanding of Lao-Zhuang thought as an expression of longevity ideas is a fruitful line of inquiry that eventually should cast some very interesting light on ancient Chinese philosophy and religion.

Longevity Concepts in Taoism and Buddhism

As mentioned above, the translation of Maspero's *Taoism and Chinese Religions* was an epoch-making work that greatly sped the progress of Taoist studies in Japan. However, aside from its importance for Taoist studies, it has also had a tremendous impact on research on longevity ideas and practices. I myself, in my contribution to the first volume of Fukui Kōjun's *Taoism* (1983), "Longevity Techniques," found that one of the most important works in the area was Maspero's. In addition, those of his works that deal specifically with the arts of nourishing life have been translated separately. All these efforts have deepened our understanding of the concrete practices of longevity.

Where Maspero deals primarily with practices before and during the Tang, Sakauchi Shigeo, in an article entitled "The *Zhong-Lü chuandao ji* and the Concepts of Inner Alchemy" (1985), describes the concepts and practice of inner alchemy after that period. This is the first major study of these materials in Japanese, and again it owes a great deal to Maspero. It describes on the basis of one of the major texts of inner alchemy how Taoist practice developed from breathing exercises and the circulation of *qi* to the full system of inner alchemy as it flourishes first under the Song. Another work that deals with Taoist practice is Mugitani Kunio's "An Inquiry into the *Huangting neijing jing*" (1982). Describing this text as one of the early scriptures that were used in the establishment of Taoism as a way of making universal salvation in immortality accessible to everyone, Mugitani provides some interesting insights into the theory of the five organs of the body and their various divine residents as well as into the practice of visualizing the body gods as a way of attaining long life and immorality.

Taoist Meditation and the Dating of Scriptures

In recent years the dates of several important Taoist scriptures have become the center of a heated discussion among Japanese and French scholars. Those in question are in particular the *Taiping jing* 太平經 (Scripture of Great Peace) and two *Daode jing* commentaries, the one by Heshang gong and the *Xiang'er* 想爾. A major participant in this discussion is Harada Jirō, with two articles, one on the *Xiang'er* (1983) and one on the *Taiping jing* (1984). In both papers, the author outlines the differences between the longevity concepts in the works in question as a clue to their dates. In addition, there are

Yoshioka Yoshitoyo's work on the practice of "guarding the One" (1976);[12] Kusuyama Haruki's contributions on the *Heshang gong Commentary* (1966) and the longevity practices mentioned in it, notably the correlation between body and state and the theory of the five inner organs (1972); and Naitō Motoharu's paper on the same text and its meditation methods (1977).

However, since all of these studies deal with longevity techniques mainly in connection with the problems of dating the texts, none of them clarifies the concrete practices involved. A more relevant contribution is found in Kusuyama's comprehensive study of the Laozi legend (1979). He distinguishes between two major sets of longevity concepts, a philosophical Taoist one and a religious Taoist one. The former emphasizes psychological efforts: lessening desires, calming the spirit, controlling the senses. The latter favors a physical approach: gymnastics, breathing, drugs, and so on. In the commentary by Heshang gong, so Kusuyama holds, the practices are mixed together, while the religious longevity theory was attached later. On the other hand, it appears that although the two different approaches may be described as nourishing the spirit versus nourishing the body, they were never really incompatible. From the oldest documents onward, the texts state again and again that

> it is most important to nourish the spirit, it is of secondary importance to nourish the body. The spirit should be pure and tranquil, the bones should be stable. This is the foundation of long life. (*Wenzi 9*)

One may well distinguish two dimensions on the theoretical level. In actual practice, however, there is a unity between meditation, visualization, guiding the *qi*, embryo respiration, and the various other longevity techniques.

Physical Exercises

Among the more physically oriented practices, gymnastics in particular have received a fair amount of attention. Before the war, Ishihara Yasuhide published his book on Chinese medicine and gymnastics (1933), recently reedited by Hayashima Masao (1979). It is an invaluable aid for the historical understanding of Chinese gymnastics. There have also been some interesting archaeological finds in this area in recent years, especially the *Daoyin tu* 導引 圖 (Gymnastics Chart) from the tomb of the Marquess of Dai at Mawangdui in Changsha (Hunan Province). A discussion of this fascinating document is

---

12. For more details on these see chapter 5, "Guarding the One: Concentrative Meditation in Taoism."

found in my paper "On Gymnastics" (1978). A historical survey of the practices and sources of ancient Chinese physical therapy is moreover contained in my introduction to Kitamura Toshikatsu's nineteenth-century account of gymnastics (Kitamura 1986). Unlike the various works on the history of physical techniques, this introduction places a strong emphasis on Chinese materials after the Song and texts found in Japan.[13] The theory and practice of Qigong, the modern development of gymnastics and Taiji quan has been discussed by Miura, as mentioned above.

Alchemy: Outer and Inner

Operative outer alchemy, one of the two types of alchemy, is the central immortality technique in Ge Hong's *Baopuzi*. This text, with its various prescriptions, was first studied by Chikashige Masumi in his book *Far Eastern Alchemy* (1933). Another work in the same field is Kōda Roban's study of the *Zhouyi cantongqi* ([1957] 1978), which goes beyond the realm of operative alchemy and also discusses the principles and concepts of later inner alchemical practice. Later, Yoshida Mitsukuni published an appreciation of the alchemy of the *Zhouyi cantongqi* and the *Baopuzi* from the viewpoint of the history of science (1963). There is no doubt that this is one of the most important studies of the subject, and certainly in the future more scholars formally trained in chemistry will turn their attention to the traditional practices.

In the more historical study of alchemy as a longevity technique the work of Sanaka Sō is indispensable (1975), especially his chapters on "The Development of Drugs and Dietetics in Relation to the Longevity Methods of the *Baopuzi*," "The Rise of Cinnabar or On the Interaction of Pharmacology and Immortality Beliefs," "Drugs in the Tang," and "Changes in the Meaning and Practice of Cinnabar." Another important contribution on the question of alchemy is the work of Murakami Yoshimi who has studied especially the *Baopuzi* (1956) and Taoist ideas and practices in the Six Dynasties (1974). Murakami has also contributed the section on alchemy in Fukui Kōjun's *Taoism* (1983).

The volumes dealing with chemistry and alchemy in Joseph Needham's series on *Science and Civilisation in China* (1973, 1974, 1976, 1980, 1983) are another set of invaluable research aids. It is especially regrettable that the latest volume, *Spagyrical Discovery and Invention: Physiological Alchemy*, has not yet been translated into Japanese. It does appear in the Chinese

---

13. The section of this introduction that deals with Japanese sources is translated above as "Sources from the Eleventh to the Nineteenth Century."

translation of Needham's entire series by Pan Jixing 潘吉星 , and parts of it have appeared in Yamada 1977 and Sakai 1977. Parts of the work of the American scholar Nathan Sivin have also been translated; his article "Chinese Alchemy and the Manipulation of Time" is of particular interest (Sivin 1976). His famous study of Sun Simiao's alchemical enterprises (1968) has unfortunately not yet been translated, although a Chinese version has appeared in Taiwan.

Inner alchemy, which as mentioned above began to flourish on the basis of operative alchemy and meditation from the Tang and Song dynasties onward, has as yet hardly been studied at all. Textual studies are scarce, theoretical inquiries into its ideas and concepts have not appeared, and its concrete methods and practices await analysis.[14] Because of this, the reprint of Itō Kōen's book, *Methods of Alchemical Cultivation* (1987), is greatly welcome. It gives a straightforward and clearly understandable outline of the practices of inner alchemy and will certainly be very useful to scholars. On the other hand, since its original, the *Jinxian zhenglun* 金仙証論 (True Account of the Golden Immortal), by Liu Huayang dates from the late eighteenth century, it can be used as a description of the practices of an earlier period only in a limited way.

Liu Huayang was a prolific writer. He also wrote the *Huiming jing* 彗命 經 (Life in Wisdom Scripture), which was published in 1794. This text, together with the *Taiyi jinhua zongzhi* 太乙金華宗旨 (Comprehensive Instructions Regarding the Golden Flower of the Great One), is contained in the famous book by Richard Wilhelm and with a preface by C.G. Jung, *The Secret of the Golden Flower* (1962), a work that also made use of the *Huiming jing*.

Other studies dealing with inner alchemy are Imai Usaburō's "The *Cantongqi* and Song Philosophy" (1960), Suzuki Yūjirō's *Studies of the Han Dynasty Yijing* (1963) and *Zhouyi cantongqi* (1977), and Fukui Kōjun's "On the *Zhouyi cantongqi*" ([1972] 1974). All these studies deal particularly with the theoretical concepts behind inner alchemy; how those concepts apply to longevity practice in a practical way has yet to be explored. I have recently studied some material of the Six Dynasties that bears on the *Zhouyi cantongqi*, some works by the poet Jiang Yan 江淹 (444–504), who apparently practiced the techniques of a certain Gugangzi 孤剛子 , allegedly a contemporary of the famous Wei Boyang 魏伯陽 (Sakade 1988).

The following works should also be taken into account: Miyakawa Hisayuki's discussion of Chen Xiyi (1973) and his study of Bai Yuchan 白玉

---

14. In the West things look only slightly better, as is evident from the reference list attached to chapter 10.

噡 (1978), and Imai Usaburō's work on the *Wuzhen pian* (1962), his study of the Southern School of Taoism (1961), and his article on the philosophy of Bai Yuchan (1963). Again, all these works tend to be very much concerned with textual lineages and philological problems. They tell us little about the actual living conditions and activities of the practitioners. I hope that in the future, the more concrete aspects of Song Taoist practice and especially inner alchemy will be brought to light.

Confucian Thought and Buddhism

Another area that has received some scholarly attention is the problem of the influence of inner alchemical theory on Neo-Confucian thought. Here we have notably Miura Kunio's work on "Zhu Xi and Breathing" (1983) and Azuma Jūji's paper on his interpretation of the *Zhouyi cantongqi* (1984). These studies show that Zhu Xi did indeed have a deep appreciation of inner alchemy and was to a certain degree influenced by Taoist thought.

We know practically nothing about inner alchemy in the Qing. About the only studies of the subject are Miyakawa's discussion of Liu Yiming's 劉 -明*Wuzhen zhizhi* 悟箏直旨 (Pointers to 'Awakening to Truth'), which was published in 1950, and my own paper on the *Jinxian zhenglun* (1987).

The important issue of the influence of religious Taoism on Buddhism in China has not received much scholarly attention to date. A discussion of the application of breathing exercises in a Buddhist context is found in Michihata Ryōshū (1961), and the relationship of certain Taoist techniques to the practices of esoteric Buddhism was studied by Yoshioka Yoshitoyo (1964, 1972), Kuriyama Shūjun (1973), and Tanaka Fumio (1984). More than that, the promising area of the mutual influence of Tiantai Samatha-Vipaśyanā techniques and Taoist forms of meditation, inner vision and inner alchemy has hardly been touched upon either. Here we have in particular the works of Andō Shunyū (1970) and Yamano Toshio (1984, 1985), who are specifically interested in the possible usage of Tiantai meditations for the healing of diseases.

Conclusion

Japan can look back on a long and fruitful tradition of Chinese longevity techniques, of both spiritual and medical practices. Today's scholars are heirs to this long tradition, and they honor their ancestors best by continuing to try to understand their techniques and their worldview on both theoretical and practical levels.

I have given here a rough outline of the history of Chinese longevity techniques in Japan, pointing to certain fundamental problems of theory, such as the distinction between mental and physical practices, and between philosophical and religious Taoism. There are many areas that should be developed further, and as I have emphasized, the main shortcoming of the studies to date has been that they do not deal with concrete issues—they hesitate to ask what was really going on in these practices. It goes without saying that this survey can only be a sketch of the history of longevity techniques and that it reflects the author's preferences and prejudices.

One big scholarship problem is on the best way to being solved: the complexity of the fields related in one way or another to Chinese traditional longevity techniques. Recent publications have shown how harmonious and fruitful cooperation among scholars in different areas can be when they are joined together by a common interest in one intriguing aspect of Chinese culture.

The concerted effort that made this book and my own possible is the result of unceasing progress in the field, which has brought specialists from a large variety of different areas together. Not only the medical, but also the philosophical and religious issues as well as a number of wider subjects related to traditional Chinese longevity ideas and practices have become the focus of scholarly attention. The result is that this fascinating phenomenon of ancient Chinese culture can now be grasped much more comprehensively and from a variety of different angles.

On the other hand, even with this concerted effort, only a small step has been taken on a long road. The study of traditional Chinese longevity ideas and practices involves Chinese ancient philosophy, religion, medicine, chemistry, and many other areas, which in themselves require much further research. More than that, many questions about the influence of Indian, Persian, and possibly even European worldviews and medicine on this area of Chinese culture remain largely unexplored. Only through the continued cooperation of specialists of all these different fields can further understanding progress. More and wider international and interdisciplinary projects are needed and desired, and it is my sincere hope that the study of this field will progress further, in my country and in yours.

References

Fukui, Kojun. 1974. "A Study of *Chou-i Ts'an-t'ung-ch'i*," *Acta Asiatica* 27 (1974), 19–32.

Maspero, Henri. 1971. *Le taoisme et les religions chinoises.* Paris: Gallimard, 1971. Originally published as *Mélanges posthumes sur les religions et l'histoire de la Chine.* Paris: Bibliotheque de diffusion du Musée Guimet, 1950.

Maspero, Henri. 1981. *Taoism and Chinese Religion.* Translated by Frank Kierman Amherst. University of Massachusetts Press, 1981.

Needham, Joseph. 1973. *Science and Civilisation in China. Chemistry and Chemical Technology: Spagyrical Discovery and invention.* Vol. V.1. Cambridge: Cambridge University Press, 1973.

—— 1974. *Science and Civilisation in China. Spagyrical Discovery and Invention: Magistries of Gold and Immortality.* Vol. V.2. Cambridge: Cambridge University Press, 1974.

—— 1976. *Science and Civilisation in China. Spagyrical Discovery and Invention: Historical Survey, from Cinnabar Elixir to Synthetic Insulin.* Vol. V.3. Cambridge: Cambridge University Press, 1976.

—— 1980. *Science and Civilisation in China. Spagyrical Discovery and Invention: Apparatus, Theories and Gifts.* Vol. V.4. Cambridge: Cambridge University Press, 1980.

—— 1983. *Science and Civilisation in China. Spagyrical Discovery and Invention: Physiological Alchemy.* Vol. V.5. Cambridge: Cambridge University Press, 1983.

Sakade, Yoshinobu. 1986. "The Taoist Character of the 'Chapter on Nourishing Life' of the *Ishinpō*," *Kansai daigaku bungaku ronshū* 1986, 775–798.

Sivin, Nathan. 1968. *Chinese Alchemy: Preliminary Studies.* Cambridge: Harvard University Press, 1968.

Sivin, Nathan. 1976. "Chinese Alchemy and the Manipulation of Time," *Isis* 67 (1976), 513–527.

Wilhelm, Richard. 1962. *The Secret of the Golden Flower.* New York: Harcourt, Brace & World, 1962.

in Chinese and Japanese

Akazuka Kiyoshi 赤塚忠 1987
Akazuka Kiyoshi chōsaku shū 赤塚忠著作集
Vol. 4. Tokyo: Kenbunsha, 1987.

Andō Shunyū 安藤俊雄 1970
"Shibyōhō to shite no tendai shikan" 治病方 としての 天台止觀
Otani daigaku kenkyū nenpō 大谷大學研究年報 23 (1970), 1–58.

Azuma Jūji 吾妻重二 1984
"Shu Ki 'Shūeki sandōkei kōi' ni tsuite" 朱熹周易參同契考異について
Nippon chūgoku gakkaihō 日本中國學會報 36 (1984), 175–190.

Chen Guofu 陳國符 1983
"Daozang jingzhong waidan huangbaifa jingjue chushi chaodai kao"
道藏經中外丹黃白法經訣出世朝代考
Zhongguo kejishi tansuo 中國科技史探索
Shanghai: Guji, 1983.

Chikashige Masumi 近重箏澄 1933
Tōyō renkinjutsu 東洋煉金術
Tokyo: Uchida rōkakuho, 1933.

Fukui Fumimasa 福井文雅 1987
"Zenshinkyō no Hannya shingyō jūyō" 全真教の 般若心經受容
Hannya shingyō no rekishi teki kenkyū 般若心經の 歷史的研究
Tokyo: Shunjūsha, 1987.

Fukui Kōjun 福井康順 et al. (ed.) 1983
Dōkyō 道教. 3 vols. Tokyo: Hirakawa, 1983.

Fukunaga Mitsuji 福永光司 1964
Sōshi: kodai chūgoku no jitsuzon shugi 莊子古代中國 の實存主義
Tokyo: Chūō koron sha, 1964.

Harada Jirō 原田二郎 1983
"Rōshi sōjichū no chōsei no riron" 老子想爾註の長生の 理論
Chūtetsu bungaku kaihō 中哲文學會報 8 (1983), 1–18.

—— 1984. "Taiheikyō no seimeikan, chōseisetsu ni tsuite"
太平經の生命觀長生說について
Nippon chūgoku gakkaihō 36 (1984), 71–83.

—— 1987. "Yōseika no nikutai hyōyō ni tsuite" 養生家の 肉體表象について
Tōhōgaku 東方學 72 (1987), 48–62.

Hayashima Masao 早島正雄 1979
Tōyō igaku tsūshi: Kampō, shinkyū, dōin igaku no shiteki kōsatsu
東洋醫學通史: 漢方針灸導引醫學 の史的考察
Tokyo: Shizensha, 1979.

Hiraki Kōhei 平木康平 1976
"Yōseiron o meguru Kei Kō to Shō Shū no ronnan"
養生論をめぐる 稽康と向秀の 論難
In *Chūgoku tetsugakushi no tenbō to mosaku* 中國哲學史の 展望と模索
pp. 381–403. Tokyo: Sōbunsha, 1976.

Ikeda Festschrift
Ikeda Suetoshi hakase koki kinen Tōyōgaku ronshū
池田未利博士古稀記念東洋學論集
Tokyo: Tōhō gakkai, 1978.

Imaeda Jirō 今枝二郎 1959
"Hōbokushi naihen ni arawaretaru yōsei shisō ni tsuite"
抱朴子内篇に現われたる養生思想について
Kambungaku kenkyū 漢文學研究 7 (1959), 24–36.

Imai Usaburō 今井宇三郎 1960
"Shūeki sandōkei to Sōgaku" 周易参同契と 宋學
Tōkyō kyōiku daigaku bungakubu kiyō 東京教育大學文學部紀要 27
(1960), 1–47.

—— 1961. "Dōka nanshu no keifu ni tsuite" 道家南宗 の系譜について
Kangi bunka 漢魏文化 2 (1961), 9–16.

—— 1962. "Goshinhen no seisho to shisō" 悟真篇の 成書と 思想
Tōhō shūkyō 東方宗教 37 (1962), 1–19.

—— 1963. "Kintandō kenkyū: Nansō no dōshi Haku Gyokuzen no shisō"
金丹道研究: 南宋の道士白玉蟾の 思想
Tōkyō kyōiku daigaku bungakubu kiyō 42 (1963), 91–126.

Ishida Hidemi 石田秀實 1982
"Kakujū suru seishin" 擴充 する 精神
Tōhōgaku 東方學 63 (1982), 1–15.

—— 1987. *Ki: Nagareru shintai* 氣: 流れる 身體
Tokyo: Hirakawa, 1987.

Ishihara Yasuhide 石原保秀 1933
Kōkan igaku oyobi dōin no shiteki kōsatsu 皇漢醫學及よび 導引の史的考察
Tokyo, 1933.

Itō Kōen 伊藤光遠 1987
Rentan shūyōhō 煉丹脩養法
Tokyo: Taniguchi, 1987.

Itō Festschrift
Itō Sōhei kyōju taikan kinen Chūgokugaku rombunshū
伊藤瀨平教授退官記念中國學論文集
Tokyo, 1986.

Kaga Eiji 加賀榮治 1982/83
"Rōsō to yōsei" 老莊と養生
4 parts, *Kokugo* 國語 219, 221, 223, and 225 (1982/83).

Kanaya Osamu 金谷治 1983
Chūgoku ni okeru ningensei no tankyū 中國における人間性の探求
Tokyo: Sōbunsha, 1983.

Kanō Yoshimitsu 加納喜光 1987
Chūgoku igaku no tanjō 中國醫學の誕生
Tokyo: Tokyo Daigaku, 1987.

Kitamura Toshikatsu 喜多村利且 1986
Dōin taiyō 導引體要
Tokyo: Taniguchi, 1986.

Koda Roban 辛田露伴 1978
"Sensho sandōkei" 仙書參同契
Kōda Roban zenshū 辛田露伴全集
Vol. 18. Tokyo: Iwanami, 1978. Originally published in 1957.

Kuriyama Shūjun 栗山秀純 1973
"Kōkyō daishi no 'Gorin kuji myōhimitsushaku' to chūsei nihon bunka ni okeru gozōkan shisō" 興教大師の五輪九字明秘密釋と中世日本文化における
五藏觀思想
Kōsōden no kenkyū 高僧傳の研究 Tokyo: Sankibō, 1973.

Kusuyama Haruki 桐山春樹 1966
"Rōshi kajōkō chū no shisōteki kōsatsu: Toku ni ichi no go o chūshin to shite"
老子河上公注 の 思想的考察: 特に一の語を中心として
Tōhōshūkyō 28 (1966), 1–20.

—— 1972. "Rōshi kajōkō chū no shisōteki kōsatsu: Chishin chikoku no ron ni tsuite" 老子河上公注の思想的考察: 治身治國の論について
Suzuki Festschrift, 231–251.

—— 1979. *Rōshi densetsu no kenkyū* 老子傳説の研究
Tokyo: Sōbunsha, 1979.

Makio Festschrift
Makio Ryōkai hakase shōju kinen ronshū Chūgoku no shūkyō to kagaku
牧尾良海博士頌壽記念論集: 中國の宗教と科學
Tokyo: Kokusho kankōkai, 1984.

Maruyama Yoshihiro 丸山吉廣 1958
"Ryōshi shunjū ni arawareta yōsei no setsu" 呂氏春秋に現われた養生の説
Kambungaku kenkyū 6 (1958), 8–18.

Maruyama Toshiaki 丸山敏秋 1986
Ki: Rongo kara nyū saiensu made 氣: 論語からニューサイェンスまで
Tokyo: Tōkyō bijutsu, 1986.

Michihata Ryōshu 道端良秀 1961
"Donran no Chōjuhō" 曇鸞の長壽法
Tōhō shūkyō 18 (1961), 1–16.

Miura Kunio 三浦國雄 1983
"Shushi to kokyū" 朱子と呼吸
Kanaya 1983: 449–521.

—— 1986. "Ki no fukken: Kikō to dōkyō" 氣の復權: 氣功と道教
Itō Festschrift, 203–233.

Miyakawa Hisayuki 宮川尚志 1950
"Ryū Itsumei no Goshin chokushi ni tsuite" 劉一明の悟真直旨について
Okayama daigaku hōbungakubu gakujutsu kiyō
岡山大學法問學部學術紀要
3 (1950), 49–58.

—— 1973. "Dōkyōshi jō yori mita godai" 道教史上より見た五代
Tōhō shūkyō 42 (1973), 13–34.

—— 1978. "Nansō no dōshi Haku Gyokuzen no shiseki"
南宋の道士白玉蟾の事跡
Uchida Festschrift, 499–517.

Mori Mikisaburō　森三樹三郎　1959
"Sōshi ni okeru sei no shisō" 莊子における　性の思想
Tōhōgaku 18 (1959), 1–13.

—— 1986. *Rōsō to bukkyō*　老莊と佛教
Kyoto: Hōzōkan, 1986.

Mugitani Kunio　麥谷邦夫　1982
"Kōtei naikeikyō shiron" 黄庭内景經試論
Tōyō bunka 東洋文化　62 (1982), 29–61.

—— 1985. "Rōshi sōjichū ni tsuite" 老子想爾注について
Tōhō gakuhō 57 (1985), 75–109.

—— 1985a. *Rōshi sōjichū sakuin*　老子想爾注索引
Kyoto: Hōyū shoten, 1985.

Murakami Yoshimi　村上嘉實　1956
Chūgoku no sennin　中國の仙人
Kyoto: Heiraku shoten, 1956.

—— 1974. *Rikuchō shisōshi kenkyū*　六朝思想史研究
Kyoto: Heiraku shoten, 1974.

—— 1984. "Chūgoku igaku shisō kara mita seimeikan"
中國醫學思想から見た生命觀
Makio Festschrift, 471–488.

Naito Motoharu　内藤軏治　1977
"Kajōkō chū Rōshi no yōseisetsu ni tsuite"
河上公注老子の養生説について
Yoshioka Festschrift, 319–340.

Onimaru Tadashi　鬼丸紀　1980
"Ojū no Yōseiron"　王充の養生論
Chūgoku tetsugaku 中國哲學　9 (1980), 1–11.

—— 1983. "Kanshi shihen ni okeru yōseisetsu" 管子四篇における養生説
Nippon chūgoku gakkaihō 35 (1983), 59–69.

Saiki Tetsurō　齋木哲郎　1986
"Shin, Seikanki ni okeru yōsei shisō to tenjin sōkansetsu"
秦西漢期 における 養生思想と天人相關說
Tōhōshūkyō 68 (1986), 25–43.

Sakade Yoshinobu　坂出祥伸　1978
"Dōinkō: Kodai ni okeru yōseisetsu to igaku to no kakawari"
導引考：古代 における 養生說と醫學との關わり
Ikeda Festschrift, 225–240.

—— 1983. "Shinsen shisō no shintaikan: Yōkei to naikan o chūshin ni"
神仙思想の身體觀：養形と内觀を中心に
Risō 理想 9/1983, 63–75.

—— 1986a. "Chō Tan 'Yōsei yōshū' itsubun to sono shisō"
張湛の養生要集佚文とその思想
Tōhōshūkyō 68 (1986), 1–24.

—— 1987. "Kinsen shōron to sono tampō" 金仙證論とその丹法
Itō 1987: 1–14.

—— 1987a. "Chūgoku no yōsei shisō" 中國の養生思想
Daihōrin 大法輪 June–July 1987.

—— 1988 (ed.), *Chūgoku kodai yōsei shisō no sōgōteki kenkyū*
中國古代養生思想の總合的研究
Tokyo: Hirakawa, 1988.

—— 1988a. "Shūeki sandōkei to kōen no shi oyobi kogōshi"
周易參同契と江淹の詩および孤剛子
Kōza kagakushi 講座科學史
Vol. 4. Tokyo: Baifūkan, 1988.

Sakai Tadao　酒井忠夫　1977
Dōkyō no sōgōteki kenkyū 道教の總合的研究
Tokyo: Kokusho kankōkai, 1977.

Sakauchi Shigeo　坂内榮夫　1985
"Shōryō dendōshū to naitan shisō" 鐘呂傳道集と内丹思想
Chūgoku shisōshi kenkyū 中國思想史研究 7 (1985), 39–76.

Sanaka Sō　佐中壯　1975
Sengoku Sōsho ken no shinkō to gijutsu no kankei
戰國宋初間の信仰と技術の關係
Tokyo: Kogakkan daigaku, 1975.

Sawada Takio 澤田多喜男 1965
"Senshin no yōseisetsu shiron" 先秦の養生説試論
Nippon chūgoku gakkai hō 17 (1965), 19–35.

—— 1983. *Sōshi no kokoro* 荘子の心
Tokyo: Yuhikaku, 1983.

Shibata Kiyotsugu 柴田清瀞 1982
"Ryōshi shunjū no yōseisetsu to seiji shisō" 呂氏春秋の養生説と政治思想
Tetsugaku 哲學 34 (1982), 1–16.

Suzuki Festschrift
Suzuki hakase koki kinen Tōyōgaku ronsō 鈴木博士古稀記念東洋學論叢
Tokyo, 1972.

Suzuki Yūjirō 鈴木由次郎 1963
Kan'eki kenkyū 漢易研究
Tokyo: Meitoku, 1963.

—— 1977. *Shūeki sandōkei* 周易参同契
Tokyo: Meitoku, 1977.

Tanaka Fumio 田内文雅 1984
"Taiheikyō no kanshinhō ni tsuite" 太平經の還神法について
Makio Festschrift, 291–303.

—— 1984a. "Gorin kuji hishaku no heikei shisō ni kansuru ichi kanken"
五輪九字明秘密釋の背景思想に關する一管見
Hōzan kyōgaku daikai kiyō 豊山教學大會紀要 October 1984.

Tsuda Sōkichi 津田左右吉 1926
Dōka no shisō to sono tenkai 道家の思想とその展開
Tokyo: Tōyō bunko ronshū 8, 1926.

—— 1964. *Tsuda Sōkichi zenshū* 津田左右吉全集
13 Vols. Tokyo: Iwanami, 1964.

Uchida Festschrift
Uchida Ginpu hakase shōju kinen Tōyōshi ronshū
内田吟風博士頌壽記念東洋史論集
Tokyo, 1978.

Yamada Keiji 山田慶兒 1977
Higashi to nishi no gakusha to kōshō 東と西の學者と工匠
Tokyo: Wade shobō shinsha, 1977.

Yamano Toshio 山野俊郎 1984
"Moka shikan byōkankyō no kenkyū" 摩訶止觀病患境の研究
Otani daigaku daigakuin kenkyū kiyō 大谷大學大學院研究紀要
1 (1984), 105–124.

——— 1985. "Tendai chigi no igaku shisō josetsu" 天台智顗の醫學思想序說
Shinshū sōgō kenkyūjo kiyō 真宗總合研究所紀要
3 (1985), 115–142.

Yoshida Mitsukuni 吉田光邦 1963
Renkinjutsu: Senjutsu to kagaku no aida 錬金術：仙術と科學の間
Tokyo: Chūko shinsho 9, 1963.

Yoshioka Yoshitoyo 吉岡義豐 1964
"Gorin kuji hishaku to dōkyō gozōkan" 五輪九字秘釋と道敎五藏觀
Mikkyō bunka 密敎文化 69/70 (1964), 77–97.

——— 1972. "Sangō shiki to gorin kuji hishaku no dōkyō shisō"
三敎指歸と五輪九字秘釋の道敎思想
Taishō daigaku kenkyū kiyō 大正大學研究紀要 57 (1972), 1–13.

——— 1976. *Dōkyō to Bukkyō* 道敎と佛敎
Vol. 3. Tokyo: Kokusho kankōkai, 1976.

Yoshioka Festschrift
Yoshioka hakase kanreki kinen Dōkyō kenkyū ronshū
吉岡博士還歷記念道敎研究論集
Tokyo: Kokusho kankōkai, 1977.

Chapter Two

Body and Mind: The Chinese Perspective

Hidemi Ishida

Introduction[1]

How did the ancient Chinese conceive of the body and the mind?[2] How, for that matter, did they conceive of the self? These are the questions that will concern us here, and I will try to answer them by looking at materials that deal with Chinese medicine and longevity techniques. The inquiry pursues two aims: first, to clarify the relation of the Chinese concept of body and mind to the Western notion of the self, to the puritanically inflated ego of the individual and to Descartes's dualistic understanding of body and mind; second, to explore and illustrate the meaning of such typically Chinese phrases as "body and mind are one" or "empty mind" in their original background setting. In the end, the most obviously non-Western notions of the body/mind phenomenon as well as the specifically Chinese concepts of human life, developed entirely free from Western influence, should become clearer.

Naturally, in light of these aims, I prefer not to follow a historical order when presenting and examining the material. Rather, I shall select, from the vast amount of information left behind over thousands of years in many

---

1. I should like to thank the Niwano Peace Foundation for its financial support of my research on the concepts of body and mind in ancient China.

2. I use the word mind in its broadest sense, including all conscious feeling, thinking, and willing, the subconscious and the unconscious, and also the deep underlying level of pure spiritual energy (spirit).

different parts of the huge realm of the Chinese empire, all the texts that reveal an underlying pattern of typical Chinese concepts. Because this method encompasses an enormous amount of material, I shall limit my inquiry to the period between roughly 400 B.C. and 200 A.D., from the Warring States to the Later Han dynasty. In this period, not only did a wide variety of philosophical schools flourish, and not only were the philosophical ideas connected to all those schools compiled, refined, and published, but new theories of natural science and cosmology were also developed, especially under the then newly unified realm.

In examining the body/mind concept in ancient China, one is not necessarily limited to abstract philosophical discourse. One can (and should) also try to understand the concrete and practical ways in which people dealt with the human body and mind. I intend to approach a theoretical and encompassing view of the body/mind concept in ancient China through materials that show how it was understood and applied: texts on medicine and longevity techniques.

Two Models of the Body

Textbooks of traditional Chinese medicine use two different methods to depict the human body. One is similar to Western illustrations, showing the shape of the digestive organs and the intestines. As can be seen in figure 1, these depictions are sometimes extremely detailed in their analysis. Most such illustrations, however, resemble the one shown in figure 2, which gives a rather stereotyped lateral view of the inside of the body. This type of diagram is called Chart of Inner Lights or Chart for Visualizing the True Ones. In their oldest forms such charts depicted the organs along with the gods or Radiant Ones residing in them. They were used primarily to illustrate the objects of Taoist meditation. A good example of this is found in Hu Yin's 胡愔 *Huangting neijing wuzang liufu buxie tu*   黃庭內景五藏六府補瀉圖 (Systematic Chart of the Five Orbs and Six Repositories of the Inner Light Scripture of the Yellow Court; see figure 3). Originally meditation instructions relating to the gods of the five orbs and six repositories are found in the *Taiping jingchao* 太平經鈔 (Selections from the Scripture of Great Peace) in the section called "Methods to Invite Happiness and Drive Out Disaster" (Wang 1979: 14).[3]

---

3. "Orbs" here is a translation of *zang*, commonly rendered "intestines," while "repository" is used for *fu*, commonly known as "organs." The traditional Western terminology does not

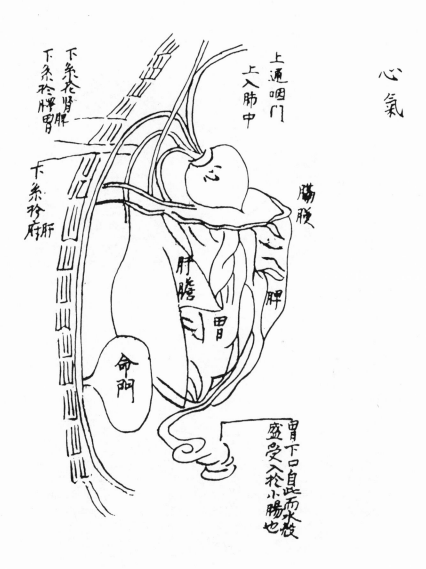

Fig. 1. Illustration of digestive organs and intestines. *Source: Hua Tuo xuanmen neizhao tu* 華佗玄門脈訣內照圖

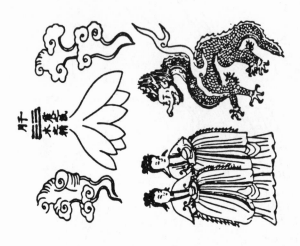

Fig. 3. The orb of the liver with its resident spirits.
Source: Huangting neijing wuzang liufu buxie tu

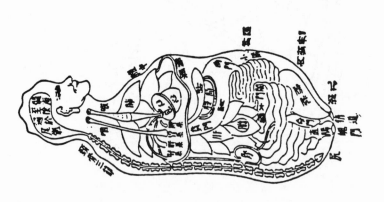

Fig. 2. Chart of Inner Lights. *Source:*
Leijing tuyi 類經圖翼 , p. 129

We can now draw four basic conclusions about the organization of the mind, as it was understood in ancient China.

1. Among the five basic aspects of the mind (material soul, spirit soul, will, intention, and spirit), the spirit, the spirit soul, and the material soul are most fundamental.
2. Within the mind, spirit arises first.
3. The two souls are characterized by movement.
4. Underlying the mind, there is a still more original and fundamental force, essence.

According to the words of Zichan in the *Zuozhuan* 左傳 (Mr. Zuo's Commentary; Shao 7, 535 B.C.) and their interpretation in later commentaries, the material soul is the power of the physical shape, while the spirit soul is the power of the *qi* energy (44.764a). Both, in comparison to the spirit, which is very similar to our idea of mind, are more what we understand by soul. The spirit, it appears, is the foundation and the leader of the two moving aspects of the mind, the spirit and material souls. This role is also evidenced by the fact that the texts frequently combine spirit with essence, with the force that lies at the back of the mind and represents it in its more original form; both taken together, as "essence and spirit," pervade the whole person.

The two other aspects of the mind, the will and the intention, represent the more specific functions of the mind. This is made quite explicit in the *Lingshu*.

The thinking aspect of the mind is called intention. The function which fixates intention on things, we call the will. (2.14a)

Here a gradual system of understanding appears to emerge. Will and intention stand for different phases of the same mental process, which one can understand as a flux going on within the individual. However, the two terms are frequently linked in the same text in order to describe the basic mental function of intentionality.[9]

Will and intention control essence and spirit, they keep the spirit and material souls in the body, they regulate the temperature of the body and harmonize its various emotions, such as joy and anger. (*Lingshu* 7.14a)

---

9. The concept of several active functions or even agents of the mind in one individual provides the basis for the understanding of spirit as gods or divinities of the body in later Taoism.

To summarize: the concrete functions of the mind are called will and intention, while spirit denotes a more abstract concept. It is the agent that keeps the entire human being in order, it represents the mind as a whole. On the other hand, spirit soul and material soul are responsible for the upkeep and demise of the body. They indeed reveal a character close to the Western concept of the soul.[10]

More specifically, the will is a resident of the essence, the body energy associated primarily with the kidneys. It is made up from the parents' energy of primordiality (Former Heaven) and of the energies that are won through the nourishment of life (Later Heaven), which makes it a fundamental factor in human existence. As a resident of the essence, one of the most basic life-forces of human beings, the will is a powerful factor. It is the mental function that controls this force.

A very similar relationship exists between the intention and the blood. The blood, the vital fluid of the liver, is created through a transformation of constructive energy originally associated with the spleen. The spirit flows along with the energy of the blood, the spirit soul follows the movements of the spirit. It is the life-force representing the energy of heaven. It is also called the yang soul and is juxtaposed with the material soul, the life-force representing earth and belonging to the realm of yin (*Zuozhuan*, Shao 7).

Following this analysis and applying the yin/yang division to the functions of the mind, we get the following schema:

yin	yang
will	intention
material soul	spirit soul
essence	spirit

earth	heaven

Thus there are two divisions, each consisting of three different levels or kinds of mind that can be easily distinguished but are parallel. At the bottom

---

10. The same idea is further developed in the three spirit and seven material souls of later Taoism.

That these energy channels and conduits are also the routes by which the mind pervades the body is made clear in the following citation from the *Lingshu*:

> The nodal points are the spots where spirit and energy come and go, enter and leave. (1.4b)

Nodal points are the points of contact where the various parts of the body meet. There are 365 of them, and they are used in healing with acupuncture, acupressure, and moxibustion, so they are also known as pressure points (*tsubō* in Japanese). Special care has to be taken in the concrete practice of healing.

> Pull out the needle only when the patient is inhaling, because then spirit and energy won't leave the body, but stay right where they are. After extracting the needle, press down on the spot and rub it for a while until the open wound has closed, so that spirit and energy remain within. (*Suwen* 8.10b)

The relation between the mind and the various sense organs is similarly expressed in terms of fluids.

> The energies of the five orbs tend to move toward the outside. They circulate around the seven orifices in the upper section of the body.
>   If the energy of the lungs passing through the nose is in good condition, the nose can smell good and bad smells. If the energy of the heart passing through the tongue is in good condition, the tongue can taste the differences of the five tastes. If the energy of the liver passing through the eyes is in good condition, the eyes can distinguish the five colors. If the energy of the spleen passing through the mouth is in good condition, the mouth can tell the differences between the five grains. If the energy of the kidneys passing through the ears is in good condition, the ears can properly perceive the five tones. (*Lingshu* 4.13a)

Wherever the energies of the five orbs are at a given moment, the mind also is. Thus, to ensure proper functioning of the various senses perceived through the seven orifices of the upper section of the body—eyes, ears, nose, and mouth— one must take care that one's intestinal energies are in good condition. As we have pointed out in discussing the senses, the good condition of their respective energies is directly related to the good condition of the mind. Because the conduits pervade the entire body and correlate many different kinds of energies passing through them, the categorization according to the five orbs of the *Lingshu* is comparatively limited in scope and by no means exhausts the complexity of the system.

In another chapter, the *Lingshu* explains the intricate interrelation of energies, organs, and senses in more detail. For example:

> The eyes are constituted by the essences of the five orbs and six repositories. There are also the constructive and protective energies, nourished with the help of the spirit soul and the material soul. The eyes are where the energy of the spirit arises. . . . They are the direct messenger of the mind, the mind is the residence of the spirit. (12.12b)

Thus, all the subtle energies of the body as well as most of aspects of the mind are present and active in the eyes. The act of seeing involves not only the energy of the liver—the blood (as directly corresponding to the eyes)—and the intention that resides there, but also the combined activities of many different energies and mental functions. In schematic form, the participation of these energies in the organic makeup of the eyes can be described as follows (based on *Lingshu* 12.12a):

pupils:	marrow of the bones (essence of the kidneys/the will)
iris:	essence of the muscles (blood of the liver/the intention
eyeball veins:	essence of the pulse (pulse of the heart/the spirit)
whites:	essence of the protective energy (energy of the lungs/the spirit soul)
eyelids:	essence of the constructive energy (energy of the spleen/material soul)

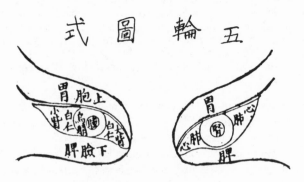

Fig. 5. The energies of the orbs and the five aspects of the mind in relation to the physiology of the eyes. *Source: Yinhai jingwei* 銀海精微   1.26a

As can also be seen in figure 5, all energies of the orbs, as well as the five aspects of the mind, play an active part in the physical constitution of the eyes and therefore in the act of seeing. The same holds true for the other senses and their related organs.

The Ways of the Mind

Can one direct the flowing mind to go in one direction rather than another? According to the textbooks of traditional medicine, the will and the intention are the guides of the mind. The same idea is found in the works of the pre-Han philosophers, although they do not explain their exact function and application as clearly. "The will guides the energy," says Mencius, "the energy fills the body. Wherever the will goes, the energy goes as well" (3.6a of the *Sibu congkan* edition).

The exact techniques and theoretical explications of how to consciously direct the mind are called the ways of the mind already in the *Liji*:

> Every human being has an inner nature which is made up from the energy of the blood in conjunction with the mind that resides therein. This mind manifests itself in a variety of emotions, such as joy and anger, sadness and happiness. The emotions develop in accordance with the appearance of their objects, thus the ways of the mind become clearly obvious. (*Liji* 38.679a)

Zheng Xuan in his commentary explains "ways" as the "locations and direction [of the mind]." Kong Yingda in his subcommentary says that "ways" refers to "the route by which the mind comes into being" and accordingly to the channels along which the mind flows. The word "ways" therefore indicates the fundamentally physical concept of the human mind.

The *Guiguzi* 鬼谷子 makes the point quite clear.[12]

> "Ways" refers to the place through which the energy of the mind passes, while the spirit functions as its guide. (3.1b)

The ways of the mind, the routes of the flowing mind, have a tremendous influence on the person, depending on whether they are basically oriented toward the positive or the negative.

---

12. On this text see Takeuchi 1978. It is cited according to the edition in *Zhongguo zixue mingzhu jicheng* of the year 1805.

More than the physical shape, the mind is of central importance
for the human being. More than the mind itself, the ways it
takes are essential. When therefore the ways are
straightforward, the mind is straightforward as well.

Thus, even when someone's face looks sinister, yet the
ways of his mind are positive, then he certainly merits to be
called a gentleman. Similarly, someone with a pleasant
countenance whose ways of the mind are negative has
definitely to be called a small man. (*Xunzi* 3.1b)

Here the quality of the mind as manifest in its ways is ranked above the mind
itself and also above the physical appearance of the person. What direction the
mind is given is of vital importance. For Xunzi the mind is like a plain white
sheet; it is *a priori* neither good nor evil, it only becomes so when it is given
direction. This direction of the mind is not only governed by the will and the
intention. As the flowing mind is a "mind turned physical" it mixes with the
various energies in the body and moves along with them and is thus subject to
the same stimulations and obstructions. Mencius describes the situation this
way:

When the will is stimulated, the energy moves. When the
energy is activated, the will moves. For example, one runs and
stumbles because one's energy moves on the inside. At the
same time one's will is activated and the mind is disturbed.
(3.6b)

According to the following passage from the *Book of Rites*, the foundation for giving a direction to the mind based on the activities of the body is
laid by conscious efforts at controlling the sensual input.[13]

Be sure that the ears never hear disturbing sounds and the eyes
always abstain from confusing sights. Make sure that lewd
music and perverted rites will not reach the ways of the mind.
Moreover, see that reckless and wicked energy never enters the
body. Only then will ears, eyes, nose, mouth, and the mind as
well as all parts of the body naturally follow straightforward
ways. (*Liji* 38.681)

According to traditional medicine, emotions are rooted in the movements and
changes of the various body fluids, in which the mind also resides.
Consequently, one should become free from their influence to exactly that
extent to which one succeeds in calming or harmonizing the movements of the
fluids.

---

13. On this subject see especially Shimamori 1976, one of the earliest works of the body/mind
question, which deals with the concept of the ways of the mind.

The interaction of the mind and the fluids is depicted as a circular and mutually conversive movement in the *Chunqiu fanlu*.

> The gentleman harmonizes the sensations in his body, he calms his desires, and puts an end to all negativity. Thereby he makes his intention straightforward. This in turn leads to the tranquility of the spirit. When the spirit is tranquil, it will expand to nourish the energy. (16.23ab)

The Mind In and Out of the Body

In a passage from the *Huainanzi* quoted above, it was mentioned that the will could be focused too much on one thing, that desires tended to become excessive. How this state comes about is explained as follows:

> When spirit is used day by day, it will go away farther and farther. It will cling to the object of desire and be unable to return to the person. The body in due course will close up and, even though it may wish to do so, spirit won't be able to enter it again. (*Huainanzi* 1.16b)

Here we should remember that in traditional medicine the nodal points together with the sense doors are thought of as the spots where the spirit enters and leaves the body. The information supplied here adds that it is the energy of the mind, guided by the will as it is fully intent on the object of its desire, that tends to leave the body through the various gates. Later, in Taoism, this concept is connected with the idea that there are numerous divinities residing in the body. For example, the *Taiping jingchao* says:

> The Tao gives life to human beings, but fundamentally they consist of nothing but the energy of essence. Within this framework there are various divinities. When the energy of essence assembles and takes up a specific shape, we speak of it as a human being. Ignorant people do not understand that one can make the energy of the spirit return and thereby keep one's body whole. Thus they lose the Tao. (Wang 1979: 723)

The energy of the spirit mentioned here is a kind of energy that has some spiritual or divine quality:

> The energies of the five agents and the four seasons enter into the human body and there manifest as the divinities residing in the five orbs. When they leave the body, they revert to being the essence of the spirit of the four seasons. (Wang 1979: 292)

The exact movements of this spiritual energy are described in the same text.

> Human energies circulate around the body, above and below. The essence of spirit uses these energies to enter and leave the body. The way in which the essence of spirit exists in the energies is just like fish live in water. When the energies are lost, spirit disperses and dies, just as fish perish when the water dries up. (Wang 1979: 727)

The second chapter of the *Huainanzi* makes the spiritual qualities of the energies in the body even clearer:

> When one continues to use the spirit, it will leave. When one gives the spirit rest, it will stay. (2.5a)

The mind is therefore the spiritual quality inherent in the energies pervading the human body. Ideally it should be restful, harmonious, and free from desires. Then the spirit will stay permanently with the person.

> When the mind (the will) is concentrated on the inside of the body, it can pervade everything just as the One or the Tao itself. As long as the mind stays unmoving, one will never know what one is doing, nor where one is going. . . . The body is like a withered tree, the mind is like cold ashes. The five orbs and the body itself are beyond one's thoughts, one knows without studying, sees without looking, accomplishes things without doing anything. Without throwing light on things one will find them clear, pushed along one will move, instinctively one will go on—flowingly, as the shadow follows the light. (*Huainanzi* 7.5a)

By remaining in a state of non-action one will prevent the loss of the mind. The commentary to the above passage explains this state as a complete "isolation of the will and the intention." By isolating will and intention one will be free from all outward relations. Then one will pervade everything. A similar concept is expressed in the "fasting of the mind" described in the *Zhuangzi* (chap. 4). The topic here is the consciousness of the empty mind. By completely emptying the mind one can realize all aspects of the envisioned object rather than being limited by the preconceptions of one's thoughts.[14]

---

14. Space does not permit a more thorough analysis of this notion here. For more information see Ishida 1985.

Other Beings and the Mind

According to this Chinese theory of mind, how does a person relate to other people and to the various creatures and objects of the outside world? Theoretically, if each and every being is possessed of a flowing mind, their interaction should be an exchange of different fluids, which however are ultimately one. There is indeed a notion in ancient Chinese sources that "I am also a being, all beings are also part of nature" (*Huainanzi* 7.3b). The underlying oneness of all things, the belief that all and everything is made up from the same basic substance, certainly present in Chinese philosophy and religion, has been interpreted occasionally as the manifestation of materialism in ancient China. However, these beings are never seen entirely as mere matter; they are never described as being without specific individual and spiritual characteristics as well as particular natural values. As the *Zhuangzi* has it:

> Beings must originally be endowed with something that makes them beings. There must be something fundamental which affirms their nature as specific entities. (chap. 2)

Seen from this angle, all beings are ultimately not determined by matter, but have a higher quality that makes them individual.

The relation between human and other beings can be described as follows:

> People are basically beings. They are those among the myriad beings that have knowledge. They receive life from heaven and energy from the prime root of all existence. They are not essentially different from the various other beings of the world. (*Lunheng* 24.1007)

According to this passage, people and other beings have their endowment with life and energy in common. "To begin with, people's essence and spirit are quite the same as those of other beings" (*Lunheng* 20.881)—their basic makeup is very similar.

All beings take part in the same cosmological pattern of origin:

> When heaven and earth are in harmony, their essence is joined as a mixture of yin and yang. When this essence is concentrated it emerges in the form of the four seasons. When each of the four seasons radiates its essences, the myriad beings are created. (*Huainanzi* 3.1a)

Everything is created through the same energy transformation. The myriad beings come to life when the essences of the four seasons radiate; they receive "life from heaven, energy from the prime root of all existence," as the *Lunheng* has it. In another section, the text states that "the bones and the physical shape are made up from energy," that "by relying on the bones and the physical shape the energy then develops consciousness" (*Lunheng* 20.874). Because all beings are created from energy, all beings are endowed with consciousness.

Consciousness emerges already at the level of pure energy. It is thus one of the primordial forces that constitute human existence. This consciousness, however, has certain tendencies of a potentially detrimental nature. When the mind (and thereby the focused power of consciousness) gets too attached to something, it may leave the person and not return. Old age occurs when the mind flows out from the body, but more commonly and before any visible physical changes take place, the vacuum that is left by the original consciousness tends to be filled by the essence and spirit of other beings. (All other kinds of beings are, of course, basically made up the same way, from essence and spirit, from energy and consciousness.) Alien energies tend to enter the individual in exchange for the original consciousness now lost. The resulting state is one of possession or dependence. The spiritual quality, the stability of mind of the individual, is lost; he or she is increasingly oriented toward others and becomes more and more dependent on outward stimulation.

On the other hand, a healthy relation between human and other beings takes place when there is a balance of impulse and response.

> Inner nature is where the energy of the spirit assembles. When inner nature is perfected, the energy of the spirit radiates with brilliance and shines out of the body. It then is able to perfectly respond to impulses it receives from other beings. (*Xinshu* 8.11b)

Here consciousness is closely related to the energy of the spirit as it leaves the body and interacts with other beings and outside things. However, this interaction is not governed by an active intention or purposeful will. It is free from attachments and desires. It is a merely automatic and instinctive response to impulse.

> The energy of the spirit rooted in the Tao and the virtue shines forth from inner nature. . . . Through changes and transformations, the energy of the spirit turns into different things. By perfectly responding to all these various changes and transformations, all can be experienced as mere transformations of spirit. (8.11b–12a)

This statement does not represent a solipsistic point of view. Rather, it emphasizes that different beings appear in different ways according to the workings of the energy of the spirit. The spontaneous response of the individual to the impulses received from beings and things on the outside is, then, an organic, natural, and life-enhancing exchange between the fluids that ultimately constitute the bodies and minds involved.

The flowing mind, as and when it emerges from the body, manifests itself as light or radiance.

> As long as the energy of the spirit remains within the body, it does not radiate on the outside. It then functions as knowledge. It may be transformed into light and as such go beyond the body and radiate brilliantly on the outside. Inasmuch as inside and outside form one whole and are part of the same continuum, one can know gain and loss, right and wrong, and the principle of things. (*Xinshu* 8.12a)

The spirit that flows around on the inside of the body turns into light and begins to radiate. In that form it interacts in a pattern of impulse and response with the mind-turned-light of other beings. This, then, is the pure awareness and knowledge of other beings. It is the basis from which everyone's everyday consciousness develops.

Conclusion

One may distinguish two major body concepts in ancient Chinese thought: the flowing body and the body as residence. It seems that the former is the more fundamental notion. The mind was also thought of as a fluid; it was part of the eternally moving flux of the human physis. As the textbooks of traditional medicine make clear, the mind was thought of as an energy residing especially in the five orbs, but it was by no means limited to these. Rather, it spread to and pervaded every minute part of the body. The flowing mind was present everywhere, it served to control and regulate the body and its various energies.

The flowing body together with the flowing mind circulate according to the ways of the mind, whose main agents are the will and the intention and whose channels are the conduits of the flowing body. The various energies of body and mind are extremely closely interrelated. Together they constitute the blood, energy, and mind circulation essential to all human beings. Body and mind are ultimately one. This does not mean that they are not clearly differentiated. Rather, it means that the mind, guided by its most practical aspects, the will and the intention, pervades the whole body without inclining more toward one part than to another. Body and mind are ultimately one and ideally function as one single unit; yet as abstract forces they are quite distinct.

The flowing mind will, when drawn to an outside object that has entered the individual's consciousness, follow it and leave the body. It may do this as a spontaneous response or with purposeful intention. In the first instance it will return in due course; in the second case, it will continue to follow the object and be lost. The consciousness of other beings will be used as a replacement, thereby creating an increased dependence on the outside world. Later, in Taoism, the same concept was personified in the divinities residing in the human body who will leave when not properly cared for. The proper way of dealing with the mind is to practice non-action and to keep the mind empty of attachments and desires, if not of all content. One must strictly abstain from all activities that might cause the mind to flow out for good.

The body is essentially fluid, and so is the mind. Beings are not solid, material entities, but are highly differentiated combinations of energies. The myriad beings originally developed from the essences of the four seasons, which contain the energy of consciousness. All beings, beginning at the lowest possible level of mere energy transformation, are therefore endowed with consciousness as soon as they take on physical shape.

References

Legge, James. 1852. *The Notions of the Chinese Concerning God and Spirits.* Hongkong: Hongkong Register Office, 1852.

Lu, Gwei-djen. 1980. *Celestial Lancets. A History and Rationale of Acupuncture and Moxa.* Cambridge: Cambridge University Press, 1980.

Omura, Yoshiaki. 1982. *Acupuncture Medicine: Its Historical and Clinical Background.* Tokyo: Japan Publications, 1982.

Palos, Stephen. 1971. *The Chinese Art of Healing.* New York: Herder & Herder, 1971.

Porkert, Manfred. 1974. *The Theoretical Foundations of Chinese Medicine.* Cambridge, Massachusetts: MIT Press, 1974.

—— 1983. "Greifbarkeit und Ergriffensein: Das Körperverständnis in der chinesischen Medizin," *Eranos Jahrbuch* 52 (1983), 389–430.

Schipper, Kristofer M. 1978. "The Taoist Body," *History of Religions* 17 (1978), 355–387.

Sivin, Nathan. 1988. *Traditional Medicine in Contemporary China.* Ann Arbor: University of Michigan, Center for Chinese Studies Publications, 1988.

Unschuld, Paul. 1985. *Medicine in China. A History of Ideas.* Berkeley & Los Angeles: University of California Press, 1985.

in Chinese and Japanese

Akatsuka Kiyoshi 赤塚昭　1968
"Sōshi chū ni okeru Kanshi Shinjutsuhen keitō no setsu"
莊子中 における 管子心術篇系統 の 說
Nippon chūgoku gakkaihō 日本中國學會報　20 (1968), 17–33.

Dadai liji 大戴禮記
Dadai liji jiegu 解詁. Taipei, 1983.

Guo Moruo 郭沫若 1944
"Song Bingyin wenzhu zuokao" 宋鉼尹文著作考
Qingtong shidai 青銅時代　(1944), 245–271.

—— 1956. *Guanzi jijiao* 管子集校
Beijing: Kexue chubanshe, 1956.

Hara Muneko 原宗子　1984
"Kanshi kenkyū no genjō to kadai" 管子研究の現狀と課題
Ryūtsū keizai daigaku ronshū 流通經濟大學論集　19.1 (1984), 1–23.

Ishida Hidemi 石田秀實 1982
"Kakujū suru seishin" 擴充 する 精神
Tōhōgaku 東方學　63 (1982), 1–15.

—— 1985. "Kanshi shihen to Junshi seimeihen to ni okeru kotoba no mondai" 管子四篇と荀子正名篇とにおける問題
Nippon Chūgoku gakkai hō 37 (1985), 47–60.

—— 1987. *Ki: Nagareru shintai* 氣: 流れる 身體
Tokyo: Hirakawa, 1987.

Kitamura Naohiro 喜多村直寬 1854
Kōtei naikei somon kōgi 黄帝内經素問講義
Edo, 1854. Reprinted Osaka: Orient, 1987.

Liu Jie 劉節 1943
"Guanzi zhong suojian zhi Song Bing yipai xueshuo"
管子中所見之宋鉼一派學說
Shuowen yuekan 說文月刊 1943.

Liu Wendian 劉文典　1974
Huainan honglie jijie 淮南鴻列集解
Taipei: Shangwu, 1974.

Lunheng 論衡
Lunheng jiaoshi 挍釋 Taipei: Shangwu, 1973.

Ma Shulun 馬叙倫　1961
Zhuangzi yizheng 莊子義證
Taipei: Hongzhi wenhua, 1961.

Qian Mu 錢穆　1959
Zhuangzi zuanjian 莊子纂箋
Taipei: Sanmin, 1959.

Shibue Chūsai 澀江抽齋 1985
Reisu kōgi 靈樞講義
Osaka: Orient, 1985. Originally published Edo 1854.

Shimamori Tetsuo 島森哲男 1976
"Genshi jukyō ni okeru jiko to rinri" 原始儒教における自己と倫理
Shūkan Tōyōgaku 集刊東洋學　36 (1976), 43–58.

Su Yu 鮮輿 (ed.) 1910
Chunqiu fanlu yizheng 春秋繁露義證
Beijing, 1910.

Takeuchi Yoshio 武内義雄 1978
"Kikokushi o yomu" 鬼谷子を讀む
Takeuchi Yoshio zenshū 全集 Tokyo: Kadokawa, 1978, vol. 6, 294–304.

Wang Ming 王明 1979
Taiping jing hejiao 太平經合挍
Beijing: Zhonghua, 1979.

Yang Shuda 楊樹達 1959
Huainanzi zhengwen 淮南子證聞
Beijing: Kexue chubanshe, 1959.

Zhang Jiebin 張介賓 1964
Leijing 類經
Beijing: Renmin weisheng, 1964. Originally published in 1624.

Chapter Three

Drug Taking and Immortality

Akira Akahori

Immortals and Drugs in Chinese History

Legends of so-called immortals (*shenxian* 神仙)[1] were widely accepted by the ancient Chinese. Although the concept of immortals was not exactly the same through the ages, some general images persisted. Immortals usually live in clean and pure places such as high mountains; they do not eat cereals; they appear only to people who perform the proper religious practices or have the right kind of destiny. Some immortals also live in grottoes underneath the sacred mountains. They can freely change their appearance: sometimes they appear in the everyday world looking like ordinary men, to test young immortal aspirants. They move very swiftly and fly through the air, sometimes using wings (see Robinet 1986).

　　Until the Song dynasty, Chinese drugs were grouped into three classes: superior drugs, which cause one to realize one's inborn vital power and fulfill one's social mission; medium drugs, which enrich one's nature; and inferior drugs, which cure diseases.[2] This classification is found already in quotations of several medical texts in chapter 4 of the *Bowuzhi* 博物志 (Record of

---

1. The image of these immortals as well as of the state of immortality has changed in the course of Chinese history. It is not clear to what extent it referred to the eternal continuation of physical existence, to a spiritual state of mind, or to access to the other world in this life or after death. For the sake of easier access in English, *shenxian* will be rendered here as "immortal."

2. For this classification see *Zhenghe bencao* (Herbal of the Zhenghe Era; Taipei: Nantian Publishers, 1976), p. 30; see also the list in figure 1 below.

Various Matters) of the third century and in chapter 11 of Ge Hong's 葛洪 *Baopuzi* 抱朴子 (Book of the Master Who Embraces Simplicity, see Ware 1966, Sailey 1978) of the early fourth century. Here the *Shennong jing* 神農 經 (Shennong's Classic) and the *Shennong sijing* 神農四經 (Shennong's Four Classics) are cited.

Earlier than that are the Wuwei Formularies, which contain two prescriptions for the cure of impotence and reduced sexual desire (*Wenwu* 1975: 84–85). The Wuwei Formularies are manuscripts written on wooden slips found in a Later Han dynasty tomb at Wuwei in Gansu. The man buried in the tomb is thought to have been a physician. The manuscript is composed of at least three formularies. All the prescriptions are written in accordance with a standardized form, and a considerable number of them are composed of various drugs with similar effects, supposedly to enhance their efficaciousness (Akahori 1978). The diseases and drugs mentioned are for the most part identical to those found in later medical literature. The prescriptions for impotence are almost entirely composed of superior and medium drugs. This suggests that the grouping was used already in the beginning of the Later Han dynasty.

After the principles of Chinese medical thought had been established during the Former Han dynasty, Chinese medicine continued to develop gradually and in diverse ways. Early Taoist movements, such as the Way of Great Peace and the Five Pecks of Rice Sect of the Celestial Masters, which began toward the end of the Later Han and developed into organized Taoism, gained followers partly through their methods of healing the sick. For this they used prayers and talismans, but they also prepared drugs, such as *dan* 丹, commonly translated "cinnabar elixir" (*Weishu* 114).

Between the end of the Later Han and the beginning of the Jin, two kinds of drugs were often prepared: *dan* and a so-called cold-food powder, *hanshisan* 寒石散 , also known as five-mineral powder. The latter was originally claimed to be effective in curing diseases and continued to be taken enthusiastically until the Tang (Yu 1938), after the philosopher He Yan 何晏 (?–249) first took it to gain relief from depression (*Shishuo xinyu* 2.14; Mather 1976: 36). However, the components of the drug are not known, and there seem to have been no standard formulas for preparing it. It frequently caused severe adverse reactions and sometimes even led to death. *Dan*, on the other hand, was believed to be the elixir of life, and its preparation was attempted many times.

During the Six Dynasties, maintaining health by means of diets, drugs, and physical exercise was a concern to both Taoists and laymen. As a result two kinds of medical literature developed: the books on nourishing life and the classics of diet. In addition, there are numerous textbooks of acupuncture, medical formularies, and pharmacological treatises (*materia medica*).

Numerous quotations of early Chinese texts dealing with various methods of prolonging life are found in Japan, especially in Tamba no Yasuyori's 丹波康賴 *Ishinpō* 醫心方 (Essential Medical Methods) of the year 984 (Sakade 1986). This medical encyclopedia is composed almost entirely of quotations from the Chinese classics, usually citing them by their title. Many of the texts used in it have been lost or were greatly revised in later times. Stimulated by the discovery of medical manuscripts at Mawangdui and Wuwei and also by the thousandth anniversary of its compilation, *Ishinpō* studies are at present being eagerly pursued in Japan. Of particular interest in our context are the first section of chapter 26, which is devoted largely to methods for lengthening one's years, and the seventh section of the same chapter, which deals with methods of abstaining from cereals. Quotations from the *Geshi fang* 葛氏方 (Mr. Ge's Formulary), the *Taiqing jing* 太清經 (Scripture of Great Clarity), the *Jinkui lu* 金匱錄 (Record of the Golden Casket), and many others contain information on the effects of crude drugs, usually elaborately processed, and of special compound preparations.

Crude Drugs Used for Immortal and Medical Purposes

Early Evidence

Several emperors of ancient China, in possession of enormous powers and riches, took great trouble to obtain the elixir of life. Shihuangdi (259–210 B.C.), of the Qin dynasty, equipped large expeditions under the command of Xu Fu and others to go abroad and get the drug of immortality from the immortals (*Shiji* 6). Emperor Wu (156–87 B.C.), of the Former Han appointed numerous magic specialists to high positions. The emperor wanted them to find the immortals for him, to prepare the elixir of life themselves, or to call back the spirits of the dead. When Li Shaojun 李少君 , a famous member of the group, died of a disease, Emperor Wu believed that he had escaped from this world as an immortal and had only left his body behind. But when the emperor found that he had been deceived by Shao Weng he had him executed (*Shiji* 12).[3]

---

3. The original chronicle of Emperor Wu's reign in the *Shiji* is believed lost. The present chapter was supposedly substituted by Chu Shaosun at the end of the Former Han.

One text of the early period, the *Liexian zhuan* 列仙傳 (Immortals'
Biographies), allegedly compiled by Liu Xiang 劉向 (77–6 B.C.) but probably
dating from the second century A.D., relates the life stories of about seventy
immortals (Kaltenmark 1953). Their methods and the drugs they used are
mentioned. Chisongzi 赤松子 , Master Redpine, for example, usually took a
drug called liquid jade. He then transformed himself by fire, ascended to
Mount Kunlun, and there lived in the stone palace of the Queen Mother of the
West. He could move freely in the air following the wind and the rain.

Just as Master Redpine's powers ultimately stem from a drug, so do
those of about half the immortals described in the *Liexian zhuan*. Among the
crude drugs mentioned in this text we find pine fruit, pine resin, China root,
cinnamon, fungus, cinnabar dust, and mica.[4] Most of the drugs in this text
belong to the superior group. Occasionally medium drugs are mentioned, such
as Chinese angelica, bitter ginseng, and scallions; only few inferior drugs
occur, such as aconite, peaches, and plums.

Shennong's Materia Medica

As shown in figure 1, most of the superior drugs in the *Shennong bencao jing*
神農本草經   (Shennong's Materia Medica) have the effects of making the
body lighter, preventing old age, prolonging life and forestalling hunger.
Medium drugs with such effects are much fewer in number, although mercury
and realgar are said to have them. These two are used as source materials for
the elixir of life, *dan*. Most immortals are said to have experienced a
lightening of the body and gained the ability to fly through the air. This
suggests a standard picture of immortals in the Former Han. Also, it implies
that lightening body weight was considered the first step in the direction of
becoming an immortal.

The *Shennong bencao jing* was compiled by Tao Hongjing   陶弘景
(456–536) around the year 500 A.D. It consists of quotations from the
Shennong bencao and the *Mingyi bielu* 名醫別錄 (Special Record of Famous
Physicians). The former is regarded as a text of the Later Han, even though no
bencao (materia medica) texts are mentioned in the bibliographical section of
the *Hanshu* 漢書 (History of the Han Dynasty; see Akahori 1978). Certain
passages of the *bencao* texts are similar to the *Wushier bingfang* 五十二病方
(Methods for Fifty-two Diseases), a formulary unearthed in the tomb at
Mawangdui (see Harper 1982). Moreover, the use of numerous drugs
according to the *Shennong bencao jing* seems to reflect prescriptions of the

---

4. For a complete list of all the drugs mentioned in this article with their Chinese characters
    see the "List of Common Drugs Used for Immortality" at the end of this chapter.

Figure 1

Numbers of Immortality Drugs and Their Effects
According to the Zhenghe bencao

Type	Origin	ZHBC chap.	all	Imm.	light body	no age	long life	no hunger
Top	Mineral	3	21	7	17	10	13	5
	Herbal	6, 7 12	101	9	82	44	36	16
	Animal	14,16 19,20	35	1	11	4	6	5
	Vegetable	23,24 27	28	3	15	9	7	10
Med.	Mineral	4	23	3	3	1	3	4
	Herbal	8, 9 13	83	-	12	5	2	-
	Animal	17,19 21	37	-	6	1	1	1
	Vegetable	23,25 28	35	-	3	2	1	1
Low	Mineral	5	23	-	-	-	1	-
	Herbal	10,11 14	85	-	4	-	1	-
	Animal	18,19 22	41	-	-	-	-	-
	Vegetable	23,26 29	21	-	-	-	-	-
Use-less	Mineral	30	26	-	6	2	6	1
	Herbal	30	132	-	16	-	11	1
	Animal	30	15	-	-	-	-	-
	Vegetable	30	-	-	-	-	-	-

Wuwei Formularies of the Later Han. Most of the drugs mentioned are also found in the *Shennong bencao jing*, but the drugs of the *Wushier bingfang* are mentioned less commonly and often only as alternate names. This suggests that many names of drugs were changed during the Han dynasty (Akahori 1978). For the *Mingyi bielu* no exact compilation date is known (Okanishi 1977: 34–37). Nevertheless, it too is believed to contain Han dynasty knowledge of drugs.

Xi Kang 稽康 (223–262), the famous poet and thinker of the Lao-Zhuang tradition who rejected government power in favor of a relaxed life, accepted the stories recorded in the *Liexian zhuan* as true. He continued to nourish his life and spirit by means of special foods and drugs that he believed efficacious for prolonging human existence (*Jinshu* 49). In his *Yangsheng lun* 養生論 (On Nourishing Life), he refers to the existence of immortals and lists longevity techniques and drugs (Holzman 1957: 83–92; see also Henricks 1983). In his answer to Xiang Xiu's 向秀 criticism of his work, he briefly quotes eight examples of immortals from the *Liexian zhuan* as proof for the efficacy of superior drugs. Another source mentions that Xi Kang took some of these drugs himself, but he does not give any specific names (*Weizhi* 21).

Crude Drugs in Taoism

The *Shenxian zhuan* 神仙傳 (Biographies of Spirit Immortals) is a compilation of Ge Hong (ca. 283–343), author of the famous *Baopuzi*. The work contains ninety-two life stories of immortals, which generally are somewhat more detailed than those found in the *Liexian zhuan*. Twenty-three immortals are described as drug takers. Among the crude drugs used are pine seeds, pine resin, fungus, mica, and *zhu*. Ten of the twenty-three supplemented their drug intake with other methods, such as breathing exercises, talismans, and elixirs. In his *Baopuzi*, Ge Hong quotes a passage from the *Shennong sijing* that describes various ways to attain longevity or even the immortal state.

> Superior drugs make it possible to keep one's body at rest, to prolong one's life, and to ascend into heaven as an immortal. One may also come and go freely between heaven and earth, control all kinds of demons, grow feathers on the surface of the body, and obtain any food one desires without difficulty. (*Baopuzi* 11; Ware 1966: 177)

Longevity drugs are discussed throughout the *Baopuzi*, but especially in chapter 11, entitled "Immortals' Drugs." The chapter is devoted exclusively to a discussion of the nature and effects of various drugs. The drug described in most detail is fungus. Many different kinds of fungus are listed, each famous for a different effect—for example, knotted fungus that allows one to fly in broad daylight, and fungus shaped like a flat peach. These two have the power to prolong human life to five hundred or five thousand years even when taken in very small doses. Fungus can be used alone and also in combination with various other drugs.

The *Zhengao* 真誥 (Declarations of the Perfected; DZ 1016, fasc. 637–640)[5] of Tao Hongjing also reports on the lives of many immortals. A typical example is the description of the life of Dai Meng 戴孟 .

> Dai Meng, a Taoist of Mount Wudang, showed an interest in the Taoist teaching from an early age; he did not enter government service, but instead withdrew from society and lived on Mount Huayang. There he nourished on *zhu*, on seeds of yellow essence, realgar, mica, cinnabar dust, and fungus.
>
> He obtained secret formulas on immortality from the Pure Numinous Realized One, himself a follower of Pei Jizhou. In particular he received the *Yupei jincheng jing*, Scripture of the Jade Pendant and the Golden Vase, and the *Shijing jinguang fu*, the Talisman of Mineral Essence and Golden Radiance. He accomplished the lightening of his body weight and traversed the sacred mountains. He could easily travel more than two hundred kilometers in one day. Thus he went to visit many places. Nevertheless, he could not transform himself fully into an immortal. (*Zhengao* 14.6a)

Tao Hongjing adds the following note: "It seems incomprehensible that Dai Meng attained only long life and not immortality despite the fact that he was bestowed the *Yupei jincheng jing* and followed its instructions."

Sun Simiao 孫思邈 (d. 682), the famous physician and Taoist of the early Tang (see Sivin 1968), is the author of the *Qianjin yaofang* 千金要方 (Essential Prescriptions Worth a Thousand Ounces of Gold; partly translated in Despeux 1987). Section 6 of chapter 27 of this text deals with longevity effects and the way eleven crude drugs and five prescriptions should be administered. Most of these drugs are also discussed in the *Ishinpō*; however, in the two sources, the methods of processing and administration are not exactly identical.

In Taoism, crude drugs are mainly associated with specific attainments, such as the lightening of the body, the lengthening of life, and the prevention

---

5. Texts in the Taoist Canon (*Daozang*, hereafter abbreviated DZ) are given according to the number of the reduced sixty-volume edition published in Taipei and Kyoto. These numbers coincide with those found in K.M. Schipper, *Concordance du Tao Tsang* (Paris: Publications de l'Ecole Francaise d'Extrême-Orient, 1975). "Fasc." stands for "fascicle" and refers to the volume number of the 1925 Shanghai reprint of the original canon of 1445 (*Zhengtong Daozang*).

of hunger. These are necessary, but not in all of the reported instances are they sufficient for the attainment of immortality.

Crude Drugs for Health: Classics on Diet

Classics on diet were compiled frequently during the Six Dynasties, but we don't know much about their contents, because they were all lost (Okanishi 1969: 1331).[6] Only short passages remain in medical texts like the *Ishinpō* (chap. 29) and the *Qianjin yaofang* (chap. 26).

The longest extant fragment of an early classic on diet is a Dunhuang manuscript of the *Shiliao bencao* 食療本草 (Herbal on Cures Through Diet; S. 76). This text was originally compiled by Meng Shen 孟詵 (ca. 622–713). It is generally regarded as a book conceived mainly as a collection of the effects of drugs for health and healing (Nakao 1929). The fragment found in Dunhuang contains descriptions of the effects of twenty-six drugs, ranging from pomegranates to taro.

Under "lotus root" the text quotes the *Shennong bencao jing*.

> Lotus root restores the weakened functioning of the middle heater [the interior organs in the center of the body; cf. *Zhenghe bencao*, p. 460] and strengthens the spirit. It increases the overall vitality and expels the various diseases. Administration over a long period of time lightens the body weight and allows adepts to tolerate extreme cold [attain old age; *Zhenghe bencao*, p. 460] and hunger. It prolongs life.

Then the text details these effects, as follows:

> The administration of fresh lotus root cures weakness, thirst, and pain in the breast as they occur after violent disturbances. Its administration over a long period of time refreshes the skin and the muscles; it keeps one's mind calm and pleasant.
>
> According to one scripture, adepts of Taoism esteem this drug very highly. Its effects are said to be too vast to describe. Its seeds are used to enrich the vital energies. It obviously is a food of the immortals.
>
> Although fresh or cold food is not to be taken after childbirth lotus root is excepted from this rule. It has a decoagulating effect on the blood. Also, it tastes good and can easily be substituted for the normal diet.
>
> Taking steamed lotus root enriches the lower heater; it improves the functioning of the intestines and the stomach.

---

6. A collection of later classics on diet together with a critical evaluation of these texts was published by Shinoda and Tanaka 1972.

玄, and from Zheng Yin 鄭隱 (died ca. 301), who had obtained them from the immortal Zuo Ci 左慈 (Needham 1976: 77; Robinet 1984: I/10, 16). Ge Hong kept them stored in secrecy for over twenty years and did not attempt to produce the elixir described, because he had difficulty raising the necessary funds for the raw materials.

Elixir Application

In his *Baopuzi*, Ge Hong lists altogether fifty-six different kinds of elixirs with effects ranging from immortality, longevity, and rejuvenation to the acquisition of magical powers and the creation of gold (Needham 1976: 90–95). To prepare an immortality elixir one first of all has to withdraw to an uninhabited place on one of the sacred mountains with no more than three companions. It is important that the place is secret, for any contact with commoners or, worse, disbelievers will upset the preparation. Then one has to undergo purification for a hundred days. It consists of bathing in water enriched with fragrant herbs[7] and cleansing one's body, of abstaining from anything considered polluting, and of practicing concentration of mind (Ware 1966: 75).

Ge Hong describes the nine tripod elixirs of the Yellow Emperor in specific detail.

The first is called Floreate Cinnabar. It is based on a substance called "dark and yellow," to which "Six-One Lute" is applied. The latter, according to *Yunji qiqian* 雲笈七籤 (Seven Slips from a Cloudy Satchel) chapter 65, is made from a base of equal amounts of alum, lake salt, a salt-sodium mixture, and arsenopyrite. These are kept simmering for twenty days, then sinistral oyster, red clay, and kaolin are added. The concoction is placed in an earthenware jar, pounded ten thousand times, transferred to an iron vessel, heated over raging flames for nine days, then pounded another ten thousand times, sorted through a sieve, and finally made into a mudlike substance with the addition of some strong vinegar. The *Baopuzi* mentions that the following materials are used in Six-One Lute: realgar solution, alum solution, salt-sodium mixture, lake salt, arsenopyrite, oyster shells, red clay, kaolin, and white lead. Six-One Lute has to be heated for thirty-six days to yield Floreate Cinnabar. Taking this elixir for seven days will transform human beings into immortals. If it is manipulated differently, the concoction may also be turned into gold (*Baopuzi* 4.5b–6a; Ware 1966: 76).

---

7. The text speaks of *wuxiang*, "five fragrant herbs." But the same expression is also used as a synonym for *qingmu xiang*, Saussurea costus (Falconer) Lipschitz, in *Bencao gangmu*, chap. 14 (see Keys 1976 for an English translation of this text).

The second elixir is called Divine Cinnabar or Divine Talisman. When one takes it for a hundred days one will be immortal and possess magical powers. Three spatulas of it will cause the three or even the nine worms[8] to leave the body immediately. Thus all diseases will be driven out.

The third elixir is also called Divine Cinnabar. Taking one spatula of this for a hundred days will result in immortality, even for animals. Also, it will make human beings invincible; spirits and demons will come to serve them.

The fourth elixir is called Reverted Cinnabar. One spatula taken for a hundred days means immortality: divine creatures come to surround the adept. When mixed with mercury and heated it will turn into pure gold. One can, moreover, apply the elixir by smearing it on one's belongings; when traded, they will return within one day. When one writes a charm above one's eyes with the elixir, evil spirits and demons flee.

The fifth elixir is called Dietetic Cinnabar. One may use it to become immortal after only thirty days. One will also become a master of demons.

The sixth elixir is called Refined Cinnabar. It will transform people into immortals within ten days. It makes them rich by turning into gold after being heated with mercury.

The seventh elixir is called Tender Cinnabar. One spatula taken for one hundred days makes men immortal, and taken in conjunction with raspberry juice it is a strong aphrodisiac. Mixed with lead and fired it turns into gold.

The eighth elixir is called Fixed Cinnabar. It turns people into immortals in one day. It scares away all demons, bandits, and tigers.

The ninth elixir is called Cold Elixir. One spatula taken for a hundred days results in immortality; divine servants will surround one; and one may levitate and fly through the air (*Baopuzi* 4.6a–7a; Ware 1966: 77).

According to another of the old elixir documents cited in the *Baopuzi*, the *Taiqing danjing*, the elixir needs to be refined nine times in order to reach its highest efficacy. The basic substances used in this prescription are red salt of Floreate Lake, black and white talismans and three-and-five divine water. When refined only once, the elixir has to be taken for three years to guarantee immortality; when refined four times, half a year will suffice; after the ninth refinement, one will become an immortal upon taking the elixir for only three days (*Baopuzi* 4.9a; Ware 1966: 82).

Numerous other methods mentioned by Ge Hong and going back to a variety of masters of old give similar recipes with comparable effects. Source materials are usually minerals, especially glistening, colorful compounds of mercury and arsenic, but also substances derived from plants or animals, like

---

8. See chapter 4, "Longevity Techniques and the Compilation of the *Lingbao wufuxu*."

the oyster shells mentioned above. Concoction takes place in a deserted spot, with few people knowing of it. Spirits have to be called on for support, mountain goblins and demons have to be scared away. There is a strong need for purification and the proper ritual procedure. The effects of the elixirs vary; the better one's raw materials and the longer and more complex the process of refinement, it seems, the stronger the resulting drug. The drug itself seems to have been a paste, mudlike, or solid, but usually not liquid. It supposedly could be dried and made into a powder, or diluted into a kind of broth. The highest elixirs would make adepts immortal in hardly any time at all when taken in minute quantities. Inferior versions would have to be applied over years and thus needed to be produced in larger amounts.

In later Shangqing Taoism, various kinds of elixirs were being prepared. They were mainly the Elixir of Nine Cycles (seven purely mineral ingredients), which resembles the nine elixirs described by Ge Hong; the Langgan Elixir (fourteen ingredients), and the Fourfold Floreate Elixir (twenty-four substances; see Strickmann 1979: 142).

Numerous stories about immortals and masters of alchemy describe the setting in which the elixir was produced and applied. A typical example, quite illustrative of the practitioners' strong desire for success, the hopes they invested in the process, and also the necessity of faith to the efficacy of the elixir, is Wei Boyang's biography in the first chapter of Ge Hong's *Shenxian zhuan*. The text is first recorded in *Yunji qiqian* chapter 109.

> Wei Boyang retired to the mountains and occupied himself with concocting the elixir. He knew that two of his three disciples lacked faith and singularity of mind. Thus, when he had prepared a small amount of the elixir, he said in order to test them: "The drug of immortality is made, but it would be as well to try its effects first upon a dog. If no harm befalls the beast, we can take some ourselves. But if the dog dies, then it is not for us."
>
> Boyang then gave the dog a dose, and immediately it fell dead. "Ah," he said, "the drug must have been wrongly compounded owing to my failure to understand the divine instructions. Whoever took it would, I fear, share the fate of the dog. What are we to do?"
>
> The disciples asked: "Will you swallow it?"—"I have renounced all worldly interests," Boyang replied, "and have abandoned my family to come here. Were I to fail in my efforts to become immortal, I should be ashamed to return home. I would therefore as soon be dead as alive, so I certainly shall take it."
>
> With these words he swallowed the elixir, but on instant that it entered his mouth he fell down lifeless. Seeing which, one of the disciples declared: "Our teacher is no ordinary

Fig. 3. Wei Boyang after his resurrection. *Source: Liexian quanzhuan* 列仙
全傳 , p. 208

mortal. There must be some deeper reason for his dying after taking the elixir." And then, swallowing some himself, he also fell dead.

The other two disciples now held a consultation. "We wanted to prepare the elixir because we wished to live forever. But this concoction obviously causes instantaneous death. What's the use of it? If we don't take it we can still live several decades on this earth instead of dying right away!" So they refrained from taking the drug and left the mountain in order to make funeral arrangements for their master and dead companion.

As soon as they were gone, Boyang rose up and placed the drug he still had in his mouth into the mouth of the disciple and the dog. Both came back to life at once. They all went off together as immortals. (Giles 1948: 67–68)

Compound drugs or prescriptions are the true stuff of the immortals. They are made of raw materials that are hard to obtain, time consuming and complicated to prepare. Not only that, the proper mental attitude and ritual purity are absolutely indispensable, as are the help of spirits and immunity from evil influences and spiteful demons. The religious aspect of alchemy is strongly emphasized in the texts. One can only become immortal by being singularly dedicated to the work, renouncing the common world completely, and being fearless even in the face of death. Utter freedom of body and mind is the ultimate reward, an immortality equal to that of heaven and earth.

Changes in the Evaluation of Longevity Drugs

Ever since antiquity, the Chinese believed in the elixir of life. Emperor Shihuang of the Qin, who sent Xu Fu and others on expeditions to find the drug of immortality, seems to have been convinced that the elixir could not be prepared by human means. In the reign of Emperor Wu of Han, however, people apparently believed that they could concoct an elixir, even though preparation was thought to be very difficult and depended on the help of spirits and demons. Emperor Wu himself believed in the powers of the magicians or technical specialists at court. Similarly, the *Hanshu* notes that many such specialists convened in Huainan, at the court of Prince Liu An 劉 安 (179–122 B.C.), where they not only discussed the methods of obtaining the elixir of life, but also conducted alchemical experiments in that direction. They joined their efforts in compiling treatises dealing with the preparation of the elixir and the creation of gold (*Hanshu* 44). Later generations believed that

Liu An himself had actually partaken of the elixir of immortality and ascended into heaven in the company of his whole family, including even the household animals (*Lunheng* 7; see figure 4). Unfortunately, none of our sources on this early period specify the source materials or preparation methods employed.

The next information we have is found in the legendary biographies of the immortals, such as the *Liexian zhuan* and Ge Hong's *Shenxian zhuan*. The former suggests that by the end of the Former Han dynasty it was believed that superior drugs had the power to transform people into immortals. Wang Chong's (27–100?) severe criticism of such beliefs in his *Lunheng* 論衡 (Discussions of Balanced Views; especially chapter 7) gives credence to this supposition. But again, he does not supply any information on the specific drugs one was supposed to take in order to attain eternal life, nor does he speak of cinnabar or details any of the crude drugs.

Assuming that the information contained in the *Shennong bencao jing* does indeed go back as far as the Later Han, one can say that in that period a large number of drugs, especially those ranking as superior, were thought to aid the attainment of long life. Expressions like immortality, prolongation of years, and never aging are found frequently in the text. Superior drugs continued to be taken for that purpose throughout Chinese history. Tao Hongjing of the sixth century, for instance, received fungus and honey as monthly supplies from Emperor Wu of the Qi after he had withdrawn from life at court in 492 (see *Yunji qiqian* 107). Also, Yan Zhitui 顏之推 records that in the sixth century, many people in Henan partook of a variety of drugs beneficial to their health. They used apricot kernels, aspen fruits, yellow essence, *zhu*, or plantain seeds. On the other hand, some people suffered from adverse effects. The prefect of Aizhou, for example, died of an excessive dose of pine resin (*Yanshi jiaxun* 15).

During of the Wei, Jin, and Six Dynasties, people apparently came to believe that they could not be transformed into immortals by taking crude drugs alone. They used those mainly to preserve their health and prolong their lives. For example, Xi Kang, the famous poet of the third century, did not expect to become immortal by taking superior drugs. Texts on immortals' biographies also reflect this change. In the *Liexian zhuan* immortals attained their aim by merely ingesting superior drugs; later texts say that successful immortals not only took crude drugs but also applied the cinnabar elixir and used talismans and sacred texts. For instance, the *Liexian zhuan* says Pengzu 彭祖 attained his enormous longevity by ingesting cinnamon and fungus, while the *Shenxian zhuan* states that he took a gold-cinnabar elixir together with cinnamon, powdered antlers, and mica (*Shenxian zhuan* 1).

Therefore, from the third century onward, the cinnabar elixir became a substitute for the crude drugs used during the Han. This may have to do with

Fig. 4. Liu An ascending into heaven. *Source: Liexian quanzhuan*, p. 251

the fact that people experimented with crude drugs and found that they did not actually turn human beings into immortals. Disappointed with the results of ingesting crude drugs, people would then begin serious attempts to prepare a compound elixir. The *Weishu* 魏書 (History of the Wei Dynasty; chap. 114) and the *Baopuzi* (chap. 4) both state that the followers of Zhang Daoling 張道陵, the first Celestial Master of the second century, could produce gold and jade. Ge Xuan, the cousin of Ge Hong's father, is said to have received the *Taiqing dan jing*, the *Jiuding dan jing*, and the *Jinyi dan jing* Zuo Ci, who consequently would himself have been working on its active preparation around the end of the Han. His life can tentatively be dated to about 196–220 (Robinet 1984: vol.1: 17). In the third century, theoretical aspects of the undertaking were formulated in the *Zhouyi cantongqi* (Yoshida 1963). All this culminated in the *Baopuzi*, which greatly propagated the alchemical way to immortality and from which we now gain our deepest insights into elixir theory and methods. The *Baopuzi* clearly states that crude drugs are only good for prolonging life; the cinnabar elixir is what transforms human beings into immortals. This evaluation has become standard: the effect of immortality is mentioned only for twenty-three drugs in the *Zhenghe bencao* (see figure 1).

However, the emphasis on the religious and ritual aspects of the undertaking indicates a further disappointment. People could not actually be transformed even by the elixir. Taoists listed numerous conditions that had to be fulfilled completely in the process of elixir preparation if the resulting substances were to be effective—possibly in order to explain their notoriously unsuccessful attempts. They claimed, for example, that nobody could ever expect to prepare an effective elixir unless he or she was properly prepared, if not actually destined, for the work. Any mistake in the prescribed ritual procedure before and during the treatment of the materials would inevitably lead to failure. In addition, the basic source materials had to be of the highest possible quality.

As a matter of fact, elixirs frequently caused immediate death. The cinnabar elixir was particularly feared for its toxicity. The *Weishu* relates the following incident (note the explanation).

Dong Mi presented numerous volumes of the *Immortal Diet Classic* to the emperor. He duly appointed an official to the rank of Immortal Scholar and had a preparation chamber established. Cinnabar was refined by heating and the addition of various drugs. The finished elixir was given to criminals under death sentence. Many of them died and were not transformed into immortals. This is because they had no sincere longing for immortality. (*Weishu* 114)

Both mercury and realgar were known as toxic substances, but cinnabar dust was generally considered harmless (*Zhenghe bencao* 107, 101, 79). On the other hand; it was also thought that cinnabar dust would change into mercury (*Zhenghe bencao* 78), as which it then could eliminate toxic substances present in that substance, such as gold, silver, copper and tin. Then it would revert back into cinnabar (*Zhenghe bencao* 107). This suggests that a detailed knowledge about the interaction of various metals was developed as early as the Later Han dynasty. Cinnabar as such is a nontoxic red mineral that, when heated, decomposes into toxic vapors of sulphur and metal. Vaporized mercury, upon cooling down, condenses again into a thick, silver liquid.

Again, mercury amalgamates various metals, including gold, which traditionally is regarded as a symbol of constancy and immutability. This process probably lies behind the mysteries associated with mercury and its sulfide, cinnabar. On the other hand, the old Chinese thought that cinnabar and realgar were not entirely pure substances but were contaminated by various impurities. The impurities may have been transferred to the original drug from various substances while the elixir was being prepared. Since no two preparation procedures were ever identical, it is hard to judge the overall toxicity and probable effects of the resulting elixirs. The Taoist texts' demands that the source materials for the elixir be of top quality therefore sound quite reasonable; contamination was a very real danger.

Cases of poisoning through an elixir were widely known, but the deaths caused in this way were sometimes interpreted as successful transformations into immortality. However, actually attaining immortality required that the body be transformed. So cases in which the elixir was applied and that actually proved the efficacy of the process were very rare. The result was that fewer and fewer people believed in immortality through drugs and elixirs. Moreover the source materials for the elixir were rare and valuable, and one had to spend enormous amounts of time and money to acquire them. Only the rich and powerful could do so. Common people never attempted to produce elixirs, so the number of people who actually suffered from elixir poisoning remained limited. Common folk instead took drugs that were easier to get, like cold-food powder (which, though actually less toxic, would cause a greater number of deaths).

Elixirs of life based on cinnabar continued to be produced even after the Six Dynasties; they frequently caused severe intoxications, and six emperors of the Tang dynasty actually died from taking them (*Ershier shi zaji* 19). In Taoism, the alchemical process was from a rather early date internalized as inner alchemy. From Song times onward, the elixir of life was exclusively interpreted as the refined substance that was attained in the process of mutating and transforming the various vital energies in the body.

Until very recently drugs named after the elixir—cinnabars—were sold as medicines in China. Many of them contained mercury (Okanishi 1963: 290–306). They were used for a variety of ailments, but their name suggests that they were believed to have some positive effect on longevity. In contemporary China, there are also drugs that are not called cinnabar but do contain mercury or even arsenic. Such prescriptions might go back to the ancient elixirs, just as certain methods of preparation—for example, heating materials in tightly sealed containers—seem to be derived from the procedure of elixir concoction.

References

Despeux, Catherine. 1987. *Préscriptions d'acuponcture valant mille onces d'or*. Paris: Guy Trédaniel, 1987.

Giles, Lionel. 1948. *A Gallery of Chinese Immortals*. London: John Murray, 1948.

Harper, Donald J. 1982. *The "Wu Shih Erh Ping Fang": Translation and Prolegomena*. Berkeley: University of California Ph.D. Dissertation, 1982.

Henricks, Robert. 1983. *Philosophy and Argumentation in Third Century China: The Essays of Hsi K'ang*. Princeton: Princeton University Press, 1983.

Holzman, Donald. 1957. *La vie et la pensée de Hi K'ang*. Leiden: E. Brill, 1957.

Kaltenmark, Maxime. 1953. *Le Lie-sien tchouan*. Peking: Université de Paris, Publications du Centre d'Etudes Sinologiques, 1953.

Keys, John D. 1976. *Chinese Herbs*. Rutland: Tuttle, 1976.

Mather, Richard B. 1976. *A New Account of Tales of the World*. Minneapolis: University of Minnesota Press, 1976.

Needham, Joseph. 1976. *Science and Civilisation in China. Spagyrical Discovery and Invention: Historical Survey, from Cinnabar Elixir to Synthetic Insulin*. Vol. V.3. Cambridge: Cambridge University Press, 1976.

Robinet, Isabelle. 1984. *La rèvèlation du Shangqing dans l'histoire du Taoisme.* 2 vols. Paris: Publications de l'Ecole Francaise d'Extrême-Orient, 1984.

—— 1986. "The Taoist Immortal: Jester of Light and Shadow, Heaven and Earth," *Journal of Chinese Religions* 13–14 (1985–86), 87–106.

Sailey, Jay. 1978. *The Master Who Embraces Simplicity: A Study of the Philosophy of Ko Hung (A.D. 283–343).* San Francisco: Chinese Materials Center, 1978.

Sakade, Yoshinobu. 1986. "The Taoist Character of the 'Chapter on Nourishing Life' of the *Ishinpō*," *Kansai daigaku bunka ronshū* 1986, 775–798.

Sivin, Nathan. 1968. *Chinese Alchemy: Preliminary Studies.* Cambridge, Massachusetts: Harvard University Press, 1968.

Strickmann, Michel. 1979. "On the Alchemy of T'ao Hung-ching." In *Facets of Taoism*, pp. 123–192. Edited by H. Welch and A. Seidel. New Haven & London: Yale University Press, 1979.

Ware, James R. 1966. *Alchemy, Medicine and Religion in the China of A.D. 320. The Nei P'ien of Ko Hung (Pao-p'u tzu).* Cambridge, Massachusetts: MIT Press, 1966.

in Chinese and Japanese

Akahori Akira 赤屈昭   1978
"Shinnō honzōkei ni kisai sareta yakukō," 神農本草經に記載された藥效
Nihon ishigaku zasshi 日本醫史學雜誌 24 (1978), 1–13.

Nakao Manzō 中尾万三 1929
"Shokuryō honzō no kōsatsu" 食瘰本草の考察
Shanghai shizen kagaku kenkyūjo ihō 上海自然科學研究所彙報   1.3 (1929).

Okanishi Tameto 岡西爲人 1963
"Chūgoku igaku ni okeru tampō" 中國醫學における丹方
In *Chūgoku chūsei kagaku gijutsushi no kenkyū* 中國中世科學技術史の研究
edited by Yabuuchi Kiyoshi.
Tokyo: Kadokawa, 1963.

——— 1969. *Song yiqian yiji kao* 宋以前醫籍考
Taipei: Guting, 1969.

——— 1977. *Honzō gaisetsu* 本草概説
Osaka: Sōgensha, 1977.

Sakade Yoshinobu 坂出祥伸 1986a
"Chō Tan 'Yōsei yōshū' itsubun to sono shisō"
張湛の養生要集佚文とその 思想
Tōhōshūkyō 68 (1986), 1–24.

Shinoda Osamu 篠田統 and Tanaka Seiichi 田中靜一 1972
Chūgoku shokukei sōshu 中國食經叢書
2 vols. Tokyo: Shōseki bunmotsu ryūtsūkai, 1972.

Yoshida Mitsukuni 吉田老邦 1963
"Chūsei no kagaku (rentan jutsu) to senjutsu"
中世の化學(錬丹術)と仙術
In *Chūgoku chūsei kagaku gijutsushi no kenkyū*. Edited by Yabuuchi Kiyoshi.
Tokyo: Kadokawa, 1963.

Yu Jiaxi 余嘉錫 1938
"Hanshisan kao" 寒食散考
Furen xuezhi 輔仁學誌 7 (1938), 29–63.

List of Common Drugs Used for Immortality

basha 巴沙   cinnabar yielded in Sichuan (Bazhou)

cheqian 車前   (seeds of) Plantago asiatica L.

chishi zhi 赤石旨   red kaorinite containing oxides of metals

danggui 當歸   root of Angelica sinensis Diels

dansha 丹沙   cinnabar

fanshi 礬石   alum

fuling 茯苓   Poria cocos Wolf

fuzi 附子   tuber of Aconitum Carmichaelii Desbaux

gouqi 枸杞   fruit of Licium chinense Mill.

gui 桂   cinnamon

huangjing 黃精   (rhizome of) Polygonatum sibiricum Red. or P. mulitiflorum L.

huashi 滑石   halloysite

hufen 胡粉   carbonate of lead

huma 胡麻   sesame

jin 金   gold

jiu 韭   Allium tuberosum Rottler

kushen 苦參   (root of) Sophora flavescens Ait.

li 李   plum

luyan 鹵鹽   table salt mixed with sodium sulfate, magnesium sulfate, and others

mijiao 麋角   antler of Cervus davidianus M. Redw.

muli 牧蠣	oyster
ou 藕	lotus root
quepen 缺盆	fruit of Rubus Tanakae O. Kuntze and other Rubus species
rongyan 戎鹽	table salt yielded at salty lakes or from salty soils in northwestern China
shilianzi 石蓮子	lotus seed
shiliu 石榴	Punica Granatum L.
shuiyin 水銀	mercury
shuiyu 水玉	rock crystal
tao 桃	peach
tong 銅	copper
xi 錫	tin
xingren 杏仁	apricot kernel
xionghuang 雄黃	realgar
yin 銀	silver
yu 玉	jade (jadeite and nephrite)
yu 芋	tuber of Colocasia antiquorum Schott. or C. indica Kth.
yunmu 雲母	mica
zhi 芝	Formes indicus Fr.
zhu 朮	Atractylodes ovata (Thunb.) D.C.

Chapter Four

Longevity Techniques and the Compilation of the *Lingbao wufuxu*

Toshiaki Yamada

Introduction

The *Taishang lingbao wufuxu* 太上靈寶五符序 (Highest Explanation to the Five Talismans of the Numinous Treasure *Daozang* 388, fasc. 183),[1] in three scrolls (hereafter called the *Wufuxu*), is one of the earliest Lingbao scriptures. It places an enormous emphasis on dietetic techniques leading to the attainment of immortality.[2]

In its present form the text dates from the beginning of the fifth century, but its oldest parts go back as far as the Later Han dynasty; they are based on the writings of the magic specialists of this era. The *Wufuxu* includes a variety of magical and mystical longevity techniques, to a large part based on a

---

1. Texts in the Taoist Canon (*Daozang*, hereafter abbreviated DZ) are given according to the number of the reduced sixty-volume edition published in Taipei and Kyoto. These numbers coincide with those found in K.M. Schipper, *Concordance du Tao Tsang* (Paris: Publications de l'Ecole Francaise d'Extrême-Orient, 1975). "Fasc." stands for "fascicle" and refers to the volume number of the 1925 Shanghai reprint of the original canon of 1445 (*Zhengtong Daozang*).

2. For a discussion of this scripture see Bokenkamp 1986; Ishii 1984; Kaltenmark 1960; Robinet 1984; Yamada 1984. Among these, Bokenkamp's article contains an English translation of the Lingbao myth found in the first scroll. This story goes back to the apocryphal *Hetu jiangxiang*. Ishii's work assembles numerous materials in connection with the *Wufuxu*. A discussion of the position of the text among Taoist scriptures is also found in Robinet's work.

cosmology that correlates celestial, mundane, and human phenomena. In the Han dynasty that cosmology was most clearly formulated in the commentaries on the classics. Maxime Kaltenmark especially has emphasized the close relation of this text to the apocrypha (*chanwei* 懺緯) of the Han (Kaltenmark 1960).[3]

These so-called apocrypha are new interpretations of the classics that were well known at the time but not officially allotted the same status of orthodoxy as the classics themselves. *Chan* were originally different from *wei*; the former were oracle books and popular prophesies, while the latter were exegeses in the limited sense. Both types of literature strongly propagated a rather rigid cosmology based very strictly on the system of the five agents and ancient mythology. Correlations were seen between natural occurrences, movements of the stars, calendar organization, government affairs, and human life in general. Numerous old prophesies as well as myths were reinterpreted in the light of the new worldview (Tjan 1973: 100–120).

The interregnum of Wang Mang as well as the development of religious Taoist groups during the Later Han were accompanied, by popular prophesies and prognostications, if not actually stimulated by them. Partly due to their political importance, most of the original apocrypha (both *chan* and *wei*) are lost today. However, a certain number of texts have been restored on the basis of quotations in later literature, beginning with the fourth century. The Japanese scholar Yasui Kōzan in particular has contributed enormously to our knowledge of these materials (Yasui 1966, 1972, 1979; see also Dull 1966).

Here I am concerned with the impact such apocryphal texts and the activities of their authors, the magic specialists, had on the development and lineage organization of early Taoism. I will begin with the assumption that a large number of the ideas and the practices described in the *Wufuxu* go back to the magic specialists and the apocryphal literature of the Han. To show this relation I shall try to delineate the concepts underlying early Taoist dietetic techniques found especially in the second chapter of the present *Wufuxu*. Professor Kaltenmark has referred to this problem many times, but unlike him I would like to link the question with the historical editing process of the text. To do so I will attempt to identify specific dietetic methods as they were transmitted under the names especially of the immortals Lezichang 樂子長 and Huaziqi 華子期 . The relation of these methods to the ancient techniques

---

3. He thinks that the original text—that is, the oldest explanation of the five talismans—is found in sections scattered throughout the version extant today, but I believe that the introductory myth in the first chapter performed this role. I intend to elaborate this point in future work dealing with the origins of the *Wufuxu* and its talismanic character. Apocryphal materials play an important role in the development of Taoism in general; see Seidel 1983. On Han dynasty magic specialists see DeWoskin 1983 and Ngo 1976.

of Lingbao together with the way in which they have been incorporated into the *Wufuxu*, to a certain degree reveal the history of the compilation of the book.

Textual studies are the backbone of critical scholarship dealing with the history of Taoism. Numerous texts in the Taoist Canon are not clearly dated, and frequently no individual author is known. The texts as we have them today may date from as early as the Tang dynasty. Sometimes there may even be correlating data among the manuscripts found in Dunhuang,[4] but even then materials contained in individual texts may date from a variety of periods and may have been incorporated by several authors or editors.

To gain an understanding of the development of the Taoist religion, both must go together: the critical evaluation of sources and the analytical study of ideas and practices. One is quite impossible without the other, since often as not the structure of the texts tells us more about the development of the religion than does the analysis of the concepts involved. On the other hand, Taoist texts have been dated on the basis of the understanding and interpretation of philosophical and cosmological ideas.[5]

Applying this methodology to the *Wufuxu*, I will present the dietetics of Lezichang and Huaziqi by discussing their possible historical origins and date of integration into the text. In addition, the question of the nature of the original *wufu*, Five Talismans, of which the *Wufuxu* claims to be the explanation, will be raised. And by looking at other, not directly dietetic, longevity techniques, I will identify another lineage leading to the development of organized Taoism. Certain meditation methods, it appears, were not based primarily on the individual search for health by means of drugs and diets, but depended on an organized system of beliefs popular in certain local communities. Taoism as a religion owes much to the magic specialists of the Han, but it is also a direct heir of Han popular religion. Examining the nature of various important longevity techniques and their different lines of transmission makes the historical development of the *Wufuxu* clearer. It also helps us to understand the concepts and methods of immortality in early

---

4. For Taoist materials found in Dunhuang see Yoshioka 1969, Ōfuchi 1979, and Tonkō kōza 1983.

5. A telling example is the *Xiang'er* commentary to the *Daode jing*, which tradition ascribes to Zhang Lu, the grandson of the first Celestial Master, Zhang Daoling. Accepting the traditional ascription on the basis of a reign title mentioned in the text, scholars dated it to the middle of the third century. Recently Mugitani Kunio has revised this dating on the basis of a critical analysis of the philosophical concepts represented in the text. He claims that it cannot have been written before the fifth century (Mugitani 1985), which theory will question, if not render obsolete, quite a number of our ideas about the early Celestial Masters that were based on this text.

Taoism as well as the formation and inner organization of the Taoist religion as a whole.

Wufuxu Dietetics and Lezichang

Among the numerous immortality techniques found in the second chapter of the *Wufuxu*, three major types of dietetics can be distinguished.

1. ingestion of sesame;
2. expulsion of the three worms;
3. intake of alcoholic beverages and various other methods.

I will not discuss the third item here, because it includes many different kinds of dietetic techniques that go back to a variety of origins and need to be treated in a special study. Most of those techniques seem to have been incorporated into the present *Wufuxu* very late, if not actually added after the basic compilation of the text had been completed. Some of them, however, are related to methods mentioned in Ge Hong's 葛洪 *Baopuzi* 抱朴子 (Book of the Master Who Embraced Simplicity) of the early fourth century. These, then, have to be considered early.

The other two items, ingestion of sesame and expulsion of the three worms, are also among the immortality methods advised by Ge Hong. Unlike the *Baopuzi*, the *Wufuxu* specifically links them with the names of Lezichang and Huaziqi. One of the numerous methods of taking sesame, listed under the heading *Lingbao jusheng zhongfa* 靈寶巨勝眾注 , the "Method that Yu Received from the Realized Ones," is described in a commentary as having been transmitted by a certain immortal, Huo Lin 翟林 , to Lezichang, who then lived secluded on Mount Lao in Shandong (2.4a).[6] Lezichang in turn made the method more popular, and it came to be named after him. Other closely related, if not actually identical, methods went from an unknown immortal to Huaziqi, who in turn was especially associated with them. It seems, therefore, that certain sections of the *Wufuxu* were at one time transmitted by Lezichang and Huaziqi respectively. Those sections may be identified as texts handed down from those masters.

Huaziqi's biography in the *Wufuxu* is very similar to the account of his life in Ge Hong's *Shenxian zhuan* 神仙傳 (Biographies of Spirit Immortals). It states that Huaziqi received three magical texts on immortality: the *Hetu*

---

6. It is not certain who the author of this commentary was. He may have been the main transmitter of the text, who, as suggested by the *Lingbao jingmu* found in Dunhuang, was Lu Xiujing of the fifth century. But this is by no means clear at present.

yincun fu   河圖隱存符   (River Chart Talisman of Appearance and Disappearance), the *Yinluo feigui* 尹雒飛龜 (Flying Turtle of the Yin and Luo Rivers), and the *Pingheng* 平衡 (Equalizer; see *Wufuxu* 1.11b). Similar texts are mentioned in the *Baopuzi* as parts of the Lingbao scriptures.

> Among the Lingbao scriptures there are three booklets, called the *Straightener*, the *Equalizer*, and the *Flying Turtle*; all contain recipes leading to immortality. (12.6a; Ware 1966: 209)

It is not clear what kind of practices were described in these texts. The *Wufuxu* says that "when one follows their instructions one will become more vigorous every day and develop the complexion of a young girl." Thus they were obviously concerned with longevity techniques. The close connection between the *Baopuzi*, the *Shenxian zhuan*, and the *Wufuxu* suggests that the methods referred to in all three were very similar, if not identical. One may thus use the technical information found in the *Wufuxu* to supplement the biographical data and general outlines of the other two texts. This means that the magical methods Huaziqi received were likely related to the ingestion of sesame, the technique most closely associated with his name in the *Wufuxu*. We will return to Huaziqi later.

Lezichang: His Life and Work

About Lezichang the *Wufuxu* relates the following:

> The *Lingbao shangxu* and the *Zhuanchu fuyu zhi wen* were originally written in an old script that could not be read by modern people. Lezichang obtained these scriptures, edited them and made them accessible. (3.2b–3a)

According to this passage, the methods transmitted under the name of Lezichang go back to two kinds of sacred, or revealed, texts: the *Lingbao shangxu* 靈寶上序 (Highest Lingbao Explanations) and the *Zhuanchu fuyu zhi wen* 撰出服御之文 (Specially Selected Materials on Diets and Body Control). Since Lezichang's methods make up a large portion of the *Wufuxu*, the text itself can be said to go back to these ancient scriptures.

The specific techniques Lezichang transmitted can be glimpsed from his biography. His life is recorded in the *Xianyuan bianzhu* 仙苑編珠 (Well-Arranged Pearls of an Immortal's Garden 1.19b; DZ 596, fasc. 329–330) and in the *Sandong qunxian lu* 三洞群仙錄 (Record of the Host of the Immortals of the Three Caves 13.11a; DZ 1248, fasc. 992–995).

Lezichang was originally from Qi (modern Shandong). He
once met an immortal known as Huolin and from him received
the methods of sesame ingestion and the pharmacological
recipes of Master Redpine.

There is no well-known immortal by the name of Huolin, but there is some
information on an immortal resident of Mount Huolin in Shandong: Han
Zhong 韓眾 is a famous immortal of eastern China who lived under the reign
of Emperor Shihuang of the Qin dynasty. The star of the immortals, Chisongzi
赤松子   or Master Redpine, whose pharmacological methods Lezichang
received in particular, was from the same time and place. (Figure 1 is a
portrait of Master Redpine.)

Both immortals are mentioned in the *Shiji* 史記   (Records of the
Historian), the *Liexian zhuan* 列仙傳   (Immortals' Biographies), and in Ge
Hong's *Shenxian zhuan*. Lezichang's biography therefore places him in a
lineage of magic specialists or immortals of eastern China, a lineage known as
the Way of Immortality Methods (*Shiji* 28.10b) and closely associated with
the names of Han Zhong and Master Redpine. The earliest evidence for this is
found in a fragment of the *Fengsu tongyi*   風俗通義 (General Explication of
Popular Customs) cited in the Song dynasty encyclopedia *Taiping yulan* 太平
御覽 (Imperial Encyclopedia of the Era of Great Peace).

Lezichang came from Qi [modern Shandong]. Even as a child
he was attracted by the Tao. Later he withdrew to Mount
Huolin where he became an immortal by means of the ingestion of sesame and the methods of Master Redpine. (662.5b)

All later biographies of Lezichang are based on his early characteriza-
tion in the *Fengsu tongyi*. He was a mountain ascetic who specifically
practiced a dietetic method based on sesame and some drug taking in
accordance with Master Redpine's recipes. The ingestion of sesame is
explicitly linked with his name in the *Wufuxu*. Thus Lezichang was one of the
magic specialists or immortals of Shandong in the early Han who became
particularly famous for his diet practices. His methods were duly transmitted
in close association with his name.

The *Zhengao* 真誥 (Declarations of the Perfected; DZ 1016, fasc.
637–640) includes the following divine report on Lezichang:

I once met Lezichang in Nanyang. He struck me as a very fine
and pure person, but since he wasn't my acknowledged teacher
I didn't receive any instruction from him. Lezichang himself
did not attain longevity or deathlessness. Rather he ascended to
paradise after death and had his name entered into the registers
of immortals. He then held the post of a gate attendant in

Fig. 1. Chisongzi, Master Redpine. *Source: Liexian quanzhuan* 列仙全傳 ,
p. 41

heaven. This is a rank just below that of a full immortal. (8.12a)

Tao Hongjing 陶弘景 (456–536), the author of the *Zhengao*, remarks that this report was a later forgery which had been added to the original text of the revelations by Lu Xiujing 陸修靜 (420–477), who edited and catalogued Taoist scriptures in the fifth century. Whether or not this short report was actually added later is not as important for our problem as the evidence it provides for the fact that Lezichang actually lived in the Nanyang region of Shandong or that there was at least a tradition that clearly associated him with the place. Also, we learn that he was not considered a full immortal, but one who ascended to heaven after death and then occupied only a lower rank.

We can see that Lezichang was famous in the Shandong tradition. Although he was later believed to have actually attained a certain immortal status by ingesting sesame and applying the drug recipes of Master Redpine, originally he was one of the magic specialists of Shandong who followed and transmitted these methods.

The Ingestion of Sesame

The effects of the ingestion of sesame described in the *Wufuxu* are quoted from an apocryphal scripture, the *Xiaojing yuanshen qi* 孝經援神契 (Pointer to the Spirit of the Classic of Filial Piety; see Yasui 1966: 455; Yasui and Nakamura 1972: vol. 5: 21–60).

> The *Xiaojing yuanshen qi* says: "Ginger and pepper increase the vital forces (*qi*), sweet flag strengthens wisdom, and sesame extends one's years." (*Wufuxu* 2.2b)

A similar citation is found in the *Baopuzi*.

> Pepper and ginger protect against the effects of dampness, sweet flag sharpens the hearing, sesame protracts the years, and resin puts weapons to flight. (11.1a; Ware 1966: 177)

It is not known when the *Xiaojing yuanshen qi* was first compiled. It is quoted in the *Baihu tong* 白虎通 (Discussions in the White Tiger Hall; translated in Tjan 1973) of the Later Han and also in the *Hou Hanshu* 後漢書 (History of the Later Han). Moreover, the bibliographic section of the *Suishu* 隋書 (History of the Sui Dynasty) mentions that the text was in seven scrolls and had a commentary by Song Jun 宋均. It is also referred to by Fan Hua 范曄 of the fifth century in his commentary to the *Hou Hanshu*. Taken together, the evidence suggests that the *Xiaojing yuanshen qi* was an apocryphal text of the

Han dynasty that was rather widely known and accepted during the Six Dynasties. It recorded the techniques of the magic specialists and as such was integrated into both the *Baopuzi* and also in the *Wufuxu*.

The Expulsion of the Three Worms

Other immortality techniques closely associated with the name of Lezichang are those of Master Redpine. The *Wufuxu* describes one practice associated with this immortal.

> When you cut the nails of your hands and feet on the sixteenth day of the seventh month, you can drive out the three worms from your intestines. (2.14b)

The *Baopuzi*, too, refers to the methods of Master Redpine in connection with the expulsion of the three worms.

> The *Commands of the Book of Changes*, the *Classic of Master Redpine*, and the *River Chart Life Talisman* say that the gods of heaven and earth who are in charge of evil deeds make deductions from people's life spans according to their wrongdoing. . . The three worms mount to heaven every 57th day of the sixty-day cycle and report everyone's sins and misdemeanors to the Administrator of Destiny. (6.4b; Ware 1966: 177)

The dietetic techniques transmitted by Lezichang and associated with Master Redpine therefore have to be understood against the background of the concept of the three worms. Various recipes for their expulsion are also given in the *Wufuxu*, for example:

> Pluck peach leaves on the third day of the third month; crush them to extract seven pints of juice. Then mix in liquor and heat it five or six times. Take it before meals and the three worms will be driven out. (2.11a)

In addition, the text mentions mercury elixirs as effective against the three worms. These are applied when one wants to become an immortal, while the herbal concoctions are helpful in attaining long life; living out one's given life span may then be followed by the deliverance of the corpse—ascension into heaven upon bodily death (see Robinet 1979).

We do not know when the concept of the three worms first developed. Textual evidence suggests that it first appeared in the section of the *Baopuzi* quoted above, which in turn is based on apocryphal scriptures like the three texts it cites by title. In any case, it is clear that the pharmacological methods of Master Redpine, and thus the dietetics of Lezichang, belong to the milieu of the magic specialists of the Han and were first recorded in their texts, the apocrypha. Similarly it is their conceptual framework in which these methods were applied and found effective. The texts associated with Lezichang, the *Zhuanchu fuyu zhi wen*, must belong to the same environment.

No solid evidence exists for the dating of Lezichang's life. His standard biography, as explained above, connects him with Qin and early Han immortals like Han Zhong and Master Redpine. These two were already famous during the Former Han dynasty. They are especially mentioned in connection with reports on the life of Emperor Wu (140–87 B.C.), who was very keen on becoming immortal himself (*Shiji* 12, 28; see Miyakawa 1983: 52; Kaltenmark 1953: 1–45). Lezichang, a master following their tradition, would therefore have to be placed in the Han dynasty himself, but there is no way of telling at exactly what point. Similarly, the apocrypha have to be considered Han dynasty materials, but as they were lost and only exist in fragments and quotations, one can never be sure that they really represent beliefs as ancient as the first or second century B.C.

The Techniques of Huaziqi

The first chapter of the *Wufuxu* contains a biography of Huaziqi that hints that certain Lingbao methods of making oneself invisible that were incorporated into the text came from him.

> Huaziqi came from Jiujiang [in southeast China]. Ever since he was a child he was attracted to the Tao of immortality. Later he withdrew into the mountains, gathered herbs and lived on drugs. He stayed in the wilderness for over twenty years.
> Once he met Master Jiaoli and received the Lingbao methods of immortality from him. These methods were transmitted in three texts; the first was called the *Hetu yincun fu*, the second the *Yinluo feigui*, and the third was the *Pingheng*. In following the instructions laid down therein one has to prepare certain drugs. Taking these over a period of time one will become younger every day. (1.11b)

More than that, the *Wufuxu* incorporates a long text on the ingestion of the energies of the five directions that supposedly was transmitted from Master Jiaoli 角里先生 to Huaziqi and was later written down by Lezichang. This suggests not only that Lezichang lived later than Huaziqi, but also that substantial parts of the *Wufuxu,* not just the specific methods associated with the names of these two immortals, were believed to go back to them.

The Ingestion of the Five Sprouts

Huaziqi's method of the ingestion of the energies of the five directions is mentioned in the *Wufuxu* in a citation of the *Xianren yifu wufang zhutian qi jing zhu* 仙人挹服 五方諸天 氣經注 (Commentary to the Scripture on the Immortal's Ingestion of the Breaths of the Five Directions and All the Heavens). This scripture states that Huaziqi received the teachings in oral transmission from Master Jiaoli, while Lezichang was inspired directly by the gods. The ingestion of the energies of the five directions is probably what became known later as the ingestion of the five sprouts of the various directions. That method is described in fuller detail in the *Chishu yujue* 赤書玉訣 {The Jade Formula of the Red Book; DZ 352, fasc. 178), where the five sprouts are identified as the essences or energies of the five orbs (30a–31a).

The practice proceeds this way. In order to ingest the sprout of the east—of the orb of the liver—one should rise very early on the first day of the New Year. In the meditation chamber one should bow to the east nine times, then sit erect, clap one's teeth nine times and visualize the green fresh energy of the East. The energy is seen to descend towards oneself, thick as a cloud and light as mist. It enters the body through the mouth and goes directly to the orb of the liver, which it supports (*Chishu yujue* 2.5a).[7]

The method of ingesting the breaths of the five directions that was transmitted by Huaziqi according to the *Wufuxu* is also mentioned in a quotation of the *Taishang taiyi zhenyi zhi jing* 太上太一真一之經 (Highest Scripture of the Great One and the True One; *Wufuxu* 3.21a) that is taken up again by the *Chishu yujue* in connection with the ingestion of the five sprouts (2.6b). Huaziqi therefore seems to have been an early practitioner of the ingestion of the five sprouts.

The Expulsion of the Three Worms

Another tradition associated with Huaziqi appears in the *Hetu yincun fu.* Like other River Chart texts, it seems to have described the theoretical, cosmological framework in which techniques of immortality were being

---

7. A very similar technique is described in the *Taiping jing* (Wang 1979: 292). Here the five orbs are visualized through the colors of their respective energies, while in the later Lingbao version the Five Old Ones, personal divinities and messengers from the Highest Lord Lao, Taishang Laojun, are their representatives.

practiced. The River Chart was a powerful talisman and insignia of rulership
in ancient China (Seidel 1983). The *Hetu jiming fu*   河圖紀命符 (River Chart
Life Talisman) mentioned above in a quotation from the *Baopuzi* contains a
long passage describing the theoretical framework in which the various
methods of long life and immortality were applied. This passage has survived
in a quotation in Tamba no Yasuyori's 丹波康頼   *Ishinpō* 醫心方 (Essential
Medical Methods).

> In heaven and on earth there are gods who supervise human
> behavior. In accordance with the sins and transgressions
> committed by every individual they subtract time from his or
> her life span. A major transgression leads to the subtraction of
> a whole year of life, a minor one causes the loss of one day. . . .
>   Three worms reside in the human body. They are
> somewhat like the various souls [that is, one cannot see them].
> They wish the person to die early so that they can feed on his
> body. Therefore they report all human transgressions to the
> cosmic administration, leaving on every sixth day of the sixty-
> day cycle. On the basis of their report the heavenly officials
> subtract time from the individual's life span.
>   Consequently, if one wishes to become immortal one
> must first of all get rid of these three worms. One can do this
> by performing good deeds and by taking drugs. Thereby one
> can become an immortal. (*Ishinpō* 26; Yasui and Nakamura
> 1972: vol.6: 113)

The agents of human mortality are therefore identified as the three
worms (for a depiction see figure 2). They are body parasites who live on
decay and death and who report everyone's behavior to the administration of
the cosmos. One can expel them only by doing good deeds so that they don't
have anything to report and consequently lose their jobs. One can also get rid
of them by taking specific longevity drugs, which starve them so that they
eventually have to leave and find another host.

Huaziqi and Lezichang are masters of such worm-starving diet
techniques. Methods of expelling the three worms are, as noted above,
associated closely with the name of Master Redpine, whose methods were
then transmitted by Lezichang. The *Wufuxu* insists that Huaziqi's techniques
make people younger every day, which indicates that they were not aimed at
immediately transforming humans into immortals. They did not consist of the
concoction of a cinnabar elixir. Rather, they served to allow adepts to live out
the life spans originally granted them by heaven, uninterrupted and
undisturbed by the parasitic activities of the three worms. Transformation into
an immortal would then be attained only upon graduation from worldly
existence.

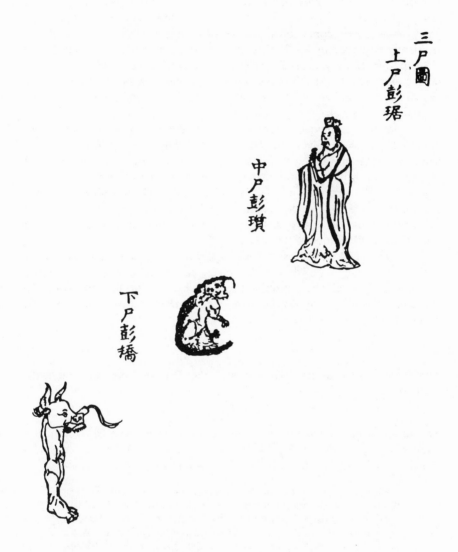

Fig. 2. The three worms. *Source: Taishang chu sanshi jiuchong baosheng jing* 7a–8a; DZ 871, fasc. 580

The talisman used for the correct practice is consequently not a protective device to expel and ward off the three worms, but an auspicious sign from heaven, a positive means to attain long life. In this sense it is not an amulet but can be compared to the red-letter charms commonly used and frequently described by the Taoists. It is probable that the text transmitted by Huaziqi, the *Hetu yincun fu*, was such an auspicious charm, containing instructions regarding to the expulsion of the three worms. As a text it may have been very similar, if not identical, to the *Hetu jiming fu*, of which several fragments have survived in quotations.

Longevity techniques aimed at expelling the three worms can therefore be traced to both Lezichang and Huaziqi. Lezichang received them under the name Methods of Master Redpine, Huaziqi in the *Hetu yincun fu*. They represent two different traditions based equally on the concept of the three worms and the necessity of getting rid of them. In the other two texts transmitted to Huaziqi, the *Yinluo feigui* and the *Pingheng*, there are references to the other two methods associated with him, the ingestion of sesame and the ingestion of the five sprouts.

As indicated in the last chapter of the *Wufuxu*, the central documents dealing with this method, around which the text developed, were the *Zhuangchu fuyu zhi wen* transmitted by Lezichang (3.3a) and not works by Huaziqi. However, as the *Wufang zhutian qi jing zhu* has it, Huaziqi also made a contribution to this text.

The Compilation of the *Wufuxu* and the Transmission of Longevity Techniques

The history of the *Wufuxu* is made clearer if one examines a fragment of Lu Xiujing's *Lingbao jingmu* 靈寶經目 (Catalogue of the Lingbao Scriptures) found in Dunhuang (see Ofuchi 1974; Bokenkamp 1983):

> The *Taishang dongxuan lingbao tianwen wufu jingxu* [the *Wufuxu*] . . . originally consisted of only one scroll. The oldest version of this was compiled by Emperor Yu of the Xia Dynasty on the basis of the revealed Lingbao Scriptures. After he finished the text he hid it on the north side of Mount Laosheng. Later Lezichang received the sacred scripture from the immortal of Huolin and made it known to the world. The version that the Immortal Ge (Xuan) obtained in his lifetime consisted of two scrolls; in the meantime the text has grown to the size of three. (P. 2256; Ofuchi 1979: 727, lines 20–24)

In this fragment of Lu Xiujing's catalogue no mention is made of Huaziqi, which means that in the fifth century version of the *Wufuxu* the biography of Huaziqi, which is found in the first chapter of the present edition, had not yet been integrated into the text. This in turn indicates that the earliest longevity methods put down in the scripture were the ones described in Lezichang's *Zhuanchu fuyu zhi wen*. The methods of Huaziqi must therefore have been transmitted independently, at least until the fifth century.

The *Wufuxu* itself has grown gradually. It began as one scroll; it consisted of two when Ge Xuan 葛玄 , the cousin of Ge Hong's father, obtained it in the third century; and by the time Lu Xiujing was writing, in the fifth century, it had grown to three. Two thirds of the edition extant today were therefore added to an original nucleus over a long time. According to Lu Xiujing, Ge Xuan's edition already contained the methods of Lezichang. This tallies with the description found in the third chapter of today's text. The old original was based on Lezichang's edition of the *Lingbao shangxu* and the *Zhuanchu fuyu zhi wen* (3.2b–3a). It may well be that the one scroll that existed originally *was* the text of the *Lingbao shangxu*, to which Ge Xuan added the *Zhuangchu fuyu zhi wen*, because they were also closely associated with Lezichang in his time. That is to say, Ge Xuan added the practical instructions—the expulsion of the three worms as transmitted according to the methods of Master Redpine, and the ingestion of sesame. The three scrolls catalogued by Lu Xiujing therefore consisted of the old original and Ge Xuan's addition plus a variety of similar longevity methods added over the years on grounds of their similarity to the techniques already described in the text. More instructions were added after Lu Xiujing saw the *Wufuxu*, but it is safe to assume that today's edition was almost finished by his time, the information on Huaziqi probably being incorporated then.

The final compilation of the *Wufuxu* from Ge Xuan onward took place in the region of Jiangnan, in the south of China near present-day Nanjing. All the texts produced in this region in medieval China show strong connections to the magic specialists of Shandong in the eastern part of the country. The *Baopuzi*, though written in the South, incorporates methods from a variety of places: Ge Hong's father-in-law, Bao Jing 鮑靚 , and his teacher, Yin Changsheng 尹長生 (see *Shenxian zhuan* 4), for example, were Henan people. Ge Hong describes the origins and lineages of the techniques mentioned in the *Baopuzi* in his autobiographical postface (Ware 1966: 6–21; Yamada 1983: 371); it is clear that they came from different places in the north, to be traced back ultimately to Shandong. For example, the teacher of Yin Changsheng, himself from Henan, was Ma Mingsheng 馬鳴生 , who was a magic specialist of the Shandong area. He prepared a cinnabar elixir for the immediate ascension into heaven and practiced gymnastics, breathing, and dietetics for the attainment of long life (*Shenxian zhuan* 2).

Various longevity techniques recorded in texts compiled in the South, therefore, go back to practices of magic specialists of the East. Independently of one another they seem to have placed enormous emphasis on applying specific diets. Both the *Baopuzi* and the *Wufuxu* are thus collections of different methods leading to long life or immortality. But unlike the *Baopuzi*, which is an intentional collection of various such recipes, the *Wufuxu* seems to have been originally limited to one specific lineage.

Other *Wufuxu* Origins

Spiritual Protection: The Five Lingbao Talismans

The last chapter of the *Wufuxu* contains pictures of the five essential Lingbao talismans after which the text was named. They were originally transmitted by Emperor Yu of the Xia dynasty and are arranged according to the system of the Five Agents—that is, associated with the five directions, five colors, and five emperors.

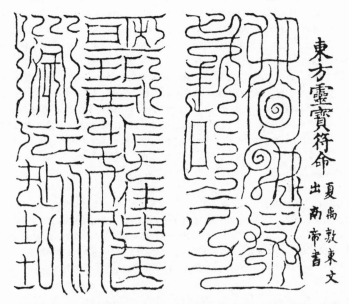

Fig. 3. The Eastern of the Five Lingbao Talismans. *Source: Wufuxu* 3.9b

What were these five talismans? The *Baopuzi* mentions them in several contexts. First, it mentions a set called "Laozi's five Lingbao talismans for entering into mountains." These are protective devices used to ward off evil spirits and negative influences when adepts go into the wilderness of the mountains to search for rocks, plants, herbs, and other raw materials used in the preparation of longevity or immortality drugs.

> There are five types of excrescences: rock, wood, herb, flesh, and the tiny; each of them has almost a hundred species.
> The rock ones are semblances of mushroom in stone. They grow on the sacred mountains by the sea. Along island streams they are formations of piled rocks resembling flesh. Those seeming to have head, tail, and four feet are the best. They look like something alive. They are attached to boulders, and prefer high, steep spots, which sometimes seem inaccessible. . . .
> Small ones cannot be seen unless one has fasted long and with effort and is wearing Laozi's five Lingbao talismans for entering mountains on one's belt. Whenever excrescences are encountered, an initiatory and exorcising talisman is placed over them, then they can no longer conceal or transform themselves.
> Then patiently await the lucky day on which you will offer a sacrifice of wine and dried meat. Pluck them while chanting an incantation, always approaching them from the east in the fashion of the Steps of Yu[8] and with your breath well controlled. When you gather a rock that resembles a mushroom, grind it with a pestle 36.000 times and take three spoonfuls every day. After taking a pound, you will live to be a thousand; after ten pounds, to ten thousand. (11.2b–3a; Ware 1966: 179–180)

The five talismans described above are protective charms. The *Baopuzi* also mentions a set of five talismans used as positive reinforcements for the attainment of immortality.

---

8. Instructions are given in *Baopuzi* 17.5a, Ware 1966: 286.

> Stand straight; advance the right foot while the left remains behind. Then advance the left foot and the right foot alternately, so that they are both side by side. This constitutes step one. Advance the right foot, then the left, then bring the right side by side with the left. This is step two. Advance the left foot, then the right, then bring the left side by side with the right. This is step three. These three are the steps of Yu.

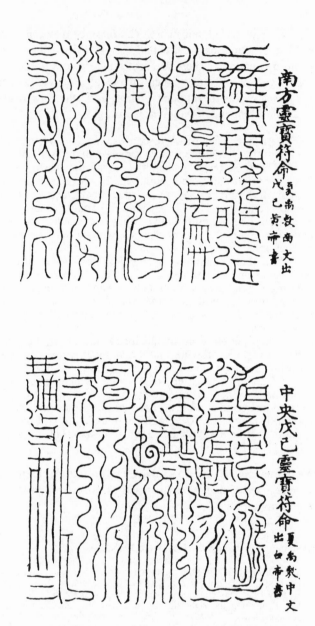

Fig. 4. The southern and central of the five Lingbao talismans. *Source:* *Wufuxu* 3.10ab

The Talismans of the Five Emperors written with cinnabar elixir will prevent death. (4.10a; Ware 1966: 83)

The association of a set of talismans with the five emperors is also found in the *Wufuxu*. The five emperors as gods of the five directions (north, south, east, west, and center) were officially established during the Han dynasty. (Figures 3, 4, and 5 depict the five talismans of the five directions.) They play an important role in the apocrypha, and occur elsewhere in the *Wufuxu* as the Five Heavenly Administrators of the cosmos. So it seems that the five talismans depicted in the *Wufuxu* were both active helpers in the search for immortality and protective charms to ward off evil.[9]

One applies them, as described in the *Baopuzi*, by hanging them from one's belt when entering a mountain (*Wufuxu* 3.9a).

The sacred mountains of ancient China were considered very dangerous spots. Without proper protection one might easily fall prey to wild animals or evil spirits there. Yet it was necessary to enter them, because the best raw materials for the drugs of long life and immortality could be found there. Ge Hong has a whole chapter on the various precautions one has to take when going into the mountains. He says:

> All mountains, whether large or small, house various spirits and higher powers. The strength of these divinities is directly proportional to the size of the mountain. To enter the mountains without the proper recipe is to be certain of anxiety or harm. . . . Lack of preparation may cause you to meet with tigers, wolves, or poisonous insects that will injure you. Mountains are not to be entered lightly. (*Baopuzi* 17.1a; Ware 1966: 279–280)

Since most of the drugs described in the ancient texts were based on materials found in the mountains and often had to be prepared there as well, it is understandable that the scriptures also contain detailed descriptions of protective measures to be taken at the beginning. The *Wufuxu* was composed for precisely this purpose.

---

9. Other protective talismans, separate from the original set of five, are also found in later Lingbao scriptures, such as the *Chishu yujue*; see Kobayashi 1982.

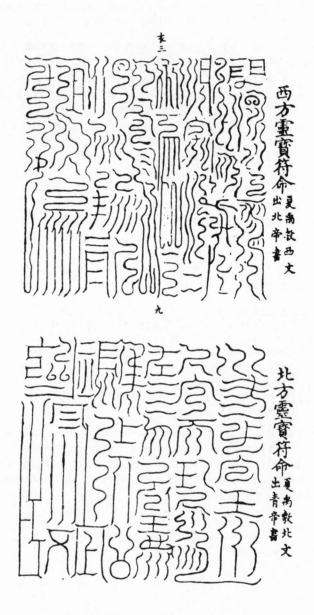

Fig. 5. The western and northern of the five Lingbao talismans. *Source: Wufuxu* 3.11ab

Visual Meditation: The Absorption of Stellar Essences

The *Wufuxu* contains a variety of methods aimed at prolonging life that have
nothing to do with either drugs or diets. Among them we find especially
techniques for absorbing stellar essences, of the sun and the moon in
particular (1.18b–19b, 25a–26a); meditations on the essences of the five orbs
of the body (1.16b–18b); and visualizations of the gods of the universe and the
body (1.19b, 23a). The ideas behind these methods are already described in
the apocrypha, notably in the *Xiaojing yuanshen qi*. Here the inner structure of
the human body as related to the forces of the cosmos and in particular to the
essences of the stars is described. Similar ideas can also be detected in one of
the earliest scriptures of organized Taoism, in the *Taiping jing*   太平經
(Scripture of Great Peace).

The absorption of solar and lunar energy is described as follows in the
Wufuxu:

> By nourishing on the essence of the sun one can attain long
> life. Every month on the morning of the first, third, fifth, sixth,
> ninth, and fifteenth day you should face the sunrise with open
> hair and closed eyes.
> Concentrate on the sun and visualize a small child
> dressed in red in your heart. His garments are embroidered in
> the five colors and he emits a bright red radiance. Then
> massage yourself with both hands from the face down to the
> heart; repeat this twelve times. You will see the red radiance of
> the sun and a yellow energy will appear before your eyes.
> Make this enter your mouth and swallow it twice nine times.
> Then rub your heart and recite the following incantation:
> "Ruler of the Sun! Let your primal yang energy merge its
> power with me! Let us together raise the immortal child in the
> scarlet palace of the heart!"
> Concentrate a little longer and the child will descend
> from the heart to the lower cinnabar field in the abdomen. He
> will stay there and make you live long.
> By nourishing the essence of the moon you can
> strengthen the root of the kidneys and make white hair turn
> black again. Get up at midnight and visualize a white energy
> floating around in your kidneys. Circulate it around the whole
> body until it reaches the head, then lead it down again into the
> feet. This method of becoming one with nature is easy to
> understand but difficult to practice.
> The essence of the moon can be ingested at full moon, on
> the fifteenth day of every month. Then, stand outside facing the
> moon and chant the following words:
> "Ruler of the Moon! Let your primal yin energy merge
> its power with me! Let us together raise the immortal child in
> the cinnabar field!"

Close your eyes and visualize the white of the moon. A
yellow energy will appear before your eyes. Make this enter
your mouth and swallow it thrice seven times. Thereafter rub
your torso to send it down into the cinnabar field where it will
stay. (1.18b–19b)

By ingesting the essences of the sun and the moon one can attain long
life. This technique is fundamentally different from the dietetic methods
discussed so far; it is a breathing and visualization technique by which the
adept incorporates the vital forces of the celestial bodies through the act of
swallowing.

Defining the Traditions

The *Wufuxu* instructions on ingesting the essences of stellar bodies are similar
to the meditation methods outlined in the *Taiping jing*. Here adepts are taught
to visualize the energies of the five orbs and the One as a light appearing in a
variety of colors (Wang 1979: 291; see also chapter 5, "Guarding the One:
Concentrative Meditation in Taoism"). Where the *Taiping jing* demands that
practices be undertaken in a closed chamber, the *Wufuxu* insists that they work
best when done in the mountains. A more fundamental difference between the
two, however, is in emphasis. The *Taiping jing* stresses the meditation itself;
the *Wufuxu* concentrates on the energy one is to ingest. Both meditation
practice and energy ingestion play an important role in early Taoism. Both
were originally used mainly for healing purposes, to establish a perfect
physical condition as the basis for long life and eventual immortality. The
mystical ideal of becoming fully one with the cosmos by identifying with the
sun and the moon seems secondary in comparison. That is to say, a state of
union with some universal force was not the final goal of the practice; rather,
it was a means for realizing longevity.

Unlike the dietetic practices discussed above, these methods are
intensely religious in nature. They are not medical and empirical. They rely on
a specific system of beliefs about the human body and the nature of the
universe. Moreover, they include visualizations of the various divinities and
incantations or prayers addressed to them. Their whole conceptual framework
is fundamentally different from the ideas underlying dietetic practices.

Consequently, it seems reasonable to assume that dietetics and the
meditation methods of energy ingestion were transmitted in two independent
traditions, that the meditation methods of the *Wufuxu* were not integrated into
the text through either Lezichang or Huaziqi but went back to other Taoists or

magic specialists of the Han. The strongly religious nature of the practices suggests that they might originally have been related to popular local cults. Practicing the methods cited above, for instance, presupposes a belief in personal gods of the sun and the moon as well as in personified vital forces residing in the human body. The former may well go back to popular worship of the celestial bodies, which included exposure to the sun and the moon, addressing the sun god and the moon god in prayer, and concentrating on their power. Similarly, the *Taiping jing* requires a belief in the life-giving power of the five orbs and the divinities residing in them.

The Lingbao scriptures include several layers or levels of Chinese religion. They cannot, for one, be understood without reference to the Way of the Celestial Masters; but one must also take the influence of popular religion into account, as is evidenced by certain sections of the *Wufuxu*. The integration of these different strands of Chinese religion is the special accomplishment of the Lingbao school. Fully formulated Lingbao rituals include both communal worship of divinities and the practice of meditation. For example, when officiating at a ritual, the master of ceremonies is to visualize the spirits of the five directions coming to the sacred area and providing divine protection (*Taishang huanglu zhaiyi* 太上黃籙齋儀 1.2a; DZ 507, fasc. 270–277). This is more obvious in the canon, formulated at the end of the fourth century, than in the early Lingbao materials. The finished Lingbao canon includes a large number of Buddhist beliefs, which were consciously incorporated by Ge Chaofu 葛巢甫 (Bokenkamp 1983). The Buddhist impact is most obvious in the highest god of the Lingbao canon, the Heavenly Worthy of Prime Beginning. This title represents an adaptation of the Han dynasty title of the Buddha, the World-Honored One. In the case of certain meditative and ingestive practices, however, the revealing deity is the Venerable Lord of the Yellow Center. This deity is associated with early popular cults and also with the communal Taoist movements of the Later Han.

The meditative practices of the *Wufuxu* seem to go back to popular beliefs and cults of the Han dynasty and before, and the dietetic techniques discussed above can be traced to specific masters or magic specialists (*fangshi*) of the Han. Both types of longevity techniques were equally esteemed by Ge Xuan, who first edited the text, and by Ge Chaofu, who compiled the Lingbao Canon in the late fourth century. According to Ge Xuan, the highest god, who revealed the scriptures and talismans, was the Zhonghuang laojun; with Ge Chaofu the era of the Buddha in Taoist guise, of Yuanshi tianzun, had begun. In the *Lingbao jingmu*, which survived in Dunhuang, a clear distinction is made between these two types of Lingbao scriptures: those revealed by Zhonghuang laojun and those going back to Yuanshi tianzun.

The development of the *Wufuxu* and, implicitly, of the Lingbao scriptures, can thus be depicted in four stages: popular folk religion, magic specialists, Ge Xuan, and Ge Chaofu. The two main sources of the *Wufuxu* can be defined more specifically as the dietetic techniques transmitted by Lezichang and the meditation methods that grew out of the popular cults. Both types of longevity methods were to be undertaken in a mountain setting, so the text itself was probably put together as a technical manual by mountain ascetics and used in conjunction with the protective five Lingbao talismans. Individual methods included in the book differ greatly, but they have all been associated with one or the other of the two main sources.

To these foundations, other techniques were added later—for example, drinking alcoholic beverages, and various other methods. It is not clear yet who transmitted these methods and where they originated. They are different from anything listed in the *Baopuzi*, yet some of them have been associated with Ge Hong in Taoist scriptures. This may imply that certain parts of the *Baopuzi* have been lost to us but were recovered by certain Taoists; it may also imply that entirely independent lineages were intentionally linked up with the mainstream represented by the Ge family.

References

Bokenkamp, Stephen. 1983. "Sources of the Ling-pao Scriptures." In *Tantric and Taoist Studies*, edited by Michel Strickmann, vol. 2, pp. 434–486. Bruxelles: Institut Belges des Hautes Etudes Chinoises, 1983.

— "The Peach Flower Font and the Grotto Passsage," *Journal of the American Oriental Society* 106.1 (1986), 65–79.

Dewoskin, Kenneth D. 1983. *Doctors, Diviners, and Magicians of Ancient China*. New York: Columbia University Press, 1983.

Dull, Jack. 1966. *A Historical Introduction to the Apocryphal (Ch'an-wei) Texts of the Han Dynasty*. Seattle: University of Washington Ph.D. Dissertation, 1966.

Kaltenmark, Maxime. 1953. *Le Lie-sien tchouan*. Beijing: Université de Paris, Publications du Centre d'Etudes Sinologiques, 1953.

— "Ling-pao: Note sur un terme du Taoisme religieux," *Melanges Publiées par l'Institut des Hautes Etudes Chinoises* 2 (1960), 559–588.

Ngo Van Xuyet. 1976. *Divination, Magie et Politique dans la Chine ancienne*. Paris: Presses Universitaires de France, 1976.

Ofuchi Ninji. 1974. "On *Ku Ling-pao ching*," *Acta Asiatica* 27 (1974), 33–56.

Robinet, Isabelle. 1979. "Metamorphosis and Deliverance of the Corpse in Taoism," *History of Religions* 19 (1979), 37–70.

— 1984. *La révélation du Shangqing dans l'histoire du Taoisme.* 2 vols. Paris: Publications de l'Ecole Francaise d'Extrême-Orient, 1984.

— 1986. "The Taoist Immortal: Jester of Light and Shadow, Heaven and Earth," *Journal of Chinese Religions* 13–14 (1985–86), 87–106.

Seidel, Anna. 1983. "Imperial Treasures and Taoist Sacraments: Taoist Roots in the Apocrypha." In *Tantric and Taoist Studies*, edited by Michel Strickmann, vol. 2, pp. 291–371. Bruxelles: Institut Belges des Hautes Etudes Chinoises, 1983.

Tjan, Tjoe Som. 1973. *Po Hu T'ung: The Comprehensive Discussions in the White Tiger Hall.* 2 vols. Westport, Connecticut: Hyperion, 1973. Originally published Leiden: E. Brill, 1949.

Ware, James R. 1966. *Alchemy, Medicine and Religion in the China of A.D. 320. The Nei P'ien of Ko Hung (Pao-p'u tzu).* Cambridge, Massachusetts: MIT Press, 1966.

in Chinese and Japanese

Ishii Masako 石井昌子 1984
"Taijō reihō gofujo no ikkōsatsu" 大上靈寶五符序の一考察
Makio Ryōkai hakase kinen rombunshū 牧尾良海博士記念論文集
Tokyo: Kokusho kankōkai, 1984.

Kobayashi Masayoshi 小林正美 1982
"Ryūsō ni okeru reihōkyō no keisei" 劉宋における靈寶經の形成
Tōyō bunka 東洋文化 62 (1982), 99–139.

Miyakawa Hisayuki 宮川尚志 1964
Rikuchōshi kenkyū: Shūkyō hen 六朝史研究：宗教篇
Kyoto: Heirakuji, 1964.

Mugitani Kunio 麥谷邦夫 1985
"Rōshi sōjichū ni tsuite" 老子想爾注について
Tōhō gakuhō 東方學報 57 (1985), 75–109.

Ofuchi Ninji 大淵忍爾 1979
Tonkō dōkei 敦煌道經

2 vols. Tokyo: Fukutake shoten, 1979.

Tonkō kōza 敦煌講座 1983
Tonkō to Chūgoku dōkyō 敦煌 と中國道經
Edited by the Editorial Committee of the Dunhuang Lectures. Tokyo: Daitō, 1983.

Wang Ming 王明 1979
Taiping jing hejiao 太平經合校
Beijing: Zhonghua, 1979.

Yamada Toshiaki 山田利明 1983
"Shinsendō" 神仙道
In *Dōkyō* 道教. Edited by Fukui Kōjun et al., vol 1, pp. 329–371. Tokyo: Hirakawa, 1983.

— 1984. "Reihō gofu no seiritsu to sono fuzuiteki seikaku"
靈寶五符の成立とその符瑞的性格
In *Zen'i shisō no sōgōteki kenkyū* 讖緯思想の總合的研究
Tokyo: Kokusho kankokai, 1984.

— 1987. "Futatsu no shinfu" 二つの神符
Tōyōgaku ronsō 東洋學論叢 12 (1987), 147–165.

Yasui Kōzan 安居香山 1966
Isho no kisōteki kenkyū 緯書の基礎的研究
Tokyo: Kangi bunka kenkyūkai, 1966.

— 1979. *Isho no seiritsu to sono tenkai* 緯書の成立とその展開
Tokyo: Kokusho kankokai, 1979.

— and Nakamura Chōhachi 中村璋八 1972
Isho shūsei 緯書集成
6 vols. Mimeographed edition, 1972.

Yoshioka Yoshitoyo 吉岡義豐 1969
Tonkō bunseki bunrui mokuroku 敦煌文獻分類目錄
Tokyo: Tōyō bunko, 1969.

Chapter Five

Guarding the One:
Concentrative Meditation in Taoism

Livia Kohn

Everything returns to the One,
Where does the One return to?

—*Biyanlu*

Introduction

The term *shouyi* 守一 , here translated as "guarding the One," is a general term
for meditation in Taoism. Its use dates from the texts of philosophical Taoism
before the Han through the organized Taoist tradition to the new Taoist sects
that developed under the Song. In addition, it has played a certain role in the
Chinese Buddhist school of Chan, where a fundamental meditation exercise is
"to guard the One and not move."

Since Taoism itself consists of many traditions, each based on a
different revelation of the Tao, there are also various meditation practices, and
the meaning of the term *shouyi* has changed in the course of time. For
different texts and different schools, meditational exercises related to guarding
the One are quite dissimilar. In this discussion I will attempt a representative
(and certainly not exhaustive) survey of the main methods referred to as
guarding the One.

As the term implies, the practice of guarding the One consists primarily in keeping the One, constraining awareness, or holding the mind under control. As a preliminary definition in terms of meditation studies, guarding the One may be said to represent a concentrative type of meditation as opposed to techniques of ecstasy or of insight. Concentrative meditation is defined by contemporary psychology as a state in which the conscious awareness of the individual is fixated on one single object to the exclusion of all others (see Walsh 1984: 28). A basic training in concentration is usually a prerequisite to entering higher or altered states of consciousness.

In some respects the exercise of guarding the One is indeed the foundation of all extended meditation practice and spiritual experience in Taoism, so it is understandable that the practice has been applied by different schools and that the term has been reinterpreted in light of the concepts and ideals of each one. However much one narrows down the definition, the term still carries a double implication: it is both a general term for meditation and a name for specific spiritual exercises.

Although it is often used as an introductory practice, guarding the One is by no means an inferior technique. The texts frequently emphasize that the continued and intense application of the exercise will in itself ensure the immortality of the practitioner. But the definition of the immortality that will be gained varies as much as the specific instructions on how to guard the One do. This suggests that studying the different techniques of concentrative meditation should provide some deeper understanding of the religious ideals of the Chinese.

My study will proceed in three steps. First, I will deal with the philosophical implications of the One in Taoism and what it means to guard, attain, or hold on to it. Next, I will give some examples of the mythology of the One as a god in Taoism and Chinese religion. Third, I will present a representative (not exhaustive) survey of practices called guarding the One in Taoism. To conclude, I will briefly discuss the use of the term in the context of Chinese Buddhism and summarize the range of practices.

The Philosophy of the One[1]

In Taoist philosophy—in the texts of the Lao-Zhuang tradition (commonly known as philosophical Taoism) and in the philosophical works contained in the Taoist Canon—[2] the One may refer to four different things. First, it is the primordial state of the world before things and beings were created. Second, it is the principle according to which creation took (and still takes) place. Third, it is the primordial force of creation, that which sustains all life; it is a power, a material energy. Fourth, it is the basic characteristic of all there is, an abstract characteristic of existence.

These four meanings of the One are not usually clearly distinguished in the texts; rather, one must read any reference to the One as including all of them. One or the other aspect may be predominant, but the other three are latently present as well. This multiple reference frame or—to our understanding—polysemy of the term should always be kept in mind when the One is being discussed.

Primordial Oneness

The One denotes the state of nondifferentiation of the universe, the primordial state of great unity (*taiyi* 太一). In this sense the One is identified with the cosmic chaos Hundun in the *Huainanzi* (chap. 14). Similar notions continue also in later organized Taoism: According to the *Taiping jing* 太平經 (Scripture of Great Peace) of the second century A.D., the One is the first of all numbers, it is the Tao of all life. Primordial energy first arises from the One, it is where heaven receives its mainstays (Wang 1960: 60: Yoshioka

---

1. Although this discussion is limited to Taoist implications of the One, the idea of the One is by no means limited to this tradition of Chinese thought. The early dictionary *Shuowen jiezi zhu*, for example, defines the One as "the great beginning" and says that the Tao itself is established in the One. Further on, it specifies that the character for heaven, for "that which is highest and cannot be surpassed," is composed of the One and the Great (*Shuowen jiezi zhu* 1A.1a). In the *Yijing*, the complexity of the world is analyzed in terms of the One (yang, one single line) and the Two (yin, a divided line). The One is ultimate primordiality. Moreover, Confucius is reported to have said: "My way is that of the One which embraces the universe" (*Lunyu* 4.15). Also, in later theory of art, the beginning of all painting and writing is said to lie in the "one stroke of the brush" (Ryckmans 1970: 9).

2. Texts in the Taoist Canon (*Daozang*, hereafter abbreviated DZ) are given according to the number of the reduced sixty-volume edition published in Taipei and Kyoto. These numbers coincide with those found in K.M. Schipper, *Concordance du Tao Tsang* (Paris: Publications de l'Ecole Francaise d'Extrême-Orient, 1975). "Fasc." stands for "fascicle" and refers to the volume number of the 1925 Shanghai reprint of the original canon of 1445 (*Zhengtong Daozang*).

1976b: 321). The *Xisheng jing* 西昇經 (Scripture of Western Ascension) of the fifth century says: "Heaven, earth and all beings are born following the One" (14.1; Yoshioka 1976a: 304).[3]

The One as Principle

The One is the highest unity, the formless omnipresent primordial principle of the cosmos. As such it is identical to and yet subtly different from the Tao itself. Thus the *Daode jing* says:

> The Tao produced the One;
> The One produced the two
> The two produced the three;
> The three produced the myriad beings. (chap. 42)

And the *Zhuangzi* has:[4]

> In the Great Beginning there was non-being;
> There was no being, no name.
> Out of it arose the One.
> Thus there was One, but it had no form.
> Beings realized and came to life.
> This was called their life-force. (chap. 12)

The One as Vital Energy

The vital energy or life-force one gets by obtaining the One as the principle of creation can be identified with the One itself. Already in ancient mythology the realization of the One resulted in the ideal state of the subject.

> Heaven obtained the One and became clear.
> Earth obtained the One and became settled.
> Spirit obtained the One and became powerful.
> The Valley obtained the One and became full.
> All beings obtained the One and lived and grew.
> Kings and barons obtained the One and became rulers of the
>   empire. (*Daode jing* 39; see also *Baopuzi 18*)

---

3. The *Xisheng jing* is quoted according to sections and lines as found in the edition by Chen Jingyuan in DZ 726, fasc. 449–450.

4. The *Zhuangzi* is quoted according to *A Concordance to Chuang-tzu*, Harvard-Yenching Institute Sinological Index Series, Supplement no. 20 (Cambridge, Massachusetts: Harvard University Press, 1956).

Similarly, the *Zhuangzi* describes the effect of obtaining the primordial force of the universe.

> Xiwei got it and held up heaven and earth. Fu Xi got it and entered into the mother of energy. The Northern Dipper got it and from ancient times has never wavered. The sun and the moon got it and from ancient times have never rested. . . . The Yellow Emperor got it and ascended to the cloudy heavens. Zhuan Xu got it and dwelt in the dark palace. . . . Pengzu got it and lived from the age of Shun to the age of the Five Dictators. (16/6/34; Watson 1968: 81)

Applied by an individual practitioner, what other effect than eternal life could the One produce? Thus Guangchengzi can exclaim:

> I hold on to the One, abide in its harmony, and therefore I have kept myself alive for 1200 years. And never has my body suffered any decay. (*Zhuangzi* 27/11/39)

Later, in religious Taoism, the deified Laozi instructs Yin Xi 尹喜, the Guardian of the Pass, according to the *Xisheng jing*.

> I cast off the ordinary, reject and leave the common world, embrace the prime and guard the One, go beyond all and attain spirit immortality. (7.12–13)

All Is One

The One is not only the underlying force of the world, but also its basic characteristic. All beings are *one* in that they all stem from the Tao. Thus the *Zhuangzi* says, "Realize what makes them one and thereby be one with all" (55/21/30; Watson 1968: 226). Here the sense of One is no longer the same as Tao or primordial energy, but refers quite literally to the oneness, the fundamental identity of all that exists. Similarly, the *Huainanzi* has, "Heaven and earth revolve and pervade each other, the myriad beings are ultimately one with them. When one knows the One, there will be nothing that remains unknown" (chap. 7; see also *Lüshi chunqiu* 3).

Three-in-One

The primordial oneness of the universe is also interpreted as its substance. The One is divided into the two forces yin and yang, and they are its functions. However, in the course of their interaction in the world, the two forces establish a harmony. Thus there are three, the third being a newly found, recovered unity on the basis of the One that was divided originally. The number three consequently implies a totality as complete as was the original unity of the One. Three is a oneness on a more complex level. The same notion holds true for all powers of three—the numbers nine, twenty-seven, eighty-one, and so on, because they in turn represent the recovered unity on a higher level (Robinet 1979: 189).

The concept that results from this reasoning is triple oneness, or one-in-three-ness, so to speak. The notion is then associated with other classical sets of three, such as the three main agents of the universe—heaven, earth, and humanity (*Baopuzi* 18). It is also applied to the three basic forces within human beings—spirit, essence, and energy. According to the *Taiping jing*, these correspond to the three cosmic administrations of heaven, earth, and water.[5] They are called the *sanyi* 三 一 or Three-in-One. They are also linked with the eyes, the ears, and the nose of human beings as well as with the basic characteristics of the Tao in the world: the invisible, the inaudible, and the subtle (*Daode jing* 14: *Yunji qiqian* 49.4a: ed. DZ 1032, fasc. 677–702). In their appearance as the three basic universal energies—mysterious, primordial, and original—the Three-in-One constitute the body of the true sage (Robinet 1977: 150, 156–167).[6] As the *Xuanmen dalun* 玄門大論 (Great Treatise on the Gate of the Mystery) puts it:

> The Three-in-One are the depth of the invisible and the inaudible, the pivot of spirit and energy. When you know how to use them, you will see how things come to be. When you know how to return to them, all will be one for you and there will be no more things. This is its essence. . . .
> Essence, spirit, and energy mix and become one. Essence is void and wonderful. It represents merit in the radiance of wisdom. Spirit is without bend. It represents function in the abandonment of all bondage. Energy is omnipresent. It represents the method of form and appearance. (*Yunji qiqian* 49.3b–4a; *Daojiao yishu* 5.1a–3a; DZ 1029, fasc. 762–763; Robinet 1977: 174)

So, where the One refers to the original state of cosmic nondifferentiation, the Three-in-One implies the same state, together with the newly found reunification. Any guarding, embracing, or realizing of the One as original purity or in its triple form will therefore bring about oneness with the primordial or with the recovered harmony of the universe. Any realizing of the

---

5. See also *Taiping jing shengjun bizhi*; DZ 1102, fasc. 755.

6. A detailed discussion of the three basic universal energies can be found in Robinet 1977: 156–167.

One allows the realizing subject to become what he or she (or it) was originally meant to become, to fulfill his or her (or its) proper destiny in the cosmos. The true nature of human beings is to be healthy and long lived, to participate willingly in the changes of the world. Successful practitioners of guarding the One should therefore become incomparably richer in primordial harmony; they should become healthier and increase their life spans, if not become as immortal as the One itself.

Realization of the One as Recovery

Realizing the One does not merely merge the self with all existence. It creates power over the world as well. The state of helpless involvement with the affairs of this world is ended once and for all when the One is truly attained.[7]

> *Zhi shouyi wanshi bi* 知守一萬事畢
> Once knowing how to guard the One
> The myriad affairs are done!

This sentence expresses the contrast between unity and multiplicity (the One and the myriad), between concentration and activity (guarding and affairs). Proper knowledge, mastery, or pervasion of the One will end all mundane struggle.

> The sages of high antiquity. . . rested tranquilly in non-action. They were endowed with the true energy of the world and their essence and spirit were guarded within. How could they ever be sick? They achieved this state because their will remained withdrawn and they cherished few desires. Their mind remained at peace and they knew no fear. (*Huangdi neijing suwen* 1.5b; DZ 1018, fasc. 649–660)

This perfect health, together with omniscience ("When one knows the One, nothing remains unknown," *Huainanzi* 7) and power of the material world, is one aim of Taoist meditation, of the practice of guarding the One. It can be summarized in the words of the *Santian neijie jing* 三天內解經 (Esoteric Explanation of the Three Heavens; DZ 1205, fasc. 876) of the fifth century.

---

7. The following quotation is found frequently in the texts: *Zhuangzi* 29/12/6; *Wufuxu* 3.22ab (DZ 366, fasc. 183); *Baopuzi* 18.2b; *Taiping jing shengjun bizhi* 7a; *Huangting neijing jing* 25:9; *Santian neijie jing* 2.4a (DZ 1205, fasc. 876); *Xisheng jing* 25.9, 39.11, 39.14; *Daomen jingfa* 1.9b (DZ 1128, fasc. 762); *Yuanqilun* 21ab (*Yunji qiqian* 56); *Xuanzhu xinjing zhu* 8b (DZ 564, fasc. 320), and *Daoshu* 32.1b (DZ 1017, fasc. 641–648).

Laozi's teaching consisted mainly of instructing humanity to
guard his root and to strengthen his origin. Man comes to life
through the energy of the Tao, and as soon as he loses it he
dies. Thus Laozi ordered all men to meditate on the True, to
recollect the Tao, to harden and strengthen their root and
origin. Thereby man should reach a state in which he never
loses his original source of life and can live forever. (2.1a)

The text speaks not of the One but of the origin of humanity and of the
primordial root of all beings, which terms are then identified with the Tao and
the true. Later, however, the text explicitly states that losing one's hold on the
root, no longer guarding the source of the One results in countless sufferings,
in the development of passion and desire. This loss is responsible for a
ceaseless agitation and wearing-out of the spirit. Loss of spirit becomes
obvious first when various sicknesses begin to afflict the body (*Santian neijie
jing* 2.4a). The complete loss of the One means the death of the individual,
just as its complete recovery means eternal life (*Taiping jing*, Wang 1960: 96).

Since originally everybody shares in the One, the process of Taoist
meditation should therefore be understood as a gradual recovery of whatever
one has lost of the One. As this recovery proceeds, the body becomes healthy
and strong and one's spirit begins to radiate with energy and joy. Passions and
desires are eliminated completely, there is no more suffering. Immortality
itself is reached when one is able to guard the One permanently and without
interruption.

Realization as Oneness

Under the influence of Mahāyāna Buddhism, the relation of practice and
realization was obscured in Taoism. Practice was necessary, but it was
actually nonpractice, noncultivation, a resting rather than an active progress.
Guarding the One, according to the understanding of Tang dynasty Taoists,
was no longer a process of gradual recovery of primordiality lost, no longer an
active cultivation, but a state of realization that existed originally and would
exist to eternity.

An example of this interpretation of guarding the One is found in two
sets of poems revealed in the middle of the Tang dynasty by Jiao Shaoxuan 焦
少玄 , the wife of Lu Chui 盧陲, in Fujian. Originally an immortal from the
heaven of Highest Clarity, she had already departed this world, leaving behind
only an empty coffin, when her husband implored her to give him some
instructions regarding the Tao. So she returned to earth once again and
revealed the poems. They were published with commentaries under the title
Xuanzhu xinjing zhu   玄珠心鏡註 (Annotated Mysterious Pearly Mirror of

the Mind; DZ 574, 575, fasc. 320) on Mount Wangwu, the former residence of Sima Chengzhen 司馬承禎 , in 817.

The first poem speaks of the restraint which with one must seek to guard the One.

> Attainment of the primordial power of the One
> Is not a gift from Heaven.
> Realization of Great Non-being
> Is the state of highest immortality.
>
> Light restrained, a hidden brilliance
> The body one with nature:
> There is true peace, won but not pursued.
> Spirit kept forever at rest
>
> In serenity and beauty: this is true being!
> Body and inner nature, hard and soft
> All is but cinnabar vapor, azure barrens.
> One of the highest sages—
>
> Only after a hundred years
> The tomb is discovered empty.

The commentary explains that the One here stands for primordial energy, the beginning of the universe, the cosmic chaos Hundun. Becoming one with it means to enter into the formlessness of universal creation. This state is not naturally given. It has to be attained by practitioners, but not actively. Rather, they must restrain their light and hide their brilliance— assemble their yang energy within rather than waste it on the world without. The peace of mind and the permanence of the body that will eventually be found come about quite naturally in the end; they are "won but not pursued." Adepts keep their spirit at rest within, relax in serenity, and naturally develop a cosmic consciousness. In due course they will vanish to take up their residence in the higher realms: they have become fully part of the One. Much later they are recognized as true sages. The second poem emphasizes the noncultivation even more strongly.

> The Tao does nothing, yet nothing is left undone.
> Purity of mind does not come from knowledge and wisdom.
> What is knowledge? What is purity?
> Knowledge is to give up all wisdom. Purity is to be empty in going
>   along.
>
> Going along, not following: this is pervasion of mind.
> Pervade the One and all affairs are done!
> The One is the root, affairs are the gate.

When affairs return to the One, the One is always there.

It is there, yet nothing is—so we borrow a term and speak of
    guard.
By just guarding emptiness and non-being you can naturally live
    forever!

The God Taiyi, Great One

The One in the Stars

The Great One as a personified god has been most commonly venerated as an astral deity in the official cult ever since the Han dynasty. It was due to the advice of the court magician Miao Ji that the god of the Great One was installed as the god of the center of the universe during Han times. He then occupied the place formerly reserved for the Yellow Emperor, Huangdi. The system of the five divine emperors or gods associated with the five colors and the five directions had been taken over from the preceding dynasties. As the Great One became the highest god in the official cult of the Han, the five mythical emperors were relegated to the position of his attendants, the Yellow Emperor being established between the Red and the White—between summer and autumn. According to a variant system valid in the same period, the Great One is served by the two attendants Dajin and Siming (*Shiji* 28).

Before the Han dynasty the god of the Great One is mentioned in the *Chuci* (The Songs of the South) as the mythical god of the East. Even during the Han the Great One was especially associated with the south of China. Emperor Wu offered a sacrifice to him before embarking on a campaign against the southern states. He also fought under a banner which showed the sun, the moon, and the Northern Dipper, as well as the Great One in the shape of a flying dragon (*Shiji* 28).

With the organization of Taoism in the second century A.D. the lofty principles of the ancient philosophers were personified by the deities of the Han pantheon, just as the philosopher Laozi was then deified as the Highest Venerable Lord, Taishang Laojun (Seidel 1969). Gods thought of as personal forces governing the universe were then identified with parts of the human body, which—though always understood as a microcosmic image of the world (see *Guanzi* 13)—was now mapped and outlined in great detail.

The One in the Body

In due course the One came to be identified with various parts of the human body.

> On the head, the One is the top;
> Among the seven orifices, it is found in the eyes;
> In the center of the body, it is the navel;
> Among the five orbs, it is the heart;
> Among the members of the body, it is the hands;
> Among the bones, it is the spinal column;
> In the flesh of the body, it is found in the five orbs and the
>   stomach (*Taiping jing*, Wang 1960: 13; Robinet 1979: 188).

According to the *Baopuzi* 抱朴子 (Book of the Master Who Embraces Simplicity), the One is "0.9 inch in length in the male, and 0.6 inch in the female. Sometimes it is in the lower cinnabar field 2.4 inches beneath the navel. At other times it is in the central cinnabar field, i.e., the golden gate or purple palace, in the heart" (chap. 18; Ware 1966: 302).

Later the One was defined as the central divinity of the human body (*Wushang biyao* 無上秘要 5; DZ 1138, fasc. 768–779; see Lagerwey 1981). He then was thought to reside in the scarlet palace of the heart or in the purple chamber in the head, i.e., the upper cinnabar field. This is the center of vital energies in the upper part of the body, just as the heart is the center in its midsection. According to standard iconography, the body god of the Great One is called the Perfect Great One of the Yellow Center of Great Purity. He is clad in purple robes and sits on a golden throne. He looks like a newborn baby. In his left hand, he holds the handle of the Northern Dipper, the pivot of Taoist astral mythology. In his right hand he has the polestar.[8]

The One as Laozi

As a divinity outside of the human body, the One is identical with the deified Laozi:

> The One when dispersed is the energy of the world; when concentrated he is the god Laozi. Then he resides on Mount Kunlun and reveals the teaching of the Tao. (*Xiang'er Commentary to the Daode jing*; Rao 1956: 13; Seidel 1969: 78)

---

8. An excellent summary of the mythology of the Great One can be found in Anna Seidel, *Mythologie des Taoismus*, currently in preparation.

The *Laozi zhongjing* 老子中經 (Central Scripture of Laozi; *Yunji qiqian* 18–19) describes the Great One as "the father of the Tao, older than heaven and earth. He resides in the heaven of Great Clarity (Shangqing) above the nine heavens." He came into being before the universe was created and is a personification of its primordial energy. After he was born, in a second emanation, the Lord of the Tao was brought forth. Thereafter, in a third emanation, the Queen Mother of the West and her male counterpart, the King of the East, came into being.

The Goddess of the Great One

In later Taoist mythology, the Great One also appears in female form as the teaching aspect of the Holy Mother Goddess who is otherwise mainly characterized through her act of giving birth to the Tao on earth (*Yongcheng jixian lu* 1.1b; DZ 783, fasc. 560–561). The Goddess of the Great One instructs the newly born Venerable Lord in the basic principles of the world and the Tao as well as in the secrets of the various Taoist techniques. She is part of cosmic primordiality, one with Tao and versed in its arcana (*Daode zhenjing guangsheng yi* 2.2ab; DZ 725, fasc. 440–448; *Lishi zhenxian tidao tongjian houji* 1.8b; DZ 298, fasc. 150).

The Three Ones

Together with the Female One and the Male One, the Great One—here also called Emperor of the One—forms the Three-in-One of Shangqing Taoism. The three Ones are the gods of the upper, middle, and lower One, who reside in the three cinnabar fields of the body respectively. The scriptures sacred to them are the *Dadong jing* 大洞經 (Great Grotto Scripture), the *Ciyijing* 雌一經 (Scripture of the Female One), and the *Suling jing* 素靈經 (Scripture of Immaculate Numen). They are born directly out of primordial energy in the constellation of the Northern Dipper. They are closely related to astral forces and divinities (Robinet 1979: 183; Andersen 1980: 43).

According to another tradition, the Three Ones are identical to the Yellow Venerable Lord and his two attendants Wuying jun and Boyuan jun (*Wushang biyao* 5). They are also called the Three Realized Ones, and are said to reside in the second of the nine palaces in the head. Figure 1 depicts the Three Ones descending from the Dipper.

In its personified, deified form the Great One is therefore a direct emanation of primordial energy. It is the first shape brought forth from the cosmic chaos of Hundun. As god of the center, the Great One is the main divinity in the official pantheon of the Han. According to Taoist revelation, he resides alone or together with two similar deities in the innermost human life centers (the cinnabar fields) and in those of the universe (the Northern Dipper). The color most frequently associated with the One is red and he is usually depicted as a male. But the One may also incorporate both male and female principles or appear as female, as the matrix of the world.

When this central deity of the human body and the universe is kept in its proper place, everything is in perfect order. As Zhang Wanfu 張萬福 of the Tang puts it,

> The One is the emperor of the body. By guarding the emperor he will remain. And when the emperor remains none of the 36,000 gods of the body will dare to be absent. Thus by meditation on him, the various demons can be expelled. (*Zhongjie wen* 1.9b)

Methods of Meditation

The earliest documents concerning Taoist meditation describe it as the focusing of the mind on the inner organs of the body then considered to be the most direct representations of primordial energy in humans. Concentrating on or visualizing these centers was thought to enhance the given life-force of human beings.[9]

The One as Light

In the *Taiping jing*, the main method of meditation is already called guarding the One (Kaltenmark 1979: 42; Yoshioka 1976b: 316).[10] It is described as a complete mental fixation on the inner light of the body as the visible

---

9. These organs are either the five intestines (*Xianger*; Rao 1956: 63; Mugitani 1985: 97; Seidel 1969: 72), the three cinnabar fields (Inscription for Wangzi Qiao, AD 165; Seidel 1978: 152), or the gods residing in them (Seidel 1983: 327).

10. The date of the *Taiping jing* as we have it today is not entirely certain. A text of this title was revealed to Gan Ji during the Han dynasty, but it was lost in the following centuries and then revised and edited under the influence of Shangqing Taoism toward the end of the Six Dynasties. See Kandel 1979; Mansvelt-Beck 1980. The edition by Wang (1979) most commonly used today supplies some chapters which are missing from the beginning of the *Taiping jingchao* of the later Tang dynasty. It is in *Taiping jing*-type texts of this period that the most lucid meditation instructions are found. It is thus not clear exactly what the practices of the early Taiping Taoists consisted of.

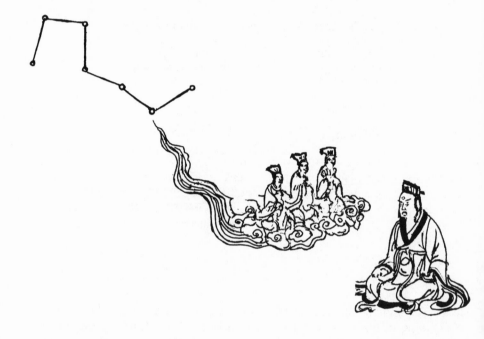

Fig. 1. The Three Ones descending from the Dipper. *Source: Shangqing jinque dijun wudou sanyi tujue* 上清金闕帝君五斗三一圖訣 9b–10a (DZ 765, fasc. 534)

manifestation of the cosmic forces of creation. However, before the light actually begins to shine forth, the meditator must undergo a lengthy training in concentration of mind. One begins by setting up a meditation chamber and continues by increasing mental one-pointedness with the help of various spirits.

> To keep the Tao [in the body as spirit, essence, and energy] one has to prepare a meditation chamber. One must lock the doors securely and never let anybody enter. Then one should examine oneself. If one finds oneself not able to concentrate properly, one had better leave the room again. There is no way to enforce the practice. Only by gradually attaining concentration and by slowly maturing in the practice will one eventually attain peace.
>
> In a state of mental peace one does not wish to move again from the room, the mouth has no desire to speak to anybody. One will still need food and drink, but one can otherwise easily be without others' company. Concerned only with inner refinement one accumulates goodness. Then one can turn one's mental gaze to the inside and observe one's body and physical appearance. They should be seen as if in a mirror, one should be able to inspect oneself as if one saw one's reflection in clear water.
>
> Thereby the myriad affairs will begin to take care of themselves naturally. (Wang 1979: 723; Yoshioka 1976b: 317)

Besides the practice of guarding the One in which meditators are assisted by the god of Heaven, the *Taiping jing* also mentions "guarding the Two" with the help of the god of earth, "guarding the Three" with the assistance of the spirits of the dead, as well as "guarding the Four" and "the Five," in which practice help is offered by the myriad beings. Successfully attaining the goals of these practices will give the adept eternal life, control over bad times, power over chaos, and prognosticative abilities, respectively (Wang 1979: 12–13; Yoshioka 1976b: 318). In the *Xiang'er* commentary to the *Daode jing* a distinction is made between "guarding the One"—yang and life—and "guarding the Two"—yin and death (Rao 1956: 64).

Having practiced guarding the One for a prolonged period of time, one will have the following experience:

> A radiance or light will arise. It will shine brilliantly in the four directions. In following this light one can travel afar, thoroughly examine oneself, one's physical body and appearance. The host of spirits will assemble. Thus one can transform oneself into spirit. (*Taiping jing shengjun bizhi* 1b; DZ 1102, fasc. 755; Yoshioka 1976b: 319)

Again, the practice of guarding the light within the body is specified in detail:

> In a state of complete concentration, when the light first arises, make sure to hold on to it and never let it go. First of all, it will be red, after a long time it will change to be white, later again it will be green, and then it will pervade all of you completely. When you further persist in guarding the One, there will be nothing within that would not be brilliantly illuminated and the hundred diseases will be driven out. (*Taiping jingchao*; Yoshioka 1976b: 319)

In addition, the *Taiping jing shengjun bizhi* 太平經聖君秘旨 (Secret Instructions of the Lord Regarding the Scripture of Great Peace 2b; DZ 1102, fasc. 755) gives a specific interpretation of the different colors, as perceived by the adept. Black is the radiance of greater yin, white of lesser. Green is the radiance of lesser yang, and the red light of greater yang means that the adept is about to go beyond the world. The yellow light is the radiance of the centered harmony of the universe. It signifies true peace.

The One as the Power of the Center

Rather more magical feats can be accomplished by one who has mastered the technique of guarding the One, according to the *Baopuzi*. "He can travel thousands of miles in an instant, enter among armed troops and ford large rivers without any need to divine the right day and hour. . . . Harmful things will find no place in him" (chap. 18; Ware 1966: 304; Schipper 1982: 176).

Two major methods of guarding the One are distinguished, guarding the Mystery One and guarding the True One; Yoshioka 1976a: 291–298).[11]   The former consists of

> imagining oneself as being divided into three persons. Once these three have become fully visible, one can continue to increase the number to several dozen, all like oneself, who may be concealed or revealed. All of them are automatically in possession of secret oral formulas. (*Baopuzi* 18; Ware 1966: 306)

The text mentions that this method is similar to a practice called Bright Mirror. Adepts use a magical bronze mirror in which they see themselves in multiple form. The mirror is a means of bringing the innermost forces of

---

11. The methods described in the *Baopuzi* are later taken up by Sun Simiao of the early Tang in his *Sheyang zhenzhong fang, Yunji qiqian* 33.11b–12a.

oneself, one's true form into focus, just as adepts, according to the directions above, would use the mind to gain creative control over the true inner powers and thus attain multilocation.

Guarding the True One seems to be a technique of visualization. The god of the Great One is seen as residing in his celestial palace and at the same time in one's own body. Ge Hong has transmitted the following formula to us:

> Visualize the One in the center of the Northern Culmen and deep inside yourself
> In front—the hall of light [in the head]; behind—the scarlet palace [in the heart].
> Imposing: the Flowery Canopy [the lungs]; lofty: the Golden Pavilion [the kidneys?].
> Left—the *Gang* Star; right—the *Kui* [of the Northern Dipper].
> Rising like a wave, sinking like the void itself.
>
> Use the mysterious mushrooms covering the cliffs, the vermilion herbs growing in thickets.
> White jade from the mountains, and the radiance of the sun and the moon.
> Pass through fire and water! Traverse the dark and the yellow [heaven and earth]!
> Enter the maze of halls and gateways, full of lustrously gleaming awnings and hangings!
>
> Helped by dragon and tiger guards and spirit-man attendants
> Don't relax, don't give in—keep the One in its place!
> Don't dawdle, don't rush—keep the One in its chamber!
> Once at ease and comfortable, the One will never leave.
>
> Guard the One and visualize the True One, then the spirit world will be yours to peruse!
> Lessen desires, restrain your appetite—the One will remain at rest!
> Like a bare blade coming towards your neck—realize you live through the One alone!
> Knowing the One is easy—keeping it forever is hard!
>
> Guard the One and never lose it—the limitations of man won't be for you!
> On land you will be free from beasts, in water from fierce dragons.
> No fear of evil sprites or phantoms,
> No demon will approach, nor blade attack! (*Baopuzi* 18)

The One as the Tao

In the *Huangting waijing jing* 黃庭外景經 (Scripture of Outer Light of the
Yellow Court), presumably the older of the Huangting scriptures (Schipper
1975; Mugitani 1982; Robinet 1979: 85), guarding the One is used as the
equivalent of cultivating the Tao, meditating on the Tao, or simply practicing
meditation. The main method cited in this text is visualizing or actualizing the
gods in the body. Thus the verb *shou* alone is frequently used to express the
state of mental one-pointedness on one particular object. It is used in connection with some part of the body—for example, the spleen—residence of the
Highest Venerable Lord, or the kidneys. Also, the adept is advised to
concentrate on some cosmic principle, such as emptiness and non-being, or
spirit as such. The text emphasizes that although "all men have the One, they
don't know how to guard it" (B 15).

   Properly meditating on the One will stabilize the body, and permanently
upholding the meditational state will result in immortality.

The Three-In-One

In Shangqing Taoism guarding the One is most commonly practiced as a
visualization of the Three-in-One (Robinet 1979: 192; Robinet 1984: vol. 1:
30; Yoshioka 1976a: 301–303). Early versions of such a practice can be found
in the *Lingbao wufuxu* 靈寶五符序 (Introduction of the Five Talismans of
the Numinous Treasure 1.24ab; DZ 388, fasc. 183; Robinet 1984: vol. 1: 32),
but the standard technique was transmitted from the sage Xuanzi 肙子 to Su
Lin 蘇林 . It is found in the *Suling jing* (24b–41a; DZ 1314, fasc. 1026;
Robinet 1984: vol. 2: 285) as well as in the *Jinque dijun sanyuan zhenyi jing*
金闕帝君三元真一經 (Lord Goldtower's Scripture of the Three Primes
and the True One; *Yunji qiqian* 50.10b; Andersen 1980: 39) and also in the
Tang text *Daomen jingfa* 道門經注 (Canonical Methods of the Gate of the
Tao; DZ 1128, fasc. 762).

   Adepts actualize the Three-in-One as a manifestation of the three kinds
of primordial energy in the three cinnabar fields. These in turn govern the
twenty-four fundamental energies of the human body, which correspond to the
twenty-four energies of the year and the twenty-four constellations in the sky.
The exact procedure of the meditation varies according to different seasons,
but it is always best when performed at the solstices and the equinoxes.

   To prepare for the practice, adepts have to purify themselves by bathing
and fasting. They enter the meditation chamber at midnight, the hour of rising
yang. Then they light incense and grind their teeth thirty times. Facing east,
they close their eyes and visualize the Northern Dipper slowly descending

Fig. 2. An adept meditating under the protection of the Dipper. *Source: Shangqing jinque dijun wudou sanyi tujue* 16b

toward them until it rests right above their heads with the handle pointing straight east. This preliminary measure serves to protect adepts from evil influences during the practice. Figure 2 shows an adept meditating under the Dipper.

Then they start with the upper One. First they visualize a ball of red energy in the Niwan Palace at the center of the head. Within this ball of energy a red sun with a radius of about nine *cun* will appear. Its brilliance envelops practitioners to such a degree that they enter a state of utter oblivion of self and others. As soon as they have reached this state, the god Red Child will become visible in the upper cinnabar field. He is the ruler of the Niwan Palace. In his hand he holds a talisman of the White Tiger, the sacred animal of the West. He is accompanied by an attendant, the god of the subtle essences of the teeth, the tongue, and the skull, who in turn holds a copy of the *Dadong jing* in his hands.

The middle One resides in the scarlet palace in the heart, the central cinnabar field. His energy is scarlet, and the sun that arises before he appears is seven *cun* in radius. After adepts have again fallen into a state of rapture, they will see the August Lord of Primordial Cinnabar in the middle of the scarlet ball of energy. This deity holds the talisman of the Female One in his right hand and the planet Mars, the symbol of the phase of fire and celestial representative of the color red, in his left. His attendant, the god of the subtle essences of the five intestines, holds the radiant pearl of life in his hands.

The third of the Three-in-One in Shangqing Taoism is the ruler of the Gate of Life. He resides in the lower cinnabar field, about three inches beneath the navel. To actualize his presence, adepts visualize a ball of white energy with a radius of five *cun* in this area of the body. After the adept attains forgetfulness, the god Ying'er will appear. He is called the Primordial King of the Yellow Court. He holds a copy of the *Suling jing* as well as the planet Venus, symbol of the phase of metal and representative of the color white, in his hands. His attendant is master over the limbs of the body, the senses, and the blood as well as the inner organs (Robinet 1979: 192–195; Andersen 1980; Maspero 1981: 369). Figure 3 represents an adept visualizing the Three Ones.

The Three-in-One together with their attendants are in control of the whole human body. They represent the primordial forces of the universe from which the body was first conceived and shaped. These three Ones are found in everyone, but since normal people never take the trouble to nourish and visualize them, they gradually lose their strength and die. As they pass away, the parts controlled by them become weaker and weaker, and eventually the person is bound to die with them.

Fig. 3. An adept visualizing the Three Ones. *Source: Taishang chu sanshi jiuchong baosheng jing* 太上除三尸九蟲保生經 25a (DZ 871, fasc. 580)

On the other hand, one can attain long life by keeping the Three-in-One active and well cared for. It is best to practice guarding the One without any interruption whatsoever.

> During all kinds of activities, in the midst of thousands of affairs, one must always be thinking of the One. While eating or drinking, think of the One! When happy, think of the One! When anguished, think of the One! When sick, think of the One! Whether passing through water or fire, always think of the One! And especially when you are agitated, think of the One! (*Suling jing* 30b–31a; Robinet 1979: 185)

Maintaining One-Pointedness

In the fifth century, Shangqing Taoism became the leading Taoist school of China, a position it owed mainly to the efforts of Tao Hongjing   陶弘景 (456–536) and was to occupy all through the Tang dynasty. In the course of its development, Shangqing Taoism incorporated certain parts of other religious teachings then current, the Taoism of the Lingbao school and Buddhism. The texts of Lingbao Taoism had been compiled by Ge Chaofu 葛 巢甫 in the last years of the fourth century in an attempt to raise the position of his ancestor Ge Xuan 玄 in the heavenly hierarchy that had been established on the basis of the Shangqing revelations after 364. Ge Chaofu not only included the Shangqing texts themselves in his new set of scriptures but also drew heavily on the library of Ge Hong, author of the *Baopuzi*, on Han dynasty correlative thought, and on Buddhist sutras (Bokenkamp 1983: 445). Of all the Taoist schools Lingbao is the most strongly ritually oriented, and much of the ritualization of Shangqing Taoism can be traced back to its influence. The Buddhist impact on Shangqing Taoism, on the other hand, is found in the development of more sophisticated meditation theories and practices and also in a heightened emphasis on the development of wisdom, *prajñā*.

An example of how the practice of guarding the One changed within Shangqing Taoism is found in a description given in the *Yannian yisuan fa* 延 年益算注   (Method of Extending One's Years and Increasing the Reckoning; DZ 1271, fasc. 1003; Yoshioka 1976a: 308), which consists of a summary of Shangqing methods. It relies strongly on the *Zhengao* 真誥   (Declarations of the Perfected) and the *Dengzhen yinjue* 登真隱訣   (Secret Instructions for the Ascent to Perfection), by Tao Hongjing, as well as on the *Taidan yinshu* 太丹 隱書 (Secret Writing of Great Cinnabar). Its later origin is revealed not only in these quotations but also in its emphasis on ritual (Robinet 1984: vol. 2: 417).

Guarding the One in the *Yannian yisuan fa* stands for the fundamental ordering of the body and mind before higher levels of meditation practice can be attained. Three distinct sections describe the Method of Laozi to Order Oneself and Guard the One. The practice should best be undertaken three times every day, at sunrise and sunset and before the main meal. It always includes massages so that the body feels warm and begins to glow; breathing exercises; swallowing saliva and grinding the teeth a certain number of times; and reciting invocations and calling the names of the particular deities associated with the practice. Figure 4 shows an adept invoking the assistance of the moon.

In actual application, however, guarding the One here appears to be mainly a fight against strong emotions.

> The foundation of guarding the One is found in a strong sense of humility. Thus, when you feel an evil urge, think of the flying immortals. When you are pestered by jealousy think of the wonderful gods. When you are driven mad by desire think of the realized ones. (*Yannian yisuan fa* 3b)

Yet, in its close association with the Northern Dipper, the center of the constellations in the sky, the practice is similar to earlier forms of guarding the One.

> When in your exercise of guarding the One you find it hard to attain proper one-pointedness of mind, think of your own death and imagine yourself to be frightened and terrified by horrible demons. Then get up and look at the Pu-Star of the Northern Dipper. The Pu-Star is the sixth star of this constellation. Then think of the One and the hundred evil influences will disperse. The body will no longer be subjected to calamities. Should this happen on a rainy day so that you cannot see the stars of the Dipper, then just concentrate your mind and meditate on the One. (3b)

Applying this method properly and consistently will sustain the three spirit souls, the yang forces that make people live and keep them strong. One will be completely free from disasters and misfortunes of all kinds. Demons and evil spirits won't be able to inflict any harm. This state of complete well-being of body and mind reflects the central ideal of Taoism. A Buddhist influence can be seen in the next instruction, that adepts should arouse a sense of compassion for all beings. Doing so will strengthen the inner hidden virtue of the adepts, the power that will survive throughout the transformations of the world and will be beneficial either for themselves in a later life or for their descendants.

Fig. 4. An adept invoking the assistance of the moon. *Source: Shangqing jinque dijun wudou sanyi tujue* 15b–16a

Another Shangqing text, tentatively dated to the Tang, describes the practice of guarding the One as an exercise in concentrative meditation based on the observance of moral precepts and leading to the attainment of Taoist wisdom.[12]

> Whenever someone has courage and daring, and is able to observe the rules and precepts, when he furthermore wants to order and control his body and mind, so that he will accumulate merit and grow in virtue and ultimately become a great sage, then he must begin with guarding the One. The One is basically shapeless, yet it goes along with everything. . . . Guarding the One is wisdom, losing it is foolishness. Foolishness leads to death, wisdom helps to preserve life. (3.1a; Yoshioka 1976a: 300)

The theory outlined in this text describes the One as the basis of creation, from which energy first arises. In the course of transformations, energy separates and is joined again as Three-in-One. The three fundamental energies of the cosmos are original, primordial, and mysterious energy (Robinet 1977: 156). One must keep all three in oneself in order to attain long life. Wisdom, an adaptation of the Buddhist *prajnā*, is realized when "the spirit of man is pervasive and brilliant" (2ab).

The concrete practice of guarding the One here begins with writing and applying talismans, paying obeisance to the gods, and burning incense. Then the Three-in-One are visualized in the three energy centers of the body as described above.

Enlightenment through the One

More of a Buddhist influence is found in certain Shangqing materials of the Tang dynasty that emphasize a strong connection between the practice of guarding the One and moral goodness. One example is the *Zhongjie wen* 眾戒 文 (On All Precepts; DZ 178, fasc. 77; Yoshioka 1976a: 307), which states categorically that "in the practice of guarding the One the proper observance of the precepts is first. As long as one obeys the moral rules and does not do wrong, evil cannot enter."

The practice described here is simpler and more mind-oriented than earlier Shangqing methods. The flow of thoughts should be interrupted, all evil should be eliminated, one should right oneself and turn fully to the Tao,

---

12. The *Zhihui xiaomo zhenjing* (DZ 1344, fasc. 1032) contains two chapters of genuine Shangqing revelation. The sections beginning with the third chapter on guarding the One are compilations of a later date (Robinet 1984: vol. 2: 185).

the spirit, and the One. Visualizations and incantations of specific deities have no part in this type of guarding the One.

> Guarding the One and not losing it is at first very hard to attain. Myriad thoughts follow one another in quick succession which cannot be interrupted for even an instant. However, once the flow of thoughts has been interrupted for a short moment, evil will be opposed.
>
> Once evil has been opposed, the screens (of the mind) will be set right. Once the screens have been set right, the gateway (to the Tao) will be established. Once the gateway has been established, one can see one's errors. Only after one has realized one's errors will one sink really into suffering. Suffering will then reach an extreme point—at that the thinking will revert. Consciousness and spirit will be activated and one will attain enlightenment and go beyond all.
>
> As a next step one can proceed to stabilize one's thoughts as they follow one upon the other. The consistent practice of this method for a long period will bring about a state when the energy of the One inundates the whole body.
>
> As body and spirit deeply pervade the universe, one will radiate with light and undergo transformations without end. This is the benefit of knowing how to properly guard the One. (*Zhongjie wen* 2.9ab)

A similar interpretation is already found in the *Xisheng jing* of the fifth century, according to which Laozi advised Yin Xi, the Guardian of the Pass:

> Get rid of all impurity and stop all thoughts, calm the mind and guard the One! (39.10; Yoshioka 1976a: 304)

Li Rong 李榮 , philosopher of the Twofold Mystery school and protagonist of Taoism in the Buddho-Taoist controversy of the early Tang, explains this advice.

> When intention is free from bondage all thoughts are stopped: when neither within nor without there are any attachments, the mind is calm. The spirit concentrated on the Tao, the will applied without wavering is what we call guarding the One. (6.17b)

Again the text states:

> Give up all thinking and guard the One, then the myriad affairs are done. (39.14)

Li Rong adds:

When one honors the precepts in one's heart and follows the
scriptures in one's deeds so that one produces no more karma
one really guards the One. Because of the practice all
defilements and bondage will soon be gone, one will establish
oneself in non-action, in truth, in the Tao. Full of wisdom and
abounding in virtue, all one does will be done naturally. Thus
all affairs are done. (6.18a)

Although certain Tang Taoist documents say that the practice of guarding the One consists of purifying the mind and describe it in mostly Buddhist
terms and concepts, the final realization is not envisioned as enlightenment in
the Buddhist sense. The practice always leads to physical health and strength.
When the body is full of the One, energy is concentrated in the lower cinnabar
field and there will be no more hunger or thirst (*Yunji qiqian* 33.11a). The
adepts will also recover their true identity as part of the Tao. They will lose
themselves as personal beings to gain themselves as part of the Tao itself.
Then they will be able to ascend to the heaven of Highest Clarity above and
take up positions in the hierarchy of the Tao.

The One in Inner Alchemy

The prevalent method of Taoist meditation under the Song was inner alchemy.
Neither visualizing deities nor interrupting the ceaseless flow of thoughts
formed the central part of the practice. Rather, the three major components of
the body—energy, essence, and spirit—were refined to higher levels of purity
in accordance with the system of operative alchemy. In this context the One is
associated with yang and permanence and yin is aligned with the concept of
change and with the number two (*Neidan shouyi zhending jing* 1a; DZ 644,
fasc. 342).

The *Daoshu* 道樞 (Pivot of the Tao; DZ 1017, fasc. 641–648), in its
outline of the ideas of Chongzhenzi 崇真子 (19.4ab), describes the central
idea of Taoist practice as consisting of actualizing the three and guarding the
One. The "three" are energy, essence and spirit; they are also called the
"Three Treasures." Guarding the One means to preserve the origin of life, the
pure energy of yang. This is done by alchemically mutating the life forces as
found in the body. The two major centers of the body, according to inner
alchemical theory, are the heart and the kidneys. They are associated with fire
and water, the trigrams Li and Kan, the South and the North, respectively
(Baldrian-Hussein 1984: 59). Fire, or the dragon, is the symbol of yang; in
human beings it is also represented by inner nature. Water, or the tiger, is the
symbol of yin; in human beings it is found as their destiny. Both these oppos-
ing energies are necessary to activate the mutations leading to ever higher

levels of refinement. Guarding the One means that one "uses energy to guard essence, uses essence to guard spirit, and uses spirit to guard energy." When one has managed to keep these three forces permanently guarded, the spirit will be firm and strong, energy will exist in perfect harmony, and immortality can be realized.

A similar description of guarding the One can be found in the *Xiuzhen jing* 脩真經 (Scripture on Cultivation of Perfection; DZ 41, fasc. 29) of the Southern Song (dated 1261). The section on "Guarding the One and Keeping the Spirit Alive" (15b) merely presents advice on how to keep the One at rest. In a later paragraph, the text links the meditation to morality (17ab). This text shows that guarding the One has changed from a technique of assembling, preserving, and nourishing the vital energy of the Tao into a practice of self-examination. The critical evaluation of oneself in terms of moral propriety can be considered typical for the new Taoist sects of the Song and Yuan which tended to heavily emphasize Confucian ethics and Buddhist precepts. The meditation methods of Shangqing Taoism were therefore popularized in the later sects as methods of critical, moral self-examination (Yoshioka 1976a: 309).

Guarding the One in Buddhism

Beginning with the early translations of Buddhist texts, the term *shou* was used to denote the effort of concentration of mind. The *Anpan shouyi jing* 安般守意經 (*Anāpānasmrtisutra*; T.15, 163–173), first translated by Chen Hui 陳慧 during the Han dynasty, even uses *shou* in its title. The technique described in this text consists of the observation of respiration as it enters and leaves through the nostrils (*ānāpāna*), with the aim of a state of mindfulness (*smrti*) and ultimately absorption of mind (*dhyāna*). It outlines the six basic stage of counting the breath, following the respiration, calm, observation, returning, and purifying (T.15, 164a; see Nakajima 1985: 89). The last two stages are explained as "unifying the mind" and "guarding the mind."

The expression "guarding the mind" occurs quite frequently in later translations of Buddhist texts (T.1, 57ab; 241a; 835c; T.3, 469b; 476b; 521c; T.4, 568c; T.8, 482a; 564a). It is used for concentration of mind, unification of mind, attainment of a unified mind, and so on, practices that in the end supposedly led to absorption of mind (Yoshioka 1976b: 326–330). In Buddhist sources, guarding the One may have been a literal translation of *ekāgrata*, "holding the One," but the term was also used as a general term for such varying concepts and technical terms as *dhyāna*, *samādhi*, or *smrti*

(Chappell 1983: 100). On the whole, in Buddhist sources the expression guarding the One is by no means used consistently, and an exact delineation of its varying connotations in different contexts and by different schools would require much further study. However, in light of the strong presence of the term in Taoist materials it seems evident that even numerous occurrences in Buddhist sources cannot justify the claim that guarding the One as either a technical term or a technique is ultimately of Buddhist origin, as proposed by Tang Yongtong (Tang 1938: 71). Not only can the expression be found in texts that predate the introduction of Buddhism, but it is also used in a very specific sense by the various schools and traditions of Taoism.

Where the *Anpan shouyi jing* leads adepts to distinguish between a mind not yet arisen, a diseased active mind, and a past regretful mind, the Chan tradition interprets Buddha-nature as the pure mind as such and uses it as the prime object of its meditation. In this tradition, the most indigenous form of Buddhism in China, two techniques using the term *shou* are prominent. The first, guarding the mind, can be interpreted as "to maintain constant, undiscriminating awareness of the absolute mind or Buddha-nature within oneself" (McRae 1986: 136). Guarding the mind emphasizes the awareness of the presence of the absolute mind. It consists of visualizing the golden orb of the sun, representative of the pure, radiating Buddha-nature. It may also be practiced by focusing attention on the movements of one's own discriminative mind. In doing so one concentrates on the clouds that obscure the radiant sun of the absolute mind (McRae 1986: 137). The second method in Chan that is described as "guarding" is "guarding the One and not moving." Its general implication is very similar to the idea of guarding the mind; in actual practice it consists of a detailed contemplation of the body that should ultimately be seen as nonsubstantial and pure (McRae 1986: 138; Sorensen 1986).

The main obvious distinction between the use of *shouyi* in Buddhist and Taoist sources is that the One as a philosophical concept, as a name for the primordial energy of the universe, or as a personalized deity does not occur in the Buddhist context. It is this lack of recognition of the One that Taoists themselves consider the most serious failure of Buddhism, or the Lesser Vehicle as they call it.

> The Buddhists follow the Lesser Vehicle. They sit quietly and count their own respiration. When they reach ten they begin anew. For years and years they continue this practice without letting off even for a moment. Buddhism does not teach the visualization of the gods in the body. . . . as the Taoists do who follow the Greater Vehicle.
> They constantly meditate on the true images of their body gods, visualize their garments and their typical colors. . . .

Thus the spirits and realized ones descend into their bodies and
their minds are free from affairs.
The followers of the Lesser Vehicle, on the other hand,
are bound by numerous affairs. They fret over a million
worries and are fettered by innumerable outward bondage. . . .
They must give careful consideration to words and phrases. . . .
while the students of the Greater Vehicle concentrate on the
practice of gathering in their vital energy and guarding the One.
They value their bodies above all else. . . . Know that all is
regulated by the One and the myriad affairs are done! (*Santian
neijie jing* 2.4b; Yoshioka 1976a: 299)

Conclusion

In Taoism the One can be understood either metaphysically or mythologically.
Metaphysically, it is first a name for the primordial state before creation;
second, the principle of creation; third, the primordial force of creation; and
fourth, the underlying characteristic common to all created things. In addition,
the primordial oneness, after being divided into the two forces yin and yang in
the course of creation, is then harmonized again on a new level, thereby giving
rise to the notion of the Three-in-One.

Mythologically, the One is either a cosmic deity, a god of the human
body, or a combination of both. As a cosmic deity, the One may reside in the
stars, preferably in the Northern Dipper or the Polestar. It may also be
identified with Taishang Laojun, the deified Laozi, and abide in the paradise
on Mount Kunlun. According to another variant, the One is depicted as the
matrix, the creator goddess of the universe. In all these cosmic appearances,
the One is closely associated with the center. Within the human body, the One
is first identified with various parts, to be later localized either to the spleen
(when associated with Laozi) or to the three cinnabar fields (when described
as the Three-in-One, the Male, Female, and Great Ones). Here again, the notion of the center plays an important role. The One as a god within or without
the human body is a personification of the central power of life and the
universe. Most frequently, the One is a combination of both astral and
physical deity; it appears simultaneously on the macrocosmic and
microcosmic levels.

Next, the notion of guarding, embracing, attaining, or realizing the One
may refer either to the recovery of a primordial oneness lost in the course of
life on earth or to the realization of an original unity that has always existed
and will exist in eternity. Among the actual practices leading to a realization

of the One in Taoism, seven representative methods may be distinguished. In each case, the immortality attained is defined slightly differently.

First, according to the *Taiping jing*, a practitioner may guard the One by visualizing light. The aim of the practice is initially to restore complete physical health and ultimately to transform into spirit itself. Immortality here could be described as a mystical union with the light of the universe.

Second, following the instructions of the *Baopuzi*, one may realize the One by visualizing the central deity of the universe and the human body. The result of the practice is the attainment of magical powers over oneself and the world. Multilocation, invulnerability, flying through the air, and diving into water, together with extending one's life at will, are thus the typical powers of immortals according to this tradition.

Third, the *Huangting jing* uses the expression guarding the One to describe a visualization of the various gods in the human body, especially of Laojun in its center, the spleen. Successfully applying the technique will enhance physical strength and make the body gods stay together, thus providing eternal life.

Fourth, we have the visualization of the Three-in-One in Shangqing Taoism. Three distinctly described deities are actualized as residents of the three human energy centers, the cinnabar fields. As long as they are there, firmly established, life will continue. Attaining complete oneness with the three central gods of the body and the cosmos will ensure eternal survival despite the physical end of a particular body on this earth.

Fifth, according to the *Yannian yisuan fa*, one guards the One by controlling the emotions and attaining one-pointedness of mind. This leads to the sustenance of the three spirit souls, keepers of the vital energies. The result is freedom from all disasters and misfortunes, a state of harmony with all, expressed actively in a feeling of compassion.

Sixth, the *Zhongjie wen* describes guarding the One as gaining control over the ceaseless flow of one's thoughts and establishing a perfect unity of mind. Stability of thoughts means not only limitless energy in the body and the end of all physical discomforts like hunger and thirst but also mystical oneness with the Tao in the mind. Immortality here consists of longevity and health plus freedom and independence of mind.

Seventh, in inner alchemy, guarding the One is the rhythmical mutation of the three inner human forces, energy, essence, and spirit. When the three forces are guarding each other permanently, a state of harmony within and without will come about. This in turn will allow adepts to increasingly refine themselves into pure energy, pure spirit, and ultimately the Tao itself. Immortality is the creation of a pure body made of spirit or of the Tao. It is in this body that adepts ascend into heaven, where they will enjoy eternal life.

All in all, guarding the One generally means concentrating the mind on one object, whether through visualization or abstract focusing of attention. Successful practice always results in the physical strengthening of the adept, explained through the metaphysical identification of the One with the primordial energy of the universe. Final realization differs according to the school in question; immortality may be defined as a permanent keeping of the body gods, as a mystical union with spirit or the Tao, as a mixture of both in the creation of a spirit body that is one with the Tao and as such will reside in heaven; it may also imply a freedom of body and mind, whether through the attainment of magical powers or through the realization of one-pointedness of mind and oneness with the Tao.

References

Andersen, Poul. 1980. *The Method of Holding the Three Ones*. London and Malmo: Curzon Press, 1980.

Baldrian-Hussein, Farzeen. 1984. *Procédés secrets du joyau magique*. Paris: Les Deux Océans, 1984.

Bokenkamp, Stephen. 1983. "Sources of the Ling-pao Scriptures." In *Tantric and Taoist Studies*, edited by Michel Strickmann, vol. 2, pp. 434–486. Bruxelles: Institut Belges des Hautes Etudes Chinoises, 1983.

Chappell, David. 1983. *The Teachings of the Fourth Ch'an Patriarch Tao-hsin (580–651)*. Berkeley: University of California Press, 1983.

Kaltenmark, Max. 1979. "The Ideology of the *T'ai-p'ing-ching*." In *Facets of Taoism*, pp. 19–52. Edited by H. Welch and A. Seidel. New Haven & London: Yale University Press, 1979.

Kandel, Barbara. 1979. *Taiping jing*. Hamburg: Gesellschaft für Natur- und Völkerkunde Ostasiens, 1979.

Lagerwey, John. 1981. *Wu-shang pi-yao: Somme taoiste du VIe Siècle* Paris: Publications de l'Ecole Francaise d'Extrême-Orient, 1981.

Mansvelt-Beck, B.J. 1980. "The Date of the *Taiping jing*," *T'oung-pao* 66 (1980), 149–182.

Maspero, Henri. 1981. *Taoism and Chinese Religion*. Translated by Frank Kierman. Amherst: University of Massachusetts Press, 1981, 431–554.

McRae, John R. 1986. *The Northern School and the Formation of Early Ch'an Buddhism*. Honolulu: Hawaii University Press, 1986.

Robinet, Isabelle. 1977. *Les commentaires du Tao to king jusqu'au VIIe siècle*. Paris: Mémoirs de l'Institute des Hautes Etudes Chinoises 5, 1977),

——— 1979 *Méditation taoiste*. Paris: Dervy Livres, 1979.

——— 1984. *La révélation du Shangqing dans l'histoire du Taoisme*. 2 vols. Paris: Publications de l'Ecole Francaise d'Extrême-Orient, 1984.

Ryckmans, Pierre. 1970. *Shitao: Les propos sur la peinture du moine Citrouille-amère*. Paris: Collection Savoir Hermann, 1970.

Schipper, Kristofer M. 1975. *Concordance du Houang-t'ing king*. Paris: Publications de l'Ecole Francaise d'Extrême-Orient, 1975.

——— 1978. "The Taoist Body," *History of Religions* 17 (1978), 355–387.

——— 1982 *Le corps taoiste*. Paris: Fayard, 1982.

Seidel, Anna. 1969. *La divinisation de Lao-tseu dans le Taoisme des Han*. Paris: Ecole Francaise d'Extrême-Orient, 1969.

——— 1983. "Das neue Testament des Tao," *Saeculum* 29. 1978), 147–172.

——— 1983. "Imperial Treasures and Taoist Sacraments: Taoist Roots in the Apocrypha." In *Tantric and Taoist Studies*, edited by Michel Strickmann, vol. 2, pp. 291–371. Bruxelles: Institut Belges des Hautes Etudes Chinoises, 1983.

Sorensen, Henrik H. 1986. "Methods of Meditation in Early Chinese Ch'an." Paper presented at the 32nd ICANAS, Hamburg, 1986.

Walsh, Roger. 1984. "An Evolutionary Model of Meditation Research." In *Meditation: Classic and Contemporary Perspectives*, edited by Duane H. Shapiro and Roger N. Walsh, pp. 24–32. New York: Aldine, 1984.

Ware, James R. 1966. *Alchemy, Medicine and Religion in the China of A.D. 320. The Nei P'ien of Ko Hung (Pao-p'u tzu)*. Cambridge, Massachusetts: MIT Press, 1966.

Watson, Burton. 1968. *The Complete Works of Chuang-tzu*. New York: Columbia University Press, 1968.

in Chinese and Japanese

Mugitani Kunio 麥谷邦夫 1982
"Kōtei naikeikyō shiron" 黄庭内景經試論
Tōyō bunka 東洋文化 62 (1982), 29–61.

—— 1985. "Rōshi sōjichū ni tsuite" 老子想爾注 について
Tōhō gakuhō 57 (1985), 75–109.

Nakajima Ryūzō 中島隆藏 1985
Rikuchō shisō no kenkyū 六朝思想の研究
Kyoto: Heiraku shoten, 1985.

Rao Zongyi 饒宗頤 1956
Laozi xianger zhu jiaojian 老子想爾注校牋
Hongkong: Tong Nam Publishers, 1956.

Tang Yongtong 湯用彤 1938
Han Wei liang Jin Nanbeichao fojiaoshi 漢魏兩晉南北朝佛教史
Beijing, 1938.

Wang Ming 王明 1979
Taiping jing hejiao 太平經合校
Beijing: Zhonghua, 1979.

Yoshioka Yoshitoyo 吉岡義豐 1976
Dōkyō to Bukkyō 道教と佛教 . Vol. 3.
(Tokyo: Kokusho kankōkai, 1976).

—— 1976a. "Bukkyō no zempō to dōkyō no shūitsu"
佛教の禪法と道教の守一
In *Dōkyō to Bukkyō*, vol. 3, pp. 287–314. Originally published in 1964.

—— 1976b. "Taiheikyō no shūitsu shisō to bukkyō"
太平經の守一思想と佛教
In *Dōkyō to Bukkyō*, vol. 3, pp. 315–351. Originally published in 1968.

Chapter Six

Visualization and Ecstatic Flight in Shangqing Taoism

Isabelle Robinet

The World of Images

Taoist practices have to be understood as processes of a specific inner order, processes that make use of images to transform psychic contents. In meditation practice, the active value of the image is first, not its theoretical or discursive importance. Mere philosophical propositions don't play a significant role in this context, because Taoism as a practice is essentially pragmatic. The scriptures delineate the practices to be followed and describe the results that can and must come about. Each practitioner must live them and turn them into reality.

The active Taoist undertakes a certain representation of the universe, of the body, and of himself or herself. This representation comes alive, it becomes visible to the mental eye and is perceived by the inner being of each and every adept. The aim of the practice is to integrate personal individuality into a coherent and harmonious unity. More than that, the representation as it is actively and consciously produced by the practitioner and his or her living experience has to be encompassed in the greater unity: respiratory and visionary practices provide a new and newly integrated understanding of the body as well as of the divinities who cause it to be alive. The body, through the inner vision of the divinities, is seen as a complex of a higher dimension; thus the meditator's understanding of the universe is reorganized and his worldview reconstructed. With all attention focused on the deep inner life of

159

the body, a series of mental exercises centering on a symbolic and nonrational vision of the world is undertaken.

The newly developed perception creates an utterly new body, a body that consists as much of the physical body proper as of the idealized image actively created. The physical body is the basic working material of the Taoists, their *materia prima*: all Taoist practices begin with the body, and one may well say that this is a characteristic common to all the various schools of the religion. The aim of the practice is therefore to establish the perception of a new body, called the "spiritual body" by Tao Hongjing 陶弘景 in the fifth century and the "yang body" in the texts of operative and inner alchemy. In addition, it results in a new personality of cosmic dimensions, where the physical and the imaginary body, the individual and the cosmos, are intimately merged, where the ordinary human being has become a true Taoist saint, such as described by Zhuangzi.

In terms of actual efforts, an adept of Taoist meditation becomes the center and the subject of his or her own organism, which is essentially of the same nature and the same structure as the universe at large. Undergoing a gradual progress, he attains unity or the One, a state of primordial oneness that nourishes and sustains the numerous diverse manifestations of being. All these manifestations are ultimately related to one another through the intervention of this central, unifying pole. While the adept moves—without ever interrupting the continuity of meditation practice—on the personal as well as the celestial and the cosmic level, he or she yet remains in close touch with all other levels. This is especially obvious in the case of inner alchemy, where the various planes intermingle ceaselessly. Yet, despite all the movement, there is a single dwelling only: the essential unity beyond all multiplicity.

Taoist meditation takes place in an intermediary world, in a world of images "where the spirit is embodied and the body is spiritualized," a psychological world Mircea Eliade calls "creative imagination" and Henri Corbin calls "active imagination" (Corbin 1953). This world lies between the unfathomable hidden mystery and the world of animated physical forms. It is not yet the realm of the unknowable, which one can neither name nor see, the world of the void, which even when touched is yet beyond expression (as the Taoists say and then duly opt for silence). Nor is it any longer the world of sensual and solidified realities. Theirs is a world of play, of polysemy and metaphor, real-unreal, quite close to that which the psychoanalyst D.W. Winnicott calls "a third space truly described neither in terms of inner psychological reality nor in terms of outer factuality." It is a world placed in the so-called transitional or liminal, located in a "realm of potential between the infant and the mother," in an area "related to play and cultural experience," thus circumscribing an intermediary way of living, situated "between the reality within and the reality without." This state is characterized by a creative mode that helps to dissolve the "paradox of being at the same time oneself and not oneself, neither within nor without," offers a resolution that gives a subjective feeling of "omnipotence" (Winnicott, quoted in Atlan 1986: 263–265). This world is unreal in that it is imaginary, but it is real in that the individual lives in it and through it creates a new self: it is unreal-real, like the world of the Buddhists, which has a metaphoric character one must never forget—a net used to catch one's prey, a creative, playful globe.

This world is founded on the interrelation of various levels: spiritual, imaginative, physical. It supposes a doctrine of "microcosm," a cosmology that claims a complete correspondence between the structure of the human body and the organization of the universe at large, in which "every point of contact holds a relation with its correlate on every other homologous level" (Corbin 1953: 80). In China we find this concept first in the school of yin and yang and the five phases, outlined in the "Seasonal Commands" chapter of the *Liji* 禮記 (Book of Rites), in the *Yijing* 易經 (Book of Changes), later it is central to Taoist liturgy and the worldview of all the various Taoist schools. This view of the universe is solidly rooted in Chinese culture and constitutes its unique character.

The universe of the Taoists is thus opposed to logical ways of thinking, to discursive and linear modes of thought, to chains of cause and effect. Their world is a realm of its own, a realm of meditation limited in space to the chamber of the practitioner, surrounded by the sacred spirits of the four poles, which are summoned for protection when one begins the exercise. It is also limited in time by the specific periods assigned for the different practices. It is a playful universe, full of chants, of dances, of metamorphoses, where the rules of the game are revealed by the gods—that is to say, they are sacred and inviolate. It is not a game without rules, would only reflect the primordial undifferentiation of all potential creation, but the rules are minimized so as to provide a basic, stable ground from which creativity can fully grow and blossom. They are constraints forming a clear framework for productivity. The special domain of the active meditator is firmly delimited, to guard against the danger of universalization. It serves to place the spiritual world of meditation in the position of an absolute, over and against any other. This prevents one from jumping from one game to another, because the rules used in one are never quite valid for any other. For instance, the rules of the visualizations in the mode of the Shangqing tradition are quite incompatible with those of the circulation of energy in the manner of the internal alchemist. One cannot easily move from one to the other even though they have certain points in common. The limitations are comparable to those between two languages: one cannot easily mix them, nor can one switch between them without making certain transitions.

In Taoism, the most ancient texts that bear testimony of visualization techniques are those of the Celestial Masters, the *Sanhuang wen* 三皇文 (Writings of the Three August Ones), and the *Lingbao wufuxu* 靈寶五符序 (Highest Explanation to the Five Talismans of the Numinous Treasure). However, it is in the documents of the Shangqing tradition, revealed to Yang Xi 楊羲 between 364 and 370, that we find visualizations described in most detail and with the most elaboration in a coherent and relatively well-organized corpus. One can show that this corpus—as regards visualizations—is based on sources that go back at least to the Han and—in terms of its cosmology—is rooted in Chinese thought of the Warring States period and before (Robinet 1984: vol. 1: 11–75).

The characteristic feature of Shangqing practices is found precisely in their preference for visualization over all other meditation and longevity techniques, even though the practice is always accompanied by other traditional methods, such as doing breathing exercises, writing and offering charms, ritually reciting texts, fasting, and so on. The essential contribution of this school of Taoism, besides that of forming a link between the heritage of the past that it reorganizes and develops and the later tendencies of the religion, is its detailed formulation of the techniques of visualization, which were never practiced this way before or after in the Chinese tradition. In the same vein, it enriched Taoism with an enormous pantheon of gods residing in the stars and in the human body, with a complete system of imaginary cosmology. The ecstatic visualizations of the far ends of the world and of the heavens as practiced in Shangqing Taoism will be the subject of our discussion.[1]

---

1. For the visualizations of single deities in the human body see chapter 5, "Guarding the One: Concentrative Meditation in Taoism."

Excursions on Earth

The World and Its Boundaries

Ecstatic excursions have a long history in China: already the *Zhuangzi* 莊子 evokes such images in the first chapter on "Free and Easy Wanderings," according to which several personages "bestride the sun and the moon," "mount on the truth of heaven and earth, ride the changes of the six breaths (of the six directions) and frolic through the boundless" or "wander around the four poles" (Watson 1968: 32). Liezi shows us how King Mu of Zhou is carried off by a magician as far as the realm of the Queen Mother of the West (Graham 1960: 64). The *Chuci* 楚辭 (Songs of the South) describe the ecstatic trip of the poet to the four ends of the world and to the Gate of Heaven (Hawkes 1959: 81). The tradition is further continued in the twelfth chapter of the *Huainanzi* 淮南子 , according to which Lu Ao "wanders around the Northern Sea, jumps over the Great Yin, enters the Dark Gate, and reaches the hill of Menghu" (Robinet 1979: 260). The same idea is attested in the mirrors of the Han, which represent immortals "who amuse themselves in the regions of the four seas."

The ecstatic journey is possible because Taoists, knowing how to "retain their spirit souls," are deeply concerned with the flying and the fleeting. They know how to make their spirits wander far off, and thanks to the guidance of sacred scriptures (when acquired properly!) they are able to control and direct their travels. They know the exact location and structure of the spirit routes. The scriptures revealed by the gods inform them of the roads of the divinities, the ways of the Yin and the Yang, the passes and the gates of the various heavens, the landmarks of the earth. They become familiar with the paths and the directions leading from the earth to the heavens, they learn to navigate along the stations of the sun and the moon, they know the exact ways by which the sun brings light to the earth and by which the stars and the moon draw shining patterns and constellations on the nocturnal sky. All these celestial activities correspond to the ways in which the gods move in the human body—that is, in the subtle body inherent in all human beings, which is an image and a country, a counterpart and exact replica of the cosmos. Active practitioners know all the passwords, hold all the necessary passports, and are initiated into the science of celestial and human topology and nomenclature that rules communication with, evocation of, and unification with the divine forces.

The foundation of the exercises is found in the basic analogy of the human body to the cosmos, which in turn is based on the correspondence system of the school of the five elements (or agents, or phases): one explores the universe within and without, on the earth, in the body, and in the heavens. These planes are merely relative phenomena, closely interrelated and quickly overcome once one has entered the visionary mode. The vision of the five orbs, of the spirits residing in the body, of the five primordial forces within is thus at the same time a vision of the five cardinal poles of the sky.

Which are these poles?

Beyond the Four Seas that enclose the known world, there are the strange lands, the wild countries of the fringes, the barbarian realms, where monsters and wonderful beings live. Here is the world of the unusual, of the extraordinary already described in detail in the *Shanhai jing* 山海經 (Classic of Mountains and Seas) and alluded to in the *Huainanzi*. The poles are the arena of the mythical explorations of which we find fragmentary evidence in the *Chunqiu* 春秋 (Spring and Autumn Annals), for example. In this extended world the isles of the immortals are located. In the East, there are the Green Hill, the Mulberry Forest, the Fusang Tree, and the Lake of the Sun. In the West, one finds the Mountain of Stones, heaped up by Yu the Great, as well as Mount Gunwu.

These polar areas are inhabited by celebrated mythical beings, who are the four pillars of the earth, and by their Taoist counterparts, who are the four emperors or the five old ones, after which the four poles have been named. These emperors are very closely related to the Five Agents and the five orbs—they correspond to one another and come to nourish their respective florescences during meditation. Moreover, they hold the registers of life and death and so control the destiny of any adept who tries to have his or her name inscribed in the registers of immortality.

The distant marshes, the isles of the immortals, and Mount Kunlun abound in wonderful beings and marvelous objects that the son of heaven summons as pledges of the reach of his power. These supernatural phenomena of the periphery sometimes were originally crude or barbarian forces that have turned into auspicious powers. The Taoist gets hold of such wonderful things by sinking deep in rapture within the confines of the sacred space of his meditation chamber and traveling through the world searching for virtue and instruction. The places he visits are precisely the untamed wild areas that are richest in numinous power, where one can absorb those precious spiritual energies. Here the followers of the Tao go to find magical plants, talismans, and sacred scriptures.

The Sprouts

To begin with, adepts absorb the sprouts of the four poles in an important practice that is already documented in the *Wufuxu*. The great Taoist and Shangqing patriarch of the Tang, Sima Chengzhen 司馬承禎 , describes it in an essay. One method left behind by Wei Huacun 魏華存 , who initiated Yang Xi into the Shangqing arcana, is described here. The basic procedures are very similar. One swallows saliva while chanting invocations to the sprouts of the four directions (*Fuqi jingyi lun* 服氣精義論 , Discourse on the Essential Meaning of the Absorption of *Qi*; HY 829, fasc. 571;[2] Engelhardt 1987: 88–99). Another typical method outlined by Tao Hongjing and cited in many places is called "Method of Mist Absorption."

The sprouts are originally the "germinal essences of the clouds" or "mist." They represent the yin principle of heaven—that is, the yin within the yang. They manifest in human saliva, again a yin element in the upper, yang, part of the body. They help to nourish and strengthen the five orbs. The *Daodian lun* 道典論 (On the Code of the Tao; HY 1122, fasc. 764) explains that they are very tender, comparable to the fresh sprouts of plants, and that they assemble at dawn in the celestial capital, from where they spread all over the universe until the sun begins to shine. Turning like the wheels of a carriage, they ascend to the gates of the nine heavens, from where they continue to the medium level of the world—to the five sacred mountains ruled over by the five emperors of the five directions—and finally descend into the individual adept. They thus pass through the three major levels of the cosmos (4.9b–10a).

The virtue of these sprouts is twofold. They are "emanations of the highest poles" and as such full of the power of the borderlands. At the same time, they are yet "tender like freshly sprouted plants" and as such contain the entire potential of being in its nascent state. In particular, the potential, the small and imperceptible that is as yet in a state of becoming, is the main object to which the future sovereign, the sage-to-be, and thus the Taoist practitioner, must pay most attention. The idea of the sprouting includes prevalence of the soft over the hard already found in the *Yijing*, the power of the yin over the yang that Laozi describes in the *Daode jing* 道德經 . Here yin is represented by the saliva that adepts absorb. The practice is undertaken at dawn, the time when everything awakens to life. This is the time of potential, when the "two breaths [yin and yang] are not yet separated," and so the most auspicious

---

2. Works in the Taoist Canon are cited according to their number in the *Harvard-Yenching Institute Sinological Index Series* no. 25 (Taipei: Chinese Material Center, 1966), abbreviated HY. "Fasc." refers to the volume number of the 1925 Shanghai reprint of the Canon.

moment to absorb the sprouts afresh and start one's meditation. Like the sovereign who takes nourishment from the "essence of all that is alive in the universe" (Granet 1950: 395) by feeding on the delicacies of the four corners of the world, the Taoist partakes of the efflorescences of the luminaries and "eats" the universe in its most subtle form.

The absorption of these sprouts is also used as a preparatory practice for the "abstention from cereals," which is necessary to dispel the three worms, who represent the principle of death within the human organism. By and by the sprout intake substitutes for the regular nourishment of the adept and allows him to identify with the germinal energy of the sprouts. He thus can become lighter, fly, and appear and disappear at will.

The Vision of the World

While the practitioner assembles the basic polar forces of the universe in the body by absorbing the sprouts, he or she learns to search for the sprouts in the far-off corners of the world in various other exercises. The inward-turning movement is thus complemented by a turn toward the outside.

One method is called the "Superior Method to Send For the Void and Deeply Contemplate the Heaven," also known as the "Meditation on the Four Directions." It is described in the *Zidu yanguang shenyuan bianjing* 紫度炎光神元變經 (Scripture on Spirit Prime Transformation Through Purple Beyondness and Brilliant Light; HY 1321, fasc. 1030), a Shangqing text, from which it is quoted in many other sources.

According to this technique, one visualizes, one after the other, all the mountains, rivers, plants, animals, barbarians, and immortals of the four directions, beginning with the closest and going toward the more distant. When the vision is clear and complete, the immortal administrator of the sacred mountain of the direction in question will appear, accompanied by a clamor of drums. This divine agent will give the adept a drink of the taste corresponding to the direction and agent. When toward the end of the exercise the adept returns to himself, the mountains, plants, animals, and barbarians of the directions visited will come and render homage.

The visionary journey is an impressive replication of the ancient inspection tours the kings and emperors of China paid to the borderlands of their realm, the way in which they assembled their treasures to concentrate the entire power of government in their capitals. At the same time, it is obvious how, in their meditations, Taoist adepts make themselves into emperors of the whole world and their bodies its center.

In other Shangqing texts the same topic is treated slightly differently. According to the *Taishang jiuchi banfu wudi neizhen jue* 太上九赤班符五

帝內真訣 (True Esoteric Writing of the Five Emperors' Charms of Nine Red Stripes; HY 1318, fasc. 1029), faithful practice will enable the adept "to have an appanage, to control the Five Sacred Mountains, and to order the Spirits of Water about." Here yin is symbolized by the water, and yang by the mountains. The concrete method consists of entering the Five Mountains and visualizing their respective emperors. The quality of the practice is judged by the color one perceives at that precise moment. The indication is auspicious when the color corresponds exactly to the emperor one visualizes or the next one. It is inauspicious when the color is that of the opposite direction. The adept then buries a charm of the given direction and in due course has his or her name inscribed in the registers of immortality presided over by the envisioned emperor. Another very similar exercise follows; it helps the practitioner obtain the same administrative measure from the Emperors of the Four Seas. To perform it, one throws a charm into flowing waters in each of the four directions.

The *Waiguo fangpin qingtong neiwen*   外國方品青童內文 (Esoteric Scripture of the Pure Lad on the Distribution of the Outer Regions; HY 1362, fasc. 1041), another Shangqing text, repeats the description of the isles of the immortals found in the *Shizhou ji* 十洲記 (Record of the Ten Continents; HY 598, fasc. 330; *Yunji qiqian* 26) attributed to Dongfang Shuo 東方朔. The first work shows a certain influence of Buddhism and the Taoism of the Lingbao school, which means it is slightly later than the other Shangqing scriptures. It is a travel guide to the "six outer regions," one in each of the four directions, one above, and one below. These outer regions correspond to the thirty-six subterranean and thirty-six celestial realms. The world is thus divided into the three levels of heaven, earth, and underworld. The outer regions are also known as the "secret regions." Their names, organized in a double system of traditional Chinese and esoteric mantras based on Sanskrit syllables,[3] are used in chants and invocations. They are essentially divine sounds that were already chanted by Laojun, the Highest Venerable Lord, when he set out to convert the barbarians. The meditator intones these names with the effect that, after a certain number of years, he is able to fly to the far-off lands and converse with the barbarians who render due homage. In addition, once the tour of the whole universe is completed, the kings of the thirty-six heavens enter his or her name into the registers of immortality.

---

3. Among the latter one finds the Buddhist names for the four main continents of the world.

Excursions to the Stars: The Sun and the Moon

The sun, the moon, and the stars play an important role in the ancient Chinese organization of the world. They form a triad that, especially for the Taoists, corresponds to numerous other sets of three and assumes a relevance of the same dimension, yet on different levels. The importance of the number three is found in the Three Breaths, divine entities that created the cosmos—the original, the primordial, and the mysterious. More than that, it is found in the cosmological triad of heaven, earth, and humanity, which (on the microcosmic level) corresponds to the Three Primordials. In dualistic terms, the sun and the moon are the celestial manifestation of yin and yang. This concept is taken up by the Taoists. The moon is the lady of ice and rules over a court of frost; she is the material (yin) soul of the earth. The sun is the spirit (yang) soul of the sky. The dualism of yin and yang, water and fire, earth and heaven, governs their role within the human body. The sun belongs to the left, the yang side, the moon to the right, the yin side. The sun is placed in the upper, the moon in the lower part of the body. The sun/fire reigns the heart, the orb belonging to the South; the moon/water rules the kidneys, the orb of the North. The sun and the moon are the eyes of heaven to which the eyes of the human body correspond: the right is the moon, the left is the sun.

Practices centering on the sun and the moon generally encompass three aspects: the adept accompanies the stars on their heavenly journey; he nourishes on their efflorescences; he frolics in the paradise protected by them, where the divinities originate and reside.

The Course of the Sun and the Moon

The texts of Shangqing Taoism (for example, the *Huangqi yangjing jing* 黃氣陽精經 , Scripture of Yellow Energy and Yang Essence; HY 33, fasc. 27) take up the theme of the sun's journey across the sky that is already formulated in the *Chuci* and in the *Huainanzi*. In some details the Shangqing elaborations retain the images of the earlier texts, in others they develop their own.

At the equinoxes and the solstices the sun and the moon pass through the polar regions: the Golden Gate in the East is entered in spring; the Palace of Universal Yang in the South is visited during the height of summer; the Eastern Pool, the Gate of the Moon, is reached in fall; and the Palace of Eternal Frost in the North is passed in the winter. Each of these palaces is a paradise complete with a tree of life, where birds with golden feathers nest and the fruits of immortality grow, and with a spot of water, spring, or lake, where the sun and the moon purify their rays. The rulers of these paradises are the kings and queens whose names are (with certain variants) the same as those of the tutelary spirits of the respective direction, who—already in ancient Chinese mythology—reside on the poles and regulate the "auspicious powers" of the four regions of space.

Each time an adept reaches one of the astral stations, he or she has to do ablutions with water rendered sacred through a talisman. Then he imagines himself ascending on the rays of the sun (or the moon) until he reaches the palace where the star resides at the given time of the year. Here he meets the king or the queen of the region, who gives him fruits from the tree of life typical for the specific area. In the periods between these excursions (limited to the equinoxes and the solstices, when the sun and the moon are present in the palaces) the practitioner is taught to visualize the sun and the moon in the area of the body that corresponds to the given season. Figure 1 depicts an adept visualizing the sun.

There are other, simpler, practices of the same type. For example, one ingests a bowl of water that has been left outside to be enriched by the rays of the sun or the moon. Then one enters the meditation chamber to visualize the energy of the star—purple for the sun, yellow for the moon. The practitioner swallows the energy which enters the orbs.

Another method, called *Yuyi jielin* 鬱儀結璘 after the sacred names of the sun and the moon, consists of an invocation of the names of the kings of the sun and the queens of the moon. Here a formula is used that is found again and again in liturgies of later centuries: it makes the divinities descend, clad in the five colors of the four cardinal directions and the center. In the end the adept ascends with them to the stars. This method is part of many rituals and has given its name to an important talisman.

In all these exercises, the subject exchanges qualities with the sun and the moon. Their qualities are most clearly documented in their names: the moon is the Yellow Energy in reference to its color; the sun the Yang Essence in reference to its nature. Specific qualities of the stars are also considered in the concrete practice as well as in the names of the palaces—for example, the Gate of the Moon, which is the pool in the East. The two heavenly bodies are sometimes thought of as consisting of fire and water.

The rhythm of the exercises follows the celestial movements of the two stars. The sun and the moon are the sign of the alternating movements of yin and yang, at the same time opposed and complementary but always inseparable. The practice is thus not the expression of a mere solar cult, but the emphasis is placed on the veneration of the joint action of the sun and the moon, of the harmony in their movements. The sun and the moon are representatives of a world governed by the interplay of yin and yang and

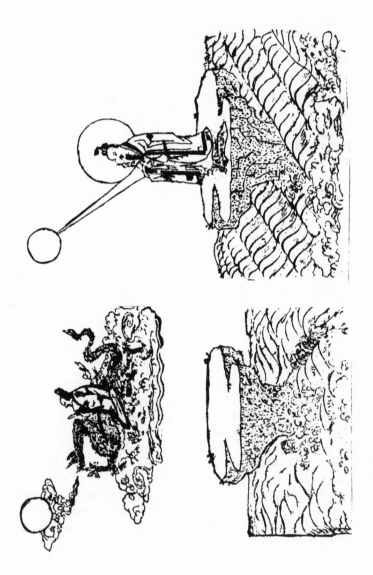

Fig. 1. An adept visualizing the sun. *Source: Yuyi jielin* 5ab

measured by the four directions. It is a world determined by the polarity of two forces on their double journey.

Human beings are a third entity in this picture, that of the center. Remaining always within their meditation chambers, adepts of Taoism wander around the whole world to its final horizons, just as the king does in his Hall of Light. They measure the periods of time and the limits of space, the temporary phases and the cardinal stations of the stars, while at the same time synchronizing them. One year in this system corresponds to one creation, continuation, and disappearance of one universe: one full cosmic cycle, one complete world.

The stars purify their rays in the lakes or water spots found at the palaces, just as described in the *Shanhai jing* (where the Mother of Stars bathes them) and in the *Huainanzi*. The procedure is quite like the royal bath taken by the ruler, as is shown in the work of Marcel Granet (1926: 449, n. 5). In their practices, Taoists of the Shangqing school similarly purify themselves with water that has been saturated with the rays of the stars. The purifying power of the sun and the moon is made most obvious here. It is taken up again in the rituals of purification by fire or water, which are performed under the auspices of the sun and the moon.

On the other hand, it may be worth noting that these practices take place on all three planes, or in the three worlds that ultimately coincide. One is the outer and material world, measured by the course of the stars and the passing of the seasons; next comes the symbolic world, marked by the four palaces where the kings and queens reside and where the four poles are represented as dynamic stages of a journey; the third is the inner world of the adept, simultaneously material and symbolic, the human body, where the stars are visualized in accordance with their positions in the outer and the symbolic universes. Human existence within the framework of the body repeats the universe and the life of the cosmos.

Nourishing on Light

The practitioner absorbs the essences of the stars and guides them to remain in certain parts of the body. They may also be circulated around the entire body. These essences appear in concrete form in a honey-like liquid that collects under the tongue and is swallowed together with the saliva. Another form of applying the astral powers is gathering them around oneself. As the *Huangqi yangjing jing* says: "The purple breath of the sun assembles and descends to envelop the entire body of the adept. Thus wrapped in a cloud of solar breath, he ascends to the Palace of Universal Yang."

According to the *Yuyi jielin jing* (Sacred Scripture of the Sun and the Moon; HY 435, fasc. 196), the meditator must "make the light of the sun embrace his or her entire person, reaching within as far as the corners of the stomach and giving him the feeling of being completely illuminated within and without." Whoever gives himself over to these exercises regularly will acquire a "rosy complexion," and his or her "whole body will be luminous and shine brilliantly." He or she may also "radiate a marvelous light; from a round spot on the nape of the neck the light will reach into the eight directions." Here again the adept becomes as luminous as the stars themselves. Like Guangchengzi in according to the *Zhuangzi*, he becomes like the sun and the moon; he is like the Great Man of the *Huainanzi*, who has "the same radiance as the sun and the moon."

In all these apotheotic exercises the sun and the moon are usually accompanied by the Northern Dipper, the central object of important visualization techniques and one of the main divinities of Taoism, whose layout is shown in figure 2.

Excursions to the Stars: The Dipper

The stars with which the sun and the moon form a typical triad are, at least in the texts of the Shangqing school, the stars of the Great Bear (Ursa Major, the Northern Dipper of the Chinese) and the planets. Let us look at the various roles the Dipper plays in these techniques.

According to the texts, this constellation consists of the Scoop, made up of four stars, and of the Handle, which unites the three remaining ones. In addition there are two invisible stars, Fu and Bi, which are related to the planet Mars and to the Polestar respectively. They are the assistants of the Dipper to the right and to the left, flanking him like the sun and the moon. These two stars do not become visible unless certain strict conditions of purity are fulfilled. One who does see them receives a life span of several hundred years. The Dipper therefore consists of nine stars all inhabited by various divinities. In addition, the constellation has a corresponding counterpart, a mirror image, consisting of "black stars" that form its spirit and material souls of yin and yang nature. Here female divinities reside, the spouses of the kings of the stars of the Dipper. These black stars form another Dipper outside the first, radiating in the dark so as to obscure itself and illuminate the other (see figure 3). Within the human body, the goddesses of the dark Dipper reside in one of the nine palaces in the head, the Hall of Light, while those of the visible constellation make their home in the heart.

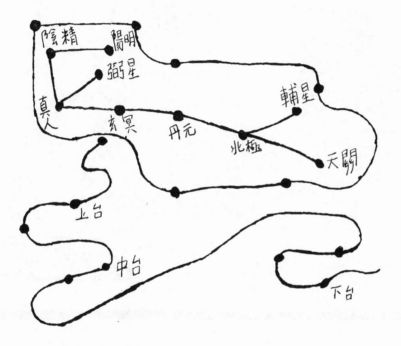

Fig. 2. The layout of the Northern Dipper. *Source: Bu tiangang fei diji* 1ab

Fig. 3. The White and Black Dippers. *Source: Tianguan santu* 9b–10a

On every star of the Dipper there is a palace made up from "watery essence and lapis lazuli." There a tree grows, full of colorful fruit and inhabited by gilded birds. There are fragrant, supernatural plants, of which one mouthful will suffice to ensure a life span of several ten thousands of years. The palaces on the stars of the Dipper are thus very similar to the paradises at the four poles of the universe visited by the sun and the moon.

Meditation Practice: The Cloak of Stars, the Celestial Bed, and the Celestial Network

Three kinds of practices center around the Dipper: invoking it for protective purposes; making its stars descend into one's body; ascending to and pacing on it.

The Northern Dipper is first of all a divinity of the North and of the underworld, and as such it has an important protective function, guarding the faithful adept against all kinds of malevolent forces. Adepts may, for example, cover themselves with the stars of the Dipper by visualizing them descending and arranging themselves right above the head, in front or behind. It is best to imagine the stars of the Dipper all around: three on the upper left side of the body, near the palm, elbow and breast, the fourth (the middle one) above the heart, and the remaining three on the lower right side of the body, near the stomach, the knee, and the foot. The two invisible stars Bi and Fu should, finally, be below the navel and above the head, or they are placed within the cinnabar fields.[4]

A relation between the three cinnabar fields and the Dipper is also found in the *Feixing yujing* 飛行羽經 (Scripture of Winged Flight; HY 1340, fasc. 1033), where it is recommended that one make the divinities of the Dipper enter into one's three cinnabar fields in a set order and on precise dates. In the Scoop of the Dipper one will then in each case see one of the three Great Spirits of the Nine Essences, which are actually emanations of the original triad formed by the Three Primordial Breaths. In the practice of guarding the One the adept ascends to the constellation in the company of the Three Original Rulers of the cinnabar fields and their assistants.

Most commonly the exercises refer to the role of the Dipper as an exorcistic agency and end by an ecstatic flight to this constellation. However, the latter may also be practiced independently. Such imaginary ascensions to the Dipper may take various forms. One of them is described in the *Jinshu*

---

4. The role of this exorcism was amplified in later centuries and has emerged as the one characteristic function of the Dipper in Taoism. Many divinities of this constellation have turned into warrior gods and frightful demon eaters.

yuzi 金書玉字 (Jade Words of the Golden Book; HY 878, fasc. 581); it consists of Sleeping in the Dipper, sketched as it were on the adept's sleeping mat. Meditating in this position, adepts visualize the essences of the nine stars turning into one divinity who comes down to receive them in a chariot. The essence of the divinities of the Dipper then will illuminate the whole body of the practitioner.

In another technique, adepts visualize the Dipper as the vehicle that carries them all around the heavens. They concentrate on the Dipper and together with him turn about the sky; individual stars bring them, one after the other, to each of the Three Gates of the Nine Heavens.

The best-known practice concerning the Dipper, which has been most elaborately used in a variety of rituals, is the pace on the planets or on the Dipper. It is documented already in Han dynasty materials, dating at least from the first century A.D. (Robinet 1984: vol. 1: 13–14), but the texts of Shangqing Taoism seem to be the earliest that describe it in any detail. The pace basically follows the steps of Yu the Great, who delimited, measured, divided, and organized the world and thereby became the prototype of the sage as the regulator and ruler of the universe by means of a sacred chart like the River Chart or the Writ of the Luo River. The chart serves as a golden rule by which exact measures and configurations are established.

The practice of pacing the net, that is, pacing the Dipper, which is a kind of celestial network, has developed from the pattern of "three paces and nine traces that is called the Pace of Yu" (*Yunji qiqian* 61.4b). This pattern, the text continues to explain, corresponds to the "Three Primordial Breaths and nine stars," but also to the number of great Yang (the number nine) and reenacts the union between yin and yang. The main emphasis is on the combination of the numbers three and nine, which thus are aligned with the three original breaths of the universe and the nine divinities of the stars of the Dipper (which are equivalent to the nine primordial heavens of the Shangqing system). Both numbers, three and nine, are equivalents of the cosmic totality, of the One.

In the Shangqing scriptures the Pace of Yu is described in more detail than in the *Baopuzi*, which seems to have preserved an older and more original form of the exercise. In later rituals numerous variants and embellishments have transformed the simple pattern into a complex liturgy. The essential novelty in the later developments is the practice of the steps on the stars rather than on earth, their transformation into a "pace of the network of heaven" or a "pace of the void" (see Schafer 1981). In any case, the pace assumes great importance in later rituals. "Pacing the celestial network," one of the liturgical texts says, "is the essence of the flight into the heavens, the spirit of the pace of the earth and the truth of all movements of humanity." It is thus a dance that joins heaven, earth, and humanity; it imitates the union of yin and yang, of water and fire, as well as of the three and the nine, the equivalents of the One.

In the practice as outlined in the Shangqing scriptures, the adept must first draw the stars of the Northern Dipper on a piece of silk that is then locked into a casket and only displayed during the actual performance of the exercise. After having delineated a sacred area by ordering the planets to take up guard around himself, he covers himself with the stars of the Dipper. Then he or she ascends into the constellation by turning along with it on the outside, by pacing its spirit and material souls as represented by the black stars, the counterpart or mirror image of the constellation which is arranged in a circle around it.

While doing this, the adept invokes the female divinities residing in this constellation, by calling their names and visualizing them with all their typical attributes. Only then can he or she pace the Dipper itself, visualize the divinities of every star on which he places a foot. The first pace is followed by nine others based on the Pace of Yu. Then the adept covers himself again with the stars of the Dipper, wraps himself in a vivid red cloud, ascends into the constellation, and revolves with it nine times. Finally, the meditator returns to the astral chart drawn on the earth, rubs the eyes, squeezes the nostrils, and chants a last invocation.

The exercise called "pacing the celestial network" is made up of several elements. The invocation formulas may change, but the principle remains the same. The exercise always consists of four parts.

First, "in one's mind," one begins by circumambulating the stars counterclockwise. Then one paces the Dipper after the fashion of the Pace of Yu, beginning with the first star and never setting more than one foot on each section.

Second, one walks around it clockwise, beginning with the last star and retracing one's earlier steps.

Third, one returns moving in the same fashion as in the first pace; one again begins with the first star, but now goes clockwise and sets out with the right foot. This is basically the yin replica of the first movement.

Fourth, one ends by going over all the stars again, however, this time one places both feet on every part.

On the basis of this fundamental, if rather complex, exercise, later Taoists have developed innumerable variants, such as "pacing the network of the Three Primordial Breaths" or "pacing the network of the Nine Phoenixes." The latter tend to be exorcistic dances of a cosmic character. The pace of the Dipper is also combined with similar exercises relating to the planets, the trigrams, and other objects.

The Center-On-High

What is the function of the Dipper? "The Dipper," says Sima Qian, "is the carriage of the emperor; it is placed in the center, . . . governs the four cardinal points, separates the yin and the yang, and determines the four seasons. It balances the five agents and arranges the divisions (of time) and the levels (of space). It fixates the various measures" (*Shiji*; Chavannes 1967: vol. 3: 342). It is quite remarkable to what degree Sima Qian already summarizes the major characteristics of the Dipper as they are found later in the Shangqing scriptures. More that merely inheriting the mainstream lineage of Chinese cosmology, of which Sima Qian is the spokesman, Shangqing Taoism also developed the tradition toward a higher precision and greater detail.

For the Taoists the Dipper means first of all the center of the universe, which establishes its inherent order. It is situated in the central palace of heaven, it is the foundation of the world, "the mysterious principle of the two symbols (yin and yang)." It is the "pivot of all creative transformations," "the mysterious root of the Nine Heavens, the bridge between the sun and the moon, the source of the ten thousand beings." The "myriad phenomena issue from there, the myriad spirits are its subordinates." Its character as the center of all is emphasized throughout: "The center is what people call the Northern Dipper," "the Northern Dipper is the great brilliant star of the central pole."

The Dipper is in fact an exultation of the center on earth, it is a vertical center where the middle of the earth is horizontal. What the Dipper is in the skies, Mount Kunlun is on earth: the vertical axis of the world. Whereas the symbolism of the sun and the moon was focused on the earth and could be imagined on a horizontal plane, situated between the four cardinal points stretched out through space, the relevance of the Dipper has to be seen in its role as the vertical, polar center of the cosmos. Where the sun and the moon were bipolar, the Dipper is polar. The North of the sky is the highest point of heaven; it symbolizes the unity of the universe on the plane of the zodiac. "The northern pole is the center of heaven," and the center of the earth is only its reflection. The sun corresponds to the human heart, made up of the element fire; the moon is related to the kidneys; and the Dipper is aligned with the spleen, the organ of the center. Here the essence of the Dipper assembles, and the Lord of the Dipper takes up his residence.

Great Unity

Positioned in the very center of the universe, the Dipper is also a symbol of the Great Unity, Taiyi. The *Dadong zhenjing* 大洞真經 (True Scripture of Great Pervasion; HY 6, fasc. 16–17) and the *Laozi zhongjing* 老子中經 (Central Scripture of Laozi; *Yunji qiqian* 18–19) both emphasize that the god Taiyi, the Lord of the Northern Pole, resides in the Dipper. Already Sima Qian notes that the banner of the god Taiyi contains the representation of the sun, the moon, and the Dipper.

Frequently the practices dealing with the sun and the moon are accompanied or followed by techniques involving the Dipper, such as a meditation on the constellation or a visualization of the Great One. More than that, the characteristics of the god Taiyi are very similar to those of the Dipper. Both are localized either in the skull, the representation of Mount Kunlun within human beings, in the heart, or in the navel. The points are the three human energy centers where the Three Primordial Breaths reside, often described as the Three Ones. These Three Ones are closely related to the Dipper already in their original shape as three primordial energies.

In its symbolism the Dipper is therefore very similar to the star of the central pole, to the god Taiyi. In one exercise adepts even meditate on the stars Fu and Bi together with the Polestar, thus forming a triad. This strongly indicates their similar nature. In the same vein, all symbols that represent the connection between unity and multiplicity, between the one and the many, the three original energies and the Three Ones, are closely associated with the Dipper.

The North: Matrix of Transformations

The North is the place of origin, the area of cyclical change where the embryonic stage and the process of gestation are located (at the cyclical signs *zi* 子, *ren* 壬, or *gui* 癸). The direction is symbolized by the agent water, which is where all life begins. In the North, the sun reaches its lowest point and in the middle of winter begins a new ascent. Here the germ of rebirth of the sun and the yearly cycle is found. For the same reason the Dipper is also called "the natural fire contained in the yin."

This general idea is borne out by the texts of Shangqing Taoism. The Northern Dipper is related to everything germinating, beginning, growing. Its stars open the seven orifices of the embryo and give him life. Its nine stars correspond to the nine transformations of Laozi in the course of the centuries and also to the nine mutations of the sacred cinnabar, the elixir of eternal life.

Nine, the number of the stars in the Dipper, relates the constellation to everything on earth and in the heavens that is related to this number: the Nine Breaths that give life to human beings, the Nine Regions of the earth, the Nine Palaces in the subtle physiology of the human head. Nine is the number of perfection, beginning with the transformations of the One.

The Northern Dipper is at the same time a place of origin and of return. The fact that certain days called Return to the Prime are dedicated to the divinities of the Dipper implies that its resident divinities preside over the changes that take place at the outset of life. They are actually the governors of "the changes, of the secret, and the return to the origin," they are the rulers who "protect the embryo and all the transformations of physical shape." The method of "opening the Three Passes" that causes the divinities of the Dipper to help is also called "method of joining and of the ten thousand transformations." On the level of space, the Dipper corresponds to the development of the primordial state, which develops in the world in myriad transformations and permutations and creates all life. It contains in concentrated form the essences of the five directions, represented by five of its divinities.

The Double Center: North and South, Life and Death, and the Underworld

The four cardinal points are marked by the Dipper in the center. This is true for Taoism as well as for ancient Chinese cosmology. The Dipper establishes the rhythm of the seasons, distinguishes good and evil, and decides about good fortune and disaster. Its essence is concentrated in one single star that shines on the top of the head of the good person but rests in darkness when the individual does evil. In that way it announces future happiness or misfortune. The texts describe the role of the Dipper as governing, directing, surveying, and judging. The Shangqing scriptures, unlike those of the Lingbao school, do not distinguish between several Dippers, but know only one Northern Dipper, which has a corresponding Carriage in the South. The Northern Dipper stands for the realm of the underworld, while the Southern Carriage leads adepts to eternal life. The divinities of the Northern Dipper are invoked to help them pass for registration in the Southern Carriage, where the true registers of immortality are kept (*Tianguan santu* 天關三圖 ; HY 1355, fasc. 1040).

The North is the area of the Great Yin that presides over death. It is located at the deepest bottom of yang and also found deep within the earth. In Taoist cosmology, there is one long central axis between North and South, heaven and earth, above and below, which crosses the horizontal line that connects the sun and the moon. The underworld is situated at the lowest point of the earth, which however reflects the highest point of heaven and is the exact mirror image of the realms-on-high. There is an essential unity between

Fig. 4. The Six Pavilions of the Underworld. *Source: Tianguan santu* 12ab

the underworld and paradise, a unity like that which joins yin and yang. The name of the first star of the Dipper expresses this symbolism: Clarity of Yang; the second is Essence of Yin.

Because the Dipper stands for both heaven and the underworld, every adept who invokes this constellation has also to know and address the six pavilions of the underworld (see figure 4) They are the counterparts to the Gates of the Heavens. Adepts must ultimately know and unify the two complementary planes, they must join them both in a perfect balance.

Celestial Darkness

Before adepts can pace the Dipper they must pass through the palaces of the female divinities surrounding it. These astral divinities radiate with a "light which never shines," they own a brilliance "without light." They are the Nine Yin, the nine goddesses of the Great Yin. A black light, a darkness floating around the pole of the sky, they are constantly in a state of non-action, of the profound tranquility that envelops the forces of nature and assembles them in their essences. In an inversion of the situation on earth, where yin (darkness) is within and yang (light) without, they are the yin that surrounds the yang within: the black halo of the radiant celestial center.

Gates and Steps: Celestial Dances

In the unity in multiplicity (one and nine) that connects North and South, yin and yang, life and death, the Dipper represents the gate of access, the passageway. Many typical characteristics reveal it in this light. The believer invokes the Dipper to pass from death to life; certain meditation methods involving the Dipper are called the Veneration of the Seven Stars Which Allow Passage. The seven passages refer to the pace of the Dipper, the seven stars are at the threshold of the Gates of Heaven. The last star of the Dipper is also known as the Celestial Gate, and sometimes the constellation as a whole is given that name. The lords of the Dipper give the practitioner the "talisman that opens the gate." They are closely related to the celestial passes and help the adept to jump over them, when he or she—after completing the pace of the Dipper—ascends to the Gates of the Heavens. The Dipper is the agent that allows the adept to pass. It judges and decides the itinerary; it secures further progress to the final goal. The adept thus turns about in the void, carried along by the divinities of the Dipper.

The passage is also symbolized by the Pace of Yu, the hero who opened the passes of the world so that the floods could flow freely. The Taoist dances

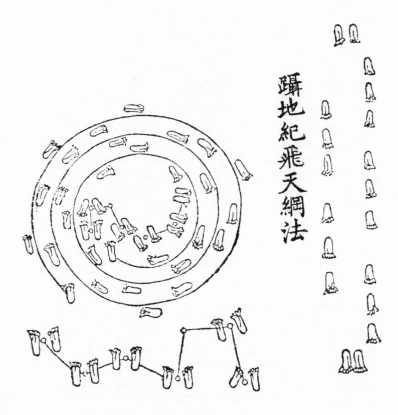

Fig. 5. The Pace of Yu. *Source: Taishang zhuguo jiumin zongzhen biyao*
大上助國救民總真秘要   3b (HY 1217, fasc. 986–987)

on the stars of the Dipper, but he also moves, following certain methods, on the networks that surround it. These are formed by the planets together with a group of twenty-five stars, black points arranged in five groups, one for each planet. A successful meditator must also complete a circumambulation of this cluster, which follows a labyrinthine course around a network both "winding and tortuous," as one text has it. This celestial network surrounds the entire center of the cosmos and serves for its defense. However, this network is also a carriage that transports the adept step by step to the last star of the Dipper, called the Celestial Gate. Here he turns and is finally elevated to the higher realms of heaven. Figure 5 depicts the Pace of Yu.

To begin with, practitioners walk the four corners of the world, to follow the sun and the moon in their courses, mark the corners of the world, and measure its four sections. Then they rise along the central axis that connects above and below, heaven and the underworld. It is right in the middle of the center of the universe, of the Dipper itself, and stands well between yin and yang. The Dipper, in conjunction with the couple of the sun and the moon, represents all the important powers of the sky concentrated in one single constellation. It assembles in one unity all that is measured by the sun and the moon.

Common Themes and Structures

Folds and Involutions

The first action a Taoist undertakes in meditation is to fold back into himself. Physically, he or she retires to the meditation chamber, to the "hall of purity," which must be isolated from normal human activities, utterly quiet and closed off. Another way to withdraw is to undertake purifying fasts and ablutions that precede the actual meditation practice. Mentally, the adept must "control the thoughts," "forget all human affairs," and "obliterate the body." Concentrating the mind with the eyes half closed keeps the vital energy within. Nothing else remains: no physical conditions, such as food or drink; no mental contents, such as visions and ideas. The meditator must be at the same time beyond the world and beyond all personal fantasies (Robinet 1979: 60–63).

Symbolically, then, the Four Heraldic Animals of the four directions, or their alter egos, the guardians of the four poles of the world, are invited to share the enclosure of the adept. Further within, these divinities are identical to the orbs of the adept's body. In a way, he or she is thus turned inside out, like a glove, with the inner organs standing by from without.

The meditation begins when "the two breaths are not yet separate," at a time that symbolizes and recovers the period of primordial chaos at the beginning of all creation. This again is a time that is beyond the world, the time when a new world makes its first appearance.

This new world, already structured in time and space, is that of Shangqing. All those adepts participate naturally in it who have legitimately received the sacred scriptures of this school. Initiation is attained only when someone is predestined for it and has special faculties for the spiritual—the so-called bones of immortality. The world of Shangqing is described in terms of the cosmology of yin and yang and the five agents. The act of receiving the sacred scriptures constitutes a contract that is absolutely necessary if the gates of this world are to be opened to the adept (Robinet 1979: 42; 1984: vol. 1: 370). The scriptures themselves are the "program" of the practitioner, the guide or vade mecum that shows the topology and nomenclature of the new world into which he or she is about to enter. The scriptures are the means by which this world can be made real, can be accessed. The gods who open the gates are described in detail, and their names are listed. More than that, they provide the necessary charms, talismans, keys, and passwords to the new realms.

Numerous symbols show the folding back of the adept, the withdrawal that is the first condition one must attain before beginning the meditation. There are the meandering curves of the Yellow River, which correspond to those of the intestines (Commentary to the *Dadong zhenjing*; see Robinet 1979: 178). Then there are the labyrinthine chambers of the Nine Heavens, which have their counterparts in the Yellow Springs and the "nine curves" of the underworld. Again, there is the design of the Pace on the Dipper, another form of the labyrinth.

Along with imitating the curved structures of the heavens, the underworld, and the abdomen, adepts clarify the forms of the various inner organs. The visualization of the interior illuminates all the divinities in the human body and makes them clearly visible. Taoists are thus their own true mirrors. They fill themselves with shapes of light and spirit. The body becomes truly a habitation of the gods. Just as if they were looking into one of those radiating mirrors, where the fire of heaven will appear and where the dew of heaven assembles, where one can see the approach of gods and demons in their "true forms," adepts look within themselves. Using mind and body as a spirit mirror, they illuminate and uncover the farthest corners of the world, where they then go to obtain rich essences, precious nourishments, and divine charms.

Folds and Repetitions

In a way meditation practice can be characterized as having a double nature. It is structurally very much like the talisman. The talisman, a very important feature of Shangqing practice, is bipartite. It is usually of two colors, cut into two halves, or written double. It is frequently written twice: one basic version and its exact mirror image. More than that, the talisman is the counterpart of the sacred scripture, the canon (see Kaltenmark 1960).

Scriptures themselves usually exist in double form. One copy is on the earth, but the true version, the original, remains always in heaven. The recitation practiced by the Taoists is a direct replica of that practiced by the gods. In addition, all gifts or tributes that adepts pay to their masters in return for instruction are double or cut in two. The *Dadong zhenjing* itself is structured in a very significant fashion: each of its thirty-nine sections encompasses two levels, one celestial, one physical. In fact, each section contains two sacred verses to be chanted to the divinities in the body, surrounded by those to be addressed to the gods above.

The Taoist universe itself is laid out on a double plan. The intestines or orbs are within what the planets are without. Whatever is below is just another version of what is above. The microcosm of the body and the macrocosm of the world correspond to and reflect one another. Whatever occurs in the body or mind of human beings happens at the same time in the heavens above. The same name is often used to refer to a place in heaven and a sacred area within the human body. The Purple Chamber, for example, is the highest palace in heaven as well as a cave within the human skull. When the adept goes there for a visit, he goes into his skull as much as into the sky.

Inversion

The movement of inversion follows the folding, repetitious movement of involution. The mirror reflects; it forms a counterpart. Yet it reflects inside out, it reverses the image. In the same way, the meditation reverses the forms, the situations, and the values of normal life.

A descent may result in being on top, in arriving in the grotto heavens, for example, which, though deep down in the earth, open toward heaven. As one transforms the bottom into the top, so one changes death into life. The same process applies to the semen. Instead of being used in sexual intercourse it is redirected to the top of the head, where it nourishes the essential life-force of human beings. Instead of giving life to another being, it is used to prolong and renew one's own. The North of heaven above corresponds to the North of earth below, yet the latter opens not toward heaven but toward the underworld, located deep within the earth. The six courts of the underworld are then invoked when the adept journeys towards the heavens-on-high.

The same holds true for the symbolism of light and darkness. The practitioner can make visible what remains commonly invisible—as for instance the gods—just as the magical mirrors show the true shapes of the demons disguised in some other form to the ordinary eye. At the same time the adept is able to make invisible what one can normally see. For this he invokes the Nine Dark Divinities of the Dipper, the Nine Queens of Yin, of the dark around the Dipper. In contrast to nature, where the deep dark yin quietly rests within itself and the radiant yang shines outside, in the heavenly spheres the yin is outside and shines with a black light and the yang is at rest within. More than that, the Taoist can also—another paradox—transform himself into light in order to make himself invisible: he "hides in and escapes to the sun."

Inversion means a reversal. This is the direction the adept sets out to in the beginning of the search for the origins (Robinet 1979: 174–176). He or she goes back to the time of birth and does not progress toward the end as normal people do. Thus the *Huangting jing* 黃庭經 (Scripture of the Yellow Court) says: "The attainment of the Tao is found in a circular movement of return; it is possible to return to one's origin by mutation. The circular return has to be repeated nine times, then one can achieve the virtue of heaven" (Robinet 1979: 136).

Patternings and Imbrications

The luminaries are joined and patterned into heaven just as the talisman is in the belly of the fish in the water. Enclosed in the body of the adept who keeps them there are the divinities who illuminate the interior. The body with its quality of yin heavily envelops the spirits, luminous and light.

Sacred time is marked by certain days and hours, imbricated into the normal time of everyday life. Supernatural space is patterned into ordinary space, such as, for example, the bed to which the adept returns when emerging from meditations. Everything is patterned and imbricated: a day in a year, the microcosm within the macrocosm, and vice versa. A small chamber doubly locked contains in itself the whole world recreated, represented in symbols and signs, special landmarks and passwords. The Taoist is within the world, and the world is within the Taoist. The symbolic world is created by the spirit of the adept, the spirit in itself is created by the world.

The male divinities of the Dipper turn about the sky surrounded by a ring of darkly shining black stars, of female deities. Yang here manifests within yang, yet at the same time yin also manifests within yang, just as within the moon there is the rabbit, and within the trigram Kan (water) there is the unbroken line of yang. This is the "yang within the yin" of the alchemists, the light hidden in the darkness, just as the celestial talisman is hidden in the belly of the fish, which itself is in the water.

The importance of saliva is evident in all the exercises mentioned. It is called "golden fluid," "jade liquid," or "sweet dew." It is the yin within the yang of the body (its upper section); it corresponds to the "energy of the kidneys," the yang within the yin.

Opening and Closing

Opening and closing play a central role in the practices of Shangqing Taoism, described, for example, in the frequently used expression *lihe* 離合 (Robinet 1979: 165). The adept withdraws to the meditation chamber, half closes the eyes, and retains the breath. The walls surrounding the chamber together with the presence of protecting divinities are positive signs, since they help the adept construct a new and sacred space. The closing movement is a positive and necessary action. Similarly, the adept closes the gates of death by expelling the breath of mortality and summoning various spirits to guard the gates. Here again opening may turn out to be harmful, because if the vital fluids are allowed to escape, the divinities might leave. Energy will be dispersed, just as knowledge is dispersed when the secrets of the school are being passed on improperly. Inversely, an opening movement may be necessary and helpful when the gods arrive from the heavens.

On the other hand, there is a negative aspect to the movement of closing. It is not desirable to close up and block the free circulation of vital energy within the body, an energy symbolized by the "knots of mortality of the embryo" (Robinet 1979: 213–219). The practitioner must loosen these knots in the meditation practice with the help of the gods. It is necessary to make oneself empty to guarantee the vital energy the utmost freedom of circulation. Emptiness here means absence of blockage and not, as in other traditions, an abyss or a moat separating human beings from the gods.

Coming and Going

To the extent the Taoist knows how to guard the souls, he or she is also able to journey with them. Ecstatic excursions to the four corners of the world are the inversion of the assembly of the four poles within the body. The extreme expansion, the outgoing movement, is the counterpart or the recovery of the far-off realms within. This is true especially for the horizontal expansion.

Vertically, the adept ascends while the gods descend. Ascent and descent intersect and mirror one another, showing at the same time high elevation and deep profundity. The gods ascend together with the adept but descend alone. The descent of the adept is the initial withdrawal to the realm within, the pivot of all the following exercises. The descent inward may lead the adept to the first encounter with the divinities in the body. The adept descends in the same manner as the gods themselves; they are the agents as well as the place of the descent.

Above: unity and fusion; below: extension and multiplicity. The Taoist unifies with the One and divides with the multiple. Along the vertical line, yang is above and yin is below; along the horizontal line, yin contracts toward the center, yang expands toward the periphery. Dissolution and coagulation, absorption and manifestation, inhalation and exhalation form a rhythmical movement. It characterizes the "opening and closing" of the *Yijing*. It is present in the meditation practice as an interiorization of the external and an externalization of the internal: light is absorbed and gushes outward.

Resolution and Fusion

Many images are set into one structure while the various movements described above are going on. Their balance is represented by the Dipper as the agent that coordinates the coming and going, ascent and descent, expansion and contraction. The very name of the stars of this constellation shows its double character: Clarity of Yang and Essence of Yin. The Pace of Yu, danced by the Taoist on the stars of the Dipper, symbolizes the passage from one sphere to another. The subtly androgynous character of the god of the Great One, called both Fatherly Peace and Motherly Essence, shows the same interrelatedness of the two spheres. Again, there is hierogamic interaction of the various attributes of the sun and the moon in their joint or alternating course (Robinet 1984: vol. 1: 287–292). The highest god holding the sun and the moon, the primordial One, is a sign of the ultimate resolution and harmony of the movements. So are the numbers three, especially in its form as the Three Ones to be visualized in the energy centers of the body, and nine (three times three), the number of completion, of perfection, of complete reunion.

Another form the merging of the extremes takes is the intervention of the deities, such as the revelation of the Shangqing scriptures by the young goddess to Yang Xi (*Zhengao* 1.14a). There are, furthermore, the "bridge" she wants to establish between "mountains and marshes" (yang and yin), the harmony she wants to ensure between the "hard and the soft" (symbols of yang and yin in the *Yijing*), the special fruits she brings to him (1.13a), and— last but not least—her spirit marriage with the seer, with Yang Xi himself.

Again, there is the image of the spiral, which represents the "tornado" (Robinet 1979: 169–183), a curled power that creates the world and moves in alternating motions of advance and retreat. The image of the spiraling wind unifies the two main concepts of time, irreversibly linear and eternally cyclical, and simultaneously contains a steady upward motion of ascent. It is at the same time a curve that bends back onto itself and a route that leads to ever further progress. The same paradox may be seen in the way Chinese in general understand things. They never stray from their emphasis on turning toward the past in order to discover the new. The tornado is a sign of the return to the origin, of the adept's rebirth as a newborn baby enveloped in clouds of light.

Light is a symbol of the recovery of time and space in a new universe. Newly created by the meditator, this universe participates in the primordial energy underlying all existence as much as it is part of the specific spirit of each practitioner. It comes into being through the active interaction of the knowledge the Taoist receives from the gods. Placed in a completely new world, it is animated by the very breaths of life and continues to be created incessantly. It is complex and consists of multiple forms, yet it has a thorough inner organization. It represents plurality resolved in ultimate unity.

In the world of the Taoist practitioner, duality only exists in unity. Unity, on the other hand is found only in the form of a fundamental duality. Both span the disjunctive tension between the two poles that activate the spiraling movement. The ultimate unreality of this world is clear. It does not exist except in the practitioner's visions, even though these visions are constructed according to a given pattern, to instructions received from the gods themselves through the sacred scriptures. Its reality is founded on a knowledge true to the individual subject, proved by his or her experience and lived out actively. It is shared by all the other adherents to the same set of beliefs, by all practitioners of Shangqing Taoism. But it remains unreal in that it is essentially a representation.

These Taoist scriptures describe and analyze, in a more tangible and more verifiable form than is common in everyday life, the nature of reality as framed by the unreal—by the conscious mind and the representations it necessarily makes of things. Mental images and abstract conceptions are ultimately what makes conscious perception of any reality possible. Yet these images and conceptions are always, if to an infinitely small degree, different from the outer objects they represent. They are in fact a translation by means of cultural tools—of which language is the first.

References

Atlan, Henri. 1986. *A tort et à raison.* Paris: Le Seuil, 1986.

Chavannes, Edouard. 1967. *Les Memoires Historiques.* Paris: Adrien Maisonneuve, 1967.)

Corbin, Henri. 1953. *Etude préliminaire pour le livre réunissant les deux sagesses.* Paris: Adrien Maisonneuve, 1953.

Engelhardt, Ute. 1987. *Die klassische Tradition der Qi-Übungen: Eine Darstellung anhand des Tang-zeitlichen Textes Fuqi jingyi lun von Sima Chengzhen.* Wiesbaden: Franz Steiner, 1987.

Graham, A.C. 1960. *The Book of Lieh-tzu.* London: A. Murray, 1960.

Granet, Marcel. 1926. *Danses et légendes de la Chine ancienne.* 2 vols. Paris: F. Alcan, 1926.

—— 1950. *La pensée chinoise.* Paris: Albin, 1950.

Hawkes, David. 1959. *Ch'u Tz'u: The Songs of the South.* New York and Oxford: Oxford University Press, 1959.

Kaltenmark, Maxime. 1960. "Ling-pao: Note sur un terme du Taoisme religieux," *Mélanges publiés par l'Institut des Hautes Etudes Chinoises* 2 (1960), 559–588.

Robinet, Isabelle. 1976. "Les randonées extatiques des taoistes dans les astres," *Monumenta Serica* 32 (1976), 159–273.

—— 1979. *Méditation taoiste.* Paris: Dervy Livres, 1979.

—— 1984. *La révélation du Shangqing dans l'histoire du Taoisme.* 2 vols. Paris: Publications de l'Ecole Francaise d'Extrême-Orient, 1984.

Schafer, Edward. 1981. "Wu Yün's 'Cantos on Pacing the Void,'" *Harvard Journal of Asiatic Studies* 41.2 (1981), 377–415.

Watson, Burton. 1968. *The Complete Works of Chuang-tzu.* New York: Columbia University Press, 1968.

Chapter Seven

Taoist Insight Meditation: The Tang Practice of *Neiguan*

Livia Kohn

Defining Insight Meditation

Contemporary psychological research on meditation and altered states of consciousness defines insight meditation or mindfulness meditation as an advanced type of meditation practice in which the practitioner maintains an open awareness to all stimuli in an undiscriminating fashion. It contrasts insight meditation with concentrative meditation, in which practitioners fixate their entire attention on a single object (Walsh 1984: 28). The two types of meditation are fundamentally different. Beginners are trained to keep their minds under control, but advanced meditators are instructed to apply the power of concentration indiscriminately to all sensual stimuli they receive. In so doing, they should come to reevaluate their experiences and worldview according to the teaching accompanying the meditation practice.[1]

---

1. This definition and distinction is based on studies of the various meditation techniques commonly available in the United States. Such techniques include Transcendental Meditation, Zen, and Tibetan Tantric as well as Theravadin practices. Since the Buddhist tradition is highly represented in the basic data, the ensuing theories also reflect Buddhist notions and systematizations. On the other hand, these contemporary theories are in no way apt to fully describe the complexity of the Buddhist meditative tradition. It is not my primary purpose here to compare Taoist and Buddhist forms of meditation; rather, I want to understand Taoist concepts and practices better. For this, I prefer to begin with a very

Psychological studies of patterns of perception in advanced mindfulness meditators of a Theravadin-type meditation, a school called Insight Meditation that follows the Burmese lineage of the Venerable Mahasi Sayadaw, found that subjects tended to perceive themselves and their environment in terms of energy-in-motion or of empty space (Brown and Engler 1984: 245). Moreover, the energies were very often seen as present within the human body:

> The number of references to bodily parts and internal organs and the psychic energy centers within the body is very high. . . One possible interpretation of this contiguity between body and energy responses is that insight into bodily (and mental) processes becomes a vehicle through which to observe the fundamental energy transformation of body/mind/universe. (Brown and Engler 1984: 248)

This description of the worldview of advanced insight practitioners applies suggestively to the higher stages of Taoist meditation as described in Tang dynasty materials, especially in texts by the famous Shangqing patriarch Sima Chengzhen 司馬承禎 (647–735) and other writers of this period like Sun Simiao 孫思邈 (581–672) and Wu Yun 吳筠 (?–778). The main text used here is the *Neiguan jing* 内觀經 (Scripture on Inner Observation) by an anonymous author. It is translated in full in the latter portion of this chapter. Other important texts cited are

1. Sima Chengzhen's *Tianyinzi* 天隱子 (DZ 1026, fasc. 672),[2] which outlines the mystical process in five stages: fasting and abstention; seclusion; visualization and imagination; sitting in oblivion; spirit liberation (Kohn 1987a);

2. Sima Chengzhen's *Zuowanglun* 坐忘論 (Discourse on Sitting in Oblivion; DZ 1036, fasc. 704), which gives the meditator's progress in seven steps: respect and faith; interception of karma; taming the mind; detachment from affairs; true observation; intense concentration; realizing the Tao (Kohn 1987);

---

general definition and to later look at specific Taoist and Buddhist descriptions pertinent to the present topic.

2. Texts in the Taoist Canon (*Daozang*, hereafter abbreviated DZ) are given according to the number of the reduced sixty-volume edition published in Taipei and Kyoto. These numbers coincide with those found in K.M. Schipper, *Concordance du Tao Tsang* (Paris: Publications de l'Ecole Francaise d'Extrême-Orient, 1975). "Fasc." stands for "fascicle" and refers to the volume number of the 1925 Shanghai reprint of the original canon of 1445 (*Zhengtong Daozang*).

3. An inscription, also called *Zuowanglun*, which is dated to the year 829 and was placed before a temple dedicated to Sima Chengzhen on Mount Wangwu (Wu 1981: 46a).

The inscription is related to Wu Yun's *Shenxian kexue lun* 神仙可學 論 (Spirit Immortality Can Be Learned; DZ 1051, fasc. 726–727; 2.9b–16a), while the appendix to the *Zuowanglun*, the *Dingguan jing* 定觀經 (Scripture on Concentration and Observation; DZ 400, fasc. 189; *Yunji qiqian* 雲笈七籤 17.1a–6b), goes back to Sun Simiao's *Cunshen lianqi ming* 存神鍊氣銘 (Visualization of Spirit and Refinement of Breath; DZ 834, fasc. 571; *Yunji qiqian* 33.12a–14b).

According to these sources, adepts of Taoist meditation first undergo periods of physical and psychological purification through fasting, bathing, and completely withdrawing from the world. Next, they control their desires and emotions by fixing their attention on the lower cinnabar field in the abdomen. Once they have attained complete physical health and full mental control, they are guided to critically examine phenomena by concentrating on the body. This process is taken over to a large extent from Buddhist models, but the results are formulated in Taoist terms: adepts increasingly realize that body and mind, they are nothing but a part of the Tao, the eternal flux of creation, the primordial energy of the universe. They dissolve to become one with creation, and the state of immortality is attained. The practice of insight meditation in Taoism may be understood as a conscious adaptation of Buddhist techniques of meditation and metaphysical concepts into the realm of higher Taoist theory and practice.

Neiguan in the Tang

How did the Tang Taoists practice insight meditation, thus understood as a technique aimed at completely revolutionizing the meditators' worldview? Let us begin with the terminology employed. The term used for insight meditation is *guan* 觀, which in the ancient dictionary *Shuowen jiezi* 說文解 字 is explained as "to scrutinize," "to examine carefully." In Buddhist texts *guan* translates *vipaśyanā*, insight meditation, which contrasts with *zhi* 止, cessation.

In Taoism *guan* goes together with *ding* 定, a borrowing from the Buddhist term for *dhyāna*, which, however, is also used together with *guan* in denoting the *śamatha-vipaśyanā* pair. To distinguish Buddhist and Taoist usages for concentrative and mindfulness meditation respectively, I use cessation and insight for the Buddhist *zhiguan* and concentration and observation for the Taoist *dingguan*. To translate *guan* as observation also has the advantage that one can give its verb form as to observe.

Neiguan, "inner observation," (often also given as "inner vision") is used in Chinese religious literature in general in a very broad sense. It refers to the active, conscious introspection of one's own body and mind. As such it is sometimes even used interchangeably with *shouyi*, "guarding the One." Not only the subtler energies of life, but also the gods and spirits who habitate the human body are thereby revealed to the practitioner who, according to the *Neiguan jing*, is instructed to see the body as part of heaven and earth, raised through yang and nourished by yin, helped and guarded by the spirit and material souls, organized in accordance with the five agents and the six tones, radiating with the power of the seven stars and eight luminaries.

The body is an exact microcosmic replica of the starry heavens above: it contains a large variety of palaces and chambers. The deities who reside in the paradises of the otherworld are as much at home in the body. Although human beings by nature are endowed in this way, they cannot comprehend it, because the senses produce delusion and cause the rise of a discriminatory consciousness.

Spirit, the primordial, formless, and ever-changing force, which in connection with the physical body causes human beings to be alive, is then no longer at rest in the mind, where it occurs in most concentrated form. Ideally, spirit working through the human mind would govern life perfectly, but instead it is wasted on sensual amusements and exertions of eyes, ears, mouth, nose, body, and mind. Confused and defiled, human beings need to be taught how to recover the primordial state.

First, one must realize the impermanent nature of the personal body. One has to see oneself as a mere assemblance of energy, essence, and spirit. Already the *Zhuangzi* has:

> The human life is a coming-together of energy. If it comes together there is life. If it scatters there is death. (58/22/11; Watson 1968: 235)[3]

Thus the body is only part of the continuous natural transformations of energy; according to Liezi, it is merely "borrowed from heaven and earth" (*Liezi* 1; Graham 1960: 29). Yet it resembles them closely in its structuring. The physical body undergoes the same transformations as all creation: it is bound to return to "dust and ashes" (*Xisheng jing* 7). More than that, it is also

---

3. The *Zhuangzi* is quoted according to *A Concordance to Chuang-tzu*, Harvard-Yenching Institute Sinological Index Series, Supplement no. 20 (Cambridge, Massachusetts: Harvard University Press, 1956).

quite unstable within itself. There is no true master of body and mind (*Zhuangzi* 2), nor do we have any conscious control over its transformations (*Zhuangzi* 58/22/25).

Next, practitioners must see that they usually are unable to let the body go on changing as it pleases. Rather, the body becomes "the reason why I have terrible vexations. If I didn't have a personal body, what vexations would I have?" This famous quotation from chapter 13 of the *Daode jing* is used frequently in Tang dynasty mystical literature. Li Rong 李榮 , one of representatives of the Twofold Mystery school of the seventh century, comments on this passage as given in the *Xisheng jing* 西昇經 (Scripture of Western Ascension; DZ 726, fasc. 449–450):

> Having a body means having vexations and adversities. Frustrated by sight and hearing, tortured by taste and smell, one is subject to pain, irritation, heat, and cold. (chap. 7; 2.9b)

Later on he says,

> As soon as there is a body, the hundred worries compete to arise and the five desires (of the senses) hurry to make their claims. (chap. 17; 4.5b)

Here it becomes clear that for Taoists the term "body" (*shen* 身) means the various emotional and psychological values attached to oneself, not simply the body as a physical entity.

Only when the negative aspects of the body and one's captivity in the clutches of the senses have been fully taken in can one turn one's attention to the heavenly qualities inherent in the body. This consitutes a third step in the practice of Taoist insight meditation. The body should now be seen as the storehouse of inner nature, as the habitation of the spirit, as the vehicle or the host of the spirit or the Tao. This resides in the body like a ruler in his country (*Huangting neijing jing* 27:6). Similarly, the body is called the "vessel" of the Tao, and one need only look inside to find the Tao right there (*Xisheng jing* 12; *Huainanzi* 11.7b). The Tao, spirit, inner nature, and sometimes even virtue are described as the rulers and inhabitants of the physical body. It is only due to their activity that the body is alive at all.

To realize the Tao within one has to understand oneself fully as part of it. One finds the Tao by looking inside, by visualizing the body as a replica of the universe. By identifying with the Tao that governs and inhabits the body one loosens attachments to the physical self and begins to develop a new and wider identity as part of the universe at large. One comes to see oneself truly as a being of spirit that is merely housed in this fragile physical framework that will be subject to all the transformations the spirit transcends.

Dealing with Everyday Life

The Tang mystical texts say that true immortality is attained only upon physical death, when the spirit-self ascends to heaven and takes up its post in the hierarchy of the otherworld; but immortals also exist on earth. For them, training in insight meditation has certain practical consequences. How does an immortal deal with everyday life?

Sima Chengzhen's *Zuowanglun* contains a section entitled "True Observation" (Kohn 1987), in which he gives practitioners concrete advice about proper attitudes toward questions of everyday life.

How, for instance, should one relate to worldly necessities like food and clothing? One should see them for what they really are: vehicles, means to an end. They are necessary but have to be abandoned in due course. Like a raft that is used to cross an ocean, they cannot be abandoned before one has completed the trip but should not be carried around afterward either.[4]

What should one do if one is still attached to sensuality? Again: see it as it is! Sensuality, Sima Chengzhen explains, is pure imagination with no solid reality behind it. He cites the famous example from the *Zhuangzi*: If there is perfect beauty in the world, why do fish or birds flee in terror at the sight of a most beautiful woman?

How does one eliminate all feelings of enmity and hatred? One must begin to see these feelings as harmful to oneself. "To see another do evil," he insists, "and give rise to enmity and hatred in one's own mind is just like seeing someone kill himself and promptly sticking out one's own neck to accept the other's blade and get killed oneself."

What if I am deeply distressed by the state of extreme poverty I am in? Try to find out who made you poor, comes the prompt advice. Heaven and earth? Why should they? Your parents? Certainly they wanted you to be happy! Spirits and other people? They are far too busy with their own troubles to make you poor. The conclusion must be that all one experiences is due to the karma produced by oneself and to the fate one has before heaven. One has to accept whatever cannot be avoided or changed.

---

4. This remark of Sima Chengzhen represents a Taoist adaptation of the Buddhist parable of the raft. In Buddhism the raft is a metaphor for the teaching of the Buddha, which, after crossing the ocean of rebirth (*saṃsāra*), has fulfilled its purpose and should not be turned into a burden; in Taoism the ocean is life in society, not the cycle of life and death, and the raft is an image for the necessities one needs to survive as a social human being. The passage shows not only the enormous concern of Taoists for social life (quite to the contrary of common Confucian prejudices), but also the limitations of Taoist ideas of liberation when compared with those of Buddhism.

What if I have some painful disease? Then it is recommended that one realize first that all this suffering originates with one's identity in a personal body. Next, one should examine this body and find that there is no true master, neither mental nor physical. The third step is to realize that all one's conceptions, plans, and ideas are just passing phenomena and only arise from delusion. Then all feelings of sickness will be thoroughly eliminated.

What if it comes to death? Death has to be considered as a change of residence for the spirit. The aging body is to be seen as "a house with rotting walls. Once it becomes uninhabitable it is best to abandon it in time and look for another place to stay." One has to learn to be as unattached to the physical transformations of this world as the Tao itself, to regard death as part of the natural process of transformation. "Desiring eternal life in this body," says Sima Chengzhen, "how is it possible?"

Meditation versus Immortality

This mystical attitude is apparently contradictory to the ideal of immortality in Taoism. Yet, as mentioned above, according to the Tang Taoists, true immortality is found only after ascent into heaven, a state that may be tasted prematurely in ecstatic excursions to the otherworldly realms above. On the other hand, the state of oneness with the Tao is as close as one can get to immortality while still alive in this world. And this state of oneness implies an utter equanimity toward life and death, health and sickness, gain and loss, wealth and poverty—a going-beyond all common human values and fears. The mental change in attitude insight meditation will produce is part and parcel of the creation of the immortal embryo, the truly immortal body made gradually from pure energy, essence, spirit, and finally the Tao itself. This physical body is "a house with rotting walls," but the spirit-body of immortality will exist forever in accordance with and yet beyond the changes, just as the Tao itself does.

Insight meditation in Taoism developed under a strong Buddhist influence, presumably of the Tiantai school. This is evidenced by the various kinds of observation given in the *Daojiao yishu* 道教義樞 (The Pivotal Meaning of the Taoist Teaching 5.5b–6b; DZ 1129, fasc. 762–763). Here we have first of all observation of energy as contrasted with observation of spirit. These are explained as concentration and insight, respectively. Second we find the threefold set of observation of real existence, observation of apparent existence, and observation of partial emptiness. In their terminology, these three closely resemble Tiantai Buddhist descriptions, but in their contents they are more similar to the practice outlined by Sima Chengzhen in his *Zuowanglun*. What comes closest to Tiantai meditation is yet another set of three, given in the *Daojiao yishu*: observation of apparent existence, observation of emptiness, and observation of the middle (Kamata 1963: 211). As an example of this more sophisticated level of insight meditation let us look at the description of the second set.

> As concerns the observation of apparent existence, "apparent" means having a temporary appearance, whereas "existence" refers to the embodiment of things. . . .
>
> For example, when it comes to understanding the fact that the five aggregates [matter, sensations, perception, mental formations, and consciousness] make up oneself, how could one know which aggregate is oneself? Thus the *Zhuangzi* [4/2/16] says: "The hundred joints, the nine orifices, the six repositories all come together and exist here. But which part should I feel closest to?"
>
> If you don't feel very close to any one part as the one that constitutes yourself, you have begun to understand the emptiness of apparent existence. This is what we call observation of apparent existence.
>
> Observation of real existence deals with the substance-reality of everything. Knowing already that all apparent existence is empty, you must now observe and examine the substance-reality underlying it. What actually is its substance-reality? Where does it come from? It must arise from something else. But if we assume that it arises from something else, we come to an endless chain of origination.
>
> If we assume, on the other hand, that this chain is not endless, then substance-reality must ultimately come from emptiness. If we now assume that it arises from emptiness, we must duly attempt to grasp this emptiness. But as emptiness is nothing in itself, how can we say that it brings forth something? This way we understand that real existence cannot be accepted either. This is the observation of real existence.
>
> Observation of partial emptiness. Here "partial" means not yet proper, whereas "emptiness" refers to a free and pervading way of seeing. This is practiced in order to get rid of all the numerous diseases of attachment which all beings are suffering. Thereby one comes to realize true emptiness little by little. (5.4b–5a)

The two major methods given here, observation of apparent and real existence, ultimately go back to the *Zhuangzi*, especially to the second chapter, "Seeing Things as Equal." Here it is stated that there is no single physical agent that controls the body and the question of the ultimate origins of all existence is asked. This early document already emphasizes the impossibility of grasping the true functioning of oneself and the world—the futility of all human knowledge. But the ultimate consequence for the meditator, the realization that he himself is as empty as his efforts, is not reached. Rather, as Guo Xiang has it in his commentary to the *Zhuangzi*, "we must understand that things are what they are spontaneously and not caused by anything else" (Knaul 1985: 19).

Buddhism in a New Guise?

The mystical ideal found in these texts appears to reflect basic Buddhist notions of salvation very closely. Adepts are made to realize that the world is as impermanent as they are. Practitioners come to see that everything is changing without interruption (*anitya*), and they are led to give up any personal identity or well-defined self (*anātman*). They are also promised complete freedom from suffering, which, caused by desires, rules all human existence (*duhkha*). The way to mystical realization, moreover, is described as a process of mental purification, and practitioners must accept certain precepts regarding their behavior. Abstention from meat, strong spices, and alcohol is required for the period of intense meditation; sexual intercourse is prohibited as well.

Can we therefore conclude that the type of Taoist theory and practice found in certain Tang dynasty documents is just another form of Buddhism? The answer is yes and no.

We may affirm the assumption insofar as much of the terminology and many of the concrete practices involved were taken from Buddhist sources. When Buddhism began to be recognized as a teaching in its own right in the fifth century, its infiltration into the indigenous Chinese religious scene did not stop. Rather, it continued to be a source of inspiration for native Chinese religious thinkers. It found its way into the Taoist Canon in many different guises: not only philosophical concepts, but also cosmological ideas (Zürcher 1980), formal rites, and everyday religious practices of Buddhism were imitated and newly interpreted by the growing Taoist community. In many of its facets Taoism has thus come to represent an intimate and more indigenous adaptation of Buddhism than the Chinese Buddhist schools themselves.

Yet the theory is also incorrect, because every single item in the description of the process of Taoist mysticism goes beyond its Buddhist appearance and is deeply rooted in the indigenous Chinese tradition. The worldview underlying the theory, and the deeper reasons behind the practices, as well as the exact procedure of practice itself, can be traced back to Chinese thought well before the Buddhist conquest.

The notion of eternal change and ongoing transformation of all things, for example, is part of the very early Chinese speculation about the world. Being and non-being are alternate states of the same cycle of existence. Change is what existence means, it is neither deplorable nor delightful. Thus in Taoist mysticism there is ultimately no search for a transcendent permanence beyond. Although many texts speak of a "going beyond of the world," the primary aim of meditation is to "equalize" all things. Equalizing as used in the *Zhuangzi* is interpreted by Guo Xiang as "in life be happy with life, in death go along with death" (chap. 18).

Again, no-self in Taoism does not suggest the denial of any personal entity whatsoever. Rather, it refers to the transformation of a self defined through social norms and values to a self going along and at one with the very agent of eternal change, the Tao itself. This transformation of self will at the same time annihilate all suffering, which, though part of all human existence as we know it, is not originally necessary in the world. The world in harmony with the Tao is free from all affliction. Suffering is thus explained in Taoism as a disharmony with the Tao or the spirit. It develops due to the arousal of desire and engagement in sensual pleasures, which squanders vital human energies. The precepts, finally, are aimed not so much at morality as at enhancing physical health. To keep the divinities in one's body strong and vigorous is a prerequisite for attaining higher stages.

The cosmological theory that is activated in the practice of Taoist insight meditation should therefore be seen as an indigenous Chinese development of Buddhist concepts, just as the actual practice is strongly influenced by Buddhist techniques. But insight meditation in Taoism is also a direct continuation of specifically Taoist cosmological concepts and meditation practices. The image of the body to be created by the meditator is based on ancient Chinese notions. It includes Taoist beliefs in the deities who reside in the microcosm of the body as much as in their astral realms. And it encompasses basic concepts of Buddhist psychology. Meditation methods include both visualization of the body gods and abstract analysis of the position of human beings in the universe. Similarly, descriptions of the realized state to be attained through the practice, though expressed to a large extent in Buddhist terms, can be traced back to the *Zhuangzi* and its adaptation in Taoism, found in texts such as the *Xisheng jing*. The ultimate goal of immortality never fades from sight.

Scripture on Inner Observation[5]

(Translation)

The Venerable Lord said:

[1b] Heaven and earth mingle their essences; yin and yang engage in interchange. Thus the myriad beings come to life each receiving a particular life: yet all are alike in that they have a share in the life-giving Tao.[6]

When father and mother unite in harmony, man receives life.

In the first month, essence and blood coagulate in the womb.

In the second month, the embryo begins to take shape.

In the third month, the yang spirit arouses the three spirit souls to come to life.

In the fourth month, the yin energy settles the seven material souls as guardians of the body.[7]

In the fifth month, the five agents are distributed to the five orbs to keep their spirit at peace.

In the sixth month, the six pitches are set up in the six repositories nourishing the vital energy.[8]

In the seventh month, the seven essential stars open the body orifices to let the light in.

---

5. The main edition used for this translation is the version found in DZ 641, fasc. 342. Frequent recourse has been taken to the variant contained in *Yunji qiqian* 17, which will in each specific case be indicated in a footnote. The page numbers indicated in brackets [ ] in the text, however, refer to the DZ edition.

6. Guo Xiang in his commentary to the *Zhuangzi* (1.1.a; DZ 745, fasc. 507–519) summarizes the meaning of the first chapter of this text by saying: "Though beings may be big or small, . . . in that they all have a share [in the Tao] they should go along with in a state of free and easy wandering, they are all alike."

7. A detailed explanation of the meaning and role of these various souls is found in *Yunji qiqian* 54. The three spirit souls are called Womb Radiance, Numen Guide, and Gloomy Essence. They are associated with heaven, the Five Agents, and earth, respectively. The first spirit soul always strives for the purity of man; the second always wishes him involved in manifold affairs; the third, finally, produces his desire for pleasure and comfortable living. The seven material souls are described as "turbid demons" in the human body (7b). Rather than retaining them as one has to do with the spirit souls, one should strive to control them. They have each a special name, too, such as Corpse Dog, Devouring Robber, Slanted Arrow, and so on. Specific methods of meditation, concentrative and visualization practices, are recommended to keep them from taking over and causing death. Figure 1 shows depictions of the various souls.

8. The five orbs are the liver, lungs, kidneys, spleen, and heart (see *Huangting neijing jing* 22:13; *Yunji qiqian* 11–12; see also Schipper 1975). The six repositories are the gall, stomach, bladder, small and large intestines, and the navel (*Huangting waijing jing* A 56).

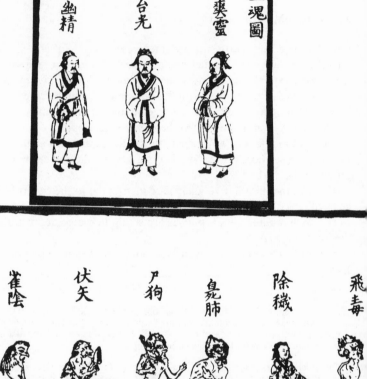

Fig. 1. The Three Spirit and Seven Material Souls. *Source: Taishang chu sanshi jiuchong baosheng jing* 太上除三尸九蟲保生經 3ab (DZ 871, fasc. 580)

In the eighth month, the eighth phosphor spirits descend with their true vital energy.[9]

In the ninth month, the various palaces and chambers are properly arranged to keep the essence safe.

In the tenth month, the energy is strong enough to complete the image.[10] Man's feeding on primordial harmony is never interrupted. The Lord Emperor of the Great One resides in the head. He is called the Lord of the Niwan Palace. He governs the host of spirits. What makes life shine forth and lets man know of the spirits is his spirit soul. [2a] Siming, the Administrator of Destiny resides in the heart. He regulates the prime energies of life.[11] Wuying occupies his left, from where he regulates the three spirit souls. Baiyuan occupies the right, from where he regulates the seven material souls. Taohai resides in the navel, where he preserves the root of the essence.

What makes the various joints of the body function together are the hundred manifestations of the spirit of life.[12] As it pervades the whole of the body, spirit is not empty. When primordial energy enters through the nose and reaches the *niwan* in the center of the head, the spirit light radiates and the body is stable and at peace. For all movement and rest, however, it fully depends on the mind. This is how life first begins.

When you now observe yourself in detail and with care, beware of the mind. As the ruler of the self it can prohibit and control everything. It is

---

9. The seven essential stars are the five planets (Mars, Venus, Jupiter, Mercury, and Saturn) plus the sun and the moon. They are commonly known as the seven stars, seven primes, or seven radiant bodies. Already in the commentary to the *Huangting neijing jing* 17:3 they are associated with the body orifices. The eight phosphors are described as the chiefs of the twenty-four gods presiding over the constructive and defensive energies in the human body (commentary to *Huangting neijing jing* 23:8; Strickmann 1979: 173; Robinet 1979: 94).

10. The same passage describing the development of the human embryo is also found in the *Hunyuan shubing pian* (*Yunji qiqian* 29.1ab). An earlier version is contained in the *Scripture on Karma and Retribution* (*Yinyuan jing* 8.1b–2a; DZ 336, fasc. 174–175). An early description of the development of the human embryo is found in *Huainanzi* 7.

11. The *Yunji qiqian* here has "source of the mind" for "prime of life."

12. The *niwan* is one of the nine palaces located in the human head. The commentary to *Huangting neijing jing* 21:14 defines *niwan* as the upper cinnabar field. The term is used to describe the god of the brain in 7:4 of the same text. As such this deity governs the various gods of the face (7:10). The other four gods named here, Siming, Wuying, and Taohai, are all described as princes of the Great One in the commentary to the *Huangting neijing jing* (15:11). Wuying especially is described as residing on the right in 11:7. Taohai is also known as Taogeng or Botao. He resides in the lower cinnabar field or in the navel (15:10). See also *Laozi zhongjing* (*Yunji qiqian* 18, 16b–17b) for a description of the gods residing in the human body.

太上老君內觀經

老君曰天地媾精陰陽布化萬物以生承其
宿業分靈道一父母和合人受其生始一月
為胞精血凝也二月成胎形兆胚也三月陽
神為三魂動而生也四月陰靈為七魄靜鎮
形也五月五行分藏以安神也六月六律定
臟用滋靈也七月七精開竅通光明也八月
八景神具降真靈也九月宮室羅布以定精
也十月炁足萬象成也元和哺食時不傳也
太一帝君在頭曰泥丸君總眾神也照生識

神人之魂也司命處心納生也无英居左
制三魂也白元居右拘七魄也桃孩住臍深
精根也照諸百節生百神也所以周身神不
空也元炁入鼻灌泥丸也所以神明形固安
也運動住止關其心也所以謂生有由然也
予內觀之歷歷分也心者禁也一身之主心
能禁制使形神不邪也心則神也變化不測
故無定形所以五藏藏五神魂在肝魄在肺
精在腎志在脾神在心所以字殊隨處名也
心者火也南方太陽之精主火上為熒惑下

Fig. 2. *Neiguan jing* 1b–2a

responsible for the propriety of the body spirits.[13] The mind is the spirit.[14] Its changes and transformations cannot be fathomed. It does not have a fixed shape.[15]

In the five orbs, the following spirit manifestations reside:
The spirit soul in the liver;
the material soul in the lungs;
the essence in the kidneys;
the intention in the spleen;
the spirit in the mind/heart.[16]

Their appellations vary in accordance with their respective positions. The mind/heart belongs to the agent fire. Fire is the essence of the South and of greater yang. Above it is governed by the planet Mars, below it corresponds to the mind/heart. [2b] Its color is red and it consists of three valves that resemble a lotus leaf. As the light of pure spirit is rooted there, it is named accordingly.

Spirit is neither black nor white, neither red nor yellow,[17] neither big nor small, neither short nor long, neither crooked nor straight, neither soft nor hard, neither thick nor thin, neither round nor square. It goes on changing and transforming without measure, merges with yin and yang, greatly encompasses heaven and earth, subtly enters the tiniest blade of grass.[18] Controlled it is straightforward, let loose it goes mad. Purity and tranquility make it live, defilements and nervousness cause it to perish.[19] When shining it can illuminate the eight ends of the universe. When darkened it will go wrong

---

13. The *Yunji qiqian* shortens this to "prohibits and controls the body spirits."

14. *Zhuangzi* 48/19/11.

15. Similarly, the *Zuowanglun* (2b–3a; DZ 1036, fasc. 704) states: "The mind is the master of the self, the master over the hundred spirits." The same text (13b), following the *Zhuangzi* (48/19/11) and the *Daode jing* (73), says: "The vacuity and mystery of the mind cannot be fathomed indeed. It really is a strange thing. If you approach its substance it does not seem to exist, if you pursue its application it certainly is there. . . . Without haste it is swift, without being summoned it arrives."

16. These correspondences go back to the theory of traditional Chinese medicine. They are also listed in the *Huangdi neijing taisu* (ed. Beijing: Weisheng, 1980) and in chapter 8 of the *Huangdi neijing lingshu* (2.4ab; DZ 1020, fasc. 661–663). Here the following emotions are associated with the orbs and their psychological correspondences: 1. anger; 2. sadness; 3. fear; 4. worry; 5. joy. The *Suwen* furthermore gives correspondences to the following physical entities: 1. blood; 2. energy; 3. semen; 4. constructive energy; 5. pulse (Ishida 1982: 3).

17. Following the *Yunji qiqian*; the DZ here leaves out "white" and "red."

18. See *Xisheng jing* (DZ 726, fasc. 449–450), sections 7 and 17.

19. This is also stated in *Qingqing jing* (2a; DZ 620, fasc. 341)

even in one single direction. You need only keep it empty and still, then life and the Tao will spontaneously be permanent. Always preserve an attitude of non-action, and the self will prosper.

The spirit is shapeless, thus it cannot be named.[20] All good and bad fortune, all success and failure only come from the spirit. Thus the sage will always preserve a straightforward relation to the ruler and the government, to the established rewards and punishments, and to the laws and regulations of the administration. He sets an example for others.[21] The reason why people find it hard to submit to rules and regulations is found in their minds. When the mind is pure and calm, all the many problems of misfortune don't arise.[22]

All ups and downs, life and death, all vicissitudes and evils arise from the mind. [3a] All foolishness and delusion, love and hate, all accepting and rejecting, coming and going, all defilements and attachments, as well as all entanglement and bondage arise gradually from becoming involved in things. Madly turning hither and thither, tied up and fettered, one is unable to get free. Thus one is bound for peril and destruction.

Oxen and horses when led properly can easily wade through the marsh.[23] When let loose, however, they will sink in deeper and deeper and can never get out again by themselves. So they have to die. People are just like this: when first born their original spirit is pure and tranquil,[24] profound and unadulterated. But then people gradually take in shaped objects. Those will in due course defile the six senses:[25]

The eyes will covet color.
The ears will be obstructed by sound.
The mouth will be addicted to flavors.
The nose will always take in smells.

---

20. The *Yunji qiqian* here has "The world thinks that the spirit . . ."

21. See *Daode jing* 8: "The sage loves order in government."

22. Already Guo Xiang assures us that the true man will "always step into good fortune" (chap. 8) and that he "will never be befallen by calamities" (chap. 1; Knaul 1985: 30; see also Robinet 1983.)

23. As concerns the comparison of the human disposition with oxen and horses see the *Zuowanglun* (5b): "Oxen and horses are domestic animals. When they are left to themselves and not tamed, they soon develop stubbornness and never accept being harnessed and charioteered."

24. Following the *Yunji qiqian* in reading "original spirit" for "spirit prime."

25. The *Daode jing* (12) has: "The five colors cause the eyes to be blind; the five tones cause the ears to be deaf; the five tastes cause the palate to be spoiled; racing and hunting causes one's mind to be mad; goods that are hard to get injure the activities."

應心也色赤三葉如蓮花神明依泊從所名
也其神也非青非黃非大非小非短非長非
曲非直非柔非剛非厚非薄非圓非方變化
莫測混合陰陽大包天地細入毫芒制之則
正教之則狂清淨則生濁躁則亡明照八表
暗迷一方但能虛寂生道自常永保無為其
身則昌也以其無形莫之能名禍福吉凶悉
由之矣所以聖人立君臣明賞罰置官僚制
法度正以教人人以難伏唯在於心心若清
淨則萬禍不生所以流浪生死沉淪惡道皆

由心也妄想憎愛取捨來去染著聚結漸自
纏繞轉轉繫練不能解脫便至滅亡由如牛
馬引重趨泥轉增陷沒不能自出遂至於死
人亦如是始生之時神元清靜湛然無雜既
受納有形形染六情眼則貪色耳則嬈聲口
則耽味鼻則受馨意隨健羨身欲肥輕從此
流浪莫能自悟聖人慈念設法教化使內觀
己身澄其心也
若君日諦觀此身從虛無中來因緣運會積
精聚炁乘華降神和合受生法天像地含陰

Fig. 3. *Neiguan jing* 2b–3a

The mind will be intent on refusing and coveting.[26]
The body will desire to be slimmer or fatter.

From all these ups and downs of life no one is able to wake up by himself.[27] Thus the sages with compassionate consideration established the doctrine to teach people to reform. They made them use inner observation of the self and body in order to purify the mind.

The Venerable Lord said:

Now observe that your self has arisen from emptiness and non-being in accordance with karma and the course of destiny. An accumulation of essence and an assemblance of energy, a coming down of florescence and a descent of the spirit—when all these come together, life is conceived.[28]

Patterned on heaven and symbolizing earth, inhaling yin and [3b] exhaling yang, your body shares in the five agents and goes along with the

---

26. The *Yunji qiqian* here has, "The mind will only embrace refusing and coveting."

27. The *Zuowanglun* (3a) has: "The mind delightfully strays in the realm of delusion, it takes this for factual reality and greatly enjoys to be in the midst of action. Who would awaken to see this as empty and wrong?"

28. For "florescence" the *Yunji qiqian* here has "karma." The notion is explained in more detail in the *Jizhong jing* (*Yunji qiqian* 31.9b–10a):

> The Heavenly Venerable said: Breath follows upon breath, seed after seed brings forth karma. Good and evil, good and bad fortune, all have their root in destiny. Yet this root is neither heaven nor earth, nor yet is it human beings themselves. Rather, it all comes straight from the mind, and the mind comes directly from spirit.

> The body is not mine. The reason why I come to be alive is found in an evolution from empty non-being and cosmic spontaneity. In accordance with karma I was entrusted to the womb, underwent several transformations and was born. The parents who conceived me are not my real origins. They are just taking the part of the parents in this world. My true parents are not here, they are noble and honored, most venerable and lofty. The parents who conceived me in this world were merely predestined to graciously give me nourishment and education. I bow to them in accordance with propriety and honor them as my parents.

> I therefore received a body but it is not ultimately mine. I only use it as a temporary residence, a shelter like a straw-thatched roof. Looking down on it I recognize it as a body; analyzing it I find it does not really exist. So the I who has realized the Tao is said to have no more body, no more self, no more spirit! Once self and body have been utterly unified with the One, the true self makes its appearance. Then I can return to the parents who first gave me life and fully realize the Tao.

four seasons. The eyes are the sun and the moon. The hair is the stars and the planets. The eyebrows are the flowery canopy (Cassiopeia). The head is Mount Kunlun.[29] A network of passes and palaces, the body serves to keep essence and spirit at peace.

Among the myriad beings, humans have the most vital energy.[30] Their inner nature and fate being in harmony with the Tao, they should always preserve[31] and love it and continue to innerly observe their bodies. In all creation only human beings are truly venerable,[32] yet they do not think of themselves as noble. Foolishly defiled by the grime of the world, they stink of impurity.[33] Disturbed and confused in body and spirit, how could they observe themselves and others and judge which is dearer and which more distant? Preservation of the Tao and long life are attained by doing good and preserving the true.[34] But normal people are ignorant and keep themselves busy with trifles, thereby bringing hardship and misery upon themselves.

The Venerable Lord said:

The life people receive from the Tao is called fate.[35]
The body people receive from the One is called inner nature.
That by which people respond to other beings is called mind.
That which the mind considers is called intention.

---

29. The concept of an anthropomorphic cosmos is reflected in the creation myth of the hero Pangu, which has also been told about Laozi. It is found in *Yunji qiqian* 3.15bb and 56.1b, with an earlier version in the *Xiaodao lun* (*Taishō Tripitaka* 52.144b):

> Laozi transformed his body. His left eye became the sun, his right eye the moon. His head became Mount Kunlun, his hair the stars. His bones were dragons, his flesh wild beasts, his intestines snakes. His chest turned into the ocean, his fingers into the five sacred mountains. The hair on his body was transformed into grass and trees, his heart into the constellation Flowery Canopy. His testicles, finally, unified and became the true parents of the universe.

30. The *Yunji qiqian* here has, " . . . is called the most numinous."

31. Added in the *Yunji qiqian* edition.

32. The *Yunji qiqian* reads, " . . . who would be more venerable?"

33. The *Yunji qiqian* has, "not tranquil" for "impure."

34. Here the *Yunji qiqian* reads, " . . . completeness of life."

35. Following the *Yunji qiqian*; the DZ version runs, "The share people receive of the Tao is called fate."

吐陽分錯五行以應四時眼為日月髮為星
辰眉為華蓋頭為崐崘布列宮闕安置精神
萬物之中人最為靈性命合道人當受之內
觀其身惟人尊焉而不自貴妄染諸塵不淨
臭穢濁亂形神熟觀物我何踈何親守道長
生為善保真世愚役役徒自苦辛也
老君曰從道受分謂之命自一稟形謂之性
所以任物謂之心心有所憶謂之意意之所
出謂之志事無不知謂之智智周萬物謂之
慧動而營身謂之魂靜而鎮形謂之魄流行

骨肉謂之血保神養炁謂之精炁清而駛謂
之榮炁濁而遲謂之衛總括百神謂之身萬
象備見謂之形塊然有閡謂之質狀貌可則
謂之體大小有分謂之軀衆思不測謂之神
邀然應化謂之靈炁來入身謂之生神去於
身謂之死所以通生謂之道道者有而無形
無而有情變化不測通神群生在人之身則
為神明所謂心也所以教人修道則修心也
教人修心則修道也道不可見因生而明之
生不可常用道以守之若生亡則道廢道廢

Fig. 4. *Neiguan jing* 3b–4a

That which results from intention is called will.
The knowledge of the various affairs is called wisdom.
The wisdom of the myriad beings is called insight.
That which moves and regulates the self is the spirit soul.
That which protects and guards the body is the material soul.
That which circulates [4a] through bones and flesh is the blood
That which preserves the spirit and nourishes the breath is the essence.
Energy when pure and swift is called constructive.
Energy when impure and slow is called protective.[36]
That which structures and combines the hundred spirits[37] is called the self.
That which relays a complete visual impression of the image is called the body.
That which keeps it clodlike and cohesive is its solidity.
That which allows appearance to be measured is called physical structure.
That which is arranged according to bigger and smaller sections is the physis.
That which cannot be fathomed by thought is called the spirit.
That which forever corresponds to the changes is the numen.
That which happens when the energy enters the body is called life.
That which occurs when the spirit leaves the body is called death.
That which pervades all life is called the Tao.[38]

---

36. *Yong* and *wei* are defined by the texts as two kinds or qualities of blood. The translation here follows Engelhardt 1987, which uses "Bau- und Wehrenergie," constructive and protective energies. In the *Huangdi neijing lingshu* (8.6b), *yong* is associated with the blood as such, whereas *wei* is said to correspond to energy in general, *qi*. When these two energies don't circulate properly throughout the body, the texts assure us, the orbs and repositories will not work and the body will be sick.

37. The *Yunji qiqian* here has "bones" instead of "spirits."

38. The *Yunji qiqian* (14.13b) gives a different list of psychological definitions:
    The coming together of the energy of life is called essence.
    The workings of essence are called numen or life-force.
    The transformations of the life-force are called spirit.
    The changes of the spirit are called spirit souls.
    The force that follows the workings of the spirit souls is called consciousness.
    The coming and going of essence is manifest in the material souls.
    The force that rules and organizes essence and the material souls is called the mind.
    When the mind touches something, there is sensual perception.
    What arises from sensual perception is called intention.
    When intention is directed towards an aim, it is called the will.
    When the will becomes clear, there is a thought.
    Thoughts regarding distant objects are called plans or ideas.
    Ideas that can be applied in reality constitute wisdom.
    It is through wisdom that consciousness arises.

When the Tao is there, it yet has no shape. When it is not there, it yet has an impact.[39] The changes of the Tao cannot be measured, it pervades the spirit and the host of living beings. When it resides in the self, the spirit light shines forth. This is called the mind.

Thus, teaching people to cultivate the Tao means to instruct them in the cultivation of the mind. Instruct people to cultivate their minds and they are cultivating the Tao. The Tao cannot be seen, so one must rely on life itself to clarify it. Life is not eternal, so one must apply the Tao to preserve it. When life perishes, the Tao is lost. When the Tao is lost, life perishes. [4b] Only when life and the Tao are combined in harmony, there will be long life and no death. Undergoing the transformation of wings one will then become a spirit immortal.[40] The reason why people cannot preserve the Tao is because they don't innerly observe their minds. By increasingly practicing inner observation, life and the Tao will remain forever.

The Venerable Lord said:

People experience ups and downs and fall into the evil ways.[41] They are in peril due to their vanities and defilements. This is due to the fact that the six senses produce delusion and give rise to the six states of consciousness.[42] These six states of consciousness in turn bring forth divisions and distinctions.[43] They cause fetters and bondage, love and hate, coming and going,

---

39. See *Zhuangzi* 4/2/16, 16/6/29.

40. The expression "transformation of wings" is already used in the *Liexian zhuan* to describe the process of becoming an immortal. Immortals were thought to be transformed either through fire or by some inner means into light, ethereal substances or creatures that could fly. Thus one finds numerous images of immortals with feathers on Han dynasty bronze mirrors. In later mystical texts, the expression denotes the ultimate metamorphosis of an ordinary mortal into a celestial being. See *Daoshu* (2.8a; DZ 1017, fasc. 641–648).

41. This refers to rebirth in a shape lower that human, by which one loses the chance to cultivate the Tao and realize immortality. This happens especially when one is given completely to sensual pleasure without realizing its bad effect on one's karma. Thus the *Zuowanglun* has: "When fox fairies seduce people they arouse loathing and distress. Hence people, even if they have to die, do not enter the evil ways." (9b)

42. These six states of consciousness arise from the six sensual roots of sight, sound, smell, taste, touch, and consciousness. For a similar description see *Dingguan jing* (*Yunji qiqian* 17.7a).

43. Already Guo Xiang, in his commentary to the second chapter of the *Zhuangzi*, points out that divisions and distinctions are the major symptoms of a loss of the Tao. "If right and wrong were not there," he says, "the Tao would still be complete. With the destruction of the Tao emotions begin to be partial and love develops fully." (Knaul 1985: 25)

accepting and rejecting, as well as defilements and attachments, passions and afflictions. Thus people are completely separated from the Tao.

This then is the reason why people should innerly observe the arising of the six states of consciousness. From where do these six states arise? Consciousness arises from the mind, the mind arises from the ego, the ego arises from desires.[44] Deluded imagining and perverted views are responsible for the fact that there is consciousness.

Now, what we call nature or non-action is originally empty and tranquil.[45] It is fundamentally free from consciousness. But as soon as there is the consciousness of divisions and distinctions, perverted views begin to arise. Once such views flourish, people will be tied by passions and afflictions, involvements and entanglements, fetters and bondage, ups and downs, life and death. They will forever be [5a] lost to the Tao.

The Venerable Lord said:

The Tao is free from life and death, but the body does undergo life and death. Thus we say that life and death are characteristics of the body, but not characteristics of the Tao. The body only comes to life when it receives the Tao. The body only dies when it loses the Tao.[46] Whoever is able to preserve and guard the Tao will live forever and never perish.

The Venerable Lord said:

To someone who is able to always keep the mind pure and calm the Tao will come to stay naturally.[47] When the Tao naturally comes to stay, the spirit light suffuses the entire self. When the spirit light suffuses the self, life will not perish.[48]

People always desire life, but they are unable to empty their minds. People always hate death, but they are unable to preserve the spirit. This is as

---

44. This follows the *Yunji qiqian* edition. The DZ has: "Consciousness arises from desires. Where do desires come from? Desires arise from consciousness." A similar emphasis on egoistic perception is found in the *Benji jing* 5, 115–125 (Ofuchi 1979: 320).

45. The *Yunji qiqian* here has "empty and pure."

46. Usually the body is contrasted with the spirit, for example, in the *Yangxing yanming lu* (DZ 838, fasc. 572; *Yunji qiqian* 32): "Spirit is the foundation of life. The body is its tool."

47. This quotation goes back to the *Xisheng jing*; it is also cited in the *Zuowanglun* 4b.

48. *Xisheng jing* 29.

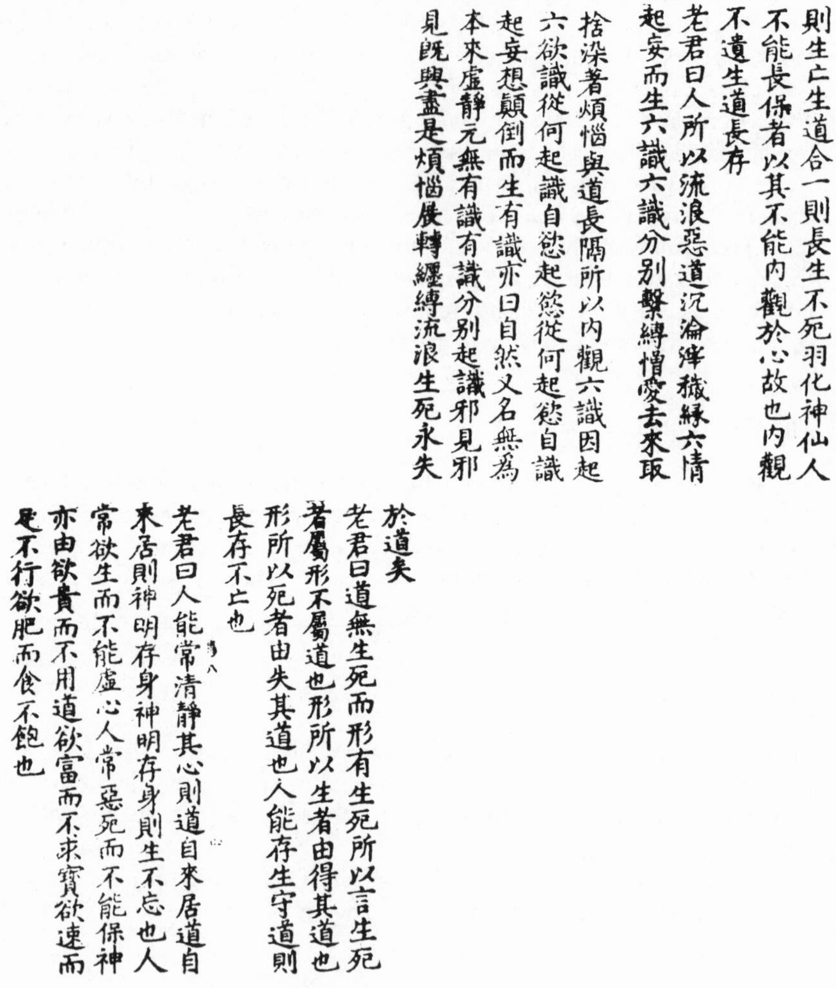

則生亡生道合一則長生不死羽化神仙人
不能長保者以其不能內觀於心故也內觀
不遺生道長存
老君曰人所以流浪惡道沉淪穢綠六情
起妄而生六識六識分別繫縛憎愛去來取
捨染著煩惱與道長隔所以內觀六識因起
六欲識從何起識自慾起慾從何起慾自識
起妄想顛倒而生有識亦曰自然又名無為
本來虛靜元無有識有識分別起識邪見邪
見既與盡是煩惱展轉經縛流浪生死永失

於道矣
老君曰道無生死而形有生死所以言生死
著屬形不屬道也形所以生者由得其道也
形所以死者由失其道也人能存生守道則
長存不亡也
老君曰人能常清靜其心則道自來居道自
來居則神明存身神明存身則生不忘也人
常欲生而不能虛心人常惡死而不能保神
亦由欲貴而不用道欲富而不求實欲速而
是不行欲肥而食不飽也

Fig. 5. *Neiguan jing* 4b–5a

道當慎擇焉

老君曰道貴長存保神固根精炁不散純白

不分形神合道飛昇崑崙先天以生後天以

存出入無間不由其門吹陰煦陽制魂拘魄

億歲春屬千載子孫黃塵四起騎羊貪人金

堂玉室送故迎新

老君曰內觀之道靜神定心亂想不起邪妄

不侵固身及物閉目思尋表裏虛寂神道微

深外藏萬境內察一心了然明靜靜亂俱息

念念相系深根寧極湛然常住杳冥難測憂

患永消是非莫識

老君曰吾非聖人學而得之故我求道無不

受持千經萬術惟在心也

太上老君內觀經

Fig. 7. *Neiguan jing* 6b–7a

The Venerable Lord said:

The Tao of inner observation lies in calming the spirit and concentrating the mind. Confusion and imagining must not arise, falseness and foolishness must not enter. Keep a firm hold on yourself and your surroundings, close your eyes and start an inspection. Within and without, both empty and still, the spirit and the Tao will be subtle and profound. Without, observe[65] all the mental projections of apparent reality; within, examine the unity of mind.[66] Once you are really luminous and restful, tranquility and confusion will both be gone. While thought follows upon thought, deep inside your root is perfectly at peace. Remain always like this deep inside. Your stillness and obscurity cannot be fathomed.[67] All sorrows and troubles forever extinguished, there are no more ideas of right and wrong.

The Venerable Lord said:

[7a] I am not a born sage, I studied the Tao and realized it.[68] Thus I had to search for it myself, but I ultimately received it completely naturally. The thousand scriptures and the myriad methods all rest within the mind in the end.

---

65. Following the *Yunji qiqian* in reading "observe" for "store."

66. The distinction between observation of the within and observation of the without is also found in the *Qingqing jing* (2a; DZ 620, fasc. 341). Here a third category is added: observation of the distant. In our within and without text refer to oneself and others; in the *Qingqing jing* they indicate that one observes oneself from the within and from the without—from the positions of mind and body. Observation of others, then, is called "observation of the distant" in the *Qingqing jing*.

67. Similarly, the *Dingguan jing* (*Yunji qiqian* 17) encourages the adept to become "like the surface of standing water" (10b).

68. This is the image of Laozi propagated by the seekers of personal immortality as opposed to the deified Laozi of primarily communal and ritual-oriented Taoism.

References

Brown, Daniel P. and Jack Engler. 1984. "A Rorschach Study of the Stages of Mindfulness Meditation." In *Meditation: Classic and Contemporary Perspectives*, pp. 232–262. Edited by Duane H. Shapiro and Roger N. Walsh. New York: Aldine, 1984.

Engelhardt, Ute. 1987. *Die klassische Tradition der Qi-Übungen: Eine Darstellung anhand des Tang-zeitlichen Textes Fuqi jingyi lun von Sima Chengzhen*. Wiesbaden: Franz Steiner, 1987.

Graham, A.C. 1960. *The Book of Lieh-tzu*. London: A. Murray 1960.

Knaul, Livia. 1985. "The Winged Life: Kuo Hsiang's Mystical Philosophy," *Journal of Chinese Studies* 2.1 (1985), 17–41.

Kohn, Livia. 1987. *Seven Steps to the Tao: Sima Chengzhen's Zuowanglun*. St. Augustin: Monumenta Serica Monographs 20, 1987.

—— 1987a. "The Teaching of T'ien-yin-tzu," *Journal of Chinese Religions* 15 (1987), 1–28.

Lu, Kuan-yü. 1964. *The Secrets of Chinese Meditation*. London: Rider, 1964.

Robinet, Isabelle. 1979. *Méditation taoiste*. Paris: Dervy Livres, 1979.

—— 1983. "Kuou Siang ou le monde comme absulu," *T'oung-pao* 69 (1983), 87–112.

Rousselle, Erwin. 1933. "Seelische Führung im Taoismus," *Eranos Jahrbuch* 1 (1933), 135–199.

Schafer, Edward H. 1980. *Mao-shan in T'ang Times*. Boulder, Colorado: Society for the Study of Chinese Religions Monograph 1, 1980.

—— 1981. "Wu Yün's 'Cantos on Pacing the Void," *Harvard Journal of Asiatic Studies* 41.2 (1981), 377–415.

Schipper, Kristofer M. 1975. *Concordance du Houang-t'ing king*. Paris: Publications de l'Ecole Francaise d'Extrême Orient, 1975.

—— 1978. "The Taoist Body," *History of Religions* 17 (1978), 355–387.

Soothill, William Edward and Lewis Hudous, *A Dictionary of Chinese Buddhist Terms*. London: Kegan Paul, Trench, Trubner, & Co, 1937.

Strickmann, Michel. 1979. "On the Alchemy of T'ao Hung-ching." In *Facets of Taoism*, pp. 123–192. Edited by H. Welch and A. Seidel. New Haven & London: Yale University Press, 1979.

Vandermeersch, Leon. 1985. "Genèse et signification de la théorie des Cinq-Agents dans le Confucianisme ancien." Paper presented at the Quatrième Colloque Pluri-disciplinaire Fanco-Japonais. Paris, 1985.

Walsh, Roger. 1984. "An Evolutionary Model of Meditation Research." In *Meditation: Classic and Contemporary Perspectives*, pp. 24–32. Edited by Duane H. Shapiro and Roger N. Walsh. New York: Aldine, 1984.

Watson, Burton. 1968. *The Complete Works of Chuang-tzu*. New York: Columbia University Press, 1968.

Zürcher, Erik. 1980. "Buddhist Influence on Early Taoism," *T'oung-pao* 66 (1980), 84–147.

in Chinese and Japanese

Ishida Hidemi　石田秀實　1982
"Kakujū suru seishin"　擴充する精神　. *Tōhōgaku* 63 (1982), 1–15.

Kamata Shigeo　鎌田茂雄　1963
"Dōkyō kyōri no keisei ni oyoboshita bukkyō shisō no eikyō"
道教教理の形成におよばした佛教思想の影響
Tōyō bunka kenkyūjo kiyō　東洋文化研究所紀要　31 (1963), 165–240.

Ofuchi Ninji　大淵忍爾　1979
Tonkō dōkei　敦煌道經　. 2 vols. Tokyo: Fukutake shoten, 1979.

Wu Shouqu　吳受琚　1981
Sima Chengzhen ji jijiao　司馬承禎集輯校　. Beijing, 1981.

Chapter Eight

Gymnastics: The Ancient Tradition

Catherine Despeux

In China, the first rays of daylight shine on the throngs of citizens in the parks, people of all ages and of all conditions who have come to wake their bodies in the purity of the rising sun. Activities of a vast range are practiced side by side: chatting, jogging, walking, badminton, martial arts, and gymnastics. Among the latter, Taiji quan and Qigong are best known to the Western observer. Certain people may well prefer to practice their exercises in the privacy of their own rooms, yet rarely will even they not perform—at some time during the day, most commonly around noon or in the early evening—some gymnastic techniques learned from a grandparent within or from a master outside the family.

The gymnastic exercises are called *daoyin* 導引, which literally means "guiding and pulling." They are known as preventives against old age and sickness, but also serve to cure certain diseases, chronic and acute. Their medical value has caused them to be classified either as part of traditional medical literature or among the various practices of "nourishing the vital principle." The latter were in due course integrated into Taoism, especially in the Shangqing, Highest Clarity, tradition.

The tradition of gymnastics goes back a long way in Chinese history. It is testified to in the writings of Zhuangzi, dated to the fourth century B.C.

> To pant, to puff, to hail, to sip, to spit out the old breath and draw in the new, practicing bear-hangings and bird-stretchings, longevity his only concern—such is the life favored by the scholar who practices gymnastics, the man who nourishes his

body, who hopes to live to be as old as Pengzu, for more than
eight hundred years. (ch. 15; Watson 1968: 167–168)

In the context of the *Zhuangzi*, however, these physical techniques were
always considered inferior to more meditative practices like "sitting in
oblivion" or "the fasting of the mind."

From the time of Zhuangzi until the present those physical practices
have never ceased to play a role—of varying importance—in Chinese culture.
The first clear testimony to certain specific sets of gymnastic practices is
found under the Han: the *Daoyin tu* 導引圖 (Gymnastics Chart) found in the
tomb at Mawangdui near Changsha.[1] During the same period the basic
theoretical principles of Chinese medicine and the fundamental notions about
the human body were first systematized. The *Daoyin tu* is a colored
manuscript that shows forty-four gymnastic movements in a series of sketches
(see figure 1). Some of the pictures are accompanied by a commentary on
their therapeutic qualities. In the following centuries, until the Tang dynasty,
the various practices flourished and were widely developed, but their original
foundations remained largely untouched.

The Sources: Han to Tang

Among the earliest documents on gymnastics there are the short commentary
to the pictures of the *Daoyin tu* and certain recently discovered texts on
bamboo slips (see Wenwu 1985). The latter were unearthed in Jiangling in
Hunan, but they have not been studied yet. One of the more extensive early
sources is a medical text dating from the Sui dynasty. Except for these, all the
texts that deal with gymnastics in this early period have been transmitted in
the Taoist Canon, which was only edited in the Ming dynasty.[2] The sources in
the Canon treat gymnastics as one of the various arts of nourishing life, and
there is only one document that concentrates exclusively on *daoyin*.

---

1. The text was discovered in the course of excavations at Mawangdui between 1972 and
   1974. For convenient reproductions see Mawangdui 1985.

2. For a discussion of the Canon, its date, and structure, see Liu 1973, Ofuchi 1979, and
   Thompson 1985.

Fig. 1. The Gymnastics Chart (*Daoyin tu*) from Mawangdui

The Yangsheng yaoji

It appears that in essence and outlook most of these later materials ultimately go back to a work of the Jin dynasty (fourth century) that today only survives in fragmentary quotations: the *Yangsheng yaoji* 養生要集 (Compendium of Essentials on Nourishing Life).[3] As the title suggests, it originally consisted of quotations and summaries of ancient sources, materials dating from the Han to the Jin, from the second century B.C. to the fourth century A.D. The latest of those works prior to the *Yangsheng yaoji* is the famous *Baopuzi* 抱朴子 (Book of the Master Who Embraces Simplicity), by Ge Hong 葛洪.[4]

The *Yangxing yanming lu* 養性延命錄 (Record on Nourishing Inner Nature and Extending Life), a text traditionally attributed to Tao Hongjing 陶弘景 (456–536) or to Sun Simiao 孫思邈 (581–682) but recently dated to the mid-Tang (Mugitani 1987), says:[5]

> The *Yangsheng yaoji* was a compendium of the sayings of the ancient sages Zhang Zhan and Daolin as well as of Huangshan and Zhai Ping. All these men were eminent specialists who gave themselves completely to nourishing life. Some of them collected statements from immortals' books and regulations regarding long life, while others obtained the longevity techniques of Pengzu and Laozi. The compilation covers the period from Shennong and Huangdi to the Wei and Jin dynasties. (1.1ab)

Among the four names mentioned, only the name Zhang Zhan 張湛 is commonly recorded in the bibliographies. He is better known for his commentary to the *Liezi* 列子 (Sakade 1986: 1). Little is known about his life, but it appears that he was a member of an aristocratic family from northern China. His grandfather was involved in the political unrest at the end of the Western Jin and first came to the South as an exile. Here he served under the Eastern Jin, who had newly established their capital in Nanjing. Zhang Zhan

---

3. The text was completely lost only after the rebellion of An Lushan in the middle of the eighth century. See Barret 1980: 172.

4. The text is dated to about 320. It has been recently edited in Wang 1980. A translation of the Inner Chapters is found in Ware 1966.

5. The text is contained in chapter 32 of the tenth-century Taoist collection *Yunji qiqian* which is found in the Taoist Canon (DZ 1032, fasc. 677–702). Texts in the Taoist Canon (*Daozang*, abbreviated DZ) are given according to the number of the reduced sixty-volume edition published in Taipei and Kyoto. These numbers coincide with those found in K.M. Schipper, *Concordance du Tao Tsang* (Paris: Publications de l'Ecole Francaise d'Extrême-Orient, 1975). "Fasc." stands for "fascicle" and refers to the volume number of the 1925 Shanghai reprint of the original canon of 1445 (*Zhengtong Daozang*).

himself at one time or another occupied the post of imperial secretary under this dynasty.

Daolin 道林 has been identified as Zhi Daolin (314–366), better known as Zhi Dun 支遁 , who is among the early aristocratic Buddhists in Chinese history (Sakade 1986: 68; Barret 1982: 41). Huangshan 黃山 presumably lived during the Later Han dynasty and is among the authors of the *Pengzu jing* 彭祖經 (Scripture of Pengzu), one of the early texts dealing with sexual longevity techniques (Sakade 1985). Zhai Ping 翟平 , finally, is mentioned in the *Suishu* 隋書 (History of the Sui Dynasty; 34.1049 of the Beijing: Jinghua edition) as the author of a certain *Yangsheng shu* 養生書 (Book on Nourishing Life) in one scroll.

As can be gleamed from fragments of the *Yangsheng yaoji* contained primarily in the *Yangxing yanming lu* and in Tamba no Yasuyori's 丹波康賴 *Ishinpō* 醫心方 (Essential Medical Methods) of the year 984 (Sakade 1986a), it consisted largely of quotations and summaries of more than thirty earlier works. The ten fundamental topics treated in the original text were:

1. strengthening of the vital spirits;
2. love of the breath;
3. upkeep of the body;
4. practice of gymnastics;
5. proprieties of language;
6. proper diet;
7. art of the inner chamber;
8. return to the common world;
9. intake of medicinal drugs;
10. different prohibitions. (*Yangxing yanming lu* 1.9b)

Thus, fragments of early texts that deal specifically with gymnastics are few in number. Those contained in the *Ishinpō* describe different massage techniques, citing a certain Master Ning (after the *Ning xiansheng daoyin jing* 寧先生導引經) who is otherwise unknown. More than that, there is a quotation from a *Daoyin jing* (Gymnastics Classic), which may or may not be identical to a work of that title contained in the library of Ge Hong and listed in chapter 19 of the *Baopuzi*. The same list also features a *Anmo jing* 按摩經 (Massage Classic).

In addition, there are about ten texts in the Taoist Canon that can be dated to before the Song and have something to say on the topic of physical exercises. Each of the texts presents a certain number of techniques useful for nourishing life in a system that reflects the tradition and tendency of its author. The texts constitute the basic corpus of materials used in the study of *daoyin* from the Han to the Tang. One important medical text has to be included: the *Zhubing yuanhou lun* 諸病源候論 (Discussion on the Origins and Symptoms of All Diseases), dated to the year 610, which we will discuss in some detail below.

The Daoyin jing

The only work in the Taoist Canon that deals almost exclusively with gymnastic movements is the *Taiqing daoyin yangsheng jing* 太清導引養生 經 (Great Clarity Scripture of Gymnastics and Nourishing Life; DZ 818, fasc. 568) which we will hereafter call the *Daoyin jing*.[6] This text is of great interest for the student of the gymnastic tradition in China.

It contains a wide range of information about a number of different schools within the tradition, for example those going back to Master Redpine (Chisongzi 赤松子), the Minister of Rain under Shennong, to Ningfengzi 寧 封子, the Minister of Fire under the Yellow Emperor, to Wang Qiao 王踽 , famous immortal of antiquity, as well as to the longevity masters Pengzu and Daolin. The mention made of Daolin or Zhi Dun, who wrote in the early fourth century, allows us to date the *Daoyin jing* to this century at the earliest. The text assembles a variety of physical exercises aimed at nourishing the vital principle in general, but it also deals with specific practices for curing diseases.

Fragments and quotations of this text are found in different places in the Taoist Canon and in the *Zhubing yuanhou lun*, in which thirty of the fifty-five movements associated with Ningfengzi are outlined together with eight of the ten practices of Pengzu, five of twenty-nine other exercises of Master Ning, nine of nineteen miscellaneous practices, as well as thirteen of the thirty-four movements that go back to Wang Qiao. In the *Shenxian shiqi jingui miaolu* 神 仙食氣金櫃妙錄　　　 (The Spirit Immortals' Wondrous Record on Ingesting Breath Kept in a Golden Casket 9a–13b; DZ 836, fasc. 571), thirty-three of the thirty-four movements of Wang Qiao are described. This text predates the Sui dynasty (Loon 1984: 130) and is ascribed to a certain Master Jingli 京里, or Jinghei 京黑. The *Shesheng zuanlu* 攝生纂錄 (Comprehensive Record of Protecting Life; DZ 578, fasc. 321) of the Tang dynasty, in its very beginning, lists six kneeling exercises ascribed to Chisongzi that are found toward the end of the *Daoyin jing* (19ab).

Most of the exercises listed in the *Daoyin jing* can therefore be dated to before the Sui dynasty—that is, to the late sixth century. On the other hand,

---

6. There are also two shorter versions of the text in the Canon, one in chapter 34 of the *Yunji qiqian*, the other in chapter 28 of the *Daoshu* (DZ 1017, fasc. 641–648) by Zeng Zao (d. 1155). The longer version in DZ 818 is not divided into sections; the shorter in the *Yunji qiqian* is.

the *Daoyin jing* itself is not mentioned in the bibliographies before the Song. It first occurs in a bibliography of the year 1145. Thus we conclude that it may have been a rather late compilation that summarizes and organizes various earlier materials. At the same time, it could still be possible that the text is in fact a fragment of the *Yangsheng yaoji*, which as a whole was only lost in the eighth century, after the rebellion of An Lushan. It may very well be the case that the same text reappeared toward the end of the Tang and the beginning of the Song and was then renamed *Daoyin jing*.

The Daolin lun

The same may be true of another document dealing with gymnastics contained in the Canon: the *Taiqing Daolin shesheng lun*   大清道林攝生論   (Great Clarity Discourse on Protecting Life by Master Daolin; DZ 1427, fasc. 1055), which we will hereafter call the *Daolin lun*. This is a short text of only twenty-four pages that describes different prescriptions and prohibitions regarding life style, living quarters, and diet. It also outlines massages, gymnastic exercises, and respiratory techniques.

As a whole it is similar to chapter 27 of the *Qianjin fang*   千金方   (Prescriptions Worth a Thousand Ounces of Gold), a seventh-century medical text written by Sun Simiao and edited by Lin Yi   林億   and nowadays conveniently available from Renmin weisheng Publishers in Beijing (1982). Chapter 27 is divided into eight sections, the second of which is called "Master Daolin's Methods of Nourishing the Vital Principle."[7]

The section that deals with massages and gymnastics is presented differently in the *Daolin lun* and the *Qianjin fang*. The *Qianjin fang* introduces the first series of massages as "Brahmanic Indian Massage Techniques" and speaks of the second series as "Massages of Laozi" (27.481–483). The *Daolin lun* does not speak of anything Brahmanic in this context. The very same techniques are, then, cited in the *Shesheng zuanlu* as "Brahmanic Gymnastics" (2a–3a). Here the instructions are followed by a number of quotations from the *Yangsheng yaoji*. The arrangement leads the reader to presume that those "Brahmanic Techniques" were included in the text from the beginning. In any case, their appearance is only a late trace of the possibly quite considerable influence of Indian ideas and practices on the Chinese tradition of gymnastics and massages.

---

7. The *Daolin lun* and chapter 27 of the *Qianjin fang* contain many identical passages, but the order is different. Also, the *Qianjin fang* adds supplementary comments to the older text. However, in the Northern Song edition of the text, as outlined in the *Song yiqian yiji kao*, the passages appear in the same order.

One source of this influence can possibly be found in the *Longshu pusa yangxing fang* 龍樹菩薩養性方 (Bodhisattva Nagarjuna's Prescriptions for Nourishing Life), quoted in the *Suishu* (34.1049) but lost today.

The *Daolin lun* probably goes back to Daolin (Zhi Dun) of the fourth century, who is among the alleged authors of the *Yangsheng yaoji* and the *Daoyin jing*. Since one can assume that as a Buddhist monk Zhi Dun had close contact with travelers from India and Indian residents of China, it is hardly surprising that he should have included some Indian techniques among his practices. Since, moreover, the *Daolin lun* not only treats the same subjects as the *Yangsheng yaoji* but also formulates its material in the same fashion, for the most part, a common origin is likely.

Passages of the *Daolin lun* that stem from the *Yangsheng yaoji* are also found in the *Yangxing yanming lu* and in the *Zhiyan zong* 至言總 (Comprehensive Collection of Perfect Words; DZ 1033, fasc. 703), by Fan Youran 范脩然.[8] Both these texts rely heavily on the *Yangsheng yaoji*. In addition, they contain quotations from Pengzu, from the *Huangdi neijing suwen* 黃帝內經素文 (Inner Classic of the Yellow Emperor: Fundamental Questions)[9] as well as from the *Baopuzi*, all established sources of the *Yangsheng yaoji*.

Nevertheless, like the *Daoyin jing*, the *Daolin lun* is not mentioned in the bibliographies before the Song (Loon 1984: 151). Since Zhi Dun is among the authors of the *Yangsheng yaoji* and since numerous important passages that survive from that work are cited identically in the *Daolin lun*, the conclusion that both the *Daolin lun* and the *Daoyin jing* as we have them today are remnants of the original *Yangsheng yaoji* seems justified.

The Shenxian shiqi jingui miaolu

The *Shenxian shiqi jingui miaolu*, allegedly by Master Jingli, is mentioned in the *Suishu* under the title *Jingui lu* as consisting of 23 *juan* (34.1048). The same author is also mentioned in the *Shenxian fu'er danshi xing yaofa* 神仙服餌丹石行要注 (Spirit Immortals' Essential Methods Regarding Dietetics and Mineralogy; DZ 420, fasc. 192). The former text consists of nine sections

---

8. Originally from Kuaiji in Zhejiang, Fan probably lived during the Tang dynasty. His work relies heavily on the various gymnastic documents mentioned so far. Chapter 2, dealing with nourishing life, takes up almost all *Yangsheng yaoji* fragments also found in the *Yangxing yanming lu*.
Citations from the *Daolin lun* are also found in 2.8a (=23a), 2.11ab (=2ab), 2.12ab (=4b), 4.9a–10b (=16b–17a and 18b–19b), 5.1a–2b (=13b–16a).

9. References are made to the edition of Beijing: Renmin weisheng, 1980.

dealing with different methods of *qi*-absorption and gymnastics, techniques that are supposed to eliminate diseases and help adepts in the prolonged abstention from cereals.

Since the main theme of this text is the absorption of *qi*, gymnastics are presented as therapeutical and additional methods that lead to the perfection of physical health necessary for the successful absorption of *qi*. More than that, in this text the practice of physical exercises is closely related to abstention from cereals. Following a general introduction on *daoyin*, the text proceeds to present thirty-three of the thirty-four movements associated with Wang Ziqiao under the heading "Formulas for the Cure of Diseases," equally mentioned in the *Daoyin jing*. The presentation then continues with a quotation from the *Yuanyang jing* 元陽經 (Scripture of Primordial Yang) based on the *Yangsheng yaoji* (as cited in *Ishinpō* 27.18a). Thus it becomes evident that the *Yangsheng yaoji* served as a source for the *Shenxian shiqi jingui miaolu*.

The Yangxing yanming lu

The *Yangxing yanming lu* is found in two versions in the Taoist Canon (DZ 838, fasc. 572 and *Yunji qiqian* 32.1a–24b). As mentioned above, it has traditionally been attributed to Tao Hongjing or Sun Simiao. Both these attributions are questionable, but it may well be that the essential concepts and ideas of the text do go back to Tao Hongjing. The text as found in the *Daozang* is divided into six sections: general principles, dietetics, various prohibitions, techniques of *qi* absorption for the healing of diseases, massages and gymnastic exercises, and alchemical practices. The second and last sections are not found in the *Yunji qiqian* version.

According to the preface, the *Yangxing yanming lu* was compiled on the basis of the *Yangsheng yaoji*, from which the author excised what seemed superfluous or redundant. The entire text is thus composed of fragments of the *Yangsheng yaoji*, newly selected and arranged by the author. In effect, one may go one step further and say that the *Yangxing yanming lu*, which only cites the *Yangsheng yaoji* once by name, is a compilation of selections from a large variety of sources, most of which are the very same materials that the author of the *Yangsheng yaoji* drew on originally. One third of the section on gymnastics and massages of the *Yangxing yanming lu* consists of extracts from the *Yangsheng yaoji*.[10]

---

10. The quotation from the *Daoyin jing* that stands at the beginning of this central section (2.4ab) is also found in DZ 578, fasc. 321 (1ab) as quoted from the *Yangsheng yaoji*. Among other passages in the same section, quotations from the earlier text that are also mentioned in *Ishinpō* (27.23a–24a) are especially found on pages 4b–5b.

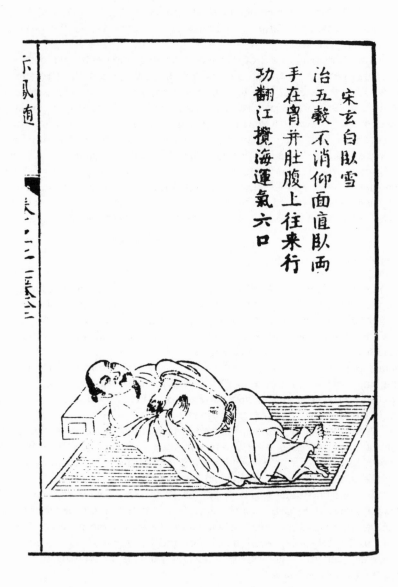

宋玄白臥雪
治五穀不消仰面直臥兩
手在胃并肚腹上往來行
功翻江攪海運氣六口

下臥趙

Fig. 2. Exercises in aid of the digestive process. *Source: Chifeng sui* 赤鳳髓 2.12a

The Laojun jue

One last source on gymnastics found in the Taoist Canon should be mentioned here: the *Taishang laojun yangsheng jue* 太上老君養生訣 (Formulas on Nourishing Life of the Highest Venerable Lord; DZ 821, fasc. 569), hereafter called the *Laojun jue*). This is a short text that rearranges a variety of gymnastic exercises. It is originally attributed to Hua Tuo 華陀, the famous physician of the Later Han dynasty.

This attribution is due to the fact that the first technique mentioned is the Five Animals Pattern, which is traditionally most closely associated with his name. The very same description of this pattern is also cited in the *Yangxing yanming lu* (2.7a–8a). The second part of the text describes six ways of expiration good for the five orbs or inner organs and the Triple Heater. The third part reveals the various secret formulas necessary for successfully undertaking the process of nourishing life. The fourth part describes the exact procedures for absorbing the *qi* with the help of visualizations, for retaining the *qi*, and for distributing it properly among the various members and organs of the body. So gymnastics here is closely associated with respiratory techniques.

Other Taoist Sources

Last but not least, the Taoist Canon contains a number of smaller sections within larger scriptures that have some bearing on the question of gymnastics, most frequently dealing with massages. There is, for example, Tao Hongjing's *Zhengao* 真誥 (Declarations of the Perfected; DZ 1016, fasc. 637–640) which describes a variety of relevant techniques (chaps. 9 and 10). The same methods are also found in the *Xiwangmu baoshen qiju jing* 西王母寶神起居經 (Scripture of the Rising and Resting of the Western Queen Mother's Treasured Spirit; DZ 1319, fasc. 1027), which precedes the *Zhengao*.

There are a number of other Taoist texts that can be dated to the Tang and contain a section on *daoyin*. However these do not, in actual fact, add any new gymnastic exercises. Rather, they limit themselves to citing or summarizing earlier materials.

1. The *Shesheng zuanlu* (DZ 578, fasc. 321). This text summarizes page 18–19 of the *Daoyin jing*. The same section is also found in *Yangxing yanming lu* 2.4ab and on pages 13–16 of the *Daolin lun*.

2. The *Zhenzhong ji* 枕中記 (Pillowbook Record; DZ 827, fasc. 570), by Sun Simiao. Here, in addition to a number of quotations of earlier

texts, the section on *daoyin* (8a–9a) corresponds to the techniques described in earlier texts, especially in the *Zhengao* (chaps. 9–10).

3. The *Zhiyan zong* (DZ 1033, fasc. 703). Here we find pages 13–16 of the *Daolin lun* reorganized in 5.1a–3b under the heading "Completing and Conducting the Breath."

4. The *Xiuzhen zhiyao* 脩真旨要 (Pointed Essentials Regarding the Cultivation of Perfection; DZ 1270, fasc. 1003). This text cites nineteen movements from the *Daolin lun* on pages 10b–11b.

An exceptional case is Sima Chengzhen's 司馬承禎 (655–735) *Xiuzhen jingyi zalun* 脩真精義雜論 (Miscellaneous Discourses on the Essential Meaning of Cultivating Perfection; DZ 277, fasc. 134).[11] This text gives a series of exercises to be practiced daily. It also insists on the importance of performing them in the proper order if they are to be effective in curing diseases and maintaining health. With this, the author presents a completely different stage of the development of *daoyin*.

The Zhubing yuanhou lun

The *Zhubing yuanhou lun* is a medical work that was presented to Emperor Yang of the Sui dynasty in 610 A.D. It had been compiled on imperial decree by a special editorial committee consisting of physicians and literati. Chao Yuanfang 巢元方 is usually named as its author, but sometimes also Wu Jingxian 吳京賢 appears in this role. It is a work of a scope unknown in China until then: for the first time, the entirety of Chinese nosology was put together in one volume. Another peculiarity of the work is that it provides therapeutic prescriptions for the cure of a large variety of diseases and conditions in the form of exercises traditionally used for nourishing life.

The book contains over a hundred quotations from a certain *Yangsheng fang* 養生方 (Methods for Nourishing Life), forty-one of which can be identified as going back to the *Yangsheng yaoji*, while two others are very close to it. Moreover, ten citations are also found in the *Yangxing yanming lu* and twelve others stem from the *Daolin lun*. On the whole it seems that the *Yangsheng fang* is more or less identical to the *Yangsheng yaoji*—or at least

---

11. On this text see Engelhardt 1987 as well as chapter 9, "*Qi* for Life: Longevity in the Tang."

based on it. In one instance, the *Zhubing yuanhou lun* even cites the text under the title *Yangsheng fang yaoji* (20.1402)[12]

The text introduces gymnastic exercises under the heading "Gymnastic Methods of the *Yangsheng fang.*" To a large extent (altogether seventy movements), it summarizes the techniques given in the *Daoyin jing.*

It is clear that among the various sources on gymnastics between the Han and Tang dynasties the *Yangsheng yaoji* occupies a central position. Most of the other works in some way or another go back to it, so it was certainly considered the standard textbook on the subject. All the sources strongly emphasize the therapeutic as well as the preventive aspects of the exercises. Yet each one integrates them into its overall system of practices differently, depending in each case on the primary concern and aim of the author.

The Principles: Origins and Purposes

The therapeutic and preventive aspects of Chinese gymnastics are fairly well known. Not so their origins, their roots in ancient practices of religion and magic. So it is important to spend a little time explaining the origins of the practices before discussing their specific purposes. All in all, one can most clearly trace *daoyin* back to ancient techniques of ecstasy—to shamanism.

Roots in Shamanism

The various traditions of *daoyin* all trace themselves back to rather well-known, albeit legendary, personages of old. There is the "Chinese Methuselah" Pengzu, there are the immortals Master Redpine and Wang Ziqiao, as well as the ancient master Ningfengzi, all mentioned in early hagiographic literature like the *Liexian zhuan* 列仙傳 (Immortals' Biographies) and associated with specific sets of exercises already in the *Daoyin jing.* The masters themselves, in addition, can be linked in one way or another to ancient techniques of shamanism.

Pengzu, to begin with the oldest, was originally the name of a local fief in the Jiangsu area that lasted there for eight hundred years. Legend then identified the place with its squire, and Pengzu, the great, long-lived sage, was born. The area was also associated with people who bore some relation to so-called "masters of fire" (Sakade 1985). At the same time, Pengzu's biography

---

12. The *Zhubing yuanhou lun* is cited after the 1980 Nanjing edition.

in the *Liexian zhuan* states that he was venerated especially as a master of the wind and the rain (Kaltenmark 1987: 83 n. 1).

Chisongzi, Master Redpine, was another of the early masters of gymnastics who is found among the immortals of the Han. He too was a master of the rain. This points directly to the tradition of shamanism, according to which the basic functions of the shaman were to secure rain at the proper time and in the proper amount. Already the *Zhouli* 周禮 (Rites of the Zhou) has:

> When there is a great drought in the realm, the chief shaman places himself at the head of his host and calls for rain while performing special dances. (chap. 25; Biot 1851: vol. 2: 102)

Besides the dances, another close connection of gymnastics to the fundamental techniques of shamanism is clearly evoked by Lü Buwei 呂不韋, the minister of Qin, who writes in his *Lüshi chunqiu* 呂氏春秋 (Mr. Lü's Spring and Autumn Annals):

> Once, under the reign of Emperor Yao, the power of yin was in abundance, there were numerous stagnations and manifold accumulations. The ways of the water were broken and obstructed, so that the flow was bad from the very sources.
> For the same reason, when the breath or energy of the individual is congested and stagnant, the muscles and the bones are contracted and don't flex well. One therefore prescribes certain dances which guide the breath and ensure that it moves throughout the body in a harmonious fashion. (5.5 of the *Zhuzi jicheng* edition)

The dances are therefore conceived of as a means of resolving the congestion and stagnation of vital energy, to ensure its healthy circulation within human beings, as much as they are used to help the flow of the rivers on the earth. The loosening of the limbs and proper guidance of the *qi* is one of the essential functions of *daoyin*. One may remember in this context the Pace of Yu, used in a large number of Taoist rituals, which, according to the original myth, was first used to "regulate the waters" and thereby establish a well-functioning spatio-temporal model of the world.

The popular dances of antiquity, which usually were held in the marketplace, had something to do with bringing rain, but they were also concerned with fertility and with death. Marcel Granet, for example, describes one function of the Crane Dance in connection with the death of the daughter of the King of Wu (r. 514–495 B.C.). This dance was carried out in the open market and signified the triumph over death (Granet 1959: vol. 1: 224). It is obvious that the crane, the symbol of the power over death, in due course would become one of the central images of the immortals. "The reason why the crane lives for a long time is that it does not have any breath of death," says the *Chunqiu fanlu* 春秋繁露 (Explanations on the Spring and Autumn Annals; 16.12a).

In addition, the crane dances remind us of another *daoyin* master: Wang Ziqiao. According to standard hagiography, he was given the *Xianghe jing* 相鶴經 (Scripture on Observation of Cranes) by his master Fuqiu gong 浮丘公. Bao Mingyuan 鮑明遠 in his *Wuhe fu* 舞鶴賦 (Crane Dance Rhapsody) describes the history of the text as follows:

> Later the art of becoming immortal by means of the crane dance as described in the text was put to good use by Cuiwenzi who hid the text in a grotto on Mount Song. Here the Eight Venerables, visitors to the court of Liu An, Prince of Huainan, found it, when they were searching for herbs. It was through them that the book became finally known to the world. (*Wenxuan* 14.10a)

Today the work is lost. However, as a work that was known to the magicians at the court of Liu An 劉安 in the beginning of the Han, it establishes a definite link between the Crane Dances and our master of gymnastics. More than that, Maxime Kaltenmark proposes the hypothesis that the Crane Dance was originally practiced on stilts, the latter being expressed in the word *qiao* 蹻, which is closely related to the second character in the personal name of Wang Ziqiao 喬 (Kaltenmark 1987: 113 n. 9).

Shamanistic dances were also used to expel evil or any sort of demonic influences, which could cause serious diseases, among other things. The shamans naturally were medicine men and women in the true sense of the term, they were conversant in medicinal herbs and simple drugs that could alleviate symptoms and heal sicknesses. In a similar way, *daoyin* is a practice that purports to drive all evil out of the body, a notion also present in the ancient meaning of the word *yin*: to pull close and expel. One still finds the term used in just this ancient sense in the *Zhubing yuanhou lun*.

> The practice consists in drawing together in one's body all the bad, the pathogenic, and the malevolent forms of *qi*, then one follows them, pulls them in and makes them leave forever. This is why the practice is called *daoyin*, to guide and pull. (22.1512)

The same sense of the term is also present in the inscriptions found in the *Daoyin tu* from Mawangdui.

Another theme that shamanistic dances and gymnastic practices have in common is their animal morphology, specifically the bird. This also connects them with the movements of Yu the Great, who in order to regulate the waters executed a bear dance. There are many other animal-inspired dances in ancient China, notably the dances of the twelve animals practiced to drive away the demons of pestilence (Granet 1959: vol. 1: 216).

In *daoyin* practice, there are a number of movements that represent imitations of animal patterns. Ge Hong says:

> Whoever can guide his breath like the dragon, pull it in and circulate it like the tiger, stretch like the bear or swallow it like the tortoise, who moreover can fly like the swallow, coil like the snake, stretch like the bird . . . he will live a long life.
> (*Baopuzi* 15; Wang 1980: 250)

Three major groups of animals may be distinguished: four-legged mammals, reptiles, and birds. It is the latter that appear most frequently in the texts dealing with gymnastics, just as they are the favorite animals of Siberian shamans, to whom auxiliary spirits equally appear in animal form.

Daoyin certainly owes a great deal to shamanism, but it is definitely distinct from it, too. Just as traditional Chinese medicine evolved from but is not identical to shamanistic medical practices, gymnastics are a later development of originally shamanistic techniques. There is strong evidence for an ongoing systematization and secularization of the exercises, which—once released from the bondage of exorcism—were no longer the prerogative of religious specialists. They became accessible to everyone and could be undertaken collectively or individually.

Gymnastics as Therapy

The *Huangdi neijing suwen*, the standard classic of Chinese traditional medicine that ultimately goes back to the Han dynasty, mentions *daoyin* in several places.[13] In it gymnastics are a form of therapy in the same vein as acupuncture, massages, and pharmacology. In one especially well-known chapter, where therapies are arranged according to the regional diversity and specific nature of the diseases, *daoyin* corresponds to the center of China. This may be where the technique originated; it certainly is where it was most prominently developed. The text says:

> The people of the central area suffer primarily from the changes between the hot and the cold breaths. It is best to take care of this condition by means of *daoyin* and massages. (4.12)

Gymnastic exercises were thus well established as a form of therapy around the third and second centuries B.C., in the Qin and Former Han dynasties. They continued to be used in the same way throughout the later periods of Chinese history. Even the oldest document extant, the *Daoyin tu* from Mawangdui, represents gymnastics in their therapeutic aspect. The manuscript shows forty-four gymnastic postures in four horizontal lines of eleven pictures each. The figures in the pictures are of men and women, younger and older people, clad in a variety of garments of red, blue, brown, and gray-green. They show different postures, mostly, however, based on an upright position.

Some of the figures are not entirely covered by their garments and some of these uncovered parts are only indicated in sketches, while others are outlined clearly and colored pink or grayish-brown. This coloring is especially visible in the head, arms, torso, and thighs. The double coloring possibly corresponds to the yin-yang dichotomy. The fact that one part of the body is colored certainly draws the attention of the observer to it and may also

---

13. The original redaction of the text dates from the first century before the Christian era. At that time, it was compiled on the basis of earlier, ancient documents that date to different periods. Some chapters are founded solidly on the theory of yin and yang but hardly ever mention the Five Agents that became the center of cosmological speculation toward the end of the Warring States period. Certain chapters (for example, chapter 3) do not mention any cyclical signs normally used to designate the time of day or the day of the month. Instead, these chapters use more ancient forms of reference. Chapters 4, 8, and 15 are considered later than the Han dynasty, because their contents, in contrast to those of the other parts of the text, are not mentioned in any way in the *Zhenjiu jiayi jing*, by Huangfu Mi of the Jin. Finally, chapters 66 to 72 are definitely dated to the Tang dynasty, when the existing edition of the work was put together.

indicate that the part in question was particularly active in the given exercise and responsible for the desired circulation of *qi*.

Originally an explanatory inscription was found next to each picture, but many of them have been erased or are hardly visible. Among those that can be read are some that indicate the therapeutic value of the practice. The problems treated are mainly related to the locomotive and the digestive systems, the two pathological areas about which most gymnastic literature was assembled in the succeeding centuries. Other common indications were deafness, inflammation of the testes, and spring fevers. The latter are caused by intensive frost in the winter. The cold settles down deep in the flesh and the bones, where it remains latent until it emerges as spring fever once it gets warmer.

Among all the gymnastic exercises that are considered useful in therapy and prevention of diseases, the Five Animals Pattern is the most popular. It is generally attributed to Hua Tuo, staff physician of Cao Cao under the Three Kingdoms. According to his official biography in the *Sanguo zhi* 三國志 (Record of the Three Kingdoms), he outlined the concepts underlying their practice to his disciple Wu Pu 吳誧 .

> The body needs a certain amount of movement. This movement serves to properly balance right and left, it helps to redistribute and assimilate the various breaths that are issued from the cereals, more than that it causes the blood to circulate properly and prevents the origination of diseases.
>
> The human body is like a door hinge that never comes to rest. This is why Taoists practice gymnastics. They imitate the movements of the bear which hangs itself head-down from a tree, of the owl which keeps turning its head in different ways. They stretch and bend the waist, and move all the joints and muscles of their bodies in order to evade aging.
>
> I myself have developed a series of exercises which I name the Five Animals Pattern. The five animals are the tiger, the deer, the bear, the monkey, and the bird. The practice of the Pattern aids the elimination of diseases and increases the functioning of the lesser members. Whenever a disorder is felt in the body one of the Animals should be practiced until one perspires freely. When perspiration is very strong, one should cover the affected parts of the body with dust. In due course one will find the body lighter, more comfortable and a healthy appetite will return. (*Sanguo zhi* 29.2a)

More detailed descriptions of the Five Animals Pattern have come down to us only from relatively late sources, the earliest of which are the *Yangxing yanming lu* and the *Laojun jue* (for an illustration see figure 3). It seems, however, that the pattern was quite popular during the Jin and the Six

Fig. 3. The immortal Fei Changfang practices the Monkey Pattern. *Source: Chifeng sui* 1.10b

Dynasties, since Ge Hong confirms its widespread use about a hundred years after Hua Tuo (*Baopuzi* 5; Wang 1980: 102; see also *Zhengao* 10.14b).

The greatest innovation in the field of therapeutical gymnastics is found in the *Zhubing yuanhou lun* of the year 610. This work gives a most exhaustive description of the pathology of the time. Whenever relevant it adds the specific gymnastic and other longevity exercises to be applied, classifying them according to pathological indication for the first time. Each general heading is divided into subsections that outline the specific origin of the disease in question, its process of development, and its major clinical symptoms. In most cases the introductory paragraph ends with these words:

> Besides decoctions, hot packs, acupuncture, and moxibustion, there are also valuable recipes for the harmonization and nourishment of the vital principle, for the correct guiding of the breath, and for its proper distribution in every part of the body. These are given below. . . .

The new classification of gymnastic movements in accordance with the origins and symptoms of a given condition represents a big step forward in the development of *daoyin*. For the first time, any interested practitioner now had an encyclopedic manual at hand in which to look up any exercise and its given indications. In the following centuries, under the Tang dynasty, gymnastics became an official part of the court medicine. The same situation was probably true already for the Sui, but it is not explicitly mentioned in the records. For this period one only knows that the Office of Medicine employed two massage specialists (*Suishu* 28.776). It is the massage specialist, however, who appears as the master of both gymnastics and massage under the Tang. The tradition of gymnastics prospered greatly in those days, both as a method of therapy and as preventive medicine. The two major medical works of that period, Sun Simiao's *Qianjin fang* of the year 652 and Wang Tao's 王燾 *Waitai biyao* 外臺秘要 (Secret Essentials of the Outer Terrace) of the year 752 contain *daoyin* exercises. The latter work in particular refers to practices already included in the *Zhubing yuanhou lun*.

Although theoretically gymnastics could be used to treat any disease in its early stages, it yet seems that there were certain ailments for which they were considered to be particularly effective. The texts refer to gymnastics especially in connection with problems of the arms and legs, with muscle tensions, rheumatism, locomotive troubles, paralyses, and so on. All these, in large part, belong to a group of ailments classified traditionally as "disorders caused by wind." In the same group one finds also digestive troubles, psychosomatic disorders, weaknesses in the circulation of blood, body fluids, or respiratory symptoms. On the other hand, fevers, epidemics, and the various disorders related to the seven orifices (ears, eyes, nose, mouth) are only occasionally mentioned as responding to gymnastics therapy. Instead, the *Zhubing yuanhou lun* especially praises mental exercises—concentrations and visualizations—for their prevention and cure.

Nourishing the Vital Principle

Already in the early period, in the *Zhuangzi*, gymnastics are described as a practice used to nourish the vital principle. They are praised as a useful means of preventing diseases and keeping the body from aging, thereby prolonging a healthy and joyful life. In that role such gymnastics flourished under the Han, the Three Kingdoms, and the following dynasties. In due course, the practices were integrated into the traditions of religious Taoism, notably by the Shangqing school. Thus they were practiced by the literati and became more and more popular among the upper classes.

The main techniques applied to lengthen life are dietetics, abstention from cereals, sexual practices, gymnastics, massages, breathing techniques, the circulation of *qi*, and visualizations of the body gods. The relationship between gymnastics and these other practices varies from age to age and among the different schools and groups. In general one may say that whenever they are arranged in a hierarchical fashion, gymnastics rank rather on the low side of the scale. They are frequently considered as being part of a preliminary phase, especially when immortality rather than health or longevity is the avowed aim. It is already clear in the *Zhuangzi* that gymnastics are somewhat inferior.

However, some adepts of longevity techniques emphasized the complementary nature of the various techniques rather than establishing a hierarchical systematization. The biography of Liu Gen 劉根, a magico-technician of the Three Kingdoms, describes them as follows:

> Generally speaking, the cultivation of the Tao of immortality consists of the absorption of drugs. Among these drugs, there are those superior and those inferior, just as there are higher and lesser immortals. When one does not know anything about sexual practices, breathing techniques or gymnastics or divine drugs, one cannot attain proper immortality. (*Hou Hanshu* 82.2746; Ngo 1976: 209)

Ge Hong takes an ambiguous stance toward the relative value of the various practices. Sometimes he insists that they are all necessary and complement each other, sometimes he ranks everything else below his favorite practice of alchemy.

The divine process leading to perfection of life
Does not depend upon offerings in honor of the ghosts and spirits

Nor upon gymnastics, bending and stretching,
The principal requirement for rising to immortality is divine
 cinnabar.
(*Baopuzi* 4; Wang 1980: 68; see also Ware 1966: 81)

Again he says:

Today, people practice gymnastics and breathing exercises,
revert their sperm to repair the brain, follow dietary rules,
regulate their activity and rest, take medicines, meditate on the
gods residing in their bodies, guard the One, undergo prohibitions and obey special precepts, wear amulets and seal from
their belts. Such people actually harm their lives and get further
away from it by employing all these techniques. (*Baopuzi* 5;
Wang 1980: 101)

When one examines these passages in the larger context of Ge Hong's work it
becomes evident that he looks upon gymnastics very much as the *Zhuangzi*
does: all longevity techniques are useful for nourishing life only when one
concentrates fully on them, but in doing that one is bound to lose sight of the
ultimate goal. This position is not a rejection of physical exercises, whose
practicability and usefulness is never questioned; it simply confirms their
limitations in relation to a higher aim. Another passage of the same work says,
in fact:

When one can guide the breath like the dragon, stretch oneself
like the tiger, hang oneself upside down like the bear, swallow
the breath like the turtle, fly like the swallow, writhe like the
snake, stretch upwards like the bird, carefully listen to heaven,
meticulously turn toward the earth and go along with the inner
luminants of the yellow and the red, without even entering the
secret grotto heavens, if one can hold on to a tree like the
monkey, be frightened like the hare, then one can live to a
thousand and two hundred years without ever experiencing any
diminishing of one's sensual faculties. (*Baopuzi* 5; Wang 1980:
103)

A similar attitude is expressed in various writings of the Shangqing
tradition of Taoism. On the one hand, physical practices are considered
inferior not to alchemy, but to the recitation and the practice of the *Dadong
zhenjing* 大洞真經 (Scripture of Great Pervasion). On the other hand, they
are accepted as necessary for the basic understanding of this text. The
Zhengao says:

When one absorbs vegetable drugs without any knowledge of
sexual practices, breathing techniques, and gymnastics, and
lacks interest in the exact procedure of absorption, one will not

attain the Tao. By means of conscious thinking one is able to activate divine forces. One can make them come forth quite without the help of vegetable drugs.

However, there may be someone who does not know the latter technique and only practices sexual techniques, gymnastics, and breathing exercises. Without undertaking the procedures of the divine cinnabar he will be quite unable to attain immortality. Once one has the golden fluid or the divine cinnabar, there are no other methods necessary, one will inevitably become immortal.

Even better get hold of the *Dadong zhenjing*! Then you have no need for the methods of gold and cinnabar either. Just recite the divine scripture a thousand times, and without fail you will ascend to the immortals. As concerns the practice of sexual techniques, gymnastics, and breathing exercises, there are numerous books about them and we don't have to go into them at this point. (5.11b)

Yet the very same text also says a little further down:

If one never practices abstention from cereals one cannot expect to even hear about the *Dadong zhenjing*. (5.15b)

Gymnastics and Fasting

Gymnastics are related to a variety of other techniques. Under the Han, for example, abstention from cereals and gymnastics were closely connected. Zhang Liang 張良 (d. 186 B.C.), the supernaturally inspired adviser of the first Han emperor, is said to have been frequently ill, so that he took to the practice of gymnastics and abstention from cereals, following the methods of Master Redpine (*Shiji* 55.2048). Similarly, in the *Daoyin tu* from Mawangdui the depictions of gymnastic exercises are preceded by a short notice on abstention from cereals.

The association of these two practices is also found in the following centuries, mentioned in the *Baopuzi* (chap. 15; Wang 1980: 245) and in a number of texts from the Taoist Canon, especially the *Shenxian shiqi jingui miaolu* and the *Xiuzhen jingyi zalun*. Even Tao Hongjing, the organizer and propagator of the Shangqing teachings, and Sima Chengzhen, the twelfth patriarch of the same school, were—at least according to their standard biographies—expert practitioners of the same two techniques (*Suishu* 35.1093; *Jiu Tangshu* 192.5127).

The word cereals in expressions like "not eating cereals" or "abstention from cereals" must be understood as referring in a general way to the common diet of the people of the day, which of course consisted in large part of cereals.

The texts specify quite clearly that the practice of abstention is not a total fasting, but rather a replacement of ordinary food with more refined and subtle materials, usually concoctions or drugs with vegetable or mineral bases. In turn, minerals and their preparation play an important part in alchemy. These subtle materials are sometimes also associated closely with the absorption of "talisman water," the ashes of a talisman dissolved in water. In describing the abstention from cereals the manuscript from Mawangdui shows how subtle and elaborate the technique already was in those days. In fact, the text reveals a level of explication quite absent from later materials. For example, it clearly spells out that, upon abstention from cereals, adepts are supposed to nourish exclusively on a certain plant (Pyrrosia lingue Thunb.). Moreover, they are to use it in quantities that correspond to the waxing and waning of the moon.

The practice of abstention from cereals may be viewed from several angles. Examples of mythological interpretations are found in the work of Stein (1972, 1973) and Levi (1983). Also significant are the socio-historical implications of the practice. It was put to good use and probably even developed especially during extended periods of famine, which were common around the end of the Later Han. Mouzi 牟子 reports that after the fall of Emperor Ling (168–189) practitioners of abstention from cereals were exceedingly numerous (*Taishō Tripitaka* 2102; 52.1b). The cases of Xun Yu 荀彧 and Han Rong 韓融 from Yingchuan are known in more detail. During the rebellion of Dong Zhuo 董卓 (189–192) the two of them fled together with a large number of refugees to mountains in the West of Mi in Henan. Here they gave themselves over to techniques of nourishing life (*Hou Hanshu* 70.2281).

When used with abstention from cereals, gymnastics are most frequently considered a complementary method that helps to eliminate bad energies and induces good energies to stay in the body. They are useful in eradicating blockages and stagnations of energy and making the inner fluids circulate more smoothly. At the same time, as documented in a Tang dynasty text, the reciprocal nature of the various practices is never lost from sight.

> Those who wish to practice gymnastics must first of all, with the help of breathing techniques, abstain from all cereals and learn how to swallow the breath. To begin with, adepts swallow only the gross breath. One holds the breath in the throat and mouth area, then swallows it for twenty or thirty times. Once the lower abdomen and the stomach area have been well filled with breath, one can hear them rumble. (*Qifa yaomiao zhijue* 5b; DZ 831, fasc. 571)

Gymnastics and Massages

Very frequently gymnastics are also associated with self-massages, if not actually merged with them. The fifth section of the *Yangxing yanming lu*, for example, is entitled "Gymnastics and Massages." Similarly, a whole series of gymnastic exercises are in fact practices of massages, so that sections with titles like "Massage Techniques" more often than not deal with gymnastics. In fact, the very same practices may appear in another text under the heading "Gymnastics."[14]

Just as gymnastics serve to eliminate blockages and coagulations of energy within the body, massages help to open the barriers and smooth the circulation of the body fluids. Normal and even perfect harmony of the various energies is thereby reestablished and maintained. But where gymnastics create harmony from the inside, using the movements of the body and the circulation of *qi* with the help of the conscious mind, massages strengthen the body from without, applying physical, outward pressure. Self-massages are especially used to warm the body, to make it glow with an outer radiance. So massages are frequently used as preliminary, warming-up exercises. They serve, as Sima Chengzhen has it, to make energy return everywhere and establish a communication of the within and the without (*Xiuzhen jingyi zalun* 2a). Figure 4 shows an adept performing a self-massage.

Finally, gymnastics are almost always presented in connection with breathing techniques and the circulation of *qi*. One may practice each one in isolation, but they have a far better effect when they are harmoniously joined together into one sequence of exercises. Thus breathing and *qi* circulation form an integral part of gymnastics. One should not be undertaken without the other.

The Practice: Positions and Movements

In the practice of gymnastics, the individual makes certain outer or inner movements of the body in correlation with breathing exercises and with special meditative techniques designed to expel negative energies and enhance positive energies.

---

14. The same techniques are found in the *Daolin lun* (13b–16b) and the *Qianjing fang* (652) as massages and in the *Zhiyan zong* (5.1–3), the *Zhengyi fawen xiuzhen zhiyao* (10b–11b; DZ 1270, fasc. 1003), and the *Shesheng zuanlu* (1) as gymnastics.

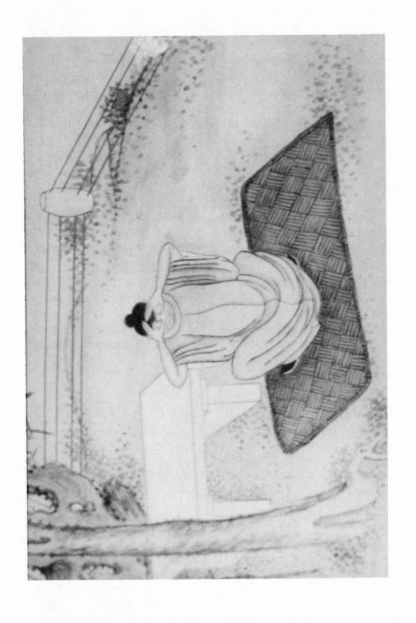

Fig. 4. Preparing for the absorption of *qi* by Beating the Heavenly Drum.

All gymnastic movements and exercises should be undertaken in a calm and quiet place, usually in a closed room rather than outdoors. One should have a mat or even a bed to sit and lie down on (*Daoyin jing* 1a). Some texts also recommend that one have a raised platform to practice on in order to avoid the possibly disruptive energies of the earth and of lower demons. As Daolin has it:

> Whenever one undertakes gymnastics, one should stretch out on a raised bed. Thus one will avoid the earthly energies which may cause upward interruption and the demonic forces which may attack people. (16b)

When one performs the exercises for the purpose of therapy, the specific direction toward which they are aimed does not seem to matter. But when they are used as longevity techniques, there are some instructions that detail the geographical orientation of the exercises. The East seems to be the most frequently mentioned direction. It corresponds to spring, to the rising energy of life, so it is an appropriate orientation for longevity exercises. Already the *Daoyin jing* cites the gymnastics of Master Redpine as following this direction, and Shangqing materials take up the same tendency.

A smaller number of exercises should be performed facing the direction that corresponds to whatever the season is (*Zhubing yuanhou lun* 19.1485; *Xiwang mu baoshen qiju jing* 15a). Certain massages should be practiced in the direction of one's "basic fate"—that is, the spatial equivalent of the cyclical sign of the day of one's birth. Others are specifically oriented toward the Northeast or Northwest in correspondence to the gates of the spirit and material souls (*Xiwang mu baoshen qiju jing* 7a–8a). On the other hand, certain directions such as the North should always be avoided, because they evoke the displeasure of the gods (*Daoyin jing* 17a).

Gymnastics are practiced only temporarily when they are used as therapy to cure a specific ailment. As Master Ning says in the *Daoyin jing*:

> Someone may suddenly be afflicted by an ailment caused by the wind, by rheumatism, paralysis, deafness, dizziness, epileptic seizures, coughs accompanied by inversion and upsets of breath, by pains in the back and hip areas. In such a case he or she should check back with the instructions and commence certain gymnastic movements. This way one will guide the breath and make it circulate all around the body. Thereby the roots of the ailment will be driven out completely with the help of one's creative consciousness. (6b)

According to Hua Tuo, perspiration is the first good sign of improving health.

> Whoever feels sick anywhere in the body should undertake the practice of one or the other of the Ánimals Patterns. The practice may be stopped when one has perspired strongly. (*Sanguo zhi* 29.2a)

As a longevity technique, gymnastics should be practiced in the same way as breathing exercises and *qi* circulation, at certain prescribed hours when the "*qi* of life" is particularly strong. These are especially the times between the hours known as *zi* and *wu*, between midight and noon (see *Daoyin jing* 2a). The *Zhenzhong ji* says:

> Swallow the saliva regularly and always during the time of day that corresponds to the *qi* of life. (8b)

At the same time, the period most preferred for the practice is dawn or sunrise. As the *Yangxing yanming lu* says:

> At the clarity of dawn, before you get up, practice some massages. . . . When the sun rises do certain gymnastic exercises. (2.4ab)

Gymnastics, therefore, should be part of everyone's daily round of activities, as life-giving and as necessary as eating, drinking, and sleeping.

The instructions that limit the practice of gymnastics to certain directions and specific times of the day provide it with a particular sense of ritual and formality. In addition, certain sources also require the observance of a number of precepts and preliminary purifications.

> When practicing gymnastics or absorption of *qi*, imagine the two arbiters of destiny turning with you to the right and the left. They should always be thought of as present. Similarly, during the practice visualize the yellow light of the inner spirit together with the brilliant moon to your right and left. These two should equally always remain present, night and day. (*Daoyin jing* 17ab)

Such preliminary meditative measures are taken whenever an adept feels them necessary in accordance with the particular tradition of gymnastics he or she follows.

Positions of the Body

Whether the whole body or certain parts of it move, or whether a particular posture is taken and maintained for a certain time, in all the gymnastic techniques—breathing, absorption and circulation of *qi*—three fundamental positions are distinguished: standing, sitting, and lying down. See figure 5 for an example of an adept performing a gymnastic exercise while lying on his stomach.

In the sources of the ancient tradition the standing position is hardly ever mentioned. Exercises are often done while the practitioner is lying down, but most common is the sitting position.

A reclining posture, on the back, the stomach, or either side, is usually aided by a pillow made from wood, bamboo, or porcelain. Its height is of utmost importance.

> When the pillow is too high, the liver is contracted. When it is too low, the lungs are squeezed. The normal height of the pillow is about four inches, it should be covered with a flexible soft material, so that equal and deep breaths are easily possible. (*Daoji jing* cited in DZ 1033, fasc. 703; 2.12b)

The height of four inches is usually given in texts associated with the tradition of Wang Ziqiao (*Daoyin jing* 7b). Another lineage, associated with Pengzu, specifies that the pillow should be exactly two-and-one-half inches high.[15]

Movements

When one considers merely the outer movements of the body, of the torso and the limbs, one is astonished at how amazingly simple the exercises are, how easy to perform. Very little space is needed, hardly any effort necessary, no difficult contortions required. So people of any class or age would ifnd them easy to perform.

The movements are essentially stretches of the limbs, especially of the legs and feet. In general, one finds that the feet play an important role in the exercises. In addition there are a certain number of stretches of the back, flexings of the torso, and swings of the hips. In most cases the movements are undertaken in a playful rhythm that ensures that the breathing stays regular and becomes increasingly deeper. Special care is taken with the areas where

---

15. The relevant passage here is found in *Ishinpō* 27.18b after the *Yangsheng yaoji*. It is later cited in the *Daolin lun* (18a), the *Zhenzhong ji* (10a), the *Shenxian shiqi jingui miaolu* (7b), and the *Zhiyan zong* (2.12b).

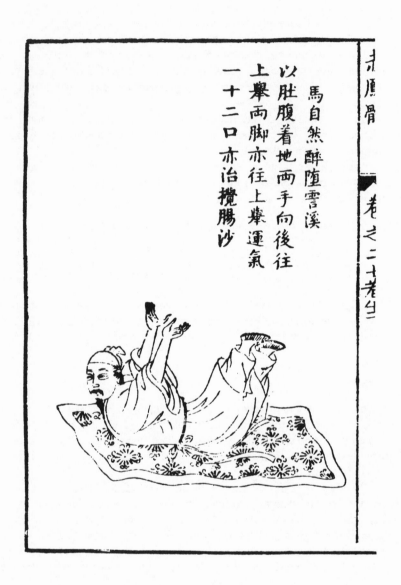

馬自然醉墮雲溪

以肚腹着地兩手向後往

上舉兩脚亦往上舉運氣

一十二口亦治攬腸沙

赤鳳髓

卷之二十卷之二

Fig. 5. Gymnastic exercises performed while lying on the stomach. *Source: Chifeng sui* 2.12b

the *qi* enters and leaves the body as well as where it tends to stagnate. The latter frequently coincide with the joints. Pathogenic energies and influences of death are carefully kept out. As Master Ning says in the *Daoyin jing*:

> Gymnastics are helpful in the elimination of all the pathogenic energies that may afflict the limbs. They are also good for guarding the proper state of the *qi* of health throughout the body. (6a)

For all functional disorders affecting the torso, exercises are used that consist of maintaining a certain posture over a given span of time while the adept mentally guides the *qi* through the body.

> Those who practice circulation of *qi* may perfect their inner state, those who practice gymnastics may cure afflictions of the limbs. (*Daoyin jing* 6b)

All movements should be executed carefully and rhythmically so that all tensions will be eliminated. Gradually the movements affect the inside of the body more and more, so that the outer practice of gymnastics is gradually replaced by the inner practice of the *qi*. The latter is a slow guiding, a circulation done at every individual's own speed. Eventually the entire body is moved by the inner circulation of *qi*, a technique vitally important in the entire process of gymnastics.

Breathing

Breathing is one of the most important elements of gymnastics. Adepts are trained to breathe in and out through the nose, in through the nose and out through the mouth, or in through the mouth and out through the nose. The oldest formula that describes breathing is "expel the old and pull in the new." Here breathing is already understood as a means of driving out impure and pathogenic and taking in pure and healthy breath. The manuscripts of Mawangdui, in describing the various practices aimed at nourishing the vital principle, again and again come back to breathing exercises used to absorb positive and energizing *qi*. The exercises are to be performed in accordance with a given direction and a specific season and only at certain hours of the day. These rules prevent the practitioners from unintentionally absorbing bad energies (see Mawangdui 1985).

Its incoming and outgoing movement makes the breathing a motor and later also a regulator for the internal circulation of the *qi*. Pure breath taken in through inhalations is still considered a universal cure for all sorts of illnesses;

it works by "attacking"[16] their evil powers in a struggle between the forces of life against the demonic forces of death. Often the fighting action within the body is supported by holding the breath, a sort of delimitation of the battle field that prevents reinforcements of evil from entering in. Once the body is properly insulated, one can heal oneself by consciously directing attention to the sick part of the body.

> Whenever you fall sick, first of all regulate the breathing, then swallow the *qi* and fixate your attention on the afflicted area. Practice holding the breath and by means of conscious attention visualize how the breath concentrates in the painful part. Imagine how the healthy breath attacks the illness and, when you cannot retain the breathing any longer, slowly exhale. (*Huanzhen xiansheng funei yuanqi jue* 6b; DZ 828, fasc. 570)

The various breathing exercises and holding the breath not only help heal diseases, but can also be used as preventive measures against all sorts of negative influences. They are in all cases part of the daily round of exercises prescribed for every practitioner of gymnastics and especially for those who wish to nourish their vital principle.

Holding the breath is a popular way to produce perspiration. It is one of the therapies most commonly employed to drive out pathogenic influences from the superficial layers of the body. It is especially found in connection with pharma-therapy. The exact procedure is described as an exercise against the influences of the wind and the cold.

> In order to bring forth perspiration by means of breathing, one should lie down on the side and practice holding the breath for as long as possible. After one round breathe again normally and wait until the breathing has become stable. Then hold the breath once more. Continue until you perspire heavily. (*Zhubing yuanhou lun* 18.1411)

Breathing on the outside of the body goes together with the circulation of *qi* on its inside. As the *Baopuzi* explains:

> Those who know breathing techniques claim that only circulation of breath can prolong life. (6; Wang 1980: 113)

Usually when a particular body posture is taken, breathing is rhythmical; an inhalation is followed by an exhalation, both through the nose. Only

---

16. Physicians or drugs commonly attack illnesses. Military terminology is used frequently in medical literature, on pharmacology or acupuncture. Pertinent examples are the expressions "defensive" and "protective" energy.

occasionally is the breath held in between. The number of respirations for which one particular posture should be maintained varies according to the different traditions. Five or seven are the most common numbers, but there are also cases in which one should hold a position for several tens of respirations.

Since breathing is a constant exchange of the inner and the outer, it also plays an important role in setting the inner circulation of *qi* in motion and in eliminating eventual blockages on the way. It also serves to harmonize the movements into a proper rhythm and to maintain a given posture.

In the gymnastics tradition of Wang Ziqiao holding the breath in certain body postures is practiced in accordance with certain ailments of the body.

> Holding the breath will cure all diseases. If one wants to get a pull on ailments affecting the head one had better raise it somewhat. In order to pull ailments of the hips and the limbs one should stretch and raise the toes. To pull on diseases of the thorax stretch the toes away from you. To deal with sicknesses of the arms keep them covered. If you want to eliminate disorders affecting the abdomen or any conditions of heat or cold in this area, begin by making it full and round. All breathing throughout the exercises should be done through the nose alone. The practice should not be continued after the condition has improved. (*Daoyin jing* 9a)

Although the various gymnastic movements of the body help to establish the proper circulation of the *qi*, the continued practice of this circulation is more a mental, meditational technique in which the energy within the body is guided along by conscious attention. The inner circulation is therefore first of all an act of the creative imagination, but it is increasingly manifested also in distinct physical sensations: adepts begin to feel light and free, they are aware of their various internal organs, they experience energy whirling all around themselves, they feel heat, tingling and many other things. All this can be described as a visualization of the circulation of energy within the body, as a creative imagination of the interior of the body in great detail that in due course gives rise to physical feelings and awareness.

Gymnastics and these techniques of the breath are equivalent and complementary at the same time. Equivalent because in many cases adepts or patients have the choice of using one or the other; complementary because gymnastics are especially helpful for all afflictions of the outer body, the limbs and the torso, the bones and the muscles, while the breath, held or circulated, affects most strongly the inner organs and circulation of the body fluids. As the *Daoyin jing* has it:

Those who are able to circulate the *qi* can perfect the inside of their bodies, those who are good at doing gymnastic exercises can cure all ailments of the limbs. (6b)

Conclusion

In the West, the tradition of physical exercise has never developed to the same degree as in China, but it has always been seen as a useful and necessary means to fuller health. With the ancient Greeks and their Olympic festivals, the concept of competition entered the understanding of physical practices, never to leave again. The result was that physical exercise became something strenuous, an area in which human beings could excel and go beyond their ordinary powers: longer, stronger, faster, farther was their aim. Physical exercises were used as a means to project a particular image of the human being as powerful and independent. They reinforced man's position in relation to himself and society, even in relation to the state and the world. Certainly, there also existed a tradition in ancient Greece of using gymnastics for therapy, but Hippocratic medicine allotted them a place of relative unimportance, on the same level as dietetics. These ancient gymnastic exercises were later taken up by Galen (130–200 A.D.) and continue to be more or less important. But it is only nowadays that people in the West have again begun to pay attention to the importance of gymnastic exercises in the overall health of the individual.

In China, therapeutic and preventive measures have been thought of very highly since antiquity. The reason is that these exercises fit in with a particular understanding of the human body, a uniquely Chinese way of looking at life and death. The movement of the body was secondary for them. It only accompanied the primordial movement of the universe, which, in human beings, is found in the spirit and mediated by the conscious attention, the creative thinking. This cosmic agent was ultimately responsible for any movement of the body, so the body in itself was neither demanded to strain to its limits nor thought of as important. Reduced to its ultimate minimum, physical exercise in China consisted only of stretches of the limbs. It served to make the joints more flexible and dissolve all blockages in the way of energy and spirit.

Associated with the various other longevity and meditation techniques of the Taoist tradition, gymnastics are found to represent a preliminary stage on the path to liberation of body and spirit. They were most closely linked with breathing exercises, diet control, and abstention from cereals, as well as with elementary alchemy (drugs), visualizations and concentrative meditations. Gymnastics could thus be employed in a variety of ways and joined with many other different practices in proper accordance with the particular tradition and process in question. Physical exercise also came to be looked on as a preventive measure used in the framework of traditional medicine, acting against all sorts of afflictions, including the inconveniences of getting older and weaker. Gymnastics were moreover a technique that, when accompanied by visualizations, aimed at refining the elixir, at recovering and harmonizing the vital forces of the three cinnabar fields. Thus used, they were a means not only to longevity but to immortality. Basically a means of expelling bad and old, used-up energies, gymnastics at the same time helped adepts absorb good, new, and vital forces. They represent an important step on the way toward harmonization of the individual with heaven and earth.

References

Barret, T.H. 1980. "On the Transmission of the *Shen tzu* and of the *Yang-sheng yao-chi*," *Journal of the Royal Asiatic Society* 2 (1980), 168–176.

—— 1982. "Taoist and Buddhist Mysteries in the Interpretation of the *Tao-te-ching*," *Journal of the Royal Asiatic Society* 1 (1982), 35–43.

Biot, Eouard. 1851. *Le Tcheou-li. Rites des Tcheou.* 3 vols. Paris, 1851.

Engelhardt, Ute. 1987. *Die klassische Tradition der Qi-Übungen: Eine Darstellung anhand des Tang-zeitlichen Textes Fuqi jingyi lun von Sima Chengzhen.* Wiesbaden: Franz Steiner, 1987.

Granet, Marcel. 1959. *Danses et légendes de la Chine ancienne.* 2 vols. Paris: Presses Universitaires de France, 1959.

Kaltenmark, Maxime. 1987. *Le Lie-sien tchouan. Biographies légendaires des immortels taoistes de l'antiquité.* Paris: 1987.

Levi, Jean. 1983. "L'abstinence des cereáles chez les taoistes," *Etudes Chinoises* 1 (1983), 3–47.

Liu Ts'un-yan. 1973. "The Compilation and Historical Value of the *Tao-tsang*." In *Essays on the Sources of Chinese History*, pp. 104–120. Edited by Donald Leslie. Canberra, 1973.

Loon, Piet van der. 1984. *Taoist Books in the Libraries of the Sung Period.* London: Oxford Oriental Institute, 1984.

Maspero, Henri. 1981. "Methods of 'Nourishing the Vital Principle' in the Ancient Taoist Religion," in *Taoism and Chinese Religion*. Amherst: University of Massachusetts Press, 1981, 431–554.

Ngo Van Xuyet. 1976. *Divination, Magie et Politique dans la Chine anciénne*. Paris: Presses Universitaires de France, 1976.

Ofuchi Ninji. 1979. "The Formation of the Taoist Canon." In *Facets of Taoism*, pp. 253–268. Edited by H. Welch and A. Seidel. New Haven & London: Yale University Press, 1979.

Sakade, Yoshinobu. 1986. "The Taoist Character of the 'Chapter on Nourishing Life' of the *Ishinpō*," *Kansai daigaku bunka ronshū* 1986, 775–798.

Stein, Rolf A. 1972. "Spéculations mystiques et thèmes rélatifs aux 'cuisines' du taoisme," *Annuaire du Collège de France* 1972, 489–499.

—— 1973. "Conceptions rélatives a la nourriture (Chine)," *Annuaire du Collège de France* 1973, 547–563.

Thompson, Laurence. 1985. "Taoism: Classic and Canon." In *The Holy Book in Comparative Perspective*, pp. 204–223. Edited by Denny, F.M. and R.L. Taylor. Columbus: University of South Carolina Press: 1985.

Ware, James R. 1966. *Alchemy, Medicine and Religion in the China of A.D. 320. The Nei P'ien of Ko Hung (Pao-p'u tzu)*. Cambridge, Massachusetts: MIT Press, 1966.

Watson, Burton. 1968. *The Complete Works of Chuang-tzu*. New York: Columbia University Press, 1968.

in Chinese and Japanese

Mawangdui 馬王堆 1985
Mawangdui Hanmu boshu 馬王堆漢墓帛書
Beijing: Wenwu, 1985.

Mugitani Kunio 麥谷邦夫 (ed.)
Yōsei enmei roku kunchō 養性延命錄順註
Tokyo: Report of the Study Group on Traditional Chinese Longevity Techniques no. 3, 1987.

Sakade Yoshinobu 坂出祥伸 1985
"Hōso densetsu to Hōsokyō" 彭祖傳說と彭祖經
Yamada 1985: vol. 2: 405–462.

—— 1986a. "Chō Tan 'Yōsei yōshū' itsubun to sono shisō"
張湛の養生要集佚文 とその 思想
Tōhōshūkyō 68 (1986), 1–24.

Wang Ming 王明 1980
Baopuzi neipian xiaoshe 抱朴子内篇校攝
Beijing: Zhonghua, 1980.

Wenwu 文物 1985
"Jiangling zhangjia shan hanjian gaishu" 江陵張家山漢簡概述
Wenwu 1985/1, 9–15.

Yamada Keiji 山田慶兒 1985
Chūgoku shinhakken kagakushi shiryō no kenkyū
中國新發現科學史資料の研究
2 vols. Kyoto: Jimbun Kagaku Kenkyūjo, 1985.

Chapter Nine

Qi for Life: Longevity in the Tang

Ute Engelhardt

Introduction

The Taoist encyclopedia *Yunji qiqian* 雲笈七籤 (Seven Slips from a Cloudy Satchel), found in the Taoist Canon (DZ 1032, fasc. 677–702),[1] contains two exemplary texts on nourishing life by means of *qi* 氣.[2] They are both attributed to eminent Taoists of the Tang dynasty: the *Fuqi jingyi lun* 服 氣精 義論 (Discourse on the Essential Meaning of Absorption of *Qi*) in chapter 57 and the *Sheyang zhenzhong fang* 攝養枕中論 (Pillowbook of Methods for Nourishing Life) in chapter 33. The former was written by Sima Chengzhen 司馬承禎 (647–735), twelfth patriarch of the Shangqing or Highest Clarity school of Taoism. The latter is attributed to Sun Simiao 孫 思邈 (581?–682), eminent Taoist, alchemist, and physician of approximately the same time.

These texts have in common that they deal with ways of avoiding illness and of prolonging life by keeping in good health. The state of perfect

---

1. Texts in the Taoist Canon (*Daozang*, hereafter abbreviated DZ) are given according to the number of the reduced sixty-volume edition published in Taipei and Kyoto. These numbers coincide with those found in K.M. Schipper, *Concordance du Tao Tsang* (Paris: Publications de l'Ecole Francaise d'Extrême-Orient, 1975). "Fasc." stands for "fascicle" and refers to the volume number of the 1925 Shanghai reprint of the original canon of 1445 (*Zhengtong Daozang*).

2. *Qi* can be translated "breath," "vapor," "cloud," or "finest influences." However, especially in the context of *qi* practices leading to longevity, it can hardly be denied that the term also connotes energy of some sort. Since there is no one translation that fits every instance of usage and that would be universally convincing, the word will remain untranslated here.

263

health, in turn, may later lead on to higher religious attainments, such as a union with the Tao itself. The techniques of nourishing life described in these texts are therefore preliminary to further spiritual development and religious accomplishment. In their main lines of argument they both rely heavily on the concepts of traditional Chinese medicine. Chinese medical techniques themselves are, of course, complex systems aimed less at eliminating specific diseases than at promoting a balanced way of life. Not only physical and psychological hygiene but also social factors are involved.

Analyzing these two exemplary texts reveals their respective traditions and underlying concepts and highlights the main lines of Taoist longevity ideas and practices of the Tang. This is of special interest because the two authors are certainly the most significant representatives of those ideas. Sun Simiao is the most famous physician of the time, and Sima Chengzhen as patriarch of the Shangqing school headed the religious life of the period.

The Authors

Sima Chengzhen

Sima Chengzhen lived in the early Tang dynasty, from 647 to 735. The date of his death has also been given as 727 (Engelhardt 1987: 27, 51). A native of Wen in Henan, he was born into a noble family that had produced numerous high officials as well as founders of dynasties.

As a young man, Sima Chengzhen lived on Mount Song near Luoyang. At the age of 21, he underwent Taoist initiation under Pan Shizheng 潘師正 (d. 684), the eleventh patriarch of the Shangqing school. In 684, he succeeded his master as the twelfth patriarch. He was the fourth direct successor of Tao Hongjing 陶弘景 (456–536), the true founder of this sect. He then settled on Mount Tongbo of the Tiantai range in Zhejiang, where, "at the beginning of the fifth century, the Shangqing texts were propagated for the first time" (Strickmann 1981: 34).

He was invited to court four times: first by the Empress Wu (r. 690–705), then, in 711, by Emperor Ruizong (r. 710–711). This emperor built a monastery for him in the Tiantai Mountains, and one of his daughters became Sima Chengzhen's disciple. The remaining two invitations were issued by Emperor Xuanzong (r. 712–756) in the years 721 and 727. He thought very highly of the Taoist master and ordered him to take up residence on Mount Wangwu, which was closer to the capital than his first retreat. According to the Shangqing tradition, Mount Wangwu contains the first of ten

司馬承禎

Fig. 1. Sima Chengzhen. *Source: Sancai tuhui* 三才圖會

large grotto heavens, so it seemed the appropriate place to house an eminent patriarch of this school. The emperor had a large monastery erected there, the Yangtai guan (Bellevedere of the Sunlit Terrace), where Sima Chengzhen spent the later part of his life.

It was due to Sima Chengzhen's influence at court that the Shangqing school could extend its influence even over the gods of the five sacred peaks. Sima Chengzhen convinced Xuanzong that these important national gods were in fact under the superintendence of the Realized Ones of Shangqing, the Heaven of Highest Clarity. Thus, in 727, the emperor ordered officially sponsored shrines to be built on the five sacred peaks.

In 735, Sima Chengzhen departed this world and his home on Mount Wangwu. According to his biographies, this event was announced by a pair of cranes and white clouds,[3] an image commonly associated with high Taoist masters.[4] Figure 1 is a portrait of Sima Chengzhen.

Sun Simiao

As in the case of Sima Chengzhen, biographical sources dealing with Sun Simiao reveal but little on the historical person. They are more of a hagiographic nature, idealizing the subject's character and embellishing his life with standard motifs of legends and myths.[5]

Sun Simiao supposedly was born in 581 as a native of Huayuan in Jingzhao prefecture, an area close to the western capital Changan. He began his studies at the age of seven, so that at twenty he not only had an extensive knowledge of the classics and of the philosophers such as Laozi and Zhuangzi, but was also familiar with Buddhist scriptures. He then went to live in seclusion on Mount Taibo in the Zhongnan range in Shaanxi, about a hundred miles from his ancestral home.

Emperor Wen of the Sui (r. 589–604) and Emperor Taizong of the Tang (r. 627–649) both summoned Sun Simiao to the capital to bestow academic titles and noble ranks upon him, but he declined those honors. In 659, Gaozong (r. 650–683) received him in official audience. It appears that although Sun Simiao entered court life around that time, he did not

---

3. "White Cloud" is also an agnomen of his.

4. There are two official biographies of Sima Chengzhen: One is found in *Jiu Tangshu* 192, the other in *Xin Tangshu* 196. For a more detailed discussion of the sources on his life and works see Engelhardt 1987: 20–61.

5. For a detailed study of the historical value of Sun Simiao's official biographies, see Sivin 1968: 81–144.

compromise himself by accepting official responsibilities. Rather, he remained in the emperor's retinue for fifteen years in some informal capacity. In 674, he requested permission to retire from the court on account of illness.

Sun Simiao presumably died in 682. To illustrate the notion that he attained immortality, the sources insist that for one month after his demise there was no change in his appearance. Moreover, when his corpse was placed in the coffin, it was as light as cloth. None of the many accounts and anecdotes recorded in his official biographies furnish reliable information regarding his life. All we know for sure are his date of birth and the fact that he was in the emperor's retinue in 673.

Yet some further information can be gathered about the exact circumstances of Sun Simiao's life and work from certain autobiographical accounts he left behind. For one thing, they show that he traveled much more widely than one would guess from his official biographies. A case in point are his repeated travels to Sichuan, which explains why he is linked with that area in a number of legends. Moreover, Sun Simiao's description of his personal medical case history informs us of his alchemical experiments, due to which he suffered from mineral poisoning several times (Sivin 1968: 136–144, Appendix A). In addition, certain passages in his *Qianjin yifang* 千金翼方 (Revised Prescriptions Worth a Thousand Ounces of Gold, chaps. 29, 30) suggest that he was personally involved with the Celestial Masters. He quotes certain exorcistic formulas that were reserved for the exclusive recital by Taoist masters of this denomination and it seems highly unlikely that someone not an initiated member would have had access to them (Sivin 1978: 312).

Soon after his death numerous different legends dealing with Sun the Immortal developed (see figure 2). Down to the present day there have been many temples dedicated to him, and he has been worshiped by the common people as a King of Medicines (see Despeux 1987: 24–34).

Fig. 2. Sun the Immortal. *Source: Liexian quanzhuan* 列仙全傳 , p. 366

The *Fuqi jingyi lun*

Context and Environment

According to Chen Guofu, Sima Chengzhen wrote or edited fifteen works, nine of which are still extant (Chen 1963: 52–59). Considering the titles of all his works, they can be generally divided into five groups: geographical descriptions, biographical works, texts on magical objects and formulas, theoretical treatises, and practical instructions.

Sima Chengzhen's high formal position as patriarch of the Shangqing school is reflected in his works, which are deeply rooted in the Shangqing tradition. For instance, he wrote a stele inscription in honor of Tao Hongjing and gave a geographical description of the thirty-six grotto heavens and seventy-two sanctuaries that play a prominent role in this tradition (see Engelhardt 1987: 62–77). Since Sima Chengzhen lived most of his life on the Tiantai Mountains, he can be expected to have also been deeply influenced by Tiantai Buddhism.

One of his works, the *Zuowanglun* 坐忘論 (Discourse on Sitting in Oblivion; DZ 1036, fasc. 704), has recently been translated and studied by Livia Kohn (1987). This text describes a systematic progress toward immortality mainly by means of mental purification. It continues the tradition of the old philosophical mystical texts and their Buddhist-influenced successors. An example of the former is that the expression "sitting in oblivion" is already mentioned in chapter 6 of the *Zhuangzi* as some sort of a meditative state of mind. The latter is especially represented in the use of terms like *karma, prajñā,* and so on. The *Zuowanglun* consists of seven sections that stand for seven consecutive steps leading to the attainment of the Tao.

A similar progress to the Tao is found in Sun Simiao's *Cunshen lianqi ming* 存神鍊氣銘 (Inscription on Actualization of Spirit and Refinement of *Qi*; DZ 834, fasc. 571; see Kohn 1987: 119). This text forms the last part of the *Sheyang zhenzhong fang* (*Yunji qiqian* 33.12a–14b), which will be discussed in some detail below. An inscription is usually only a short and specific text. This, together with the fact that the *Cunshen lianqi ming* has also been transmitted independently in the Taoist Canon, indicates that it originally circulated separately and was only incorporated into the *Shenyang zhenzhong fang* later as it is now contained in *Yunji qiqian* 33.

In this inscription, Sun Simiao emphasizes the importance of techniques like abstaining from cereals and meditating on the centers of the *qi* in the lower abdomen. Only after the adept has undergone these preliminaries will he or she be able to enter the five phases of the mind that lead to complete mental purity and tranquility. During the following seven stages of the body, the adept gradually refines himself utterly into pure *qi*; this stage is called that of the Realized One. Through the ensuing refinement of *qi* into spirit, the spirit man develops. Whoever is then able to unite the spirit with the Tao is called a perfect being. Comparing Sima Chengzhen's *Zuowanglun* and the inscription of Sun Simiao, Livia Kohn makes clear that although Sima Chengzhen focuses more on the development of spiritual abilities he does seem to have known Sun Simiao's earlier text. He may in fact have been influenced by it (Kohn 1987: 30).

Both Sima Chengzhen and Sun Simiao share a certain concern about the higher religious or spiritual development of human beings. Yet neither is content to deal only with subtle and advanced meditational practices. The *Fuqi jingyi lun* as well as the *Sheyang zhenzhong fang* bear witness to their active involvement in the more fundamental exercises of long life and health. These are related more closely to the ideas and practices of traditional Chinese medicine than to the Taoist mystical tradition.

Problems of Authenticity

The *Fuqi jingyi lun* is first mentioned in the *Shiyao erya*   石藥爾雅 (Compendium of Mineral Drugs), a lexicography on mineral drugs contained in DZ 901, fasc. 588, by Mei Biao 梅彪 The preface of this work is dated to the year 806. Before the *Fuqi jingyi lun* was incorporated into the *Yunji qiqian* around 1025, the text was not widely distributed. It is not listed in either of the standard histories of the Tang.

Only after the devastation of Kaifeng by the Jurchen in 1127 does the text begin to appear in the bibliographies. It is listed in the reconstructed catalogue of the Imperial Library as lost (2.25b). Later the bibliographical section of the *Songshi* 宋史 (History of the Song 4.5195) mentions it as a work by Sima Chengzhen comprising one scroll. In both these bibliographical sources, the name of the author is given as Master of the White Clouds of the Tiantai Mountains, a common agnomen of Sima Chengzhen.

Despite this rather sketchy information, an evaluation of the text according to the criteria of authenticity—style, place names, taboo characters, quotations from other sources, and so on—leads to the conclusion that the text was probably written in the eighth century. Moreover, in style and content it is reasonably consonant with Sima Chengzhen's other works.   Therefore it seems logical to consider him as its original author.

The *Fuqi jingyi lun* has been handed down to us in two different versions. In the *Yunji qiqian* (chap. 57), it consists of nine sections, the most complete version of the text. The *Daozang* version is divided into two independent texts, each with a title of its own. First there is the *Fuqi jingyi lun* in DZ 830, fasc. 571, which comprises the first two sections of the *Yunji qiqian* version. Then there is the *Xiuzhen jingyi zalun*　　脩真精義雜論 (Miscellaneous Discourses on the Essential Meaning of Cultivating Perfection) in DZ 277, fasc. 134. This contains the rest of the text.

Comparing the two versions leads to the conclusion that the original text, now found in the *Yunji qiqian*, was divided arbitrarily into two parts and as such was integrated into the Taoist Canon. Taken together, the two *Daozang* texts furnish a longer and more detailed variant. But, on the whole, the *Yunji qiqian* version seems more coherent in style and content.[6]

Contents of the Text

All nine different sections, the so-called discourses, of the *Fuqi jingyi lun* are structured in a similar fashion. An introduction by the author is followed by quotations from various traditional sources concerning the topic in question. Sometimes a concluding statement is appended.

To this general rule there is only one exception. The second section seems to have been written entirely by Sima Chengzhen himself. Entitled "Discourse on the Absorption of *Qi*," it is the most important of the whole text. Its subject is in fact the central topic of the entire work. Quite appropriately, this section is also the longest.

Only against the background of this initial discourse can the techniques described in the remaining sections of the text be understood properly and in their full complexity. This section establishes the systematic context of the *Fuqi jingyi lun* as a whole. Instructions given here enable adepts as well as readers to grasp the entire system of the absorption of *qi* so that they can apply the exercises in a sensible way.

The structure of the text as a whole, therefore, does not imitate a succession of phases or stages on the way to the Tao. Rather, eight discourses are grouped around a ninth and central one, furnishing detailed explanations and examples of the various techniques of nourishing life involved. This structure is strongly reminiscent of the cosmology of the *Yijing* 易經 (Book of Changes): the eight trigrams are all grouped around the Great One in the center; they issue from it and ultimately return to it.

The high degree of systematization found in the *Fuqi jingyi lun* is exceptional and outstanding. In general, early sources on nourishing life tend

---

6. An annotated translation of the text is found in Engelhardt 1987: 85–200.

to provide descriptions of different exercises without furnishing a systematic context.

It will be useful to examine a rough outline of the contents of the text.

Preface

In his short preface, Sima Chengzhen illustrates the importance of the *qi* in the origin of the cosmos. In metaphorical terms that are typical for Shangqing Taoism, he emphasizes the prominent position of humanity among all living creatures. He then goes on to mention various techniques leading to the attainment of the Tao. In a closing paragraph, he notes with regret that the instructions on how to absorb the *qi* are scattered in too many different sources of unknown affiliation. This, he says, is the reason he decided to attempt a systematic account of them himself.

Discourse on the Absorption of the Five Sprouts

In the first section, Sima Chengzhen discusses two traditional Taoist methods: the method of the five sprouts, first found in the *Taishang lingbao wufuxu* 太上靈寶五符序 (Highest Explanation to the Five Talismans of the Numinous Treasure; DZ 388, fasc. 183), which is dated to the third century; and the technique of the cloud sprouts of the four extremities, mainly documented in a commentary to the *Mingtang yuanzhen jingjue* 明堂元真 經訣 (Canonical Formula of the Primordial Truth of the Hall of Light; DZ 424, fasc. 194). The latter is generally attributed to Tao Hongjing, but may also go back to Wei Huacun 魏華存 (Robinet 1984: vol. 2: 363, 369).

Both methods refer primarily to the absorption of the *qi* of the five directions. The practice is undertaken while the adept swallows saliva and recites invocations. Sima Chengzhen elaborates on these techniques from a background of medical knowledge. He says, for example, that one should swallow saliva enriched with the green *qi* of the East. This is then guided to the *orbis hepaticus*, the liver orb, and to the first nodal or sensitive point of the energetic conduit belonging to it. From there the *qi* is visualized as circulating along the conduit, strengthening and nourishing the orb.

This method promotes the circulation of *qi* throughout the body. Sima Chengzhen considers it a basic exercise, preliminary to all further practice of *qi* absorption. The technique can also be applied in the case of illness. It then has an effect similar to that of acupuncture, except that the *qi* is guided not by needles but by concentration on specific nodal points.

In this section of the text, Sima Chengzhen refers to the vivid mental pictures of the orbs (*zang* 藏). Closely following the basic outline of the visualization of these in the various *Huangting jing* 黃庭經 (Yellow Court Scriptures), he describes their leaflike shape and their color as well as positions within the body. There is no doubt that these pictorial representations of the *zang* were not understood as referring to an anatomical substratum of the human body—a circumstance that could justify translating *zang* as "organ." On the contrary, the *zang* should be considered pictorial, visualized conceptions of the gods who reside within people in the form of blossoms.

Sima Chengzhen combines these traditional Shangqing concepts with the dynamic interplay of physiological functions as originally described in the *Huangdi neijing suwen* 黃帝內經素文 (Inner Classic of the Yellow Emperor: Fundamental Questions). Moreover, it appears that over time the traditional pictorial conceptions were overlaid, if not actually replaced, by the well-defined physiological network of their functions. That is why the word orb will be used to refer to them here. But it should be clearly understood that the organs mentioned in connection with these orbs are not organs as understood in Western medicine. Rather, a reference to any of them—for example, the liver—connotes the entire fabric of functional manifestations related to that orb. So "liver" includes the working of the muscles and sinews and also corresponds to the sense of vision and the eyes (see Porkert 1974: 117–123). To emphasize the difference between the anatomical concepts of the organs in Western medicine and the more functional Chinese approach, the full Latin terms will also be included.

Discourse on the Absorption of Qi

The second section is central to the whole text. It comprises several methods. Adepts begin by absorbing the so-called Great Clarity Talisman for the Facilitation of *Qi* Circulation. By doing so, they are enabled to gradually refrain from eating cereals. Undergoing the proper ritual purification and maintaining a strict dietetic regimen, practitioners absorb the *qi* by visualizing the first rays of the rising sun. This *qi* is then guided through the *orbis pulmonalis*, lung orb, and through the arms. From there it is taken to the *orbis stomachi*, the stomach orb, then to the *orbis renalis*, the kidney orb, and finally to the legs. The process always ends by "retaining the *qi*," making sure that whatever has been absorbed won't leave again.

Why, through the absorption of *qi*, the orbs are entered in this and no other manner can be explained with the help of quotations from the *Suwen*. In it the functions of the orbs and their relations to the *qi* are described in detail. Sima Chengzhen also points out that when one begins to abstain from cereals and lives only on the absorption of *qi*, one has first to undergo a phase of weakening and decay. However, as soon as orthopathic *qi* becomes predominant in the body, all illnesses vanish. After nine years of further practice one can rightfully be called a Realized One. Toward the end of the section, the author provides helpful invocations and mentions some additional techniques. Of the latter, one can be traced back to the *Baopuzi* 抱朴子 (Book of the Master Who Embraces Simplicity), and another is originally related to the tradition of the Celestial Masters.

Discourse on Gymnastics
Sima Chengzhen begins the third section by quoting a number of famous passages from the *Suwen* and the *Nan jing* 難經 (Classic of Difficult Issues; dated to the first or second century A.D.). He emphasizes the importance of *daoyin* exercises—which literally denote "to conduct (the *qi*) and to stretch (the body)." Seventeen different exercises are mentioned in the *Daozang* version of the text, whereas the *Yunji qiqian* gives only two. They are applied in the same order as the *qi* proceeds through the body upon absorption.

The exercises all serve to make the conducting of the *qi* easier. They eliminate internal obstructions and improve blood circulation. The latter is especially important, because long periods of quiet sitting are required for the proper absorption of *qi*. The practice of gymnastics, according to Sima Chengzhen's recommendation, should always be followed by certain exercises of self-massage. These are commonly found in combination with *daoyin*.

Discourse on Talisman Water
The fourth section deals with the ingestion of talismans. These are usually sacred characters written on paper. The paper is burnt and the ashes dissolved in water. Adepts drink the mixture to ingest the talisman, then called "talisman water," while reciting sacred formulas. The practice of drinking talisman water can be traced back to the tradition of the Celestial Masters, but it was later also integrated into Shangqing practice.

In his introductory remarks, Sima Chengzhen explains that the characters written on the talisman are pure emanations of cosmic *qi* as it is reflected in the writing. The *Daozang* version of this section contains a lengthy collection of talismans together with various formulas that differ according to the adept's purpose. Talisman water is most commonly used to avoid hunger and thirst, especially during long periods of abstention from cereals. It is also used to heal diseases and facilitate the absorption of *qi*.

Discourse on Taking Drugs
The fifth section warns against possible dangers of prolonged abstention from all cereals. Problems will arise unless cereals are replaced by drugs containing *qi*. Again the author refers to the medical classics, quoting from the *Suwen* and from the *Huangdi neijing taisu* 太素 (Inner Classic of the Yellow Emperor: Great Simplicity; edited during the Sui or early Tang). He gives two prescriptions, both not primarily aimed at healing diseases. Rather, they serve to strengthen the adept in the early stages of *qi* absorption, when his or her

Fig. 3. A practitioner clapping the teeth. *Source: Neiwai gong tushuo*
內外功圖說

overall condition is weakened due to the radical change in diet. The *Daozang* version also includes two recipes for purifying the digestive system.

Discourse on Precautions

The sixth section explains how careful preservation of *qi* within the system of the cosmos is attained through a perfect balance of the macrocosm and the microcosm—the world and the human body. When this balance is disturbed the practitioner can come to harm; therefore he must take precautions to maintain harmony within and without. Sima Chengzhen illustrates this balanced way of life by quoting the *Zhengao* 真誥 (Declarations of the Perfected; DZ 1016, fasc. 637–640), by Tao Hongjing of the fifth century.

To avoid all sorts of inner and outer harm, one should never exert oneself. During the process of *qi* absorption, too much seeing, lying down, sitting, standing, or walking will be as dangerous as any intense emotional state. As the *Suwen* (chaps. 23, 39) explains, this can harm the orbs and the *qi*. It is of essential importance to keep a regular diet, to properly balance the five sapores (*Suwen* 3, 10). Sima Chengzhen concludes this discourse with further recommendations. An increased intake of drugs in particular will help harmonize the five sapores properly. Moreover, he insists that one should avoid pungent food when the *qi* is being absorbed. This notion corresponds to the medical advice given in the *Suwen*. Here the pungent is described as the sapor of the *orbis pulmonalis*, the lung orb that is considered a primary residence of the *qi*. The pungent will drive the *qi* away and many diseases will arise.

Discourse on the Five Orbs

The seventh section gives a physiological description of the five orbs, including their correspondences to the five planets and the five sacred peaks. It is interesting to note that Sima Chengzhen hardly says anything on the topic himself. He leaves it almost entirely to the *Suwen* to explain the different functions of the orbs.

Discourse on Healing Diseases

The eighth section describes how to maintain health, which is an indispensable prerequisite for any successful practice of longevity and life-nourishing techniques. Whenever there are any malfunctions of bones or muscles, when one suffers from pains in the four extremities or in the head, one must absorb *qi* and conduct it mentally to the diseased part. This process can be intensified through *daoyin*. Even malfunctions of the orbs can be treated in this way; only indurations in the abdomen resist it. It may be necessary to apply drugs to heal them.

In the last paragraph of this section, the author also recommends applying the sounds of the twelve pitches in correspondence to the twelve months of the year. In order to eliminate the heteropathic *qi*, the pipes have to be placed on the nodal points in accordance with the respective disease. The *Zhengao* (chap. 10) mentions a slightly different method: acupuncture needles are used to almost the same effect.

Discourse on the Symptoms of Diseases
The ninth section provides instructions on how to become aware of the symptoms of various diseases at a very early stage. It will be unnecessary to consult a physician, much less to endure any suffering from the disease when it breaks out. The exact process by which different diseases arise is outlined, again relying heavily on the *Suwen*.

Medical and Religious Themes

The nine discourses in the *Fuqi jingyi lun* demonstrate how the central technique of *qi* absorption is supported by various accompanying methods. The aim of the whole process is primarily to counteract the decay of the body, achieved by gradually replacing crude nourishment like cereals with finer materials and by removing all impure substances from the body. The result is an increase in refined and cosmic substances containing *qi* within the body. The *Fuqi jingyi lun* relies on both Shangqing texts and the medical classics. This shows that in the early stages of religious accomplishment a certain medical knowledge, particularly of the medical system of correspondences, is as important as the religious striving.

The *Sheyang zhenzhong fang*

Context and Environment

Both standard histories of the Tang list twenty-two works by Sun Simiao. By now, about a thousand years after his death, the number of titles attributed to him has increased to almost eighty. These are found in various biographical and bibliographical sources (Sivin 1968: 60). Only a handful exist today, and among those only two can be ascribed to Sun Simiao with reasonable certainty. He is the established author of the *Qianjin fang*, written around the year 650, and of its revised version, the *Qianjin yifang*, which can be approximately dated toward the end of Sun's life in 682.

In addition, an early alchemical text, the *Danjing yaojue*   丹經要訣
(Essential Formulas of Alchemical Classics), now contained in *Yunji qiqian*
71, can be considered his work. This text was translated and analyzed in detail
by Nathan Sivin (1968), who considers Sun Simiao its true author, although
not entirely beyond all doubt. It is a collection of formulas for preparing
alchemical elixirs of immortality and was definitely written in Sun Simiao's
time. Moreover, it fits in neatly with the overall picture of Sun as a physician,
since, as Sivin has convincingly shown, "alchemy is a branch of Chinese
medicine, a branch whose major goal transcends the cure of diseases and
maintenance of health" (Sivin 1968: 142). More than that, the two works that
definitely go back to Sun Simiao both contain much information on
alchemical procedures as well.

The *Qianjing fang* and the *Qianjin yifang* are among the most important
sources for Chinese traditional therapeutics and are still being used in the
training of traditional physicians in China today.[7] Both works bear witness to
Sun Simiao's broad medical knowledge and his gift of exact observation.
They document his ability to integrate his various clinical experiences with
medical theory and his concern for medical ethics and the social
responsibilities of the physician.[8]

His works leave no doubt that he was not an orthodox physician. As
Sivin puts it:

> It is precisely in their eclecticism, the ease with which they
> incorporate elements from the folk traditions as well as from
> the medical traditions of other cultures into a loose rational
> structure, that Sun's books are most representative of the major
> trends in Chinese medicine. (1967: 270)

This tendency toward eclecticism is also evident in Sun's approach to
religion. For example, he supposedly wrote a treatise entitled *Hui sanjiao lun*
會三教論   (On the Reconciliation of the Three Teachings). This is lost today
but was extant in the libraries of the Tang (*Jiu Tangshu* 191). Again, he
studied Buddhism more carefully than any Chinese physician before him. His
two main works, although fundamentally Taoist in outlook, bear a clearly
Mahāyāna Buddhist imprint in certain places. For instance, in the introduction
to the *Qianjin fang*, he maintains that nobody who has not read Buddhist texts
will ever be a good physician. More than that, he seems to be the only medical

---

7. No reliable Western translations of these two important works have appeared to date, with
the notable exception of the last two chapters of the *Qianjin fang*. These deal with
acupuncture in particular and are found in Despeux 1987.

8. Sun's attitude toward medical ethics has been particularly studied by Unschuld (1975:
18–24).

author who has evidently been influenced by Buddhist medical theory and practice. Among other things, he borrowed the theory of the four elements from Buddhism. He also gives a detailed description of an Indian massage procedure (Demiéville 1985: 94–98).

How Sun himself came to be a physician and how easily medical techniques came to him no matter what their theoretical affiliation is illustrated in a passage of the preface to the *Qianjin fang*.

> In my childhood I suffered from a cold disorder due to winds, and constantly consulted physicians. My family's finances were exhausted to pay for medicine. So it was that during my student years I held the medical classics in special regard, and that even in my old age I have not set them aside.
>
> As to the reading of pulses and other techniques of diagnosis, the gathering of simples and their compounding, administration and dosage, hygiene and the various precautions associated with health—when I heard of any man who excelled me in any of these, no distance would keep me from him. I would learn what he had to teach and then apply it. When I reached maturity I became aware that I had attained some understanding. (Sivin 1967: 271)

Both his works contain chapters on the techniques of nourishing life: chapter 27 of the *Qianjin fang* and chapter 12 of the *Qianjin yifang*. Here the same attitude of eclecticism is found, as characteristic of Sun Simiao's approach to these techniques as of his view of medical knowledge in general.

Contents of the Text

The title *Sheyang zhenzhong fang* translates as Pillowbook of Methods for Nourishing Life. A pillowbook is a book that is considered so valuable that one wants to have it close at all times. Therefore it is inside the pillow—pillows being longish structures made of bamboo, rattan, wood, or porcelain, rather than cushions. The expression *zhenzhong* 枕中 —literally "inside the pillow"—is first found in the *Hanshu* 漢書 (History of the Han Dynasty) biography of Liu Xiang (chap. 36). There it refers to the Taoist scriptures that Liu An 劉安 , the prince of Huainan, kept inside his pillow. Later the expression was popular for describing Taoist texts (see *Baopuzi* 2, 16, 19), emphasizing their esoteric and precious nature.

In his preface, the author points out that the text is composed of five major paragraphs and forms one scroll. The compilers of the *Yunji qiqian*, however, abridged the text and divided it into a number of shorter sections. This becomes clear especially in comparison with a *Daozang* version of the text, the *Zhenzhong ji* 枕中記 (Pillowbook Record; DZ 837, fasc. 572). Aside from the *Cunshen lianqi ming*, which probably was not part of the original text, the *Sheyang zhenzhong fang* (*Yunji qiqian* 33) concentrates on five main subjects: prudence, prohibitions, *daoyin* exercises, conducting the *qi*, and guarding the One.

Judging from the length of the sections, it seems that the author is primarily concerned with prudence (seven pages) and prohibitions (five pages). The other practices appear to be less important, since they are discussed in less detail.

Preface
In his preface, the author points out that the awakened mind is preliminary to any further religious accomplishment. If one is not able to concentrate one's willpower, one's "affairs will not follow [the intentions] of the mind and the methods will not be effective" (*Yunji qiqian* 33.1a).

In this context, Sun Simiao mentions that in his opinion Xi Kang 稽康 (223–262), the famous author of the *Yangsheng lun* 養生論 (On Nourishing Life; Holzman 1957), became aware of the Tao only to a limited degree. Following the common practice in writing a preface, Sun emphasizes how much time and effort he invested in the work. He goes on to say that in spite of his constant search for the Tao he was not able to attain it.

Certain sentences of the preface are also found in the chapter on nourishing life of the *Qianjin fang* (12.141), which relies strongly on Zhang Zhan's 張湛 *Yangsheng yaoji* 養生要集 (Compendium of Essentials on Nourishing Life). As is evidenced in Sakade's reconstruction of this lost work, Zhang Zhan thought more highly of the nourishment of the spirit than of bodily techniques (Sakade 1986).

On Prudence
The section on prudence is by far the longest. It begins by explaining that prudence is of the utmost importance for anyone desiring to nourish inner nature and by defining prudence as living in a balanced way. The exact methods that lead to prudence are then outlined.

First, he says, "the basis of prudence is awe," and continues:

> If a son is without awe, his filial devotion will not be sincere. If a father is without awe, his parental kindness will not be manifest. If a minister is without awe, he will not be rewarded for his merits. If a ruler is without awe, the gods of soil and grain will not be at peace. (2b)

As Sivin has pointed out, this passage (of which only a short section appears here) is especially important because of its style. It is written in old text style, which the editors of the *Xin Tangshu* 新唐書 (New History of the Tang) strongly encouraged and tried to revive (Sivin 1968: 118). They duly incorporated this treatise into Sun Simiao's biography, painting him in a strong Confucian light. Their main source was an earlier account of his life found in the *Tanbin lu* 譚賓祿 (Record of Discussions with Guests), by Hu Qu 胡璩 (ca. 827–846). This is now contained in the *Taiping guangji* 太平廣記 (Broad Record of the Taiping Era) of the early Song (218.1670). Here Sun Simiao is treated in great detail and described more in terms of Taoism and Lao-Zhuang philosophy. A passage very similar to the one quoted above is found here, too, but it adds certain allusions to the *Daode jing* (chap. 50) and to the *Zhuangzi* (chap. 17).

> One who is able to understand these things is safe from harm by dragons when traveling on water, and cannot be hurt by tigers or rhinoceroses when traveling on land. Weapons cannot wound him, nor can contagious diseases infect him. Slanders cannot destroy his good name, nor the poisonous stings of insects do him harm. (Sivin 1968: 118)

When we compare the version of the *Sheyang zhenzhong fang*, as cited in part above, first to the text of the *Tanbin lu*, we find the former more detailed and more carefully phrased. One can therefore assume that the *Sheyang zhenzhong fang* is the oldest source of the passage, which was then taken up first in the *Tanbin lu* and later in the *Xin Tangshu*.

After these fundamental remarks on the problem of awe, the author names certain serious obstacles to the enjoyment of long life. He is especially concerned about the "evils of eating and drinking" and "sensual pleasures." Anyone who indulges in them will become sick or fall victim to disaster.

A list of prohibitions that will help overcome these obstacles appears next. They reflect conventional ideas of the time and are also included in the *Qianjin fang* (26.464). For example:

> Between the summer solstice and the autumn equinox do not take greasy cakes, broths, and similar food of this kind. (3a)

Prudence is not limited to avoiding specific foods. Rather, it is found in the subtle details of one's life. In this context, Sun Simiao quotes the section on the "Twelve Little Ones" from the *Xiaoyou jing* 小有經 (Scripture on Lesser Existence).

> Those who want to nourish their nature should think little, remember little, desire little, act little, speak little, laugh little,

grieve little, be little delighted, feel little joy, feel little anger, love and hate little. (3b)

The *Xiaoyou jing* has not come down to us today, but it is quoted in Tamba no Yasuyori's 丹波康賴 *Ishinpō* 醫心方 (Essential Medical Methods) after the *Yangsheng yaoji* by Zhang Zhan.[9] Like the earlier paragraphs, this quotation emphasizes Sun Simiao's basic point of view that the Tao can most of all be attained through moderation. This stance is typical of the entire *Sheyang zhenzhong fang*.

As a consequence of this predilection for moderation, Sun is convinced that recluses and even peasants have better chances to prolong their lives than members of high society who are wealthy and addicted to luxury. To illustrate the moderate way of life, the author quotes the answer Feng Junda 封君達, the Taoist Master of the Grayblue Ox, gave to the question of Emperor Wu of the Wei dynasty.

> In [moving] any part of the body, constant effort is desirable. In eating, constant restraint. Yet just as in efforts one should not go to extremes, in restraint one should not go [as far as] to deficiency. Avoid [constantly] all fat and heavy foods, control the intake of the sour and salty. Think and worry less and reduce the intensity of joy and anger. Abandon haste and hurry and be careful with sexuality. In spring and summer drain [the fields] and in fall and winter close the storehouses. (*Yunji qiqian* 33.4a; see also *Shenxian zhuan* 10)

All rules for moderation have to be accompanied by control over the mind and an attitude of morality.[10] In this context, Sun Simiao cites the words of the famous immortal Pengzu 彭祖 as they are related in the *Yangsheng yaoji*.

> Padded clothing and comfortable sleeping mats, never bearing any bodily hardships, this certainly makes you sensitive to colds. Sweets and dried meat, always feeding oneself to the brim, this certainly makes you prone to painful constipation.
>   Sexual fascination and physical beguilement lead to deficiency and loss. Lewd music and deft songs, always

---

9. The same passage is also quoted in the *Yangxing yanming lu* (*Yunji qiqian* 32.5b; Mugitani 1987: 11, 70). It is also found in the *Qianjin fang* (27.478).

10. The last two sentences of the passage can also be understood as referring to processes within the framework of the body. "In spring and summer act purgative, in fall and winter close the *yin*-orbs." This reading is further supported by the DZ variant that has "store essence." The *Shenxian zhuan* takes it to refer to general behavior: "The sages nourish *yang* during spring and summer and *yin* during fall and winter."

cheering the mind and delighting the ear, this certainly causes debauchery and addiction.

Fast riding and going places, hunting and shooting out in the wild, this certainly causes you to go mad. Planning the victory in the next battle, taking advantage of confusion and weakness, this certainly leads to pride and arrogance.

All these are proscribed by the sages as losses of principle. One should never think of them as ways of stimulation. (*Ishinpō* 27; *Yangxing yanming lu* 10b)

The author subsequently points out how one should best follow one's daily activities without growing soft and living in overindulgence.

The gist of all the rules is summarized in a famous proverbial passage based on the *Lüshi chunqiu* 吕氏春秋 (Spring and Autumn Annals of Mr. Lü):

Flowing water will never turn stale,
the hinge of the door will never be eaten by worms.
They never rest in their activity: that's why! (5a)

In accordance with this spirit, the author gives two basic instructions for exercises. One is a method of swallowing the saliva, the other is a technique of visualization. It specifically teaches how to kindle a fire in the mind in order to burn the personal body. Through this burning, the mind becomes highly concentrated and one is able to cure all diseases. A similar method is mentioned in *Baopuzi* 15.

On Prohibitions

The *Sheyang zhenzhong fang* cites four major types of prohibitions.

1. Prohibitions Found in Immortals' Classics
2. Ten Defeats to Be Avoided in the Tao of Immortality
3. Ten Precepts of the Tao of Immortality
4. Various Precautions for Students of Immortality

The first prohibitions are a set of conventional taboos mostly concerned with specific days of the month. For instance, all days corresponding to the cyclical signs *jia* 甲 and *yin* 寅 are very dangerous, because this is the time when the demons are fighting each other. Human beings become nervous because of their influence. One should take special precautions on these days—one should not "share the same mat with one's wife or husband." On the other hand, one should "only look at clean and pure things while talking to others" (5b). Other prohibitions deal with dietetic regulations. On the whole, this paragraph bears the imprint of astrology and magic.

The ten defeats are ten states of ritual impurity to be avoided:

1. debauchery
2. stealing and doing evil
3. drinking
4. uncleanliness
5. eating the meat of the zodiac animal corresponding to the year of one's father's birth
6. eating the meat of the zodiac animal corresponding to the year of one's own birth
7. eating any meat at all
8. eating anything raw or the five forbidden pungent roots (garlic, onions, leeks, and so on)
9. killing a sentient being, including even insects and worms
10. urinating while facing north.

The ten precepts are primarity taboos for individual days of the month. An example is that "on the eight annual festival days one should not carry out severe punishments." Others are that one "should not get angry during new moon" and that one "should not eat fish or reptiles on days which fall under the sign of the scale."

The precautions, finally, include advice on the general living conditions of serious students of the Tao. The adept practitioner should move frequently and not live in the company of normal people. The same idea is also found in Sun Simiao's *Cunshen lianqi ming* under the second of seven stages of the mind. He says:

> At this stage one should move to a different part of the country, choose a spot and settle down. It is better not to be a too old acquaintance of the local folk. (Kohn 1987: 122)

In addition, practitioners are admonished to keep themselves and their surroundings scrupulously clean and to always maintain a harmony of the emotions. Auditions or olfactions—imaginary sounds or smells perceived during meditation—are unlucky signs. When they occur, adepts should pray to the lords of the Tao for help.

Most interesting in this last section is the clear rejection of sexual practices and the warning against any deep involvement in sensual relationships with the other sex. Female adepts should not get pregnant, and male practitioners should not approach pregnant or menstruating women. Both should rather strive for more self-reliance and venerate the goddesses on high but not dream of engaging in sexual intercourse with them. This is contrary to the shamanistic visions frequently found in Tang poetry and also in certain Shangqing documents. Here, the goddess descends and has a physical relationship with the adept—then always male.

The section dealing with the three latter kinds of prohibitions seems to have been divided rather arbitrarily by the editors of the *Yunji qiqian*. The text

(6ab) is in fact an abridged version of the beginning section of the *Lingshu ziwen* 靈書紫文 (Numinous Writings and Purple Writs 1b–3b; DZ 179, fasc. 77). This text is a Shangqing scripture dealing with ritual rules and various prohibitions (Robinet 1984: vol. 2: 106). It begins by naming the ten defeats and goes on to list various other prohibitions. Initially the *Sheyang zhenzhong fang* fully follows the Shangqing scripture, which shows a superficial Buddhist influence in its choice of precepts and prohibitions, but later it seems to become more fragmentary. The fourth group in particular seems to include odds and ends of prohibitions and lacks a formal structure.

On Gymnastics

The section on physical practices mainly describes techniques of self-massage. It contains only one exercise that could be described as *daoyin*— guiding the *qi* and stretching the body—in a narrow sense. This particular exercise is applied to the neck and the head. It is said to harmonize essence, unattached structive energy. It also ameliorates blood circulation, with the result that the *qi* of the "wind" will not be able to affect the body. In this context, "wind" figures as one of the "six climatic excesses" of traditional Chinese diagnostics. It enters the body as heteropathic *qi* and causes various diseases (Porkert 1983: 58).

The deeper layers within the body are treated by means of a meditation in the course of which adepts visualize the five orbs. Otherwise, the *Sheyang zhenzhong fang* describes conventional massage techniques mainly applied to the neck and the face area. For instance, one should take a thick piece of silk and rub one's neck until it becomes warm. Then one should massage the face until "the complexion becomes glossy and is completely free from spots or wrinkles" (8a). Throughout, however, primary emphasis is placed on massaging the nodal points located around the eyes (see figure 4). This serves to preserve good eyesight.

The section dealing with *daoyin* concludes with the warning that one "should never touch upon the Flowery Canopy" (9a). The commentary explains that Flowery Canopy refers to the eyebrows. However, in the *Huangting neijing jing* the same term is used to denote the lung-orb. According to the *Suwen*, this orb is the seat of the *qi*, to which the eyebrows are closely related. Here, it seems, is the reason why Sun Simiao warns against any inadvertant interference with the eyebrows during exercises involving the *qi*.

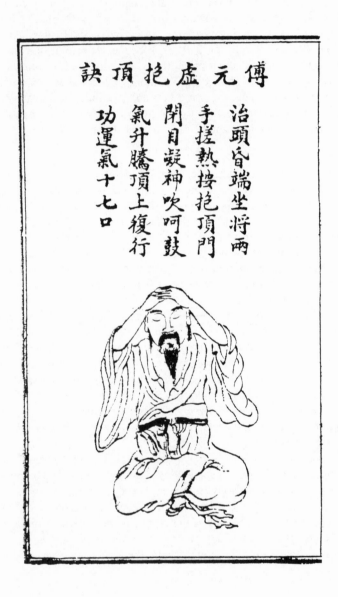

傳元虛抱頂訣

治頭昏端坐將兩
手搓熱按抱頂門
閉目凝神吹呵鼓
氣升騰頂上復行
功運氣十七口

Fig. 4. An adept performing a self massage of the upper face area. *Source: Neiwai gong tushuo*

On Guiding the Qi

There are three superior methods of immortality: preserving essence, guiding the *qi*, and taking drugs. Sun Simiao mentions the first and the last techniques only in passing but places considerable emphasis on the second. This practice supposedly cures all kinds of diseases and even epidemics.

Among the various possible ways of guiding the *qi*, embryo respiration is the most significant. This is described as follows:

> In the practice of embryo respiration, one does not use the nose or the mouth. Instead one breathes in the manner of an embryo inside the womb: who realizes this has truly attained the Tao. (9b)

The text then goes on to discuss the practice, quoting heavily from the eighth chapter of the *Baopuzi* (9ab). A strong concern for attaining magical powers through guiding the *qi* is revealed here.

Then Sun lists further methods of guiding the *qi* (10ab). Their main purpose is to retain the *qi*; that is, they make the *qi* that has been absorbed stay in the body permanently and help eliminate pain and cure diseases. Most of them are also found in chapter 27 of the *Qianjin fang*.

To stress his point, the author quotes the Chinese Methuselah Pengzu.

> Perfect Tao means freedom from trouble: just never think or worry about anything and the mind will never be labored. If, in addition, you practice gymnastics, guiding the *qi*, and embryo respiration, you can live to a thousand. If you then also practice alchemy and take drugs, you can live as long as heaven itself.[11]

He goes on to describe some techniques of visualizing the sun and the moon within the body. These have a long history within the Taoist religion and play an important role in Shangqing practice.

On Guarding the One

The last and shortest section of the *Sheyang zhenzhong fang* also consists of various quotations from the *Baopuzi*, specifically its eighteenth chapter. First, it explains where to guard the One by means of visualization: in the main *qi* centers of the body, the three so-called cinnabar fields of the head, the chest, and the abdomen. Then it summarizes the overall importance of this meditation technique.[12] It says:

---

11. The same quotation is found in chapter 27 of the *Qianjin fang* and in the *Yangxing yanming lu* 8b.

12. For more detail see chapter 5, "Guarding the One: Concentrative Meditation in Taoism."

> To prolong life and attain immortality, there are only gold and
> cinnabar; to preserve the bodily form and drive away old age,
> there is only guarding the One. (11b; *Baopuzi* 18)

In general, the text agrees with the *Baopuzi*, in that it finds alchemical
elixirs (gold and cinnabar) superior to meditative techniques of attaining
immortality. The primary purpose of guarding the One is to acquire magical
powers so that demons or mountain spirits won't dare attack the adept when
he or she goes off to the wilderness to concoct the elixir of life.

Structure and Themes

The *Sheyang zhenzhong fang* is divided into five parts that correspond to the
main topics of the text, yet its structure is by no means systematic. This is not
due to the eclectic character of the text, which is reflected in other works of
Sun Simiao, too. Rather, it seems the result of later distortion and interpolation.

In content, the *Sheyang zhenzhong fang* mainly emphasizes prudence
and a series of prohibitions. In contrast, methods like guiding the *qi* or
guarding the One are made rather subordinate. The central concept throughout
is the idea of the awakening of the mind mentioned in the beginning. The
author obviously considered this to be of paramount importance for any
religious accomplishment. The first step toward an awakening of the mind is
prudence. In this orientation, the text resembles Zhang Zhan's theory of
nourishing life, where the primary concern lies with the nourishing of the
spirit (Sakade 1986: 9). Next to the *Baopuzi*, Zhang Zhan's *Yangsheng yaoji* is
quoted most frequently in the *Sheyang zhenzhong fang*.

The Authenticity of the Text

The complete title *Sheyang zhenzhong fang* is not listed in any of the
biographical or bibliographical sources on Sun Simiao and his time. The
bibliographical section of the *Xin Tangshu* (3.5a) and Sun's biography in the
Xuanpin lu 玄品錄 (Record of Mysterious Occurrences; DZ 781, fasc. 558)
mention a *Zhenzhong sushu* 枕中素書 (Pillowbook Written on Silk) by Sun
Simiao. In addition, two Song bibliographies attribute to him a *Zhenzhong ji*
(Pillowbook Record) in one scroll and a *Zhenzhong jue* (Pillowbook Formula;
Loon 1984: 115). The *Yunji qiqian* editors frequently added classifying
modifiers to the beginnings of titles. so it seems highly probable that these
works are identical to the *Sheyang zhenzhong fang* that is now found in *Yunji
qiqian* 33.

In addition, however, there is a text in the Taoist Canon by the title of *Zhenzhong ji* (Pillowbook Record) that is not ascribed to any specific author. Since it seems to be the only surviving variant of the *Yunji qiqian* text, let us compare the two.

They differ in a number of ways. First, the *Zhenzhong ji* of the Taoist Canon begins abruptly and does not contain a preface. Second, there is a long, almost identical passage in both texts: *Yunji qiqian* 33.2a–9a equals DZ 837.1a–10a. But the *Daozang* text, unlike the *Yunji qiqian* version, continues with an interpolation from the *Xiuzhen bilu* 脩真祕錄 (Secret Record of Cultivation of Perfection 10b–13a) and ends with prescriptions on taking drugs (13a–27a). Also, in the *Yunji qiqian*, the passage is divided into numerous individual sections and the *Daozang* divides it into two parts only. Third, considering the quotations found in the passage, it appears that the *Zhenzhong ji* is more complete and closer to the respective original sources than the *Sheyang zhenzhong fang*. The latter seems abridged in comparison. This is especially true of the paragraph dealing with awe, also contained in Sun Simiao's biography in the *Xin Tangshu* and the *Tanbin lu*.

The date of the text in either variant can be established mainly from later references to it. For example, the pharmacopoeia *Jinshi zhenglei daguan bencao* 經史諡類 大觀本草 (Classified Materia Medica from Classics and Histories of the Daguan Period; dated 1108) cites a *Zhenzhong ji* by Sun, the Realized One. The text quoted here under the title *Zhenzhong ji* corresponds to passages dealing with prescriptions that are found in the last section of the *Zhenzhong ji* (DZ 837.13a–27a). This leads to the conclusion that this particular section was already integrated into the *Zhenzhong ji* during the Song dynasty and was not interpolated erroneously.[13]

Three further texts have to be taken into account before a final conclusion can be reached:

First, Tamba no Yasuyori's *Ishinpō*. Dated to 982, chapter 27 on nourishing life of this text quotes the *Qianjin fang* and a text called *Zhenzhong fang* (Pillowbook Prescriptions), by Sun Simiao (Sakade 1986a: 789–793). In comparing the quotations of the latter with the two versions of our text, it becomes clear that there is more agreement with the *Zhenzhong ji* than with the *Sheyang zhenzhong fang*. Several sentences found in the *Daozang* version do not appear in the *Yunji qiqian*.

Second, Zhang Zhan's *Yangsheng yaoji*. As mentioned above, the *Sheyang zhenzhong fang* contains several quotations from this text. These are also found in the *Ishinpō* and in the *Yangxing yanming lu*, which has traditionally been attributed to Tao Hongjing but sometimes to Sun Simiao. All

---

13. For these considerations of the *Zhenzhong ji*, the author is indebted to C. Despeux.

quotations from the *Yangsheng yaoji* in the *Zhenzhong ji* of the *Daozang* and the *Sheyang zhenzhong fang* in the *Yunji qiqian* seem closer to the *Ishinpō* than to the *Yangxing yanming lu*. This supports Mugitani's recent conclusion that the *Yangxing yanming lu* was in fact written much later than previously thought, later even than Sun Simiao (Mugitani 1987).

Third, the *Shenxian shiqi jingui miaolu*   神仙食氣 金櫃妙錄   (The Spirit Immortals' Wondrous Record on Ingesting *Qi* Kept in a Golden Casket; DZ 836, fasc. 571). This text contains almost the entire section on guiding the *Qi* as it is found in the *Sheyang zhenzhong fang*; that is, DZ 836.7a–8a equals *Yunji qiqian* 33.9a–10a. Since this passage thus shows the same abridgments as the *Yunji qiqian* edition of Sun Simiao's text, it was probably incorporated later.

It seems beyond doubt that there was a work called *Zhenzhong ji* or *Zhenzhong fang*, by Sun Simiao. Fragments of this text can still be found in the *Sheyang zhenzhong fang* as well as in the *Zhenzhong ji* of the Taoist Canon. Both texts are therefore versions of Sun Simiao's work, and both still contain much of the old original. This is especially true for the preface of the *Sheyang zhenzhong fang* and for the long passage found in both variants. The contents of these original fragments in no way contradict the ideas about nourishing life which Sun Simiao expresses in *Qianjin fang* and his *Qianjin yifang*. Moreover, the original text must have contained prescriptions on taking drugs. This is clear from the last part of the *Zhenzhong ji*, which is also quoted in the *Jingshi zhenglei daguan bencao* of the Song. The last section of the *Sheyang zhenzhong fang*, finally, the *Cunshen lianqi ming*, was either incorporated into the text by the compilers of the *Yunji qiqian* or originally existed as an appendix to the text.

Tang Ideas of Longevity

It is through comparison of Sun Simiao's *Sheyang zhenzhong fang* and Sima Chengzhen's *Fuqi jingyi lun*, these two representative works on longevity ideas and practices of the Tang, that one can understand the basic concerns and concepts of Taoist thought of the time.

One must first of all keep in mind that the *Sheyang zhenzhong fang* is fragmentary and contains many later interpolations and distortions. But a useful comparison can still be made, especially since both texts have their main purpose in common. They both accompany and instruct readers or adepts in their first steps toward a balanced way of life. This in turn is the

initial stage leading to higher religious accomplishments, and an important
attainment on the way to perfect alignment with the Tao.

It is curious to note that Sun Simiao, the famous physician, places primary
emphasis on mental discipline, while Sima Chengzhen, the Taoist master,
concentrates most strongly on the medical and physical aspects of the
undertaking. Sun Simiao claims that no progress is possible without an
awakened mind.

> I doubt that an unawakened mind will ever be able to attain
> divinity or practice inner observation, to roam in the obscure or
> gather in the true. Therefore one should not reach for small
> wisdom, nor look for constant thinking. If one plans on one's
> ability to reach it [the final attainment], one's willpower will
> not be able to preserve it, one's affairs will not follow [the
> intentions of the] mind, and the methods will not be effective.
> (*Sheyang zhenzhong fang* 1a)

Sima Chengzhen, on the other hand, says that the *qi* is the main force on
which to build attainment. The *qi*, he claims, is the exceptional gift intrinsic to
all human beings that leads them to higher accomplishments. So it is the
cultivation of *qi* that allows adepts to develop their willpower and proceed in
the direction of immortality. Using the words of the *Zhengao* (6.11a), he says:

> Who nourishes life will forever dwell in the Tao. Who
> assimilates *qi* will forever roam in the Tao. When the *qi* is
> complete, life is permanent. Only then can adepts nourish their
> willpower. Having nourished willpower, they are able to join
> the realized ones. Only then can they ascend to the sphere of
> the eternally living *qi*. (*Fuqi jingyi lun* 1b)

Qi literally means "air," "cloud," "breath," or "vapor." The character
shows vapor arising from fire or from cooking cereals (Engelhardt 1987: 1–5),
but the term equally connotes energy—more specifically, the cosmic creative
energy of the world. As such it plays an important role in classical Shangqing
cosmogony. This can be understood as a synthesis of the theory of the Five
Agents or evolution phases with traditional theories regarding the Tao and the
qi. The latter are closely related (Mugitani 1978: 273).

Sima Chengzhen begins his *Fuqi jingyi lun* with an explanation of the
paramount importance of *qi*. He outlines a typical Shangqing cosmogony.

> The *qi* is the germinating effectiveness and the subtlety of the
> Tao [*Yijing, Xici* 5]. As its germinating effectiveness, the *qi*
> sets it in motion; as its subtlety, it puts it into function.
> Thereupon it creates the oneness of all life [*Daode jing* 42].
>
> Hence the primordial chaos is complete in the phase
> Grand Transformation [*Liezi* 1]. Oneness is at the same time

> this point, essence and spirit are manifest. The ten thousand
> creatures equally receive them.
>   Among the bodily forms, only the human is upright.
> Among the essences of all manifestations, only the human is
> numinous [*Liezi* 7]. Together with the trigrams of heaven and
> earth, human beings occupy a position among the three
> potencies. Encompassing yin and yang, they belong to the elite
> of the five evolution phases. Therefore they are able to
> penetrate the obscure and to make the sages descend. (*Fuqi
> jingyi lun*, 1a)

According to Sima Chengzhen, the Tao is the primordial ruling
principle, whereas the *qi* is its active and manifest force. The *qi* as the original
life force leaves the state of original oneness and develops in phases of
diversion. Developed in a rather late phase, only human beings have the
exceptional ability to cultivate their natural endowments and especially the *qi*.
This is because a portion of the primordial *qi* is allotted to human beings at
birth. It is their task to counteract the natural dissipation of *qi*. They should
strive to strengthen, control, and increase it in order to live out their natural
life spans.

In his introduction to the second section of the *Fuqi jingyi lun*, which is
particularly concerned with the absorption of *qi*, Sima Chengzhen elucidates.

> The *qi* is the origin of the embryo and the basis of the bodily
> form. As soon as the embryo is born, essence begins to
> disperse. As soon as the bodily form moves, the fundamental
> substance begins to decay. Therefore one has to take in the *qi*
> to consolidate the essence, one has to preserve the *qi* to refine
> the bodily form. When essence is full, spirit is complete. When
> the bodily form is fully matured, life is prolonged.
>   When one's origin and basis are strong and full, one can
> live long. As to the ten thousand creatures, there is none that
> has *qi* but does not have bodily form. Nor is there one that has
> bodily form but does not have *qi*.
>   How could therefore the adept striving to augment the
> vital forces [*Daode jing* 50] not concentrate his *qi* and perfect
> his softness [*Daode jing* 10]? (*Fuqi jingyi lun* 5ab)

Sima Chengzhen thus propagates the absorption of *qi* together with
accompanying techniques, with the aim that people augment their *qi* and avoid
the decay of the body. In contrast, Sun Simiao does not think the dispersion of
qi or essence is the primary danger to the vital forces. Rather, in his view a
shortened life span is caused by a confusion of the mind and a loss of moral
attitudes like prudence and awe. He states:

When one who wants to nourish his inner nature loses awe, his mind will be confused and cannot be regulated. His bodily form will be irritable and not at peace. His spirit will disperse while his *qi* gets out of control. His willpower will dissipate while his imagination is dulled. Who responds to life with such an attitude will certainly die. (*Sheyang zhenzhong fang* 2b)

According to Sun Simiao, awe is the predominant principle that influences the relation of people, the world, and the Tao. He explains their hierarchical structure as follows:

The greatest awe is that of the Tao; next is the awe of heaven; then follows the awe of all creatures; then comes the awe of the next man; and finally there is the awe of oneself. Who is anxious about his or her own bodily form will not be controlled by others. Who is prudent in small things will have no reason to fear the large. Who is on guard in matters close to him will not be disgraced in those more distant. (2b–3a)

The two texts therefore show two fundamentally different approaches to the techniques of nourishing life. One emphasizes mental discipline, the other is primarily concerned with the cultivation of *qi*. Yet they agree as far as the prevention of diseases is concerned.

As mentioned above, health is an indispensable prerequisite for any successful practice of the techniques of nourishing life. Sima Chengzhen stresses this point already in his preface.

It is only after having driven away all diseases by means of calming the bodily form that one is able to prolong harmony and to enjoy long life. (1b)

For this reason, Sima Chengzhen deals with early diagnosis and with the treatment of diseases in the last two sections of the *Fuqi jingyi lun*. In his "Discourse on the Symptoms of Diseases" he explains his intention.

Someone absorbing *qi* may have already practiced abstention from cereals and yet his bodily form may still be subject to gradual decay. His essence and *qi* may not yet be complete, his spirit and spirit soul may not yet be fully developed.
This may be due either to a protracted disease or to a newly arisen symptom evoking an "exhaustion heteropathy" [see Porkert 1974: 54 n.]. In such a case, it is indispensable to know whence the disease arises. One must carefully examine how it should be treated.

> Therefore I will now give a rough outline as to how one can discern the different appearances of diseases oneself instead of consulting a physician. (*Fuqi jingyi lun* 18a)

Sun Simiao shares this opinion. He also thinks that everybody should be able to recognize a disease at its very beginning. Formulating the issue in a more moral way, Sun Simiao points out:

> There are people who think the disease begins only on the day it breaks out. They do not know that the origin [of the disease reaches back much further and that it] developed gradually. The prudent practitioner must therefore eliminate all diseases in their very beginning. (*Sheyang zhenzhong fang* 3b)

As noted above, the *Sheyang zhenzhong fang* identifies overindulgence of any sort as the main reason for illness. The *Fuqi jingyi lun*, on the other hand, sees the origin of illness in the imbalance of *qi* or of the "blood" within the body. In this attitude, as in the discussion throughout the text, Sima Chengzhen relies on a conception of *qi* indigenous to both Shangqing Taoism and traditional Chinese medicine (see Robinet 1984: vol. 1: 68–70; Engelhardt 1987: 189–193). Sima Chengzhen's high esteem of the latter is obvious in his frequent recourse to the medical classics, especially to the *Suwen*. In contrast, Sun Simiao, who certain evidence suggests was personally involved with the Celestial Masters, might very well have been influenced by their conception of disease. They mainly considered disease a punishment for one's own or one's ancestors' misdemeanors. As retaliation the celestial administration sent demons to attack the sinner's body. Disease was understood to be primarily caused by moral transgression, and one could attain a cure only by confessing one's sins and repenting (Robinet 1984: vol. 1: 68–70; Engelhardt 1987: 189–93). Sun Simiao may well have been influenced by similar ideas, which would certainly explain the emphasis on morality in his *Sheyang zhenzhong fang*.

The religious leader Sima Chengzhen emphasizes the more bodily and medical aspects of the initial steps to be taken toward attaining longevity and eventually immortality. On the other hand, Sun Simiao, the famous physician, mainly stresses moral aspects and mental discipline as fundamental for the quest. To him, the medical system of correspondences as formulated in the *Suwen* seems of minor importance in this context. However, one should always keep in mind that the *Sheyang zhenzhong fang* has come down to us only in fragments and with numerous later interpolations and distortions. It is impossible to define the main concerns of the original text conclusively.

Moreover, it may be that the two authors were addressing different audiences. Sun, the medical specialist, might have appealed to laymen and therefore emphasized that mental effort and discipline in daily life are indispensable. Otherwise all medical treatments remain ineffective and won't bring permanent betterment. Sima, the religious leader, might have spoken primarily to people who already had devoted their lives to religious discipline and who therefore did not need any special advice on moral behavior. At any rate, the aims of the two authors are the same. They agree that in the early stages of accomplishment adepts should be highly aware of the subtlest perceptions and devote themselves to a balanced way of life.

References

Demiéville, Paul. 1985. *Buddhism and Healing.* Translated by Mark Tatz. Boston: University Press of America, 1985.

Despeux, Catherine. 1987. *Préscriptions d'acuponcture valant mille onces d'or.* Paris: Guy Trédaniel, 1987.

Engelhardt, Ute. 1987. *Die klassische Tradition der Qi-Übungen: Eine Darstellung anhand des Tang-zeitlichen Textes Fuqi jingyi lun von Sima Chengzhen.* Wiesbaden: Franz Steiner, 1987.

Holzman, Donald. 1957. *La vie et la pensée de Hi K'ang.* Leiden: E. Brill, 1957.

Kohn, Livia. 1987. *Seven Steps to the Tao: Sima Chengzhen's Zuowanglun.* St. Augustin: Monumenta Serica Monographs 20, 1987.

Loon, Piet van der. 1984. *Taoist Books in the Libraries of the Sung Period.* London: Oxford Oriental Institute, 1984.

Porkert, Manfred. 1974. *The Theoretical Foundations of Chinese Medicine.* Cambridge, Massachusetts: MIT Press, 1974.

—— 1983. *The Essentials of Chinese Diagnosis.* Zürich: Acta Medicinae Sinensis, 1983.

Robinet, Isabelle. 1984. *La révélation du Shangqing dans l'histoire du Taoisme.* 2 vols. Paris: Publications de l'Ecole Francaise d'Extrême-Orient, 1984.

Sakade, Yoshinobu. 1986. "The Taoist Character of the 'Chapter on Nourishing Life' of the *Ishinpō*," *Kansai daigaku bunka ronshū* 1986, 775–798.

Sivin, Nathan. 1967. "A Seventh-Century Chinese Medical Case History," *Bulletin of the History of Medicine* 41.3 (1967), 267–273.

—— 1968 *Chinese Alchemy: Preliminary Studies.* Cambridge, Massachusetts: Harvard University Press, 1968.

—— 1978. "On the Word 'Taoist' as a Source of Perplexity," *History of Religions* 17 (1978), 303–330.

Strickmann, Michel. 1981. *Le Taoisme du Mao chan. Chronique d'une révélation.* Paris: Collège du France, Institut des Hautes Etudes Chinoises, 1981.

Unschuld, Paul. 1975. *Medizin und Ethik.* Wiesbaden: Franz Steiner, 1975.

in Chinese and Japanese

Chen Guofu 陳國符 1963
Daozang yuanliu kao 道藏源流考 . Beijing: Zhonghua, 1963.

Mugitani Kunio 麥谷邦夫 1978
"Dōka, dōkyō ni okeru ki" 道家道教における氣
In *Ki no shisō* 氣の思想 . Edited by Onozawa Seiichi 小野擇精一. Tokyo: Tokyo daigaku, 1978.

—— 1987 (ed.) *Yōsei enmei roku kunchū* 養性延命錄順註
Tokyo: Report of the Study Group on Traditional Chinese Longevity Techniques no. 3, 1987.

Sakade Yoshinobu 坂出祥伸   1986a
"Chō Tan 'Yōsei yōshū' itsubun to sono shisō"
張湛の養生要集佚文 とその 思想
Tōhōshūkyō 68 (1986), 1–24.

Chapter Ten

Original Contributions of *Neidan* to Taoism and Chinese Thought

Isabelle Robinet

Characteristics of *Neidan*

The term *neidan* 內丹, Inner Alchemy, is conventionally used to describe a major current of religious Taoism, of which we will presently define some elementary characteristics. *Neidan* is, quite literally, the opposite of *waidan* 外丹: the inner cinnabar, or elixir, versus the outer cinnabar. The term is not used systematically by Taoist authors, who usually prefer to speak of *jindan* 金丹 , Golden Cinnabar, when they refer to the current in question. The expression inner itself, as opposed to outer and when joined with cinnabar, tends to take on a variety of connotations in the texts we will discuss here (see also figure 1). As will become quite clear in the examples to follow, the term is always used to describe a reality or a stage that is more within, more subtle than another preceding one.[1]

I therefore use inner alchemy in contrast to proto-chemical alchemy, which has the production of a specific substance as its aim and object. The

---

1. See, for example, the different usages of these terms as pointed out by Baldrian-Hussein 1984: 15–21. Here it is quite obvious that the terms *nei* and *wai* must never be understood independently of their respective contexts. This, and because it is used rather commonly, is why I say that the expression *neidan* is entirely conventional. In addition, one may find that the expression is used to designate a personal discipline. Here it is opposed to *waidan*, which describes instruction given to someone else in an altruistic manner and for the sake of salvation (*Dadan qianyong lun* 7b; HY 922, fasc. 596).

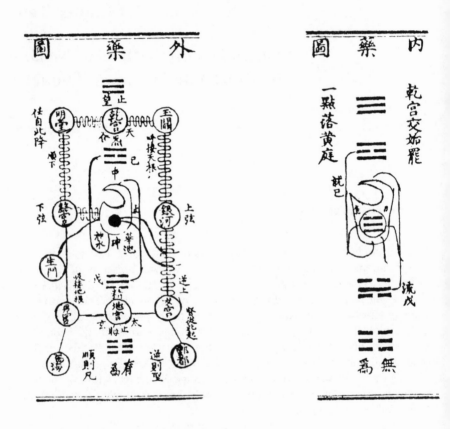

Fig. 1. The outer versus the inner cinnabar. *Source: Zhonghe ji* 2.3b

latter always takes place in a laboratory setting. Despite this obvious difference it is not altogether easy to distinguish the two properly in every instance, especially in the most ancient texts dealing with inner alchemy, because of the similarity of the language used in both practices. The essential difference is that inner alchemy never pursues the production of a specific substance; it can be described more precisely as a method of ordering the world and oneself, or even of fashioning it anew—as the authors have it. More than that, inner alchemy is a way of understanding, meant to be an existential integration and at the same time an intellectual comprehension.

As a matter of fact, inner alchemy is a method of finding illumination by returning to the fundamental order of the cosmos. This goes closely together with a regeneration of the individual, both—individual and cosmos— being axiomatically understood as connected and originally, from beginning to end, nothing but one.

As promising as this initial distinction and understanding of inner alchemy may sound, it is nevertheless insufficient. Let us go a little further.

How can we properly distinguish inner alchemy from chemical or proto-chemical or even operative alchemy, on the one hand, and from the various breathing and gymnastic exercises, from which the authors of inner alchemy distance themselves repeatedly and categorically, on the other? The most practical way seems to establish a list of characteristics uniquely *neidan*. This way one will be able to exclude all those texts, as for example the works by Zhao Bichen, that claim to be part of *neidan* but are actually in no way different from all those materials dealing with breathing techniques and gymnastics, practices that have been popular in China ever since antiquity— that is, probably at the time of Zhuangzi (fourth century B.C.) and certainly since the Han (see the *Daoyin tu* found at Mawangdui of the year 168 B.C.).

Neidan is, in fact, distinguished quite clearly from those materials in that it gives greater weight to intellectual speculation of an original and unique form.

Inner alchemy has been thoroughly influenced by Buddhism. Preceding Neo-Confucianism, to which it made some important contributions, it is in a way a completely Chinese and Taoist reaction to Buddhism. It takes care of a certain shortcoming felt by the native Chinese creed in comparison to the foreign religion: its greater pragmatism. Taoism, at least as far as we can tell from the texts extant today, had not much of a path to offer to all those more given to intellectual speculation, to all those for whom the ecstatic visions practiced especially in the Shangqing tradition were not satisfactory. This is also the reason Taoism, toward the end of the Six Dynasties and in the beginning of the Tang, absorbed a great deal of Buddhist thought, crudely though, and not sufficiently digested. There were especially the Buddhist notions about being and non-being, found frequently in texts like the *Daojiao yishu* 道教義樞 (Pivotal Meaning of the Taoist Teaching; HY 1121, fasc. 762–763)[2] and in the philosophy of the Twofold Mystery school.[3]

In order to remain faithful to the fundamental calling of Taoism, it was thus necessary to reconcile physiological training and the imaginative meditation it aimed at, on the one hand, and pure intellect, on the other. This, then, is the first characteristic of inner alchemy, its fundamental objective, the underlying bond that ties all its authors together.

The second major objective of inner alchemy is to put forward a practical synthesis of, first of all, the various techniques and practices long transmitted within Taoism, certainly a well-rooted and by no means negligible mass of material. It wished to combine those with the fundamental aspirations of Chinese philosophy, found in certain Buddhist texts as well as among Taoists (especially Laozi and Zhuangzi)[4] and, last but not least, in Confucian documents. The spirit of synthesis, of harmonization, is the second basic characteristic of inner alchemy.

In addition to the philosophical tradition of Taoism, inner alchemy adopts and integrates most importantly the heritage of: (1) practices relating to breath or energy (*qi* 氣), (2) proto-chemical efforts, from which it takes a great deal of its vocabulary, and, to a lesser degree, (3) the visionary meditations of the Shangqing school.

All of this was placed, as is common in Taoist thought, under the auspices of the School of Yin-Yang and the Five Agents. That is to say, the various teachings functioned in accordance with the systematic cosmology and the structural analogies provided by this school of thought. It brought to inner alchemy all the necessary conceptual systematization. Speaking of the general Chinese heritage proper, inner alchemy is indebted particularly to the *Yijing* 易經 (Book of Changes).

Let us point out clearly the three major heritages: alchemy in the sense of proto-chemistry (in turn an heir of pharmacology); the various practices of the *qi*; and the cosmological speculations typical for the *Yijing*. In addition, inner alchemy is a direct successor of the *fangshi* 方士 , the magic specialists

---

2. Works in the Taoist Canon are cited according to their number in the *Harvard-Yenching Institute Sinological Index Series* no. 25 (Taipei: Chinese Material Center, 1966), abbreviated HY. "Fasc." refers to the volume number of the 1925 Shanghai reprint of the Canon.

3. For details on this line of Taoist thought see Robinet 1977: 96–208.

4. It is in the texts of inner alchemy that the *Daode jing* and the *Zhuangzi* are cited most frequently of all the Taoist tradition.

of the Warring States period and the Han dynasty. It derives from them in direct lineage; with them it shares the same three lines of origin.

The tradition of inner alchemy is quite conscious of this background, as a text from one of its earliest representatives, Zhenyuan 真元 , testifies. He declares that the three fundamental texts are the *Yijing*, the *Bencao* 本草 (Pharmacopoeia), and the *Neijing* 內經 (Inner Classic [of the Yellow Emperor]). Similarly, Shangyangzi (ca. 1330) names a certain number of *fangshi* as ancestors of inner alchemy (*Shangyangzi jindan dayao xianpai* 上陽子金丹大要仙派 3ab; HY 1062, fasc. 738).

One may say that texts belonging to the current of inner alchemy are characterized by

1. a concern for training the mind as much as the body, with the mental aspect usually predominant;
2. a tendency to synthesize various Taoist currents, certain Buddhist speculations, and specific Confucian lines of thought;
3. references to the *Yijing*; and
4. references to chemical practices.

The two latter characteristics are combined: all *neidan* texts use chemical terminology—at least they speak of lead and mercury, the furnace and the cauldron—and place them in relation to the trigrams of the *Yijing*.

It seems that a text can never fall into the range of *neidan* materials if it lacks this particular trait. Without it, the text is just concerned with breathing exercises and gymnastics, the tradition of what nowadays is known as *Qigong*. Unless one limits the subject in this manner, one is faced with an incredible mass of material. More than that, all historical significance of inner alchemy would be lost. The characteristic combination of chemistry and trigrams is all the more pertinent because, at least to my knowledge, all the texts that make use of it are inspired by the very spirit of synthesis described above. They should thus properly be considered members of the same family.

On the other hand, any study of this synthesis will show clearly how *neidan* reveals the unceasing activity and the unbending creativity of Taoism, manifested, to the chagrin of the Western student, in a variety and diversity of currents and traditions. It continues to amalgamate and merge poetry, intellectual speculation, and pragmatic training. It contains the twofold aspect of Taoist life: it works quite independently of the spirit of a long Chinese heritage and yet perfectly incorporates the gifts of olden times, the remnants of ancient mythology as well as the philosophy of Yin-Yang and the Five Agents, of the *Yijing* and Han dynasty thought. To all these it adds the newly developed Chinese form of Buddhism, the ideas of the Chan school, and—later on—the worldview of Neo-Confucianism. Inner alchemy for the first time integrates these two later traditions into Taoism in a reflective, organized, and coherent manner, not merely superficially and formally as had happened earlier.

However, the great novelty that inner alchemy adds to Taoism is found in its methodology. Although its ultimate aim remains typically Taoist, its methodology is new, as we shall show below. Danyangzi   丹陽子 (1123–1183), one of its masters, was able to write that the only really important thing in alchemy was the technique of the breath. This he described as consisting of "serenity, non-action, free and easy wandering," all terms of the *Zhuangzi*, as well as "independence, freedom from defilements, and detachment," Buddhist terms. He went on to emphasize that alchemy is nothing but metaphors. In summary he said that *neidan* is nothing really new except that it uses a special language that aims at disrupting ordinary thinking by tearing apart the hardened knots, the solid barriers. Eventually this language will soften the mind in exactly the same way as the body has been relaxed previously by the various techniques of respiration.

Our description of *neidan* here will of necessity remain general; the overall framework of this discussion does not allow detailed analysis. We will therefore limit our exposition to sketching the major lines along which inner alchemy has developed, bypassing numerous aspects of higher complexity and deeper subtlety.

The history of inner alchemy will therefore be merely sketched in outline. *Neidan* will be treated not so much as an object but as a subject, that is to say, according to the principles of intersubjective criticism, as an activity one cannot understand except by using it anew. It will also be treated according to an objective principle of intelligibility, by maintaining a distance from the subject, which allows us to isolate its structure, and by attempting to discover the methods or expedient means the authors consciously used as ways of analysis and with an inclination toward geometry—to attempt a translation of Pascal's "esprit de géometrie." (One must also keep in mind the "esprit de finesse," the intriguing subtlety, that the texts evoke time and again just as they persistently come back to the indispensable intersubjectivity we mentioned above.) We will take care of the structure and the substance of the subject at the same time—its bones and its flesh, as the Chinese would say— just as the inner alchemy masters would see their subject themselves.

A Short History of Inner Alchemy

It is impossible to present more than the basic facts of the history of inner alchemy here, mainly because it has not yet been studied in great detail. The names of the most important masters are known, as well as their succession, but the differences among the lineages, often considerable, have not yet been made altogether clear. This is a very difficult problem, indeed, as those differences can sometimes be found even within one single work.

The most ancient texts inner alchemy materials refer to are the *Zhouyi Cantongqi* 周易參同契 (Tally to the Yijing; found in numerous commented editions in the *Daozang*) and the *Guwen longhu jing* 古文龍虎經 (Old Text Dragon and Tiger Scripture; HY 995, fasc. 620). Both these texts are attributed to Wei Boyang 魏伯陽 (second century A.D.), and their major characteristic is that both of them, especially the former, make use of the *Yijing* in the same way inner alchemy does. The basic trigrams are personalized: the father, the mother, the sons, and the daughters and are then associated with the Five Agents and their various characteristics. They are also the basic materials that provide the authors of inner alchemy with their rich font of images and symbols: the toad of the sun, the hare of the moon, the cauldron and the furnace in the shape of a crescent moon (see figure 2), the yellow sprout, the chariot of the river, the black mercury that contains the golden flower, and so on. In addition, the more philosophical vocabulary of inner alchemy is found here in expressions like "before heaven and earth" and "original nature."

The question of the date and authorship of these two texts has not been studied sufficiently to allow any conclusive theories. It is definitely known, however, that both were extant in the Tang, the period when the tendency toward inner alchemy is increasingly found in Taoist materials.

After those two texts is first of all the *Yinfu jing* 陰符經 (Scripture of Obscure Correspondence; HY 125, fasc. 58), attributed to Li Quan 李筌 , who supposedly "received" it in 718.[5] A constant source of inspiration for the authors of inner alchemy, it contains numerous elements typical for inner meditation, a Taoist trend strongly developed during the Tang Dynasty.[6]

---

5. The *Yinfu jing* is unknown before Li Quan, who "received" it from Kou Qianzhi of the fifth century. He also wrote a commentary to it, but one may well assume that commentary and text go back to the same author. In this text, certain characteristics typical of inner alchemy are found already; especially the tendency of synthesis, which is obvious in its usage of the Confucian Classics, Taoist scriptures, and the concepts of the Five Agents and the *Yijing*.

6. *Neiguan* type literature developed most strongly during the Six Dynasties and the Tang (see chapter 7, "Taoist Insight Meditation: The Tang Practice of *Neiguan*"). It was influenced by Buddhism to such a degree that one cannot truly call it part of the Taoist tradition of *qi*,

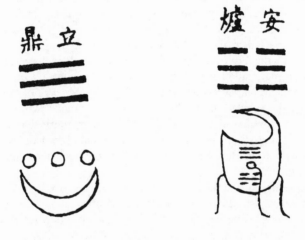

Fig. 2. The furnace and the cauldron. *Source: Zhonghe ji* 2.1ab

The first texts that, following the criteria established above, fall into the category of inner alchemy proper are dated to this period. The works of the School of True Primodiality, which probably date from the reign of Xuanzong or, more specifically, were composed after 742 A.D., already make frequent use of inner-alchemical vocabulary (see Robinet 1988). Zhang Guo 張果, the alleged author of an obviously *neidan*-inspired work, the *Jiuyao xinyin jing* 九 要心印經   (Ninefold Essential Scripture of the Seal of the Mind; HY 225, fasc. 112), lived around the same time.

In the ninth and tenth centuries, the current seemed to gain momentum, since we find numerous texts using the ideas and terminology of inner alchemy. There are, for example, the works of Cui Xifan 崔希范 (ninth century), among which the *Ruyao jing* 入藥鏡 (Mirror of Taking Medicine; chap. 37 of the *Xiuzhen shishu* 修真十書 ; Ten Writings on Cultivating Perfection; HY 263, fasc. 125) is the most prominent. It was variously edited and commented on as well as cited in the *Shangyangzi jindan dayao* 上陽子 金丹大要(Shangyangzi's Great Essentials of the Golden Cinnabar 1.8b, 9a; HY 1059, fasc. 736–738). Then there is Peng Xiao 彭曉 who wrote a commentary to the *Zhouyi cantongqi*, which is dated to the year 947. Above all, there is Chen Tuan 陳摶 (ca. 906–989) whose influence on the later tradition seems to have been considerable. He was especially noted for transmitting the concepts and methods of inner alchemy to Neo-Confucianism.[7]

Under the Song, two major lineages of inner alchemy may be distinguished: the Zhong-Lü tradition and the Quanzhen school.

The Zhong-Lü tradition is named after its two founders, Zhong-li Quan 鍾離權   and Lü Dongbin 呂洞賓 , alias Lü Yan 呂嵒. Zhong-li Quan allegedly lived under the Han, was active again under the Jin, and continued to appear to various Taoist masters under the Tang and the Song. Lü Dongbin is among his most famous disciples; even in the earliest accounts, he is a legendary figure. He came to be known as the master of quite a number of different schools and lineages within Taoism. It seems that he lived around the ninth century and was a disciple of Cui Xifan, but this has not prevented historians from recording several later appearances and activities of his.[8] The Zhong-Lü tradition itself did not take shape until the Song dynasty. More than the other schools it places primary importance on respiratory techniques and is

---

gymnastics, and breathing exercises. This literature is one of the threads that weave the background of inner alchemy, showing again its strong tendency to unify and harmonize trends that historically and logically exclude each other.

7. Li Yuanguo (1985) has shown brilliantly that the various elements of Neo-Confucianism are present already with Chen Tuan.

8. On the various appearances of Lü Dongbin in the Song see Baldrian-Hussein 1984: 25–30, 1985, 1986.

less inclined toward intellectual speculation. Nevertheless, its materials undoubtedly belong within the range of inner alchemy.

The Quanzhen school developed under the Song, too. It is a school of Taoism that, when compared to the Celestial Masters, who prefer rigid institutions and formal liturgy, shows a strong tendency toward monasticism and contemplation. The school itself divides into two groups, northern and southern. The northern group is traditionally called Quanzhen; the southern calls itself by the same name but has been distinguished by the tradition. The northern group, Quanzhen proper, was founded by Wang Chongyang 王重陽 (1113–1170). It is still active today, with headquarters in the White Cloud Monastery in Beijing. The southern school claims descent from Zhang Boduan 張伯端 (d. 1082). His major work, the *Wuzhen pian* 悟真篇 (Awakening to Truth; HY 141, fasc. 61–62), has been commented on several times and is recognized by all schools as a scripture of central importance. It is quoted frequently and still plays an important role even today. It certainly can be considered one of the central scriptures of modern Taoism. Present scholarship does not permit a clear definition of the distinctions and differences between these groups. Let it suffice to note the traditional split into northern and southern schools.

The Quanzhen school, strongly influenced by Buddhism, places an enormous emphasis on intellectual speculation. It can be clearly distinguished from the Zhong-Lü tradition because texts of the latter do not use the terms *xing* 性, "inner nature," and *ming* 命, "fate," in their expositions, nor do they use expressions like "the sparkle of the original yang" or the Mysterious Pass. The point of view of the Zhong-Lü tradition is much more physiological and a great deal less mystical than that of the Quanzhen school. In addition, both Quanzhen lineages are characterized by a strong tendency to "harmonize the three teachings" (Confucianism, Buddhism, and Taoism). They borrow heavily from Buddhism, and we know that their leaders in several cases were close friends of Buddhist monks. They also use a certain number of Neo-Confucian ideas, integrating the notions of Zhou Dunyi, Zhang Zai, and the Cheng brothers, who were contemporaries of the earliest Quanzhen masters. At the same time, Quanzhen is quite unique and clearly distinct from both Buddhism and Neo-Confucianism. Their ultimate aims may be the same, but there are always clear differences in their concrete ways and methods.

In addition to these two major lineages of inner alchemy, Zhong-Lü and Quanzhen, three more currents of the East, the West, and the center are traditionally recognized, presumably to fit in with the concept of the Five Agents and their directions. However, these distinctions have not yet been studied and we do not know to what they refer.[9]

Language Expressing Silence

In regard to the problem of expressing the ineffable by means of language, of formulating a silence that is actually sufficient expression itself, inner alchemy places itself completely in the tradition that goes back to the *Daode jing* and the *Zhuangzi*. It also uses the *Yijing* to overcome the inherent opposition between language and silence, a process necessary for transmission and teaching, which are both between the two extremes of unity (silence) and duality (language). The *Yijing*, it must be understood, had at no point ceased to be part of the Taoist tradition. Tang Changru (1955) and Michel Strickmann (1981) have shown how the study of the *Yijing* was consistently preserved in the environment of Yang Xi and the Xu family, who were closely related to Ge Hong.[10]

The *Yijing* offers a system of symbols that permits a less discursive approach to truth than that preferred by inner alchemy. However, the silence is always invoked. Only in silence can the Mysterious and the Marvelous reside, always present yet inevitably fleeting. For instance, the *Zhonghe ji* 中和集 (Collection of Central Harmony; HY 249, fasc. 118–119) says:

> Silence is language. Where language is, there is fundamentally silence. Silent language: this is the secret formula of alchemy. (6.13a)

The preface of the Qing-dynasty edition of the *Wuzhen pian* states:

---

9. For some details on these various schools see Despeux 1979 and Li 1985: 60–61. Li advances the theory that the northern school concentrated especially on the *xin* (heart/mind). However, the formulations he quotes are quite similar to those found in materials of the southern school, for example, by Bai Yuchan in *Xiuzhen shishu* 6.1b.

10. The tradition of *Yijing* study and exegesis that developed under Taoist influence and that has been conserved and developed is obviously that of the new text school. The original elements of this interpretation are as follows: the *Xici* (dated to the beginning of the Han) vision of the sage, which can easily be related to that of the *Zhuangzi*, but is slightly different; and Yu Fan's (164–233) interpretation and the *Yijing* apocrypha, which both place the trigrams in relation to the movements of the sun and the moon and to the various cyclical signs. As a consequence, the trigrams are understood as temporal divisions. This is one of the central functions the hexagrams have within inner alchemy. See Fung and Bodde 1953: vol.2: 106, 406; Needham 1956: 329–330.

> The Tao, she says, does not have a name. The sage has given it
> an artificial appellation. Names and words assemble in silence.
> . . . The Tao is rendered manifest by means of words. The
> words are forgotten by the Tao. (Lu and Davis 1939: 102)

The classic phrase that expresses this sentiment is taken up by innumerable
texts again and again. It stems from the "Great Appendix" section of the
Yijing and usually appears after following a logical argument. The texts
thereby adopt the development that was first formulated by Wang Bi 王弼
(226–249): the symbols (of the *Yijing* and of alchemy) lead to the idea; once
the idea is grasped, the symbols must be forgotten.

Inner alchemy remains constantly faithful to its proposition: open up
Unity and, while traversing the dualism that is inevitably established by
language and practice, continue to approach a Unity that in the end cannot,
paradoxically, be any other but the same Unity that is the ground of the very
dualism that is its opposite but also its face, its outer and only visible
appearance. This is why, according to Li Daochun 李道純, the process ends
in a negation of the Unity (*Zhonghe ji* 4.20b–21a). He refers to the radical
dissolution of all opposition between unity and duality.

Inner alchemy employs many techniques in order to use language and at
the same time abuse it by overstepping it and twisting it about. The trigrams of
the *Yijing*, as we said above, are used for this, and so are the innumerable
metaphors and symbols found again and again in the texts. Here one once
more discovers the fundamental tendency of Taoism to use symbolic thinking
rather than intellectual speculation, such as found in the Mādhyamika, for
example. Moreover, there are a variety of literary means to make silence
speak out truly, a silence that when left in its original state will do nothing to
serve the teaching. There are poems and chants, both abundantly found in the
texts, there are diagrams and charts, paradoxes, contradictions, the kōans of
Chan, philosophical essays full of playful dialectic, and most of all, the
polysemy contained in all the images and words.

It is important to note that the texts of inner alchemy do not treat the
discipline uniformly. Their way of formulating things is just one way among
many others (compare, for example, *Panshan zhenren yulu* 盤山真人語錄
HY 1052, fasc. 728). Or, to put it differently, alchemical language is not only
used by the texts of inner alchemy in the wide sense of the term.

The *Yijing*, the *Daode jing*, and the Five Agents

Inner alchemy is a technique of enlightenment, but it is also a technique of teaching. To that end, the Chinese traditon has long found a form of language that approaches if not hits the truth. It is in this area that inner alchemy furnishes some innovation.

There is, actually, a certain similarity between the methods of Mādhyamika and the procedures of inner alchemy in that they both use the combination of binary and dialectical opposites in a systematic fashion to convey their meaning. However, despite the fact that the intellectual oppositions used in Mādhyamika are integrated into inner alchemy (existence and nonexistence, truth and illusion, and so on), they are lost among many other examples taken from the deep vein of Chinese intellectual and symbolic thinking. It furnishes a multiplicity so rich that its expressions are practically uncountable.

The principle of binary systems is represented by the couple Yin and Yang. The One (the Taiji 太極, the Great Ultimate, or the Tao), articulates itself in two (Yin-Yang), the first fraction that starts a whole series of divisions multiplying, separating, or joining ever anew. But the basic binary system of the *Yijing* (one to two, two to four, four to eight, as formulated in the *Xici*) is then combined with the pattern of the Five Agents and with a fundamentally Taoist structure (origination from one to two, two to three, three to multiplicity, formulated in the *Daode jing*).

Thus, inner alchemy adds several sets of complex patterns to the basic binary system of the *Yijing*, which when left to itself merely revolves around itself in a sterile and uncreative manner. First it integrates the Five Agents: not just four (two plus two, two couples) but five, because the One in the Center is an integral part of the whole, and together with the One, which is the fifth agent, the items assembled gather in a new level of unity. Inner alchemy continues to emphasize the importance of the agent Earth, the "one placed in the middle," which unites the two antagonists. The Center, the heart, the unfixed position is indefinable and transcendent; here the subtle combination of the two outward opposites takes place. In addition, one should keep in mind that the pattern of the Five Agents is an organized system based not on binary opposites but on correspondences and resonances, on intimate relationships.

Also, the authors of inner alchemy continue to be rather indifferent toward the cosmogony of the *Yijing*, where the Taiji is divided into two, the two are divided into four. They much prefer the system found in the *Daode jing*, where the Tao produces the two, the two produce the three, and the three produce the multiple. Where the *Yijing* proposes a multiplication by way of division, using, in fact, the word *fen* 分, "to divide," the *Daode jing* embraces a development through emanation, expressed in words like *sheng* 生 , "to produce," or *hua* 化, "to transform." Moreover, the symbolism inherent in the *Daode jing* means something different from that found in the *Yijing*: the world comes forth not from a division of the One to the infinite, but from the division into two, which then reunite into three. It is this reunion that can forge the multiplicity of all beings into one. Related to the notion of division is the idea of the couple. Li Daochun expresses it with the word both or dual, a term used in the *Yijing* to refer to the two basic principles Yin and Yang, and explicitly states that he means something different from the simple Two.[11] It is through union that there is a response, and because of the response that there is transformation and communication.

This, then, is an example of how the procedures of *neidan* use various and even contradictory systems in order to provide different and yet complementary visions of the world. On the one hand is the binary system based on division (one-two-four-eight); on the other is a process of emanation and a dialectical pattern (one-two-three). On all of these the principle of response and of intimate relations is superimposed, a principle fundamental to the system of the Five Agents.

An heir to thinking in terms of the Five Agents, alchemy thus remains faithful to the relational character of this system. Again and again neither the images nor the concepts, the terms, or the subject are really of central importance in the texts; the Center is the relations that unite all of them. Their organization and the way they function within the context justify their very existence. The function of a given term is most important in understanding it correctly, it makes sense only because of its role within the entire system. For example, *xin* 心 (mind), when opposed to *shen* 身 (body), means the intellect, but when used alone and in an absolute sense of its own it refers to the Center, the heart of things. The same phenomenon is found in connection with the word Yang. It may be part of the dualism of Yin and Yang, but it may also be placed on an absolute level and be a synonym for enlightenment. Depending on the context, the Dragon and the Tiger may denote the Breaths of the liver and the lungs, or they may indicate the Spirit and the Breath. In all these examples, the change in function reveals a change in the level of meaning, which again corresponds to a change in the level of consciousness. The literature abounds with examples of this kind, as will become very clear as we go along, because the constant change of levels and the polysemy of terms that goes with it are an integral part of the mental discipline of inner alchemy to which every student must submit.

---

11. See *Quanzhen jixuan biyao* 8a; HY 251, fasc. 119.

transcendent and impossible to locate. This spark forms the first impulse of the work, the acknowledgment of the fundamental desire to accomplish the task and to realize the true vision in the sense of alchemy. At this point one becomes conscious of the existence of the three basic constituents, *jing, qi,* and *shen.* One realizes that they are but one and that they are fundamentally different from the ordinary human forces known by these names. The latter are merely materials for outer alchemy (*Zhonghe ji* 2.6a), which here refers to the classical respiratory and physiological practices of Taoism.

In other words, inner alchemy begins where the various exercises of the gross breath end. At this stage, adepts must know the exact moment of unfolding and properly catch hold of it, "just as one would catch a thief," says Zhang Boduan in his *Jinbao neilian dan jue*　金寶內煉丹訣　 (Golden Treasure Formulas for the Inner Refinement of the Elixir, 2.13b; HY 240, fasc. 114). This moment is marked by the hexagram Fu and the cyclical sign *zi* 子. It is the moment of rebirth, when one gathers the true ingredients, the moment that sets the alchemical dynamic in motion, which also sees the beginning of its folding back.[15] Here is where the return begins, the climb back from the level of mundane or posterior time to the anterior stage, the time of alchemy.

The second stage, going from *qi* to *shen,* is frequently described as representing inner alchemy in the strict sense. It is the phase of yang-ization, when one moves from the hexagram Fu to the hexagram Qian. During this stage one begins to activate and circulate the ingredients, one makes them rise and descend. In other words, one now activates the various forces that one has discovered during the first stage. First the activation is careful, very methodical and fully conscious; later, when a certain mastery is attained, it becomes increasingly spontaneous. This stage the texts describe in most detail in the terms outlined above: simultaneously physiological and alchemical (see Baldrian-Hussein 1984).

In contrast, the third stage is not discussed a great deal. Here one returns to emptiness, to the Tao as such, to one's original nature. The final stage is the immobility that contains all action, the non-action that follows from all the conscious practices undertaken earlier. The second part of the regulation of the fire is a process of yin-ization in the sense that the Yin is the principle of immobility and invisibility. The adept is compared to a dragon guarding a pearl, to a chicken hatching an egg, to a fish in the water. His actions, which

---

15. The rich theme of the countercurrent is one of the important topics dealt with again and again in the texts, but we cannot take it up here in any detail. To "go along with the current" means to create something, to bring forth something else. To "go against the current" means to turn one's physiological, psychological, and creative energies inward, to produce the cinnabar, the elixir within, to create immortality within.

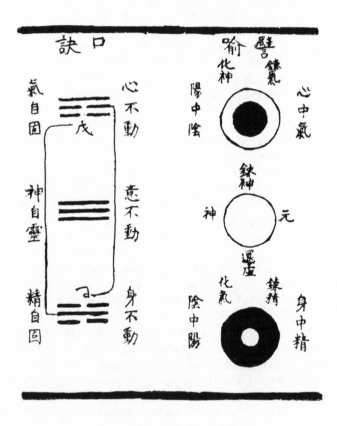

Fig. 5. Symbols of attainment. *Source: Zhonghe ji* 2.2ab

arise subtly and tenuously, are described as the cooking of tiny fishes, already mentioned in the *Daode jing* (chap. 60).

In a diagram by Li Daochun (*Zhonghe ji* 2.5a; see figure 5), the third stage from *shen* to emptiness is represented by an empty circle. However, this circle is not placed at the top. Instead it is found between a black circle with a white center below, which stands for stage one, and a white circle with a black center above, which represents stage two. The third stage is thus the central, the essential undertaking. Unless one manages to attain, to gather true emptiness, unless one practices non-action, one has only done half the work (*Jinbao neilian dan jue* 15b).

Li Daochun also explains that the three stages stand only for outer alchemy (*Zhonghe ji* 2.5a). He uses the term outer in a unique sense, meaning that—as also emphasized by other authors—the three stages as formulated can only stand for a pattern, a way of expression, not for the thing as such. The distinction between the stages is only made for teaching purposes. In inner alchemy the one and only thing of importance is the spark of true eternal Yang. It is represented by the central line of the trigram Kan, which insofar as it unites with Kun, the trigram of complete Yin, is identical to the central line of the trigram of complete Yang, Qian. It is essential in alchemical practice to isolate this spark of true eternal Yang and make it return to the ancestral breath. This is different from ordinary respiration, it is the original breath, the primordial breath of the cosmos, the creative force of the universe. The aim of the practice is to cross Yin with Yang in a way that allows the Yin line of Kun to enter into Qian and form Li.

Instantaneousness

The question of the sudden attainment of the goal, of instantaneousness, is a notion that fundamentally negates the idea of stages outlined above. The question is discussed amply by *neidan* authors. Although they all inherit the strong emphasis Taoism places on nature and on spontaneity, they tend to be fundamentally gradualists. They all describe a teaching, a culture, a training that cannot be learned in any other way but gradually and progressively over a long time.

But this does not keep them from insisting that there is a "simultaneous grasping" that is essential for the entire undertaking. In a way it accompanies the whole process of mental refinement. It is an intuitive and all-encompassing vision, a concrete manifestation of the unity it accompanies, beyond and yet underlying the duality that is inherent in both practice and language. It is this

knowledge that makes Chen Nan 陳南 , also known as Master Cuixu 翠虛先
生 (d. 1213), among others, state that all returns to Unity, to "one single time,
which is but one single place, which in turn is nothing but one" (*Cuixu pian*
14a; HY 1082, fasc. 742). Li Daochun similarly emphasizes that the time of
the work, the moment of first opening and initial gathering, is not common
time, nor is it outside of time, without which one cannot begin the work
(*Zhonghe ji* 3.31a).

    This moment, described as a flash, where suddenly something arises
that transports, is most frequently illustrated as an opening. It is a Mysterious
Pass, so called in accordance with the notion of the Three Passes in the spinal
column. It is also known as the Opening of the Mysterious Pass or the
Mysterious Female (taken from the *Daode jing*). This Pass, the authors assert,
is located neither in the cinnabar field nor in the kidneys, as one would expect
from reading ancient Taoist accounts of spiritual physiology. In inner alchemy
it lacks any precise location. It is an undefined opening anywhere in the
eternity of time and the infinity of space. It is beyond time, it is so great that
none is beyond it, so small that none is within it (a formula traditionally
applied to the Tao), as Zhang Boduan describes it (*Jinbao neilian dan jue*
2.11b). All is contained in it, the winter solstice, the traditional beginning of
respirational exercises and alchemical work, the ingredients, the regulation of
the fire, the purification, the conception of the embryo, and the ultimate
deliverance. It encompasses all: the beginning, the process, and the end.
Zhang Boduan, who discusses the opening in some detail, uses a language
known primarily from Chan Buddhism: it cannot be transmitted other than by
mind and mouth, it can only be known immediately and through one's entire
being (*Jindan sibai zi* 金丹四百字 , in *Xiuzhen shishu* 5.4ab).

    Both—a deep inner rootedness and a wide universal range—are united
in the process of the inner alchemical work. They are expressed in a large
variety of ways, too diverse and numerous to be more than touched on here. Li
Daochun is certainly not the only one who insists that the one unifying instant,
the "one single thought," must be repeated without interruption. In tiny
minuteness there is the tenuity of a single thought; in the vast expanse it
becomes the whole world. In this special moment one may accomplish the
work of an entire year, but when it is repeated continuously, it accords with
the passing of a real year and thereby is aligned with the regulation of the fire
(*Zhonghe ji* 4.3b). Through its constant presence, this very moment, in its
fundamental negation of history and of binary thinking and in its fundamental
permanence of unity and oneness, goes beyond the evolution of multiplicity. It
becomes a part of the eternal negation of the entire system, a negation that is
fundamentally contained in it.

breath. The regulation of the fire works according to the rhythm of the seasons in the course of one year. The Mysterious Pass is located in the Niwan Palace in the center of the head, the highest spot of the body, and not in the lower cinnabar field in the abdomen as one might have expected. The aim of the practice at this level is to merge essence and spirit. The techniques are part of the larger tradition of nourishing the life span. The level of the work as a whole has moved from the more physical to the more psychological.

On the third level, the greater vehicle, the cauldron and the furnace are Heaven and Earth, water and fire are the sun and the moon. Dragon and tiger stand for inner nature (pure and tranquil) and passions or emotions (mixed and moving). The Mysterious Pass is located in the center, in the heart. The aim at this level is to realize the oneness of inner nature and the passions. The practice has moved completely to a cosmic and psychological level: the life that is being strengthened and extended is called *sheng* and no longer *ming*, the latter expression bearing the stronger physiological connotations.

The highest and unique vehicle that is placed above all the others is obviously patterned on the One Vehicle of Buddhism. Here the cauldron is the Great Void, the furnace is the Great Ultimate. The base of the elixir is serenity, its mother is non-action. Lead and mercury are *xing* and *ming*, standing for the two major poles of human personality, the spiritual/celestial and the physical/terrestrial. Water and fire function as concentration and wisdom. The aim of the practice at this level is attained when *xing* and *ming* are completely merged. There is no more question here of any bodily element, except very generally in the term *ming*. The practice has gone beyond the physical sphere.

Limiting ourselves to the survey found in the *Zhonghe ji*, one should not overlook the fact that there are numerous similar descriptions in various texts—for example, one by Li Daochun (*Xiuzhen shishu* 4.1b–2a)—that arrange the inherent principles with extraordinary clarity. However, in many cases the texts do not distinguish too clearly between the different levels. They mix their terminology, because every disciple has to grasp from the teacher's instructions that which is suitable for him at any specific moment (a fundamental rule of teaching also found in Buddhism). Thus the same word may carry a variety of connotations and be valid on more than one level. On the other hand, inconsistencies in the terminology serve to express the viewpoint of fundamental and ultimate unity of all that is said. The different levels all coexist and in the end are merged into one. They neutralize and cancel each other out without interruption; the continuous process of oneness makes the individual levels incomplete without recourse to all the others.

It is thus evident how the Buddhist system of dividing and integrating the teaching is applied and integrated into Taoism.[18] The different practices and schools are so completely united in a well-structured hierarchy that at the highest level the whole system is merged into one: the pyramid coincides in a unifying, all-transcending synthesis.

All in all, it appears that alchemy, on whatever level it is being practiced, always contains a speculative and theoretical part and an experimental and practical side. The latter may be physical, as it is in the Zhong-Lü tradition, but *it is never* purely psychological and mystical, as it is on the third and fourth levels of the scheme discussed above. Here we have the fundamental distinction between inner alchemy and respiratory or meditative practices.

On the other hand, the essential distinction between inner alchemy and Chan Buddhism, as the authors claim, lies in the fact that inner alchemy always begins at the bottom. It deals first with the *ming*, with the resisting part of human beings, on the level of concrete manifestations, physical or psycho-physiological, and by experimenting with these manifestations. Inner alchemy does not turn to the purely speculative and abstract realm without physical shape of *xing* until the more concrete sphere has been traversed. To begin with the abstract and proceed toward the concrete is to try to catch the moon in the water, as Zhang Boduan has it (*Jinbao neilian dan jue* 12ab). One must always begin with the more manifest side of things, with the *ming*, and progress to the more abstract, the *xing*. This is the first phase of the work, the rising of yang. Then one must return to the *ming* from a secure position of *xing*. In the alchemical work, this phase is a process of yin-ization. The loop is closed, the summit is reached, well earned after a long journey.

---

18. To divide the teaching refers to a system of Indian origin that was taken up and developed by various Chinese schools. In the Tiantai tradition, Zhi Yi (538–597) paid special attention to it. The system consists of a hierarchical organization of all the various teachings and traditions within Buddhism. It is based on the theory that the Buddha taught his ideas in many different ways so as to adapt it to the individual preferences and specific abilities of his listeners. This system allowed Buddhists to integrate texts from widely variant and even contradictory traditions into one organized whole. The integration of the teaching, on the other hand, completed the system of division. It is a theory that claims that whatever the form of a given teaching, it always goes back to one single original truth. This fundamental truth encompasses all its manifestations and at the same time all the manifestations contain one another (Hurvitz 1962).

Then, in the early decades of this century, several pioneering books appeared that propagated the use of traditional longevity methods in the healing of diseases. In the fifties, the first Qigong clinics were established. Even then the practitioners and beneficiaries were mainly members of an elect, cultured elite who belonged to medical or religious circles. But their amazing successes in curing chronic and even terminal diseases led to an ever-increasing popularity of the methods throughout the country.

Most outstanding among the early propagators were Jiang Weiqiao, Liu Guizhen, and later on Guo Lin. Let us examine their careers and the changing evaluations of their work.

Jiang Weiqiao 蔣維橋 was born in 1872. He was a sickly child and developed tuberculosis and lung hemorrhages as he grew up. He completely cured himself by means of meditation, an experience he described in his book *Yinshizi jingzuofa* 因是子靜坐法 (Quiet Sitting With Master Yinshi; contained in the *Daozang jinghua*). The book appeared in 1914 and became rather well known.

A typical experience related in it is the emergence of involuntary body movements.

> All of a sudden there was this intense rumbling movement in the cinnabar field in my lower abdomen. I had been sitting in quiet meditation as usual, but this was something I really couldn't control. I was shaken back and forth helplessly. Then an incredibly hot energy began to rise at the bottom of my spine, climbed up further and further until it reached the very top of my head. (Renmin 1981: 77, 175, 219)

Later he describes how the experience is being repeated several times until the hot *qi* that rises along the spine no longer leaves the body through the point at the top of the head but returns through the face and the breast area to the lower abdomen. That is, in terms of acupuncture, it rises along the governor conduit and falls following the conception conduit. He thus experienced the spontaneous establishment of the classical microcosmic orbit of inner alchemy. The hot energy is traditionally known as the Energy of Former Heaven, the inner energy, or the Great Medicine.

Jiang Weiqiao was a scholar by profession. He published works on Chinese philosophy and the history of Buddhism (see Matsuzaki 1980: 197). Well versed in traditional thought and the methods of Buddhism, he integrated the methods of Tiantai meditation into his own practice. A similar case is that of Ding Fubao 丁福保 (1874–1952), who wrote on classical Chinese literature and Buddhism and also published the *Jingzuofa jingyi* 靜坐法精義 (Essential Meaning of Quiet Sitting; see Ma 1983a: 43; Lin and Luo 1983: 11).

These early publications on traditional longevity methods are characterized by a strong emphasis on the meditative—that is, unmoving—aspect of Qigong. Those were the practices of scholars, not of the working masses, and in many ways they continued the Confucian tradition of quiet study and meditative reflection, which from Song times onward had included Taoist and Buddhist techniques of meditation.

They were duly criticized for being too spiritual and not active enough. Mao Zedong himself, then twenty-five years old, expressed the reaction as follows:

> Human beings are active animals and they love to be active. Human beings are also rational animals and thus they need a reason for their activity. Why is this?
>
> Because activity secures survival. Yes, but that is an easy explanation. Because activity secures the fortune of the homeland. Yes, and that is a weighty explanation. Neither reach the basis of the matter. Activity is ultimately what nourishes life and satisfies the mind. This and none other is the truth.
>
> Zhu Xi proposed respect, Lu Xiangshan proposed tranquility. Tranquility is meditation, and respect isn't activity either, it's but another form of being at rest. Laozi emphasized to be without activity, the Buddha wished all beings to be serene.
>
> Sitting in meditation was advised by the followers of Zhu Xi and Lu Xiangshan over the ages, the most recent example being Master Yinshi's book. He praises his method as wonderful and highly spiritual and says that activity destroys the body. This is one way of looking at things.
>
> However, I do not share these ideas. In my opinion, there is nothing between heaven and earth that is not activity. (Mao 1972: vol. 1: 39)

This reflects the fundamental battle of our century: the battle between idealism and materialism, between free will and determinism, the beliefs in the independence and in the conditioning of man. In terms of Qigong, the controversy was solved by a gradual shift to more movements in the practice, to ways of treatment that involved a high degree of active interaction between physician and patient. Steps in that direction were first taken by Liu Guizhen.

Liu Guizhen 劉貴珍 was born in 1920 in the Wei district of Hebei Province. When he was twenty years old, he developed an ulcer of the stomach. Suffering from it as well as from other chronic diseases, he engaged actively in the practice of Qigong and eventually succeeded in completely curing himself. The specific method he used, the so-called Exercise of Inner

Nourishment, had been transmitted in the Hebei area and specifically in his family since the end of the Ming.

Inner Nourishment is a kind of meditation or restful practice. It is practiced in either a sitting or a lying posture and includes breathing exercises and meditations on the cinnabar field in the lower abdomen. Frequently a given phrase is repeated along with the observation of the respiration. Thereby the conscious mind is rested while the inner organs are strengthened (Renmin 1981: 4; Lin and Luo 1983: 69).

Having by his own cure proved the effectiveness of the traditional method, Liu Guizhen became duly involved in efforts to use it in helping others. He directed various Qigong clinics, first in Tangshan (1954), later in Beidaihe (1956), and treated a large number of patients with a success rate of over 80 percent even in chronic cases (Renmin 1981: 2). For his amazing success he was given several awards by the Ministry of Health and was received formally by Chairman Mao in 1956. In 1957, his ground-breaking best-seller *Qigong liaofa shiyan* 氣功療法實驗 (Experiences in Healing with Qigong) appeared. Unfortunately he died rather early, at the age of 64, in December 1983 (see *Qigong* 1984/6: 282).

It was thus not until the fifties and sixties that Qigong became known and available to larger segments of the population. Even then, certain sentiments that it was all superstitious nonsense still lingered, its traditional connection with religion being more on people's minds than its visible success in medical treatment. The pressure was heightened during the Great Cultural Revolution, when earlier Qigong establishments, such as the oldest sanatoriums in Tangshan and Beidaihe, were demolished and progress was virtually impossible (Ma 1983a: preface).

The seventies finally saw the explosion of Qigong activities all over the country. Guo Lin 郭林, a popular Beijing actress, contributed considerably to this development. Born in 1907, she was diagnosed as suffering from cancer of the uterus at the age of 42. After six operations she was ready to die. With her last bit of strength she devised her own kind of Qigong and, miraculously, cured herself completely. She called her technique the New Qigong Treatment and in 1970 started to teach it in public parks all over the city. By 1979, she had cured twenty people in the last stage of cancer. Seven of them were able to take up part-time work and eight went back to full-time employment (Guo 1980: 6). Her new method was described on radio and television and Qigong became widely praised as a cancer cure.

Another important thing happened in the later seventies: the existence of *qi* was experimentally proven. In 1977, a joint team of the Shanghai Research Institute for Traditional Medicine and the Shanghai Nuclear Research Center developed a special sensor that could measure the *qi* that was radiated by a Qigong master. A similar experiment was completed successfully in Beijing in 1983 (Lin and Luo 1983: 38). According to the report of Lin Hai 林海 from the Shanghai Research Institute, *qi* is very much like infrared rays, electromagnetic waves, static electricity, magnetism, or the flow of tiny subatomic particles. With this, the ancient techniques finally graduated into the scientific age.

Popular Practice

Qigong practice is usually described according to different stages undergone by the practitioner. On each specific level, certain preparations involving mental concentration and bodily relaxation are necessary. Then instructions relating to the respiration and the inner circulation of *qi* are given. When all these are performed properly and regularly, health improves enormously.

General Rules

It is of utmost importance that the adept of Qigong begin his practice with a strong, good faith in the power of the method to improve his health. Guo Lin emphasizes that a successful practitioner needs most of all faith, determination, and perseverance (Guo 1983: 10; Ma 1983: 6). Once these have been solidly established, the next important prerequisite is a complete relaxation of body and mind. Already in the *Zhubing yuanhou lun* 諸病源候論 (On the Origins and Symptoms of All Diseases) of the seventh century, the relaxation of body and mind is mentioned as an important part of gymnastics used to attain long life (chap. 2). Certain Qigong schools claim that a tight control of consciousness is needed before successful relaxation can take place (Renmin 1981: 83; Lin and Luo 1983: 32). Tension and stiffness of the body are the worst conditions for a Qigong practitioner. But relaxation alone is not the final goal of the techniques. Rather, it is joined by calmness and spontaneity, and the three together form the fundamental roots of Qigong (Jiang 1983: 47).

Next, the two main pillars of active practice must be established: respiration and thinking. Calming and controlling these two has the effect of establishing not only a thorough hold over the conscious mind, but also an awareness of the circulation of *qi* throughout the body. In the long run, circulation can even be consciously controlled. At this stage there is an intense interaction between rest and movement, which have to be balanced and then worked against each other.

The breathing practiced in Qigong is first of all natural breathing, but with prolonged exercise abdominal breathing is encouraged, which in the end should lead to embryo respiration. All movements of the body are accompanied by a particular kind of breathing: just as in Taiji quan, upward and expanding movements are usually accompanied by inhalations, and downward and contracting movements go together with exhalations. While the movements of the body give an outward stimulus to the inner flow of *qi*, the respiration at the same time gives it an inner stimulus.

As it strengthens the blood and energy flow of the body, controlled respiration at the same time serves to calm the conscious thinking. In this aspect it is used as a means of entering a state of mental one-pointedness, just as in the beginning stages of Buddhist meditation practice. When the mind is fully concentrated on respiration, all irrelevant and scattered thoughts vanish completely. One method leading to this aim is propagated by Chen Yingning. He bases its description on the dialogue on "the fasting of the mind" found in chapter 4 of the *Zhuangzi*. He claims that by straining one's ears in the effort to listen to one's own respiration the mind gets concentrated. He calls his technique "Zhuangzi's method of listening to the respiration" (Renmin 1981: 34).

Actually, there is nothing particularly unusual in health practices placing a strong emphasis on respiration. What is special about its application in Qigong, however, is the use that is made of thinking (*yi* 意). Qigong thereby ceases to be merely a way of exercising the body and becomes an exercise of the mind. *Yi* is defined as "conscious mental contents, such as ideas, emotions, knowledge, and thoughts in general" (Renmin 1981: 86), but the concept also includes imagination and a general idea of feeling. In Qigong physical energy is circulated by a movement of conscious thought as much as by physical exercise. As the thinking moves around the body so does the *qi*. This concept is usually expressed in phrases like "guiding the *qi* with the thinking" or "where there is thinking there is *qi*." It is important to note that the movement of the thinking is not necessarily linked to the rhythm of the respiration, although it may very well coincide with it.

Another method frequently practiced is the fixation of the thinking on some particular part of the body, most popularly (and most effectively) the lower cinnabar field. But certain other nodal points, such as, for example, the Gate of Life behind the navel, the perineum, the soles of the feet, or the crown of the head might also be used. For patients with high blood pressure, the soles of the feet are recommended as a point of mental fixation. For those who suffer from low blood pressure it is best to concentrate on the crown of the head (Lin and Luo 1983: 15).

With prolonged practice of mental fixation, the *qi* tends to assemble in that particular spot and in due course reactions such as the spontaneous erupting of *qi* or sensations of intense heat might develop. The reason why concentration on the lower cinnabar field is considered most beneficial is found in the belief that the abdomen is the focal point of the fundamental vital force of human beings. All true primordial energy generated by the practice of Qigong tends to assemble there. The more life-force one has the stronger and healthier one is bound to become (Renmin 1981: 171; Lin and Luo 1983: 47; Tao 1981: vol. 2: 54).

The technique of focusing the thinking on a particular part of the body is also applied in the initial training of mental calmness and harmony. "One single thought replaces the myriad thoughts" is the basic principle at work here (Renmin 1981: 105). That is to say, as soon as the mind is fully fixated on one single thing, one is freed from distractions and confused thinking (Renmin 1981: 237; Lin and Luo 1983: 51–53).

The object of mental concentration might also be something outside of oneself, such as, for example, a religious edifice, a mountain, or some other feature of the landscape. Again, the object could also be something imagined by the adept (Renmin 1981: 366; Lin and Luo 1983: 54) or some specific theoretical topic (Renmin 1981: 107). One school of Qigong, however, completely rejects the use of thinking: the School of Non-Action claims that one should abstain from any conscious effort whatsoever (Lin 1983: 55).

Progress in Six Stages

A typical practice follows six distinct stages.[1]

The beginning stage of Qigong lasts for thirty days. The adept is told to breathe naturally, but exhale slowly through his mouth with the teeth lightly touching and inhale carefully through the nose. The eyes are closed; the attention is fixed on the point between the eyes, or a straight vision of an object not too far ahead is maintained.

The arms are raised and stretched sideways so that the chest may be opened up. The knees are slightly bent, the feet are positioned at shoulder width in the form of the character 八, "eight." Then the whole body is relaxed with no tension left anywhere. Breathing follows its natural course entirely.

---

1. The description that follows is not intended as a practical instruction in Qigong. It is an example of how the progress can be described. For the actual practice of Qigong, the reader is strongly advised to seek the instruction of a competent teacher. Incompetent attempts at the practice may backfire.

The adept imagines his head suspended in midair and slowly coming down while swaying freely in the draft.

The aim of the practice at this level is the widening of the ribcage. During the period of regular exercise, appetite and lung capacity should increase, and there will be a heightened feeling of physical well-being.

In the second stage, which lasts ninety days, exhalation takes place through the mouth with teeth lightly touching, the tongue pressed against the lower teeth, and the lower abdomen gradually expanding. The body is relaxed. Inhalation takes place through the nose with the mouth firmly closed, the teeth lightly touching, the tongue slightly pressed against the upper gums, and the lower abdomen contracting. At the same time, the toes grip the earth and the anus is pulled in. Respiration should be very slow and calm, but increasingly rhythmic.

During exhalation the *qi* should be guided mentally from the crown of the head to the chest and into the lower cinnabar field. During inhalation it is reverted to the crown of the head via the anus, lower spine, spinal column, and the neck. The body is relaxed, the mind tensed. This permits a free movement of *qi*. To keep the body from tensing one should pull one's arms in with 70 percent of all one's might while inhaling and stretch them out with the remaining 30 percent while exhaling. The result of this practice is a marked improvement of the lungs, the stomach, and the heart, as well as of the blood pressure. Figure 1 shows the nodal points activated in Qigong practice.

The third stage of Qigong is scheduled to last 150 days. Respiration instructions remain the same, with the addition that during exhalation the body should be felt sinking as lightly as a wild goose sweeping down; during exhalation, it should stretch out powerfully like a wild goose soaring up toward the sky.

The cycle of *qi* is now extended to the soles of the feet. Inhalation brings the *qi* all the way down, exhalation raises it up again. The health of the practitioner improves further, especially in the areas mentioned above. More than that, nervous disorders are healed.

The fourth stage, lasting another sixty days, is not much different from the third except that during respiration the movement of the lower abdomen is reversed: it now contracts during exhalation and expands during inhalation. The cycle of *qi* remains the same. All inner organs of the body are by now greatly stimulated, and all digestive and respiratory ailments in particular have been completely eliminated.

The same exercises are continued for another ninety days in the fifth stage. During exhalation, the adept leaves the lower abdominal movement to itself and concentrates on widening the throat. During inhalation, more tension is generated. The cycle of *qi* is again shortened to reach only from the crown

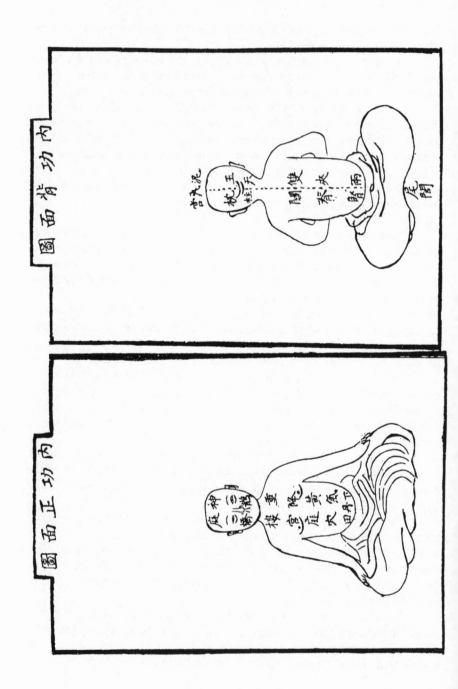

of the head to the lower cinnabar field and up again. The inner organs are strengthened.

The sixth and final stage is scheduled to last to 300 days, almost a whole year. Both exhalation and inhalation now take place through the nose, the breath becomes finer and subtler, without, however, losing its rhythm. The teeth touch lightly, the tongue slightly presses on the lower gums during exhalation, on the upper gums during inhalation. The cycle of *qi* is expanded again to reach from the crown of the head to the soles of the feet during exhalation and back up through the spine during inhalation. The Tiger Pattern is practiced. All the fine hair of the body rises and folds in accordance with the respiration. True harmony of respiration is attained. Health is now perfect: the body is energetic, vigorous, and long-lived.

The whole process lasts 750 days, slightly over two years. The main elements of the practice are respiration and the mental circulation of the *qi* through the body. The complexity and subtlety of the practice change, and so does the practitioner's health. In the end Qigong becomes the natural way of breathing and overall physical feeling; in harmony with the original rhythm of *qi*, the adept has recovered complete health and long life.

Systems and Categories

Qigong, literally "the Effort" or "the Merit of Qi," denotes one specific health practice but also includes several different lineages and teachings. The term *qigong* is of comparatively recent origin. A very early reference is found in Sima Chengzhen's 司馬承禎 *Fuqi jingyi lun* 服氣精義論 (Discourse on the Essential Meaning of the Absorption of *Qi*) of the Tang. He speaks of the "applications of *qi*"氣之爲功 (*Yunji qiqian* 57.23a;[2] Engelhardt 1987: 180), but the combination of both characters as a technical term cannot be dated to before the Ming dynasty. It occurs in the *Jingming zongjiao lu* 靜明宗教錄 (Record of the Teachings of Purity and Light). attributed to Xu Sun 許遜 (*Daozang jiyao, weiji* 4.35b, 36b). In the end of the Qing dynasty the term is

---

2. This early encyclopedia (dated 1013) is found in DZ 1032, fasc. 677–702. The abbreviation DZ refers to the *Daozang* or Taoist Canon. Texts in this collection are given according to the number of the reduced sixty-volume edition published in Taipei and Kyoto. These numbers coincide with those found in K.M. Schipper, *Concordance du Tao Tsang* (Paris: Publications de l'Ecole Francaise d'Extrême-Orient, 1975). "Fasc." stands for "fascicle" and refers to the volume number of the 1925 Shanghai reprint of the original canon of 1445 (*Zhengtong Daozang*).

found in the *Yuanhe bian* 元和篇 (On Primordial Harmony) of unknown authorship. This text contains a section entitled "Qigong Supplement."

Still, even here the term is not used in quite the same sense as it is understood today. The first reference for the current usage is found in Dong Hao's 董浩 *Fei laobing teshu liaofa: Qigong liaofa*   肺癆病特殊療法氣功 療法 (Special Treatments for Lung Ailments: Qigong Treatments) of 1934 (see Ma 1983a: 2; Lin and Luo 1983: 3). Although there is no evidence for any long-term terminological tradition of Qigong, there is a strong feeling that Qigong continues authentic Chinese health methods of old. Modern authors on Qigong therefore take frequent recourse to traditional materials. For example, Zhao Jinxiang 趙金香 , who developed the famous Crane exercise only in 1980, in his documentation traces its origins to the Former Han dynasty, more specifically to the *Daoyin tu* 導引圖 (Gymnastics Chart) found at Mawangdui (*Qigong* 1984/2: 58).

There are as yet no formally established categories and systems of Qigong. To give a clear idea of which practices the term may at some time or another imply, it may therefore be best to arrange them according to the different ways of practice. Dividing Qigong first according to martial practice and health practice, among the latter one can further distinguish the two major groups of techniques applied to others and those applied to oneself. The techniques applied to others include the laying-on of hands, massages, acupuncture, and chiropractice. In all cases the strong inner *qi* of a masterful practitioner is inserted into the body of another person, with the help of instruments and without. The techniques one applies to oneself are divided further on the basis of the degree and kind of body movement involved. There are those without body movement (restful practice or meditations), those with intentional movement (gymnastics and Taiji quan), and those with unintentional body movement (dances and trance states).

Martial Practice

The term for martial practice, *yinggong* 硬功, was defined in 1978 (Lin and Luo 1983: 174). It refers to practices like breaking a thick iron pole with bare hands, lying down naked on bare blades, or similar popular acrobatics. Whichever part of the body, hands or forehead, comes into closest contact with the stone or the metal one works with will receive its *qi* and thus be hardened (Lin and Luo 1983: 286). Until very recently most people in China associated Qigong with these martial techniques.

Qigong Applied to Others

Although martial arts have become increasingly popular and are nowadays organized on a nationwide level, the real boom in Qigong has taken place in the health practices. They are of basically two kinds: techniques applied to oneself and practices used on others. When used on others, the master or doctor infuses his or her own (outer) *qi* into the body of the patient, usually by means of laying on hands. When applied to oneself, one circulates one's own (inner) *qi*. [3] Proficient masters have so much control over their own *qi* that they can infuse it into sick persons' bodies and thus help them recover their health. Patients who submit to such treatment report sensations of soreness, congestion, numbness, heat, cold, or pressure, just as if they received additional *qi* through acupuncture (Lin and Luo 1983: 237).

In infusing the *qi* of Later Heaven from without, Qigong masters do not actually increase the absolute amount of that energy available in the universe. They take it from their own stock and are—at least until they have had a chance to replenish it through self-applied Qigong—the poorer for it (Hoshino 1984: 137). The idea that the disposable energy of the world is limited is also obvious in the Taoist sexual technique of "valuing the semen and loving one's energy," as described in the *Baopuzi* 抱朴子 (Book of the Master Who Embraces Simplicity, chap. 6).

The latest development on the Qigong market is a machine that replaces the skilled masters. Such devices are used most frequently in traditional clinics, where more and special Qigong wards are being established. In the Research Institute for Chinese Traditional Medicine in Shanghai, a device called Qigong Infusion Healing Machine has proved effective in cases of high blood pressure, asthma, insomnia, and heart disease (Lin and Luo 1983: 242). Though hard for a Westerner to believe, the infusion of energy by a Qigong master or machine is also reported effective in anesthesia. Along with similar experiments on acupuncture, infusion of *qi* has been found to successfully keep a patient without feeling for a given time. The first case occurred on May 9, 1980, in Shanghai's People's Hospital No. 8, where a patient was efficiently operated on for a case of swollen thyroid gland under anesthesia provided by a Qigong master. There have since been twenty-two other promising experiments and in each the patient remained fully conscious for the duration of the operation and experienced no unpleasant later side effects. Anesthesia

---

3. The concept of inner *qi* is based on Taoist notions. It refers to the energy of Former Heaven, the primordial power of the universe that makes up every being. Outer *qi*, the energy of Later Heaven, in Qigong refers to the *qi* that is infused into someone else, there to mingle with his own inner *qi*. The Taoists use the term outer *qi* more generally in the sense of all energy that is not within one's body, including air, water, and other forces of nature.

by means of the Qigong machine is envisioned for the future (Lin and Luo 1983: 237–239).

In ancient China, Qigong as a practice applied to others was called "spreading *qi*." The *Youzhen xiansheng funei yuanqi jue*　幼真先生服內元氣訣 (Master Youzhen's Formula on Absorption of Primordial Energy)[4] gives the following description:

> To spread one's *qi* in order to heal a sick person one must first examine where, in his orbs, the problem is rooted. Then one takes one's *qi* through the mouth and places it into the patient's body. The patient faces the *qi* master, but before he receives the *qi* he should calm his mind and cleanse his thoughts. After the infusion the patient should swallow the *qi*. Thereby demons and evil forces will be expelled; bad *qi* will be eradicated forever. (7a)

He Yuan 何遠 of the Song Dynasty provides a concrete example for this method in his *Chunzhu jiwen* 春渚紀聞 (Record of Things Heard in Chunzhu). A Taoist treats a nun by infusing *qi* through the mouth. She feels a hot liquid flow in her intestines and, to her embarrassment, unintentionally urinates (chap. 3). Normally, however, the placement or infusion of *qi* is done by laying hands on the nodal points, the points where the energy channels of the body come closest to the surface. Yet another method is found in the *Buqi jing* 布氣經 (Scripture of Spreading *Qi*), a text of unknown date. The master should place one hand on the navel, and the other on the Gate of Life, the spot on the back that corresponds to the navel in front. Then he can direct the *qi* to strengthen the center of life, from where all parts of the body derive their health (Ma 1983: 51).

Qigong Self-Applied: Without Body Movements

Qigong is usually self-applied. Various authors distinguish the types of practice in various ways. One categorizes according to practice without body movement, practice with intentional body movement, and practice with unintentional body movement. Some follow the distinction between practice with and without body movement (Lin and Luo 1983: 261), or practice with and without body movement plus a combination of both (Lin and Luo 1983: 265; Jiang 1983: 50). Others establish massage as a separate category (Hoshino 1985: 33).

---

4. The text is found in DZ 824, fasc. 569, in *Yunji qiqian* 60, and in the *Chifeng sui* (for a translation of this text see Despeux 1988).

Qigong without any movement of the body is usually practiced in a sitting position: cross-legged on the floor, in the half or full lotus posture, or on a low stool or chair. The practitioner sits very still in the chosen posture and begins by paying utmost attention to the respiration as it keeps flowing to and from the center of the body, the cinnabar field in the lower abdomen. Thus, even though the body is outwardly at rest, the exercise involves an inner movement. This is called rest within movement or movement within rest (Hu and Jiao: 8).

Qigong without body movements is not limited to the sitting posture. It can also be practiced while lying down or standing up. A popular method developed by Liu Guizhen in 1947 encourages the adept to practice not only while sitting, but also while lying on the side and on the back (Renmin 1981: 2; Lin and Luo 1983: 69; Tao and Yang 1981: vol. 2: 8). Also called *yigong* 意功, "exercise of the thinking," this technique is basically a type of meditation. Another term for this Qigong technique is *jinggong* 靜功, restful or silent practice.

The term *jinggong* appears first in the *Zhuangzi*:

> Stillness and silence can benefit the ailing, massage can give
> relief to the aged, and rest and quiet can put a stop to agitation.
> (chap. 26; Watson 1968: 301)

This, of course, does not provide any clues to the concrete methods practiced then. In later traditional materials dealing with Taoist calisthenics and inner alchemy, the term is used to refer to the practice of *qi* in general. As such it is used in the great Chinese encyclopedia *Gujin tushu jicheng*   古今圖書集成, which collects a large number of texts on Qigong under the heading "On Restful Practice." Another such general term used in the old texts is *neigong*, inner practice (see *Neigong tushuo*).

Similarly undefined is the technique of "sitting in oblivion" (*Zhuangzi*, chap. 6). Guo Moruo claims that this, rather than the Buddhist methods of *dhyāna*, is the ancestor of all Chinese meditation techniques (Guo 1959: vol. 10: 50). Although the *Zhuangzi* does not allow a clear definition of sitting in oblivion, the later *Zuowanglun* 坐忘論 (Discourse on Sitting in Oblivion) leaves no doubt that, at least in Tang times, it was a method of meditation, and one influenced by Buddhism at that.

The first documentation of Qigong without body movement might be the *Daoyin tu* found at Mawangdui. Here one sees a sitting figure with the knees drawn in. The explanation reads: "Pulling the pain of the spleen." Tang Lan 唐蘭 identifies the pose with a gymnastic exercise named after the immortal Wang Qiao 王踽.

> Squat down and hold your knees with both hands. Inhale
> through the nose. After seven deep breaths any pain in the hips
> or the back should be gone. (*Yunji qiqian* 34; Wenwu 1979)

This evidence, though scarce, suggests a two-thousand-year history for
the practice of silent or restful Qigong in a sitting posture. Circulation of *qi*
while lying down, on the other hand, seems comparatively recent. Sun Simiao
孫思邈 of the early Tang says in his *Zhenzhong fang* 枕中方 (Pillowbook
Methods; DZ 837, fasc. 572):

> Regular practice of *qi* should take place in a secret chamber.
> Close the doors and quietly lie down on a bed with a pillow 2.5
> *cun* in height under your head. Straighten the body, lie on your
> back, and close your eyes. Keep the *qi* inside and breathe with
> your chest. A down feather held before your nose should not
> move. (9b–10a)

Certain practices performed while lying down are also called sleep
exercises (*shuigong* 睡功). Zhou Tichuan calls this the turtle breath and gives
the following instructions: lie down flat and relax; listen to your respiration; if
you fall asleep that's fine (Renmin 1981: 227). There is no telling how old this
practice is in China. The Song dynasty sage Chen Xiyi 陳希夷 was
particularly famous for his sleep method, of which he allegedly produced a
description (see figure 2).[5]

The well-known poet Lu You 陸游 even praised the practice in chapter
49 of his *Jiannan shijiao* 劍南詩稿 (Poems Drafted in Jiannan; see Renmin
1981: 402).

> Stretched out facing each other in delicious sleep,
> Host and guest forget each other.
> Time is up, the guest leaves, the host awakes—
> No longer does the evening sun shine through the western window.

---

5. His *Shuigong tu* is cited with illustrations in the *Chifeng sui* of the Ming. This text is
translated in Despeux 1988; see also Qin 1984: 4.

On the other hand, today's spontaneous movements are rather played down. Modern practitioners rationalize that they occur when someone removes energy blockages and activates deeper layers of his *qi*, which then manifest in uncontrolled body movements. The modern master Zhang Huimin even accepts only the perception of inner activities of the *qi* as positive. He says, "such feelings are a sign that the energy channels have opened up, they indicate progress in the healing of diseases" (Zhang 1980: 121). He considers spontaneous outer movements of the body alarming signs, whether or not they are identical with the spirit dance.

This cautious reaction may have to do with a certain feeling of unease regarding uncontrolled physical movements in China today. Such exercises tend to evoke the general suspicions attached to practices labelled feudalistic, superstitious, or shamanistic. This, of course, goes against the newly constructed image of Qigong as a modern and scientific health practice that has nothing whatever to do with the remnants of past irrationality.

Also, very recently the enthusiasm about spontaneous practice has declined somewhat, because more and more people were found trapped in the involuntary, trancelike state. They had to be confined or even hospitalized, since they tended to hurt themselves unknowingly. The Crane exercise, closely associated with these involuntary movements, has thus lost some of its popularity.

Integrated Patterns

The Five Animals Pattern

One of the oldest categorizations of Qigong exercises is the one attributed to the famed physician Hua Tuo of the Han: the Five Animals Pattern. The five birds or beasts are the tiger, the bear, the deer, the bird (crane), and the monkey. Several early references to the Five Animals Pattern can be found in the literature (Liang 1981: 4). Qigong methods found effective in cancer cures can be traced to it (Guo 1980: 2).

The pattern itself looks back on a long history. It is quite possible that Qigong as a whole derived originally from the imitation of animals' movements. Even in the Mawangdui manuscripts, there are about ten pictures that call to mind dancing beasts. In chapter 15 of the *Zhuangzi*, "bear hangings and bird stretchings" are mentioned, the former corresponding to the eighth picture in the fourth line of the Mawangdui text on gymnastics. Judged from this pictorial evidence, one does not practice bear hangings by hanging from a tree by the legs, but by walking swayingly back and forth with one's neck stretched out (Wenwu 1979: 6).

The *Huainanzi* 淮南子 adds "duck bathings, monkey leapings, owl glarings, and tiger turnings" to the two practices of the *Zhuangzi*, thus specifying six different types of animal-based exercises (chap. 7). Others can be found in the *Baopuzi*, which lists "dragon writhings, tiger stretchings, bear hangings, and turtle swallowings together with swallow flyings, snake twistings, bird stretchings, monkey bowings, and rabbit runnings" (chap. 15). Wang Xizhi 王羲之 , the famous calligrapher, is reported to have been very strong, supposedly due to his practice of "goose fightings," another early kind of active Qigong (Ma 1983a: 26).

The most popular kind of Five Animals Pattern nowadays is the practice including unintentional movement propagated under that name by Liang Shifeng 梁士豐 in Guangdong since 1980. Each of the five exercises attempts to imitate the movements of a particular animal, and except for their emphasis on unintentional movements, which are credited with strong healing powers, they do not vary considerably from other common Qigong practices.

In theory, the five animals are part of the following systematization:

Tiger:	metal, lungs, sorrow, numbness, scarred skin, mucus from mouth and nose
Bear:	water, kidneys, fear, coldness, cracking joints, abnormalities in the ears
Deer:	wood, liver, anger, muscle spasms, watery eyes
Bird:	fire, heart, joy, throbbing arteries, fever, quickened heartbeat, rolled-up tongue
Monkey:	earth, spleen, worry, twitching muscles, movements of the lips. (Hu and Jiao: 47)

All animals are associated with one of the Five Agents, an inner orb, as well as with the specific emotion typical for it. The various symptoms listed here indicate not only the particular orb responsible for them but also the kind of Qigong most effective in treating them. The practice begins with movements based on the behavior of the respective animal. But then, theory claims, a point will be reached where movement comes to a standstill; that is, the body will be entirely calm and at peace. This in turn becomes the starting point for a new, this time unintentional, activity of the body (Liang 1981: 12).

In addition, the association of the animals with the Five Agents allows for a particular dynamic; they can either overcome or generate each other. They may be negative and destroying: tiger, deer, monkey, bear, bird, tiger. They can also be positive and enhancing: tiger, bear, deer, bird, monkey, tiger. Subtler kinds of diagnosis and treatment are found in combinations of types. Generally, all symptoms indicating a positive relation are considered healthy, and those pointing to a negative relation are signs of sickness (Liang 1981: 29).

Hu Yaozhen and Jiao Guorui present different theories regarding the Five Animals Pattern. Jiao Guorui claims that the adept should not merely practice certain body movements in imitation of one or the other of the animals, but should try to become as much like the animal as possible "in spirit and character" (Hu and Jiao: 6–7). According to him, it is important to frequently visit the zoo to study the behavior and movements of the animals. He calls this technique to "fully become an animal." Hu Yaozhen says that all active Qigong practice of the Animals Pattern should be preceded by an inner exercise or meditation. The body thus relaxed and warmed up will easily develop spontaneous movements, upon which the practice of the Animals Pattern is begun (Hu and Jiao: 94). In this case, then, the development of unintentional body movements is not the ultimaι aim of the technique.

None of the authors sufficiently explains exactly what mechanism makes the development of unintentional body movements so good for the practitioners' health. More than that, evaluations often are quite contradictory. Jiao Guorui emphasizes that it is best for the adept to completely relax all conscious control of the body and to give himself over fully to unintentional movements, but Zhou Tichuan, a practitioner of the Omei school, finds that such movements are unwanted side-effects and should be avoided as far as possible (*Qigong* 1984/3: 130–133).

The Six Sounds

Qigong is also practiced by breathing according to the six sounds (*liuzi jue* 六字訣). These are believed to have a positive influence on the health of the inner organs (Hoshino 1985: 81). They are organized in the following system:

xi	chui	si	hu	ke	xu
burners	kidneys	lungs	spleen	heart	liver
	winter	autumn		summer	spring
semi-fire	water	metal	earth	fire	wood
	ears	nose	mouth	tongue	eyes

The reason for the effectiveness of these six sounds is that they require a different positioning of the lips, the tongue, the teeth, the throat, as well as the chest and the abdomen. Thus they each have a different impact on the "orbs within the body" (Hoshino 1985: 81). This effect is enhanced in a specific exercise designed by Ma Litang　馬禮堂. He prescribes certain movements of the hands and a meditation on the circulation of *qi* in accompaniment (Hoshino 1985: 82).

Ancient texts offer some evidence about the age of the method. The *Daode jing* says: "Some breathe *xu* and some breathe *chui*" (chap. 29); the *Zhuangzi* has: "*Chui, ju, hu, xi*, that's how we spit out the old and draw in the new" (chap. 15). If it weren't for this explanation one would assume that all sounds refer only to exhalations. As it is, the *Zhuangzi* provides early evidence for the theory held later by Tao Hongjing (*Yangxing yanming lu* 18b) and today by Ma Jiren: that some of the sounds should be made while exhaling, others while inhaling (Ma 1983a: 27). Breathing exercises including sounds are also mentioned in Zhiyi's 智顗 *Tiantai xiao zhiguan*　天台小止觀 (Tiantai Samatha-Vipaśyanā for Beginners; *Taishō Tripitaka* 46.471c; translated in Lu 1964). Moreover, the phrase "make *xuxu*" often occurs in Zen texts, such as the *Linji lu* 臨濟錄 (The Record of Linji). It is likely that it is meant quite literally as a reference to a sound made in a breathing exercise. Numerous other historical documents mention similar techniques (Renmin 1981: 340; Ma 1983a: 33; Lin and Luo 1983: 10).

Modern Qigong also employs practices of breathing with the sound of *hai, hei*, or *pei* (Renmin 1981: 22, 214, 226). These are most commonly used with exhalations. In addition, a whole set of patterns including the practice of all the sounds has been developed, analogous to the continuous exercise designed for the Five Animals Pattern.

The sound method might also be connected with the ancient magic of "whistling," used before the Han dynasty to evoke the spirits of the wind, rain, clouds, and thunder, but also demons and goblins. Later *xiao* became a vocal art: it was either a long expiration through narrowed and rounded lips, a vocalization with lips kept open, or a whistling on two fingers (Sawada 1974).

Conclusion

The theory and practice of Qigong bear witness to the tremendous vitality of the Chinese tradition. Exercises developed as early as the Han dynasty and possibly before that have continued to be used over the ages by physicians and religious practitioners for better health and the fullness of life. Integrated into a variety of patterns, systematized and evaluated in many different ways, the basic techniques of meditation and physical exercise have survived with unbroken and ever renewed vigor. The main pillars of the practice are the respiration and the conscious guidance of the *qi*, which are used to coordinate and intensify the movements of the body without and control the meditation of the mind within. A technique of meditation accompanied by physical practice or a kind of exercise joined by control over the mind—either definition would fit Qigong perfectly.

The modern age of science and technology has brought changes in the understanding, description, and evaluation of the practices. Transcendence or immortality is out of the question. Spirit or spirits don't play any significant role any more. Trance states are discouraged, since traditional ways of understanding and controlling them have been lost. Scientific man shies away from the supernatural. The *qi* itself is no longer the primordial creative power of the universe, but merely one force among others, somewhat like electricity. The gods are dethroned, the cosmos is made measurable, and man remains strictly within the confines of the known.

Though the existence of *qi*, formerly an article of faith, is now scientifically proven (at least as far as the Chinese are concerned), belief in the effectiveness of the practices is still the starting point for their application. Certain feelings in the body and improvements in one's overall health, otherwise attributed to some physical condition or other, are then interpreted as caused by the activity of the *qi*. Only with the right understanding and with the proper control over the mind is successful practice possible. Is this really science? Or is it still religion?

Western doctors and natural scientists remain skeptical about Chinese reports on the use of Qigong in anesthesia and in curing terminal diseases. They don't accept the existence of either *qi* or the conduits that supposedly pervade the body from top to bottom. From their point of view, because all Qigong theory is bound by faith all Qigong practices fall into the range of religion.

The scholar of religion, on the other hand, deplores the disregard of the sacred, the loss of traditional ways of dealing with supernatural and superhuman agencies. The rationalization of Qigong can't convince him, since it seems to leave out so much of the theory and cosmology that originally made the practices sensible and attractive.

Modern Chinese interpretations of traditional practices, according to our understanding, are therefore somewhat ambiguous. They remain in the twilight sphere between the realms of science and religion. The Chinese themselves use this to advantage: they can use whatever techniques prove useful without confronting their theoretical implications. This certainly is not proper science. But is it religion?

Taoist professional interest in the practices certainly seems to point in this direction. On the other hand, the average Qigong practitioner would not wish to be considered a Taoist nor would he or she connect any spiritual aims with the techniques. Good for health and therefore for family and fatherland, fun to do and a nice way to meet people informally. A new sport for the masses—that's what it seems to boil down to.

Still, even the man in the park will probably believe in the existence of the *qi*, will at the same time be convinced that it is a scientifically proven electromagnetic force. His conviction identifies him as a believer in science without any qualified knowledge of what science actually says. Aren't we all, to a certain degree, members of the same cult?

References

Despeux, Catherine. 1976. *Taiki k'iuan: technique de combat, technique de longue vie.* Paris: Institute des Hautes Etudes Chinoises, 1976.

—— 1987. *Préscriptions d'acuponcture valant mille onces d'or.* Paris: Guy Trédaniel, 1987.

—— 1988. *La moelle du phénix rouge. Santé et longue vie dans la Chine du XVI siècle.* Paris: Guy Trédaniel, 1988.

Engelhardt, Ute. 1981. *Theorie und Technik des Taijiquan.* Schorndorf: WBV Biologisch-medizinische Verlagsgesellschaft, 1981.

—— 1987. *Die klassische Tradition der Qi-Übungen: Eine Darstellung anhand des Tang-zeitlichen Textes Fuqi jingyi lun von Sima Chengzhen.* Wiesbaden: Franz Steiner, 1987.

Lu, Kuan-yu. 1964. *The Secrets of Chinese Meditation.* London: Rider, 1964.

Watson, Burton. 1968. *The Complete Works of Chuang-tzu.* New York: Columbia University Press, 1968.

Wilhelm, Richard. 1962. *The Secret of the Golden Flower.* New York: Harcourt, Brace & World, 1962.

in Chinese and Japanese

Gu Zhenghua 谷正華 1982
Tujie baduanjin huibian 圖解疤段錦彙編
Hongkong: Yimei tushu, 1982.

Guo Lin 郭林 1980
Xin qigong liaofa 新氣功療法
Anhui: Kexue zhishu, 1980.

—— 1980a. *Xin qigong fangzhi yanzheng fa* 新氣功防治癌症法
Beijing: Renmin tiyu, 1980.

Guo Moruo 郭沫若 1959
Moruo wenji 沫若文集
Beijing: Renmin wenxue, 1959.

Hoshino Minoru 星野稔 1984
Zusetsu kikōhō 圖說氣功法
Kyoto: Hakushusha, 1984.

—— 1985. *Kikō kenkōhō* 氣功澗康法
Tokyo: Nihon bungeisha, 1985.

Hu Yaozhen 胡耀貞 and Jiao Guorui 焦國瑞 (no date)
Wuqinxi 五禽戲
Hongkong: Xinwen shudian.

Jiang Minda 蔣敏達 1983
Qigong qiangshen fa 氣功強身法
Shanghai: Jiaoyu, 1983.

Jiao Guorui 焦國瑞 1984
Qigong yangsheng xue gaiyao 氣功養生學概要
Fujian: Renmin, 1984.

Li Yuanguo 李遠國 1987
Qigong jinghua ji 氣功精華集
Chengdu: Bashu shushe, 1987.

—— 1988. *Daojiao qigong yangsheng xue* 道教氣功養生學
Chengdu: Sichuan Academy of Social Sciences, 1988.

Liang Shifeng 梁士豐 1981
Zifa wuqinxi donggong 自發五禽戲動功
Guangdong: Renmin, 1981.

Lin Hai 林海 1980
"Qigong shi fahui renti tili de yimen kexue" 氣功是發揮人體替力的門科學
Xin zhongyi 新中醫 1980.6.

Lin Housheng 林厚省 and Luo Peiyu 駱佩鈺 1983
Qigong sanbai wen 氣功三百問
Guangdong: Kezhi, 1983.

Ma Chun 馬春 1983
Majia qigong 馬家氣功
Shanxi: Renmin, 1983.

Ma Jiren 馬濟人 1983a
Zhongguo qigong xue 中國氣功學
Shaanxi: Kexue zhishu, 1983.

Mao Zedong 毛澤東 1972

Mao Zedong ji 毛澤東集
Beijing, 1972. Vol. 1. Originally published in 1917.

Matsuzaki Kakuo 松崎鶴雄 1980
Gogetsu chufū 呉月楚風
Tokyo: Kagaku sogo kenkyujo, 1980.

Qin Zhongsan 秦重三 1984
Qigong liaofa he baojian 氣功療法和保健
Shanghai: Kexue zhishu, 1984.

Renmin tiyu 人民體育 (ed.) 1981
Qigong jingxuan 氣功精選
Beijing: Renmin tiyu, 1981.

Renmin tiyu 人民體育 (ed.) 1982
Qigong di miaoyong 氣功的妙用
Beijing: Renmin tiyu, 1982.

Sawada Mizuho 澤田瑞穂 1974
"Kō no genryū" 嘯の源流
Tōhōshūkyō 東方宗教 44 (1974), 1–14.

Tao Shengfu 陶乘福 and Yang Weihe 楊衛和 1981
Qigong liaofa jijin 氣功療法集錦
Beijing: Renmin weisheng, 1981.

Wenwu 文物 (ed.) 1979
Daoyin tulun wenji 導引圖論文集
Beijing: Wenwu, 1979.

Yang Changji 楊昌濟 1978
Dahuazhai riji 達化齋日記
Hunan: Renmin, 1978.

Yang Meijun 楊梅君 and Tian Changwu 田昌五 1983
Dayan gong 大雁功
Beijing: Renmin weisheng, 1983.

Zhang Huimin 張惠民 1980
Qigong liaofa qutan 氣功療法趣談
Tianjin: Kexue zhishu, 1980.

Zhou Renfeng 周稔豐 1978
Taiji quan changshi 太極拳常識
Beijing: Renmin tiyu, 1978.

List of Contributors

Akira Akahori is the director of the research and development department of Kotarō Pharmaceutical Company in Osaka. He completed his studies of medicine at Tokyo University in 1951 and specialized in pharmacology at Osaka University, where he stayed until 1954. He has been interested in traditional medicine for a long time and is a member of the research group on ancient Chinese medicine at Kyoto University. Among his outstanding publications is the recently published volume entitled *Kampōyaku* (Traditional Drugs of China and Japan). In addition, he presented a paper on "The Interpretation of Classical Chinese Texts in Contemporary Japan: Achievements, Approaches, and Problems" at the First International Symposium on Traditional Chinese Medicinal Literature in Munich, 1986.

Catherine Despeux completed her doctorate at the University of Paris-VII Jussieur in 1974. Since then she has published widely. Her area of expertise is especially the realm of longevity techniques, Taoist inner alchemy, and Chinese traditional medicine. Her publications include: *Taiji quan, art martial, technique de longue vie* (1981), *Traite d'alchimie et de physiologie taoiste* (1979), *Prescriptions d'acuponcture valant mille onces d'or* (1987), *La moelle du phénix rouge. Santé et longue vie dans la Chine du XVI siècle* (1988). She is an active practitioner of Taiji quan, and her current research on the history of medicine has involved her with a group of scholars at the Centre National des Recherches Scientifique.

Ute Engelhardt completed her Ph.D. at the University of Munich in 1985. Her studies brought her to Taiwan as well as to the Chinese mainland. At present she is doing research on Chinese health techniques supported by a postdoctoral fellowship from the Deutsche Forschungsgemeinschaft. She has authored *Theorie und Technik des Taijiquan* (1981) and recently *Die* *klassische Tradition der Qi-Übungen* (1987). She is also an active practitioner and teacher of Taiji quan and Qigong.

Hidemi Ishida studied at Waseda University, Tokyo, and in 1978 graduated from Tōhoku University in Sendai, where he subsequently taught for several years. At present he is assistant professor at Yahata University in Kitakyūshu. A prolific writer, he has published numerous articles on ancient medical thought using traditional philosophers as well as medical textbooks. His latest publications are *Qi: The Flowing Body* (1987) and an edition of texts and commentaries of the *Huangdi neijing* (1987). A new *History of Chinese Medicine* is in press.

Livia Kohn earned her Ph.D. in 1980 from Bonn University, and then spent several years at the Institute for Humanistic Research of Kyoto University, where she studied under Mitsuji Fukunaga. After two years at the University of Michigan, she is currently teaching at Boston University. Her primary interest is focused on questions of mysticism in China and on Taoist mythology. Among other things, she has published *Leben und Legende des Ch'en T'uan* (1981) and *Seven Steps to the Tao: Sima Chengzhen's Zuowanglun* (1987).

Kunio Miura completed his studies at Osaka City University in 1964. After several years at Kyoto and Tōhoku Universities, he has been a professor at Osaka City University since 1982. His interest in Taoist longevity techniques was inspired by his studies of the Neo-Confucian tradition, and he has also written on the interaction of literati elite culture and popular health and immortality techniques. His works include monographs on Zhu Xi (1979) and Wang Anshi (1985). Recently he spent six months in Shanghai studying the practice as well as the theory of Qigong.

Isabelle Robinet is a graduate of the Ecole Pratique des Hautes Etudes of the Sorbonne, where she completed her doctorate and also earned her *doctorat d'état*. She is currently teaching at the Université d'Aix-Marseille. Her area of specialization is Shangqing Taoism and, more recently, inner alchemy. Her major publications include *Les commentaires du Tao to king jusqu'au VIIe siècle* (1977), *Méditation taoiste* (1979), and the monumental *La révélation du Shangqing dans l'histoire du Taoisme* (1984).

Yoshinobu Sakade completed his studies of Chinese philosophy at Kyoto University in 1961 after he had graduated from Osaka Foreign College. Since 1971 he has been a professor at Kansai University in Osaka. He received his formal doctorate from Nagoya Unviversity in 1984. He is the doyen of longevity and medical studies among Japanese scholars. He has published widely and is well known for his expertise and hard work. His books include *Philosophy and Science in Modern China* (1983), *Kang Youwei—The Blossoming of Utopia* (1985), and *Nourishing Vitality in Ancient China: Comprehensive Studies on Theory and Practice* (1988).

Toshiaki Yamada was trained at Tōyō University, Tokyo. Between 1978 and 1985 he taught at Taishō University and did research under the guidance of Yoshitoyo Yoshioka. For several years now he has been an instructor at Tōyō University. He is a specialist in the early period of Taoism and has published variously on the history and composition of ancient Taoist texts. Among his publications there are especially the *Index to the Shenzhou jing* (1984) and "The Tao of Immortality," published in Fukui Kōjun's *Dōkyō* (1983).

Index

Abe no Manao 1
absorption of energy (*qi*) 234ff.,
  247, 250, 271, 273, 275, 292
abstention from cereals, *see*
  dietetics
acupuncture 3f., 12f., 16, 59f.,
  244, 272, 276, 333, 343
acupuncture points, *see* nodal
  points
Akazuka Kiyoshi 24
After Heaven, *see* Later Heaven
alchemy, *see* elixir
An Lushan 7, 228
Andō Shunyū 30
ānāpāna 152
anātman 201
Anfukuden 15
animals, *see* Five Animals
  Pattern
anitya 201
Anmo jing 229
Anpan shouyi jing 150f.
apocrypha 100f., 107f., 117,
  119, 307
Asakusa 5
August Lord of Primordial
  Cinnabar 144
awakened mind 280, 288, 291
awe 280
Azuma Jūji 30

Baduan jin 15, 348ff.
Baihu tong 106
Bai Yuchan 30, 307, 313
Baiyuan, *see* body divinities
Bao Jing 113
Bao Mingyuan 239
Baopuzi 6, 18f., 28, 74, 78, 84ff.,
  92, 103f., 106f., 109, 113ff.,
  117, 122, 130f., 140ff., 146,
  155, 176, 228f., 232, 244,
  246ff., 256, 273, 279, 283,
  287ff., 343, 353
Before Heaven, *see* Former
  Heaven
beings 65ff., 68
Beidaihe 335
beidou, see Northern Dipper
Beijing 5, 332, 335f., 350
bencao, see materia medica
Bencao gangmu 85
Benji jing 215
Biyanlu 125
blood 45, 49ff., 52ff., 58, 60f.,
  66, 144, 203, 207, 213, 285,
  337ff., 343
Bodhidharma 15
bodily form, *see* shape
body 6ff., 11f., 21, 25, 27, 41–68
  passim, 79ff., 133, 135ff., 144,
  146f., 159–190 *passim*,

367